Opéra de salon

Opéra de salon

Parisian Societies and Spaces in the Second Empire

MARK EVERIST

OXFORD
UNIVERSITY PRESS

Oxford University Press is a department of the University of Oxford.
It furthers the University's objective of excellence in research, scholarship,
and education by publishing worldwide. Oxford is a registered trade mark of
Oxford University Press in the UK and in certain other countries.

Published in the United States of America by Oxford University Press
198 Madison Avenue, New York, NY 10016, United States of America.

© Oxford University Press 2025

All rights reserved. No part of this publication may be reproduced, stored in a retrieval system,
transmitted, used for text and data mining, or used for training artificial intelligence, in any form or
by any means, without the prior permission in writing of Oxford University Press, or as expressly
permitted by law, by license or under terms agreed with the appropriate reprographics rights
organization. Inquiries concerning reproduction outside the scope of the above should be sent
to the Rights Department, Oxford University Press, at the address above.

You must not circulate this work in any other form
and you must impose this same condition on any acquirer.

Library of Congress Cataloging-in-Publication Data
Names: Everist, Mark, author.
Title: Opéra de salon : Parisian societies and spaces in the Second Empire / Mark Everist.
Description: New York : Oxford University Press, 2025. |
Includes bibliographical references and index.
Identifiers: LCCN 2025004955 (print) | LCCN 2025004956 (ebook) |
ISBN 9780197695180 (hardback) | ISBN 9780197695203 | ISBN 9780197695210 |
ISBN 9780197695197 (epub)
Subjects: LCSH: Operetta—France—Paris—19th century. |
Salons—France—Paris—History—19th century. |
Paris (France)—Intellectual life—19th century.
Classification: LCC ML1727.8.P2 E93 2025 (print) | LCC ML1727.8.P2 (ebook) |
DDC 782.10944/36109034—dc23/eng/20250207
LC record available at https://lccn.loc.gov/2025004955
LC ebook record available at https://lccn.loc.gov/2025004956

DOI: 10.1093/9780197695210.001.0001

Printed by Marquis Book Printing, Canada

The manufacturer's authorized representative in the EU for product safety is
Oxford University Press España S.A., Parque Empresarial San Fernando de Henares,
Avenida de Castilla, 2 – 28830 Madrid (www.oup.es/en).

For Jeanice and Amelia

Contents

List of Illustrations	ix
Acknowledgements	xi

Introduction	1
Backgrounds and Contexts	4
Repertories and Performance Practices	8
Methodology and Terminology	11
1. *Opéra de salon*	21
Opéra—*salon*	21
Opéra de salon	28
Patterns of Publication	64
2. Performers and the Improvised Stage	81
Casts, Scoring, and Instrumentation	81
Vocal Artists	84
The Improvised Stage	95
3. Performance and Places: The *Bourgeois* and the Aristocrat	101
Spaces and Patrons 1: The Medical Profession	102
Spaces and Patrons 2: Entrepreneurs and the *Haute Bourgeoisie*	114
Spaces and Patrons 3: Government and Aristocracy	118
4. Performance and Places: Music and Letters	125
Spaces and Patrons 4: Artists and Men of Letters	125
Spaces and Patrons 5: Professional Musicians	138
Spaces and Patrons 6: Public Spaces	145
5. Contexts and Cultivation	153
Contexts for Creation	153
Salons—Concerts	154
Théâtre de société	157
Charade	161
Proverbe	163
Opéra de salon and the Regulated Theatre	166
Salon, Song, and *Séance*	171

6. Performance and the *Parloir* — 186
   Women, the *Parloir*, and *Opéra de salon* — 186
   Women Composers and Librettists — 201

7. Locating *Opéra de salon* — 209
   Time and Space — 209
   Spatialité — 211
   Geolocation — 219
   Multiplicities of Power — 225
   Opéra de salon in the Provinces and Abroad — 229

Conclusion — 240

Bibliography — 245
Index — 261

Illustrations

Figures

1.1.	Graph of the number of works and performances of *opéra de salon*, 1849–1870.	25
3.1.	Établissement Hydrothérapique des Néothermes, view of the *grande galerie*, 1831.	109
3.2.	Établissement Hydrothérapique des Néothermes, view of the *grande galerie*, 1841.	110
3.3.	Ballroom of Henri Binder modified for performance of *opéra de salon*.	117
3.4.	Carriage showroom of Henri Binder.	117
4.1.	Studio of Henri-Joseph-Charles Cordier, view through multiple arches.	130
4.2.	Studio of Henri-Joseph-Charles Cordier, view of smaller room.	130
4.3.	Studio of Henri-Joseph-Charles Cordier, general view of larger room.	131
4.4.	Raymond Poisson, engraving by Charles-Albert d'Arnoux (Berthall).	135
4.5.	Gilbert Duprez's theatre on the rue Turgot.	141
5.1.	A *séance* in a *parloir*, 1853.	174
5.2.	A *séance* in the *salon*, 1853.	174
7.1.	Honoré Daumier, *Les comédiens de société* i.	216
7.2.	Honoré Daumier, *Les comédiens de société* ii.	217
7.3.	Topographical distribution of Parisian theatres, 1850s.	221
7.4.	Locations of performances of *opéra de salon*.	223
7.5.	Autograph of Salvator, *L'esprit de foyer*.	236

Music Examples

1.1.	Félix Godefroid, *A deux pas du bonheur*, end of overture and beginning of scene 1.	35
1.2.	Charles Poisot, *Rosa, la rose*, beginning of *duo*.	36
1.3.	Charles Poisot, *Rosa, la rose*, citation of *duo* in finale.	38

1.4.	Théodore Semet, *Laide*, opening of 'Allez, beau papillon'.	40
1.5.	Victor Massé, *Prix de famille*, 'Adieu mon village', transition.	42
1.6.	Charles Poisot, *Rosa, la rose*, extract from *duo de Latin*.	44
1.7.	Félix Godefroid, *A deux pas du bonheur*, recitative embedded in finale.	48
1.8.	Charles Poisot, *Le coin du feu*, 'Il n'est pas femme à mes yeux plus charmante', accompanied recitative.	53
1.9.	Charles Poisot, *Le coin du feu*, 'Rêve enchanteur', recitative.	56
5.1.	Clairville and Jules Cordier, *L'esprit frappeur*, reconstruction of *évocation*.	178
5.2.	Victor Robillard, *Amour et spiritisme*, *évocation*.	180

Tables

1.1.	Distribution of the number of compositions in *opéra de salon*, 1850–1870.	29
1.2.	Four sample *opéras de salon*: structure and contents.	31
3.1.	Performances of *opéra de salon* at the home of Anne-Gabrielle Lesueur (Orfila).	106
4.1.	Performances of *opéra de salon* in concert halls.	146
5.1.	Sources for music in Nicolas-Auguste Dubois, *La réconciliation*.	160
5.2.	*Opéra de salon* based on *proverbes*.	163
5.3.	*Vaudevilles* and *séances*.	175
6.1.	*Opéras de salon* in *Le magasin des demoiselles*, *Le journal des demoiselles* and *Le berquin*.	190
6.2.	Structure of Alfred Driou, *Le bonhomme Noël*.	197
6.3.	Eudoxe-Françoise Péan de la Roche-Jagu, lyric output.	205
7.1.	Performances of Félix Godefroid, *A deux pas du bonheur*.	213
7.2.	Performances of *opéra de salon*, 1850–1870, by location.	224
7.3.	Repertory of the *hôtel des bains*, Le Croisic, 1858–1860.	232

Acknowledgements

Much of the research and writing for this book was undertaken during the pandemic of 2020–2021. At the moment when Europe shut down in March 2020, I was in Paris but lucky that my partner had managed to get a ticket on one of the last aircraft travelling from Göteborg to Paris before lockdown and that there were two opera singers and a pianist in my building. Every Friday evening for two months we would throw open the windows onto the courtyard and listen to a recital given by Sophie and Candace. The repertory was excellent: a good deal of Reynaldo Hahn (I learned a lot of new repertory) and several operatic excerpts. There was a video, of course, which found its way inter alia onto the website of the UK radio channel Classic FM (I deny all responsibility . . .) and onto the Instagram account of the Ministère de Culture. It was as if the day's work on *opéra de salon* during the Second Empire was coming to life in the evening as we poured drinks and leaned out of our windows to chat with our neighbours and listen to our friends' music. Like so many who survived the pandemic—and too many did not—I owe a great debt to those who managed to assuage fears and frustration through music.

Opéra de salon: *Parisian Societies and Spaces in the Second Empire* was born out of bemused curiosity. I was halfway through work on a project that attempted to make sense of the kaleidoscopic early decades of *opérette* in the same period that occupies the current book. Although I was adept at responding to works that bucked every trend that every scholar thought they understood, there was one group of works that eluded me, and as I investigated this repertory—*opéra de salon*, as it was called by its Second Empire commentators—it became larger and more clearly focussed as something that sat outside the polyvalent traditions of *opérette* in the 1850s and 1860s. There was a chapter written on *opéra de salon* as part of this *opérette* project that was as unsatisfactory as it was out of place. At this point, my Oxford University Press editor, Norm Hirschy, came to my rescue with conversation, cocktails, and costume whose style and sprezzatura aligned just perfectly with more generous views of the Second Empire; he suggested a second monograph (actually, it was a third, but that's another story), and

Opéra de salon: *Parisian Societies and Spaces* is the result. Norm was a key interlocutor during all phases of the book's gestation, and I owe him much. Not the least of his skills was being able to find sympathetic but penetrating peer reviewers for the outline and then the final typescript (I use the term loosely), and I am obviously greatly indebted to these generous colleagues who gave so freely of their time and expertise during peer review of the book.

I'm used to working in well-populated scholarly fields—the Middle Ages and the long nineteenth century—but a project on music for the improvised stage identified very few people to talk to; I enjoyed conversations with Pierre Girod and Nicole Vilkner during the early stages of the work, but much of the research and writing was conducted in an unfamiliar isolation, so I was all the more grateful to the descendents of the composer, mystic, and critic Allyre Bureau (a key figure in chapter 5), who invited me to the parental home in the Oise and gave me such a good lunch that I had to run for my train back to Paris. Gabrielle Cadier-Rey and Alexis and Philippe Bureau-Thibaut not only generously made Bureau's papers and manuscript scores available to me but also offered encouragement for a related project in which their ancestor features more prominently on music and the occult in the nineteenth century (this is 'Musique, journalisme et justice sociale: Paris entre les révolutions [1830–1851]', *Presse et musique*, special issue of *Tangence* 137 [2025]) 13–42.

Even at the height of the pandemic, I managed to read a couple of conference papers related to the emerging book, one at a round table at the online American Musicological Society meeting in November 2021 and the following month in Siena (where I swear I was the only non-Tuscan present); the latter was published as 'Opera in the Bathroom: Power, Personality and *Opéra de salon* during the *Second Empire*', *Music and Power in the Long Nineteenth Century*, ed. Fabrizio Della Seta and Massimiliano Locanto, special issue of *Chigiana: Journal of Musicological Studies* 52 (2022) 61–78. I was also invited to read the keynote at an online conference in October 2022, 'Gender, Sexuality and Eroticism on the Lyric Stage'; parts of chapter 6 found their way into the resulting article: '"Opera" off the Stage: Gender and Genre in *opéra de salon*', *Genre and the Production of Gendered Identity on the Lyric Stage*, ed. Mark Everist and Jennifer Walker, Speculum musicae 55 (Turnhout: Brepols, 2025) 223–254. Very late in the publication process, I had the good fortune to attend the 'Mapping Music History' conference in Aberdeen in April 2024, where many of the ideas in chapter 7 were discussed and where I developed the idea of an online display of the geolocative elements that accompanies that chapter. Many people contributed to discussions, formal and informal, at this event, and I am grateful to all, but I have to thank Louis Epstein, the director of the Musical Geography Project (https://musicalgeography.org/), who steered the project through the middle months of 2024, and Maeve Nagel-Frazel, who managed the technical part of the project with unalloyed brilliance and taught me a lot about ArcGIS along the way.

With the text of the book more or less established, I was lucky to have Alexander Glyde-Bates prepare all the music examples, Meagan Mason work on the index, and Wendy Keebler copy-edit the book. Rachel Ruisard at Oxford University Press has been a constant support ever since we shared a cup of coffee in New Orleans and has worked tirelessly with Norm to make the book better than it probably deserves.

From the beginning of the twenty-first century, I've shared a home with two people, whom I acknowledge every time I publish. Work on this book was denied the company of my daughter, Amelia, who left to study at the University of Maryland in 2019; she may well have considered herself lucky (she will certainly say that), but various technologies have ensured that she has been kept up to date on the project, however often it showed up on her digital doorstep. But the person who has shared most during the preparation of this book, from the courtyard concerts in Paris to online conferences from our home in Burgundy, is Jeanice Brooks. She knows what I owe her: simply everything.

Saint-Vincent de Paul, Paris
Charigny, Côte d'Or
April 2024

Introduction

Opéra de salon: *Parisian Societies and Spaces in the Second Empire* analyses a repertory and culture that are unknown to music history. As its name implies, *opéra de salon* was a type of stage work conceived for and performed in a number of types of private spaces collectively known as the *salon*. Sharing many of its features—a single act, a consistent number of compositions, and dramaturgical structure—with contemporary forms of one-act *opéra comique* and with *opérette* which emerged at the same time, *opéra de salon* was a key genre in the complex cultural network engendered by the Second Empire.[1] The book uncovers approximately 120 completely unknown works that arrayed music, prose, poetry, and drama in ways that distanced them from the broader culture of Parisian music in the theatre and placed them in an entirely different context: the environment of the mid-nineteenth-century *salon* and related spaces. *Opéra de salon* constitutes around a tenth of all Parisian works in one act premiered during the period 1850–1870; if *opérette* and related genres alone are considered—which are *opéra de salon*'s closest siblings—*opéra de salon* as a proportion of the total rises to nearly a quarter.

Characterized by its use of a single act with an average of around ten scenes and three or four characters of whom the vast majority were female, *opéra de salon* is most frequently made up of an overture and seven composed numbers. Reflecting its performance contexts, the register of its libretto is either a rural or urban domestic setting, with comedies of manners preferred to satire and politics. *Opéras de salon* were performed almost exclusively in private environments that could range from the most aristocratic or *haut-bourgeois* suite of rooms with an audience in the hundreds to the most modest *parloir* in an apartment building with perhaps fewer than thirty in attendance; in the overwhelming majority of these performances, the

---

[1] Louis-Napoléon Bonaparte was the last president of the Second Republic which had been ushered in by the revolutions of 1848. In December 1851, he staged a coup d'état supported by a referendum at the very end of the year and by a second referendum almost exactly a year later which reintroduced imperial rule in the guise of the Second Empire; the regime lasted until 1870, when it ended with the Battle of Sedan, the Siege of Paris, the Commune, and the establishment of the Third Republic.

Opéra de salon. Mark Everist, Oxford University Press. Oxford University Press 2025.
DOI: 10.1093/9780197695210.003.0001

accompaniment was entrusted to a solo piano, and all publications of *opéras de salon* were for voices and piano alone. These approximately 120 *opéras de salon* have survived in forms that range from nothing more than a single title in an account in the press to a complete array of published and manuscript sources for the score and the libretto as well as descriptions of performances and performers. Performances, especially in the aristocratic or *haut-* and *moyen-bourgeois salon*, were reviewed in the press, while those in the *parloir* fell beneath the range of any critical radar. An important part of the distribution of such *opéras de salon* destined for the *parloir* was publication in journals dedicated to the interests of young women between school and marriage—*demoiselles*—for whom cultural activities in the *parloir*, *opéra de salon* in particular, were important accomplishments and could illuminate their lives, to paraphrase Rebecca Rogers, from the schoolroom to the *salon*.[2]

A study of *opéra de salon* undertakes several different types of cultural tasks. It clearly offers a challenge to modern canonic discourses which prize a tiny handful of works for the musical stage at the expense of the simply colossal repertory—conveniently labelled as 'forgotten' to forestall possible criticism—which is equally conveniently pushed to one side and ignored as musical cultures are described and analysed on the basis of a tiny fraction of the surviving remains. Opéra de salon: *Societies and Spaces* juxtaposes a largely private musical and dramatic culture with the more public, state-regulated theatre that underpins most study of 'opera' today. The book implicitly presents challenges to the way in which music and theatre interact with both the urban and broader concepts of musical geography, while problematizing questions of listening and the preservation of attention. Identifying the exact position where performances took place allows a geolocative structure to be built, while questions of *spatialité* suggest the ways in which physical spaces—*lieux*—are transformed into performative *espaces*; both geolocation and *spatialité* may be correlated with questions of class to provide a reading of music and drama in Second Empire society. Networks of actors who engaged with *opéra de salon* behave in totally different ways from those associated with the regulated theatre, and Opéra de salon: *Societies and Spaces* attempts to disentangle the issues of professionalism and non-professionalism that lie at the heart of the genre and of its cultivation. Women are central not only to the world of *opéra de salon* as

---

[2] Rebecca Rogers, *From the Salon to the Schoolroom: Educating Bourgeois Girls in Nineteenth-Century France* (University Park: Pennsylvania State University Press, 2005); the work is a crucial source text for much of chapter 6.

salonnières but also to the composition of libretti and scores, and central to this culture lie the interests of the *demoiselles* and the support they received. In doing this, the book responds to and engages with the recent growth in the interest in and understanding of music in the *salon* across Europe and in the Americas. While *opéra de salon* remains an exclusively Parisian undertaking (with some regional presence described in chapter 7), the broader picture of music in *salon* culture, and of 'opera' beyond the 'opera house', had resonated across the world for decades before *opéra de salon* emerged. Studies of these musical ecosystems throw down the gauntlet not only before assumptions that govern the understanding of the engagement with music by women and by non-professionals in general but also before the dominance of the study of music in the concert hall and the opera house. Several recent studies have sketched out some key territory: a study of music and the *salon* across Europe and the Americas in the last forty years of the nineteenth century, an investigation of Mary Gladstone's *salon* in late Victorian London, and article-length studies in a number of collections of essays.[3]

It is all the more surprising, then, that *opéra de salon* has figured so little in accounts of nineteenth-century music. As long ago as 1980, Carl Dahlhaus suggested that 'The salon was in the first half of the nineteenth century, alongside the opera house and the concert hall, one of the places that was crucial for the history of music, and that mediated between the premises of social history and history of composition', and while it is unclear what other places Dahlhaus might consider critical (educational establishments, the open air, the military, perhaps?), the emphasis on the *salon* was at the same time remarkable but little heeded, even if it denied the *salon* any aesthetic power after the mid-century.[4] Only in the last two or three years has *opéra de salon* surfaced, but this has been in the context of general histories of music,[5] composer

---

[3] Rebecca Cypess, *Women and Musical Salons in the Enlightenment* (Chicago: University of Chicago Press, 2022); Phyllis Weliver, *Mary Gladstone and the Victorian Salon: Music, Literature, Liberalism* (Cambridge: Cambridge University Press, 2017); Anja Bunzel and Natasha Loges, eds., *Musical Salon Culture in the Long Nineteenth Century* (Woodbridge, UK: Boydell Press, 2019).

[4] 'Der Salon war in der ersten Hälfte des 19. Jahrhunderts neben dem Opernhaus und dem Konzertsaal einer der Orte, die musikgeschichtlich entscheidend waren und zwischen gesellschaftsgeschichtlichen und kompositionsgeschichtlichen Voraussetzungen vermittelten'. Carl Dahlhaus, *Die Musik des 19. Jahrhunderts*, Neues Handbuch der Musikwissenschaft 6 (Wiesbaden: Akademische Verlagsgesellschaft Athenaion, 1980) 121; trans. J. Bradford Robinson as *Nineteenth-Century Music* (Berkeley: University of California Press, 1989) 147–148. The translation has been lightly adapted.

[5] The sole exception is the short but valuable overview in Pierre Girod, 'Un demi-siècle d'opéra de salon', *Histoire de l'opéra français*, 3 vols., ed. Hervé Lacombe (Paris: Fayard, 2020) 2:560–570.

studies,[6] or studies of the urban.[7] Opéra de salon: *Parisian Societies and Spaces*, however, offers a comprehensive account of the repertory that should be read against a broader study of the origins and early history of *opérette* and related types alongside which *opéra de salon* developed.[8]

Devoting a study to the non-canonic or to the unexceptional carries many advantages. It allows the musically quotidian to emerge with some force in ways that studies of 'opera' sideline at best and ignore at worst. While a study of *opéra de salon* leads certainly to aristocratic and *haut-bourgeois* salons and to the related performers' studios and concert halls, it also offers more than a glimpse of the world of the *moyen-* and even *petit-bourgeois parloir*. Furthermore, large parts of the repertory encourage the recovery of the life and educational world of the *demoiselle*—the young woman between school and marriage—and the role that music and *opéra de salon* play in it. The study of *opéra de salon* furthermore animates a discussion of the nature and extent of *salon* culture and of '*salon* music'. Put simply, *opéra de salon* problematizes performance that is both broader than the *salon*, in the concert hall and in other public spaces, and narrower than the *salon*, in the artist's studio and the *parloir*.

Backgrounds and Contexts

In terms of its creation, function, and consumption, *opéra de salon* has almost nothing to do with what might be called the regulated theatre. But to speak of 'theatre' in Paris in the long nineteenth century is always to speak also of music. There is no theatrical genre that does not engage with music; while *grand opéra* and *opéra comique* speak for themselves, other theatrical genres—*mélodrame*, *vaudeville*, and related types—are conceived from the outset as careful blends of poetry, drama, and music.[9] But even

---

[6] Sabine Teulon Lardic, 'L'opéra de salon ou un salon à l'opéra: les contributions de Ferdinand Poise au *Magasin des demoiselles* (1865–1880)', *Presse et opéra aux XVIIIe et XIXe siècles*, ed. Olivier Bara, Christophe Cave, and Marie-Ève Thérenty, 2018 (http://www.medias19.org/index.php?id = 24101). Only one of Poise's *opéras de salon*, however, falls into the period considered in this book.
[7] Nicole Vilkner, 'Re-examining Salon Space: Structuring Audiences and Music at Parisian Receptions', *Journal of the Royal Musical Association* 147 (2022) 221–248.
[8] Such a project is close to publication. See Mark Everist, *Opérette: The First Twenty-Five Years* (New York: Oxford University Press, forthcoming).
[9] The terms to describe the genres *mélodrame* and *vaudeville* suffer from translation into English, the former because of the impossibly broad sense of 'melodrama' and the latter because of confusion with the American tradition of 'vaudeville' whose connection with *vaudeville* is tenuous at best and non-existent at worst (it aligns more clearly with *théâtre des variétés* or *music-hall* in French

seventeenth- and eighteenth-century classics at the Comédie-Française employed an orchestra for the performance of overtures, entr'actes, some songs, and melodramatic passages and played a key role in the relationship between music and drama in the city.

The plethora of unregulated theatre unleashed by the revolution of 1789 could not continue unchecked, and, taking time off from victories at Iéna and Wagram, Napoléon enacted a number of pieces of legislation during 1806 and 1807 that would control the Parisian theatrical world for more than half a century. The aim was to ensure that only one theatre performed a single type of work: so *opéra comique* was restricted to the theatre of the same name, the Théâtre-Italien held the monopoly on Italian opera in its original language, and the Académie Impérial de Musique was dedicated to through-composed works in French that included dance, which later in the century would be known as *grand opéra*, as well as various forms of ballet. *Vaudeville*, *mélodrame*, comedy, and tragedy were assigned to a small handful of theatres across the city, and all others were closed. The legislation remained in place until 1864, when it was repealed after having come under immense pressure and in some instances having largely collapsed in the preceding decade. Despite the legal emergence of a number of additional theatres in the first half of the century—the Gymnase Dramatique, the Théâtre de la Renaissance and the Opéra National (later the Théâtre-Lyrique)—the legislation nevertheless controlled the exercise of theatrical power in the city during no fewer than seven political regimes.[10] Even the emergence of the theatres dedicated to *opérette*—the Théâtre des Folies-Concertantes/Nouvelles and the Théâtre des Bouffes-Parisiens—was managed within the legislative constraints of the 1806–1807 laws.[11] The term 'regulated theatre' is used in this book to identify the places that supported theatrical works, and by extension the works

and 'variety' in English). The French terms (italicized) for *mélodrame* and *vaudeville* are therefore retained in this book.

[10] For details on individual theatres and their arrangements for governance, see Nicole Wild, *Dictionnaire des théâtres parisiens au xixe siècle: les théâtres et la musique* (Paris: Amateurs des Livres, 1989), revised and enlarged as *Dictionnaire des théâtres parisiens (1807–1914)*, collection Perpetuum mobile (Lyon: Symétrie, 2012). The ways in which genre and power were controlled and exploited within this framework are outlined in Mark Everist, 'The Music of Power: Parisian Opera and the Politics of Genre, 1806–1864', *Journal of the American Musicological Society* 67 (2014) 685–734; and a case study of the Paris Opéra during the period covered by this book is idem, *The Empire at the Opéra: Theatre, Power and Music in Second Empire Paris*, Cambridge Elements of Musical Theatre (Cambridge: Cambridge University Press, 2021).
[11] Mark Everist, 'Jacques Offenbach: The Music of the Past and the Image of the Present', *Music, Theater and Cultural Transfer: Paris, 1830–1914*, ed. Mark Everist and Annegret Fauser (Chicago: Chicago University Press, 2009) 72–98.

themselves, that were controlled by the state (including *cafés-concerts* after they started mounting sanctioned productions of *opérette* in 1867). The regulated theatre invited patrons to exchange money for a seat at a performance, and it paid actors, dancers, musicians, and a host of other agents to provide the *spectacle*; it may then be distinguished from the more private environments—the *salon*, the concert hall, the studio, and the *parloir* which are the focus of this book.

Opéra de salon was completely immune to the strictures that the licensing regulations entailed, and the number of *opéras de salon* that moved back and forth between the regulated theatre and the world of the *salon* was vanishingly small. Performers, audience behaviours, and performance cultures associated with *opéra de salon* likewise owed little or nothing to the regulated theatre. On the other hand, the anatomy of *opéra de salon*—the patterns of its libretti, the distribution of compositions within the work, the internal structure of those compositions—has much in common with that of the *opérette* which emerged at the same moment: the earliest *opéra de salon* dates from 1852, and the first theatre dedicated to *opérette*, the Folies-Concertantes founded by Hervé (Louis-Auguste-Florimond Ronger) was authorized in December 1853, followed rapidly by Jacques Offenbach's Bouffes-Parisiens, authorized in May 1855.

Much of the reason for the distance between the cultures of *opéra de salon* and the regulated theatre was geography: *opéra de salon* circulated in different and highly varied places. There are four different environments in which *opéra de salon* was cultivated that are discrete in some ways and overlap in others: the *salon* itself, the musician's studio, the concert hall, and the *parloir*. Epistemological difficulty surrounds the last of these: while performances of *opéra de salon* in *salons*, studios, and concert halls were previewed and reviewed in the press—and this material is key to understanding the genre—performances in the *parloir* were never reviewed, and the nature of such performances has to be inferred from the contexts in which works for the *parloir* were published, most importantly in journals dedicated to the interests of *demoiselles*, young women between school and marriage. Concert halls—the Salle Érard, the Salle Pleyel, and especially the Salle Herz—were venues where performances of *opéra de salon* were at their most public and therefore closest to the controls shared with the regulated theatre; in these instances, libretti had to be submitted to the censor, the police were concerned with questions of safety, and carriage traffic in the street required control. Even though some of the largest *salons* could match some public concert halls in terms of audience capacity, their invitation-only status and private premises absolved them from any intrusion by the state. Such *salons* could range from the most opulent ballrooms of the aristocracy or *haute bourgeoisie* repurposed for performances of *opéra de salon* to the rooms of *moyen-bourgeois* men of letters or—an important group—medical professionals. Similar privacy was enjoyed in musicians' studios, where performances were attended in perhaps smaller numbers than at the larger *salon* events but were similarly sheltered from state intervention. Even when the celebrated tenor Gilbert Duprez enlarged his studio to build a fully featured theatre in his home, it remained immune to the controls of the state. The *parloir*—the smallest and most intimate of all the places in which *opéra de salon* was developed—could be found in relatively modest apartments, and here the cultivation of *opéra de salon* was at its most intimate and opaque.

The different places where *opéra de salon* was cultivated triggered different listening practices. Attentiveness in the Salle Pleyel, for example, could be assumed to be the same as that for any other sort of concert, and paradoxically, what little evidence survives for listening in the *parloir* has very small numbers of individuals in a very small place that constitutes an intense zone of attention. Likewise, the professional expectations in musicians' studios might also be expected to have inspired a high level of attentiveness, although even here the possibility of other activities taking place around the edges of the performance remains great; professional commentaries on works or performers in real time would have been an almost inevitable sound track to these types of events.

Such issues raise the question of how to define the specifically *salon* culture of *opéra de salon*—as opposed to the cultures developed in concert hall, musician's studio, and especially *parloir*. *Salon* culture has a history stretching back to the seventeenth century, but its history after 1789 becomes progressively complex with each change of regime. There was almost no *salon* culture immediately after the *trois glorieuses* of the July Revolution of 1830,[12] for example, and gender balance, the subject of the *salon* (political, literary, conversational, celebrity, or musical), and competition with other emerging social structures—the *cercle* in particular—complicate the history of the *salon* ecosystem. This means that understanding the Second Empire *salon* entails

---

[12] The July Revolution of 1830 took place over three days, 27–29 July 1830, saw the final exile of Charles X and the royal family, placed Louis Philippe on the throne, and inaugurated the July Monarchy; the three days were thereafter known as *les trois glorieuses*.

recognizing its difference from that of the preceding July Monarchy and also the multiplicity of *salon* practices within the Second Empire itself.

The wide range of endeavour encompassed by the term *salon* also implies different modes of listening. In general, the highly distributed layout of spaces in a *salon* permitted a range of simultaneous activities, which in turn prompted irregular zones of attention across the space. The highly structured formality of the aristocratic or *haut-bourgeois* ballroom or large reception room, repurposed as a theatre with seating in rows, would, however, imply the same types of zones of attention as in the regulated theatre; to be sure, there was a wide range of attention across the gamut of Parisian theatres, from the Opéra to the Funambules, and this variety of engagement must have been replicated in the performances of *opéra de salon* in those aristocratic and *haut-bourgeois* settings that aimed to mimic the formal space of the theatre. This process of imitating practices at the regulated theatre was furthermore gendered, and performances of *opéra de salon* in ballrooms and analogous spaces dramatize the different behaviours of male and female. Even without the complicating presence of *loges* and other stratified forms of participation (*fauteuils*, *premier balcon*, *deuxième balcon*, and so on), the simple rows of seats were largely occupied by women, while men stood and, more importantly, circulated at the back and at the sides, very much in the same way as males and females interacted in the *coulisses* of the regulated theatre.

Repertories and Performance Practices

Opéra de salon emerged from, and functioned within, several social, theatrical, and musical practices. The best known is the concert in the *salon*, which closely imitated, in its division into the *parties vocales* and *parties instrumentales*, the more public concerts given in the halls owned by the piano manufacturers: Pleyel, Érard, Souffleto, and especially Herz. Equally important was the tradition of *théâtre de société*, which brought *comédies*, *drames* (occasionally), and *vaudevilles* out of the regulated theatre and into the private sphere.[13] This was a long tradition, and one that had constantly

---

[13] For an introduction to *théâtre de société* in nineteenth-century France, see the collection of essays *Tréteaux et paravents: le théâtre de société au xixe siècle*, ed. Jean-Claude Yon and Nathalie Le Gonidec (Paris: Créphis, 2012), especially the introduction: Jean-Claude Yon, 'Le théâtre de société au xixe siècle: une pratique à redécouvrir', 13–27.

engaged with music, sometimes to the extent (as in the case of the Abbaye de Royaumont in the 1830s) of including works known from the Théâtre-Italien or Opéra-Comique.[14] Two important elements of *théâtre de société* that had a direct impact on *opéra de salon* were the *charade* and the *proverbe*; both forms were recast as short plays and often involved some form of music, but more importantly, the concept of the dramatic *proverbe* was one that overlapped to a great degree with *opéra de salon* and was one of its key prompts. A further element in *théâtre de société* which—unlike the *charade* or the *proverbe*—intersected with the regulated theatre was the *vaudeville*, which figured across the performative field, especially in works published in journals for the *parloir*.

The four different types of space in which *opéra de salon* functioned—*salon*, concert hall, studio, and *parloir*—intersect with two groups of works separated not by their anatomy, style, or register but more by their function. There is no overlap between the two, so one group of works circulated around and between the *salons*, studios, and concert halls, while a second was restricted to the *parloir*. The first group was published via conventional means—through Parisian publishing houses—and scores and libretti could be bought according to circumstance and taste, whereas the second group circulated exclusively via publication in journals dedicated to the interests of the *demoiselle*. There is almost no evidence of a work published in a such a journal ever being performed in a *salon*, studio, or concert hall, and while *opéras de salon* published in journals were destined for the *parloir*, there is no evidence that works composed for the studio, *salon*, or concert hall appeared in the *parloir*. The overwhelming evidence for the types of works circulating in the studio, concert hall, and *salon*, however, strongly suggest that there was a difference in function but not in style, anatomy, or register between the two groups of *opéras de salon*. The book stops short of a terminological distinction between *opéra de salon* and 'opéra de parloir' simply because the former term is authorized by the nineteenth century, while the latter is not. This distinction, however, remains tacitly in place throughout Opéra de salon: *Parisian Societies and Spaces*.

In its use of a single act with around ten scenes, seven composed numbers, an overture, and three or four characters, *opéra de salon* clearly

---

[14] Jean-Claude Yon, 'Des tréteaux dans une abbaye: la comédie de société à Royaumont sous la monarchie de Juillet', *Royaumont au xixe siècle: les métamorphoses d'une abbaye*, ed. Jean-François Belhoste and Nathalie Le Gonidec (Paris: Créaphis, 2008) 137–147.

requires understanding in the context of the emerging history of *opérette*. Comparisons, however, are dangerous: while certain composers and librettists moved from *opéra de salon* to *opérette* and beyond, others restricted themselves to the *salon* alone, and performers by and large specialized in *opéra de salon* and did not explore the regulated theatre. Any movement of works themselves between that part of the regulated theatre represented by the Folies-Concertantes/Nouvelles and the Bouffes-Parisiens was negligible and usually the result of personal impulse on the part of the composer or librettist engaged in the regulated theatre itself. A difficulty with taking a comparative approach to *opéra de salon* and *opérette*, even if the repertorial and performative overlaps were trivial, is that the current view of *opérette* in the Second Empire and beyond is completely dominated by the works of Offenbach, whose penchant for burlesque libretti together with literary and musical parody is not matched by the rest of the repertory. And when it is recognized that Offenbach's works constitute only 12 percent of the works premiered during the first two decades of the genre's history, the comparison between *opéra de salon* and the remaining 88 percent of the *opérette* repertory falls into place very quickly.

The distinction between *opéra de salon* and works from the regulated theatre also plays out in issues of power. Away from the regulated theatre, *opéra de salon* was far removed from the types of competition between theatres engendered by perceived overlaps in licence and *cahier des charges* witnessed throughout the licensing period. It was also immune to the sorts of political engagement that blighted the Opéra for most of the Second Empire starting around 1854. *Opéra de salon*, however, appears to regulate itself with conventions around the anatomy of the libretto (one act, around ten scenes, and three to four characters) and the score (most frequently seven compositions and an overture) but most importantly around the subject matter, register, and tone of the libretto, which remained conservatively circumscribed with never an attempt at satire or political commentary; in this regard, *opéra de salon* shies away from the type of multi-act *opérette* in particular fostered by Offenbach after the 1858 triumph of *Orphée aux enfers* but aligns itself most clearly with the other much larger repertory of one-act *opérette*. In this self-regulating behaviour, *opéra de salon* is much more like the generalized approach to the censors taken by the entire Parisian theatre industry, in which—apart from a handful of spectacularly public examples that have disproportionately dominated the literature—most librettists knew very well the tolerances of the censors and effectively self-censored. Much more important for *opéra de salon* was the question of cultural capital and the extent to which expenditure on performers, perhaps sets, and other activities could elicit approval and admiration from one's peers.[15] This was certainly true of performances in aristocratic and *haut-bourgeois salons* or ones given by those same groups outside their homes. Even for performances in the *parloir*, *opéra de salon* could evoke the same sorts of admiration and regard, although the challenges might have been easier to surmount: the ability to find footlights, for example, or even keeping the family dog away from proceedings.

Methodology and Terminology

Opéra de salon: Parisian Societies and Spaces not only brings to light an almost completely unknown repertory but also offers new ways of looking at music for the stage, by focussing on questions of geography and urbanism, geolocation, and *spatialité*. While the book advances a view of 'opéra' that emphasizes domestic environment, location, and class, it does this with a repertory that requires description at every turn. 'Description' is a term much in need of recovery. Here, in a recent call for conference papers, for example, is a common formulation that prefers 'hypotheses' and 'connections' to 'description': 'we will favour papers that explore hypotheses and seek connections, *rather than offer only description* [emphasis added]'; and others make clear that 'On privilégiera les propositions explorant des enjeux problématisés, plutôt que les approches purement descriptives'.[16] This certainly sets the bar high for scholarship that seeks not only to 'explore hypotheses and seek connections' or 'explor[er] des enjeux problématisés'

---

[15] The concept of cultural capital, today much cited and much used, dates back to 1970 and the publication of Pierre Bourdieu and Jean-Claude Passeron, *La reproduction: éléments pour une théorie du systâeme d'enseignement*, Sens commun (Paris: Éditions de Minuit, 1970). The earliest empirical study of music as cultural capital appears to be Richard A. Petersen and Albert Simkus, 'How Musical Tastes Mark Occupational Status Groups', *Cultivating Difference: Symbolic Boundaries and the Making of Inequality*, ed. Michèle Lamont and Marcel Fournier (Chicago: University of Chicago Press, 1992) 152–186, where the authors took data from the 1982 'Survey of Public Participation in the Arts', undertaken by the US Census Bureau for the National Endowment for the Arts. Cultural capital is but one of three subdivisions outlined in Pierre Bourdieu, 'Okonomisches Kapital, kulturelles Kapital, soziales Kapital', *Soziale Ungleichheiten*, ed. Reinhard Kreckel, Soziale Welt: Sonderheft 2 (Göttingen: Schartz, 1983) 183–198.

[16] See 'Cultural Intermediaries in the Nineteenth-Century Music Market / Call for Papers / University of Bristol / June 23–24, 2023' (https://www.19cmusicmarket.com/call-for-papers); 'tosc@paris.2109—Appel à communications / 3rd transnational / opera studies / conference / Paris, 27–29 June 2019' (https://scenes-monde.univ-paris8.fr/tosc-paris-2019-appel-a-communications).

but also to recover a repertory that is completely unknown and where a lack of description would merely lead to incomprehensibility. Yet another paper on *La traviata* can take much description in previous literature for granted, whereas one that offers any sort of reading of any of the works discussed in this book has much basic explanation—description—to undertake.

The crude distinction between 'descriptions' and *enjeux problematisés*, 'hypotheses', or 'connections' is already one that has come in for harsh criticism in other disciplines. Here is Bruno Latour writing as long ago as 2005:

> And what is so wrong with 'mere descriptions'? . . . The simple act of recording anything on paper is already an immense transformation that requires as much skill and just as much artifice as painting a landscape or setting up some elaborate biochemical reaction. No scholar should find humiliating the task of sticking to description. This is, on the contrary, the highest and rarest achievement.
>
> However, we worry that by sticking to description there may be something missing, since we have not 'added to it' something else that is often called an 'explanation'. And yet the opposition between description and explanation is another of these false dichotomies that should be put to rest.[17]

Additionally, Latour invoked 'thick description' in his gloss on these comments: a direct reference to Clifford Geertz's *The Interpretation of Cultures*, which provoked so much interest in music studies in the 1980s but which has had so little impact on the discipline that denigrations of 'mere' or 'only' 'description' are now so commonplace that they have become conventional.[18]

If Opéra de salon: *Parisian Societies and Spaces* manages to elude the false dichotomy between 'description' and 'explanation' to which Latour refers, it will be because it problematizes relationships between creators, recreators, works, contexts, and environments for cultivation at the same time as it

---

[17] Bruno Latour, *Reassembling the Social: An Introduction to Actor-Network Theory*, Clarendon Lectures in Management Studies (Oxford: Oxford University Press, 2005) 136–137.

[18] Clifford Geertz, 'Thick Description: Toward an Interpretive Theory of Culture', *The Interpretation of Cultures* (New York: Basic Books, 1973; London: Hutchinson, 1975) 3–30. The precepts of *The Interpretation of Cultures* were exposed to the musicological world in Gary Tomlinson, 'The Web of Culture: A Context for Musicology', *19th-Century Music* 7 (1984) 350–362, but a decade later, Philip V. Bohlman could lament how little impact Geertz's or Tomlinson's proposals had made on the discipline, in 'On the Unremarkable in Music', *19th-Century Music* 16 (1992) 203–216.

describes those same works and contexts together with the agents that animate them. A large part of the underpinning research for the book consisted of establishing the extent of the corpus of *opéra de salon*, recovering a total of around 120 works from the appearance of the genre in the early 1850s up to the end of 1870.[19] Many of these works exist in a partial form—a libretto that reveals little about the music, a score that discloses nothing about the dramatic structure, or a reference in the press to a work that has left no other trace—and that are difficult to integrate into an analysis. However, a core of sixty-seven *opéras de salon* survives with all sources intact or recoverable, and this forms the basis of generalized observations on style and structure (see the appendix in chapter 1). Documentation of performances traverses the complete range of possibilities: some pieces are the subject of several attested performances in such journals as *La Revue et Gazette musicale de Paris*, *Le ménestrel*, *Le musée des familles*, even in the *Le journal des débats*, while other works that might exist in a complete form have left no trace of performance;[20] this is a particularly pressing issue for the *opéras de salon* cultivated in the *parloir* whose performances never claimed the attention of the press. While it may be assumed that the approximately 120 *opéras de salon* constitute close to the entire repertory, the 148 documented performances must certainly be counted as a mere fraction of the number of performances that must have taken place.[21]

Much of Opéra de salon: *Parisian Societies and Spaces* engages with the relationship between physical space and groups of individuals with varying degrees of wealth and status. The latter discussion is premised on, but by no means restricted to, Marxian categorizations of aristocracy, *haute*, *moyenne*, and *petite bourgeoisie*, inflected by the concept of *habitus* derived from Maurice Merleau-Ponty and filtered through early Pierre Bourdieu.[22] This

---

[19] There is an incomplete list of *opéras de salon* in Pierre Girod, 'L'opéra de salon à Paris [*sic*] (1851–1904)' (https://dezede.org/dossiers/opera-de-salon/). It contains sixty-nine works up to 1870, including one English piece and three by Pauline Viardot written for Baden, so only sixty-five out of the approximately 120 inventoried for this study; this is now superseded for the period covered by this book by Mark Everist, 'Music in the Second Empire Theatre (MitSET)' (http://www.fmc.ac.uk/mitset/).

[20] There is a *dossier de presse* of 211 texts relating to the performance of *opéra de salon* during the Second Empire on which much of this book is based. Mark Everist, 'Opéra de salon', FMC Collection 30 (http://search.fmc.ac.uk/#m-columnbrowser@||m-informationcontrol@url = html/home.php).

[21] In addition to the inventory in Everist, 'Music in the Second Empire Theatre', and the *dossier de presse*, the geolocative data have been used in a third digital resource to produce an interactive map of the culture of *opéra de salon*. See '*Opéra de salon*: Paris, 1850–1870' (https://musicalgeography.org/opera-de-salon/) and the discussion in chapter 7.

[22] The literature on Marx and class is vast; this study has been largely guided by A. Jordan Zbigniew, ed., *Karl Marx: Economy, Class and Social Revolution* (London: Thomas Nelson

terminology has the advantage of giving names to the middle classes whose plurality has been stressed by William Weber.[23] The *haute bourgeoisie* from at least the 1850s were associating with the aristocracy in the same domains and in search of the same cultural capital; *opéra de salon* gave them both. For the current study, the *moyenne bourgeoisie* is of particular importance since the repertories of *opéra de salon* it cultivated overlap with the aristocracy and *haute bourgeoisie*; the *moyenne bourgeoisie* is identified with the professions: architects, men of letters of all types, lawyers, civil servants, and medical professionals. In its use of the same repertory and employment of the same artists as the aristocracy and *haute bourgeoisie*, *moyen-bourgeois* Paris deployed *opéra de salon* as a way of obscuring social boundaries. But the genre also could be seen to be slightly blurring the distinction between *moyenne* and *petite bourgeoisie*, in that *opéra de salon* was cultivated both in the *moyen-bourgeois salon* and in the *petit-bourgeois parloir*. However, although the genre was basically shared between the two groups, individual works did not pass from one environment (the *parloir*, publication in journals) to the other (the aristocratic and *haut-bourgeois salon*, the concert hall, and *moyen-bourgeois* environments). In this regard, *opéra de salon* did much less cultural work effacing the boundaries of the *petite* and *moyenne bourgeoisie* than it did between the latter and the aristocratic/*haut-bourgeois* ecosystem.

Not unrelated to questions of performance environment and social structure is the status of the librettists and composers who created *opéra de salon* and of the performers who brought it to life. Casual distinctions between 'amateur' and professional, while made frequently in the study of nineteenth-century music outside the public domain, are treacherous in the extreme. The elision between ability to play and to derive revenue from the activity is nowhere near as clear as is often assumed, and the concept of the 'professional' composer or librettist—in the sense that composer or librettist could have been an exclusive career choice—is a nebulous one. For performers, at

and Sons, 1972); Edward Andrew, 'Class in Itself and Class against Capital: Karl Marx and His Classifiers', *Canadian Journal of Political Science/Revue canadienne de science politique* 16 (1983) 577–584; Ralf Dahrendorf, *Class and Class Conflict in Industrial Society* (Stanford, CA: Stanford University Press, 1959). For Bourdieu's *habitus*, a good point of departure is Karl Maton, 'Habitus', *Pierre Bourdieu: Key Concepts*, 2nd ed., ed. Michael Grenfell (Abingdon: Routledge, 2014) 48–64.

[23] William Weber, 'The Muddle of the Middle Classes', *19th-Century Music* 3 (1979) 175–185.

least, there is some nineteenth-century terminological peg on which to hang some alternatives. Within the domain of Parisian *salon* performance and of *opéra de salon* in particular, the term *artiste-virtuose* was much used and is helpful in identifying those who had professional training and who derived revenue from their performances. *Artistes-virtuoses* were distinguished from vocal artists from the regulated theatres who were usually identified in terms of the theatre or opera house at which they were currently singing: 'The lively singer from the Théâtre-Italien, Mme Nantier-Didié exhibited a verve, a spirit, an irresistible charm in the Spanish songs', for example.[24] But those who were not identified as *artistes-virtuoses* are perhaps more interesting, and separating out musical and literary ability in what this book calls a non-professional group is one of the principal tasks chapter 2.

One of the most common Parisian determinants of class in the nineteenth century was where you lived. Some areas of the city mapped directly onto specific social groupings, and the focus of each is important to the understanding the circulation of *opéra de salon*. The Faubourg Saint-Germain—the *noble Faubourg*—was the home of the aristocracy; the Faubourg Saint-Honoré was where the expensive new building was taking place and the place that attracted the *haute bourgeoisie*; and Nouvelle Athènes was the neighbourhood where artists and musicians of all types had rubbed shoulders since the 1830s. But these neighbourhoods had boundaries, and the boundaries were porous; for example, the eastern end of the Faubourg Saint-Germain, especially the area around the hospital—the Hôtel-Dieu—was populated unsurprisingly by medical professionals, and this entire region was a central location for the *moyen-bourgeois* performance of *opéra de salon*. The specific geolocation of performances of *opéra de salon* in part defines the genre and should be read alongside the analysis of the types of works, their performers, and, insofar as they can be established, their audiences.

Whatever the geolocation of performance spaces for *opéra de salon*, none of these venues was designed to support *opéra de salon* in the same way that a theatre was designed to provide a home for *opérette* or *vaudeville*. Salons

---

[24] 'La spirituelle cantatrice du Théâtre-Italien, Mme Nantier-Didiée, a montré une verve, un esprit, un charme irrésistibles dans des chansons espagnoles' (*La Revue et Gazette musicale de Paris*, 6 February 1859).

and *parloirs* were not designed predominantly for performance, nor were artists' studios, which were primarily living areas repurposed for teaching and further repurposed as performance spaces. Concert halls were designed primarily as showrooms for the piano manufacturers' products, secondly for performances using their instruments, and only finally for such activities as the performance of *opéra de salon*.

The concept of repurposing evokes various attempts to theorize *spatialité* made since the end of the Second World War, efforts that draw a distinction between the physical boundary and the material on the one hand and the use to which it is put on the other. Central to this concept of *spatialité* is Merleau-Ponty's distinction between *espace géométrique* and *espace anthropologique*; the former is homogeneous and isotropic, the latter multivalent and endless.[25] *Espaces géométriques* are susceptible to unambiguous description and can be analysed and categorized, as when Henri Lefebvre grouped them into *espaces géométriques, visuels*, and *phalliques* (although Lefebvre makes no reference to Merleau-Ponty in this regard).[26] The study of *espaces anthropologiques* for Merleau-Ponty can therefore be pursued indefinitely: there are as many *espaces (anthropologiques)* as there are distinct spatial experiences.[27] He goes on to enhance the concept with the construction of a further dimension of *spatialité* conditioned by aesthetic perception; he gives the examples of a painting that is more than the *espace* (*géométrique* or *anthropologique* is not specified) it inhabits and of dance which, according to him, uses the body in different ways from natural experience and likewise falls outside—or requires more subtle analysis of—broader concepts of *espace*.[28]

Michel de Certeau brought the concept of *spatialité* into the study of the urban and the domestic and provided a terminology that is less ambiguous than Merleau-Ponty's or Lefebvre's; it is also one that has emerged with a clear set of supporting conditions.[29] De Certeau's terms are *lieu* and *espace* (corresponding to Merleau-Ponty's *espace géométrique* and *espace anthropologique*, respectively), For de Certeau, *lieu* is a set of stable,

---

[25] Maurice Merleau-Ponty, *Phénoménologie de la perception*, Bibliothèque des idées (Paris: Gallimard, 1945; reprint 1992) 324–344 (in the 1992 reprint).
[26] Henri Lefebvre, *La production de l'espace*, Société et urbanisme (Paris: Anthropos, 1976) 328–331.
[27] Merleau-Ponty, *Phénoménologie de la perception*, 333.
[28] *Ibidem*, note 1.
[29] Michel de Certeau, *L'invention du quotidien*, 2 vols. (Paris: Union Générale d'Éditions, 1980; reprint Paris: Gallimard, 1990–1994) 1:172–175 (in the1990 reprint).

describable, and measurable relationships—between wall and floor, between *canapé* and table—where the objects have their own positions and relations to others; time does not play a role. This stability sits in contrast with *espace*, which de Certeau describes variously as an intersection of mobilities, an environment in which vectors of distance, speed, and time come into play. 'In short', writes de Certeau, '*espace is a worked lieu* [his emphasis]';[30] his example is of a street (a *lieu*) transformed into a market by the actions of vendors, the presence of stalls, and the less transitory behaviours of pedestrians, who stop to browse, bargain, and buy.[31]

It is easy to see how the constant transformation of domestic *lieux* into performative *espaces* underpins almost all performances of *opéra de salon*. Perhaps the only exception might be the theatre that Duprez built in his own home, where the *lieu* is conceived as a static performance space and no further repurposing as theatrical space is required. In general, and more or less for all performances of *opéra de salon*, *lieux* are reconfigured as *espaces* for the sole purpose of mounting a production, and the subtle contingency of this repurposing recurs throughout this book. Musicians repurposed their studios; so did sculptors. Concert halls were reconfigured with stages, and the types of ad hoc arrangement in the *parloir* were legion.

The polyvalent significance of *opéra de salon* lies first in its intrinsic impact on the rapidly changing landscape of music in the nineteenth-century Parisian theatre. Accounts of a limited repertory of *grands opéras*, *opéras comiques*, and imported works at the Théâtre-Italien constitute a very partial account of the subject; and although *opérette* is now taking its place in that cartography, most analysis is restricted to the tiny proportion of the repertory created by Offenbach. *Opéra de salon* not only sits alongside the larger share of the *opérette* repertory but also beside *vaudeville* and related genres, *ballet-pantomime*, *mélodrame*, and the music that found its way—in terms of the overtures, entr'actes, and occasional songs encompassed by the term *musique de scène*—into what the anglophone world has termed since 1737 the 'legitimate theatre'. The picture of music in the Parisian theatre not only begins to look very different from how it appeared twenty years ago but also points the way for more comprehensive accounts of music on stages in London, Vienna, Berlin, and Italian cities.

---

[30] 'En somme, l'espace *est un lieu pratiqué*' (*ibidem*, 173).
[31] *Ibidem*.

Although the fact that this book deals with the non-canonic is both obvious and essential, *Opéra de Salon: Parisian Societies and Spaces* bypasses questions of inclusion and of axiology; there is no attempt to seek integration of the repertory into the existing highly restricted cultures of 'opera' production or—equally restricted—'opera studies', nor are any claims made for the quality or modern viability of the genre. Works are treated on their own terms, and their value is more aligned with the views, opinions, and prejudices from the Second Empire than with those of the first quarter of the twenty-first century. In any case, at the level of early-twenty-first-century performance, almost nothing from the French nineteenth century rises to the status of the canonic apart from *Faust, Carmen, Pelléas et Mélisande*, and perhaps a handful of works by Offenbach; the nineteenth-century canonicity of Giacomo Meyerbeer, Daniel-François-Esprit Auber, Fromental Halévy, and Adolphe Adam remains something of an awkwardness, even an embarrassment, for modern critiques of the canon. Yet Paris is one of the environments for stage music where it is easy to see how canons were formed, even if they do not equate with, indeed if in many cases they contradict, modern ones. *Opéra de salon* is not immune from canonising pressures, although the effect is different from Meyerbeer at the Opéra, Auber at the Opéra-Comique, or even such imported repertories as Wolfgang Amadeus Mozart and Carl Maria von Weber at the Théâtre-Lyrique.

If a study of *opéra de salon*, together with *vaudeville*, *opérette* beyond Offenbach, *musique de scène*, *mélodrame*, and so on broadens the repertorial field of music in the nineteenth-century French theatre, then it also challenges to the history of institutions that support music on the stage. In contrast to the unbroken micro-rhythms of the French theatre—where the Opéra and Théâtre-Italien carefully dovetail performances in a single week so as not to compete with audiences, while the Opéra-Comique and other theatres perform every night of the week—*opéra de salon* has a completely unpredictable pulse, one more geared to the conventions of society, the regularities of *salons*, and the opportunism of *opéra de salon*'s creators and performers. It is only at the macro-rhythmic level that *opéra de salon* has any sort of convention to it, the restriction of the genre to the season that ran through the winter, and in this it matched only the Théâtre-Italien, while the Opéra and other theatres operated throughout the year.

Nevertheless, *opéra de salon* presents an opportunity to interrogate the quotidian, the unexceptional. True, there is little of the unexceptional about the performance of an *opéra de salon* in the Salle de Diane in the Louvre in the front of the imperial family, but such performances are rare; most of the performances discussed in Opéra de salon: *Parisian Societies and Spaces* interrogate private spaces and private rhythms of living in ways that other genres render impossible. By and large, the discussion leaves aside composers who enjoyed high status during their lifetimes, let alone at the hands of posterity, in favour of those who engaged with a *salon* culture that remains poorly understood. One of the challenges here is to resist the attempts made by the press to exceptionalize the culture of *opéra de salon*. It is understandable that authors writing for *La Revue et Gazette musicale de Paris* and *Le ménestrel*—the two sources that reveal most about creation and consumption of *opéra de salon*—would fall back on patterns of discourse with which they were most comfortable and that were used for performances at the Opéra and the Opéra-Comique, recitals at the Salle Herz, and so on. Such journalists constantly identify 'premieres' of *opéra de salon* in which the concept really makes little sense and frequently allude to works 'taking their place in the repertory', and this methodological anxiety speaks volumes about the very different, unexceptional, and quotidian nature of the *opéra de salon* and its cultures.

Even more broadly, the study of *opéra de salon* reveals a very different dimension of nineteenth-century music-making beyond, and in relation to, the public sphere. The private sophistication of *opéra de salon* reflects the private but also indicates very clearly the limits of its engagement with that of the public. The way the genre shares performance spaces at the Salle Herz with concerts by visiting soloists and of other types and with the—admittedly limited—regulated theatre suggests where the boundaries between private and public might fall and, most importantly, how porous they might be. With an understanding of the *salon* as something that, while ostensibly private, could be a context for display in front of two hundred or three hundred people, *opéra de salon* offers a glimpse of cultures that are both more public and more private than modern views of the *salon* allow. So the same *opéra de salon* could be performed in an aristocratic or *haut-bourgeois salon* and in the home of a *moyen-bourgeois* medical professional, but it might also be given in a space like the Salle Herz where the audience could be as big as the most ambitious *salon*. But equally, *opéra de salon*—although not with the same works as those for the *salon*, concert hall, and musicians' studios— found its way into the *parloirs* of those on the boundaries of the down-at-heel *moyenne bourgeoisie* or the aspirant *petite bourgeoisie*, where the size of the audience could be measured in the low tens, and the physical *lieu*, even when transformed into a performative *espace*, was modest in the extreme. These issues occupy the latter part of Opéra de salon: *Parisian Societies and Spaces*, but some explanation of how *opéra de salon* functions is an essential prerequisite, and that is where the book begins.

1
Opéra de salon

Opéra—salon

The term *opéra de salon* is something of a misnomer, since in general, the genre aligns itself much more closely with *opérette* and one-act *opéra comique* than with what modern—and some nineteenth-century—commentary considered *opéra*: works mounted at the Paris Opéra, Italian *melodramma* and *opera buffa*, and *opéra comique*. Many of the title pages of published *opéras de salon* use such terms as *opérette de salon* or *opéra comique de salon*, occasionally with the *salon* qualification omitted if the publication left its *salon* context in no doubt. Journalists favoured the term *opéra de salon* but were frequently unable to resist a wide range of other terms. *Salon*, furthermore, is itself a contested term and requires careful definition in the present context. Certainly, many of the performance contexts for the culture discussed in this book were what is understood to be a *salon*: a suite of rooms in a private dwelling in which the *salonnier* or *salonnière* invited guests to participate in a range of activities, from sewing to *séances* and from drawing to dancing. But equally, the artist's studio, the concert hall, and the domestic *parloir* were important environments for *opéra de salon*.

The *salon* of the Second Empire is particularly intriguing in its attempts to create a *lieu de mémoire* out of a *lieu social*:[1] to re-enact the glories of the seventeenth- and eighteenth-century literary *salons* in the very different environment of the mid-nineteenth. Most modern critical writing on the *salon* focusses on the earlier period,[2] while largely anecdotal accounts of the *salon* in the Second Empire date from the nineteenth century itself.[3] Accounts

---

[1] See Duncan McColl Chesney, 'The History of the History of the Salon', *Nineteenth-Century French Studies* 36 (2007–2008) 94–108.

[2] The literature on the *salon* of the *grand siècle* is vast. Key texts are Sonja Boon, *The Life of Madame Necker: Sin, Redemption and the Parisian Salon* (London: Pickering and Chatto, 2011); Steven Kale, *French Salons: High Society and Political Sociability from the Old Regime to the Revolution of 1848* (Baltimore: Johns Hopkins University Press, 2004); Antoine Lilti, *Le monde des salons: sociabilité et mondanité à Paris au XVIIIe siècle* (Paris: Fayard, 2005), trans. as *The World of the Salon: Sociability and Worldliness in Eighteenth-Century Paris* (New York: Oxford University Press, 2015).

[3] See Virginie Ancelot, *Les salons de Paris: foyers éteints* (Paris: Tardieu, 1858); Anaïs de Bassinville, *Les salons d'autrefois: souvenirs intimes*, 4 vols. (Paris: Victorion, n.d.); Edouard

of the fate of the *salon* after the 1789 revolution, during the two Bourbon restorations, and the revolutions of 1830 and 1848 are rare; however, several key trajectories may be traced.

Between 1789 and the Second Empire, the *salon* as an environment for the discussion of politics was clearly in a state of flux, as it confronted a number of competing intellectual ecosystems. The overriding trajectories were determined by physical spaces that broached the private and the public: the *boulevard*, the theatre, the spa (important, as it turns out, for *opéra de salon*), the café, the restaurant; but most important was the emergence at the end of the Second Bourbon Restoration of the *cercle*.[4] *Cercles* were a locus of sociability that differed from the *salon* in three important ways. First, they were partisan (legitimist, *ultra*, liberal, Bonapartist, republican, and so on). Second, as a result of such partisanship, the discussion of politics as the conversational subject was almost entirely absent (such an echo chamber is familiar from social media in the first quarter of the twenty-first century). Finally, and most important, they were all-male assemblies; there was no *salonnière*, and critically, the balance between male and female that had characterized the *salon* since the seventeenth century completely disappeared, with the consequence that the surviving *salons* tended towards female membership.[5]

Salons, then, like their competitors, began to align themselves with a much wider *mondanité*, one that reflected the growth of *tout-Paris* during the July Monarchy, and they began to develop a single-sex character that they had not known for centuries.[6] They also increased in size, to the extent that Charles-Augustin de Saint-Beuve could describe them, just before the advent of *opéra de salon*, in his famous *Causeries de lundi* as *raouts* (he blamed the move

---

Ferdinand de la Bonninière Beaumont-Vassy, *Les salons de Paris et la société parisienne sous Napoléon III* (Paris: Sartorius, 1868); Victor du Bled, *La société française depuis cent ans: quelques salons du Second Empire*, 2 vols. (Paris: Bloud & Gay, 1923). For scholarly attempts to engage with the *salon* of the Second Empire, see Laure Rièse, *Les salons littéraires parisiens du Second Empire à nos jours* (Paris: Privat, 1962); Antonietta Angelica Zucconi, 'Les salons de Mathilde et Julie Bonaparte sous le Second Empire', *Napoleonica: la revue* 11 (2011–2012) 151–183.

[4] Kale describes this change as a decline (*French Salons*, 165–199), but it really constitutes 'decline' rather than 'change' in terms only of the political rather than the literary *salon* (Kale's focus). But his diagnosis of the competition with the *salon* remains compelling. His discussion of the press and the way in which the offices of a newspaper could serve as a site of political sociability demonstrates very clearly how such a change could detract from the political importance of a *salon* (*ibidem*, 173–175).

[5] For a contemporary account of the first half century of the *cercles*' history, see Charles Yriarte, *Les cercles de Paris* (Paris: Dupray de la Mahérie, 1864); for a modern study of their importance, see Maurice Agulhon, *Le cercle dans la France bourgeoise, 1810–1848: étude d'une mutation de sociabilité*, Cahiers des annales 36 (Paris: Armand Colin, 1977).

[6] For the key diagnosis of the growth of the emergence of *tout-Paris*, see Anne Martin-Fugier, *La vie élégante ou La formation de out-Paris* (Paris: Fayard, 1993).

on the English).[7] This increase in the number of participants in a *salon* also changed their character, and with this shift came a move from *habitué* to audience member. A surge in the number of participants also aligned the *salon* much more with the performative—hardly surprising, since one of its principal competitors was the theatre—and the involvement of literary, theatrical, and musical stars as the points of focus during the *salon*'s proceedings.

Music, both instrumental and vocal, was a key part of a small number of private *salons* open only by invitation,[8] and many of these also cultivated *opéra de salon*; such private events were hosted by those with no professional stake in the performance or the work and could encompass performances in aristocratic or *haut-bourgeois* homes and performances in the homes of the professional classes: medical specialists, artists of all types, and men of letters. But the changes wrought on *salon* culture in the first half of the nineteenth century developed an environment that allowed *opéra de salon* to be cultivated elsewhere. The types of *lieux* that were repurposed as *espaces* for *opéra de salon* fell into four categories: the private *salon* (in all its complexity, as just discussed), the concert hall, musicians' studios, and the *parloir*. What would later be called the concert hall originally referred to the showrooms of the major Parisian piano manufacturers: Herz, Pleyel, Érard, Souffleto, and so on.[9] As in the case of the *salon*, the performative background to *opéra de salon* in the Salle Herz and elsewhere was the concert, with the binary division into vocal and instrumental halves of the traditional mid-nineteenth-century concert being expanded to admit a theatrical work with music. The third environment for the cultivation of *opéra de salon* was the studio of the

---

[7] Charles-Augustin de Sainte-Beuve, *Causeries de lundi*, 15 vols. (Paris: Garnier, 1851–1862) 1:103. See also Anne Martin-Fugier, 'La cour et la ville sous la Monarchie de Juillet d'après les feuilletons mondains', *Revue historique* 278 (1987) 121.

[8] Music in the *salon* has received a certain amount of recent attention: Anja Bunzel and Susan Wollenberg, 'Rethinking Salon Music: Case-Studies in Analysis', *Nineteenth-Century Music Review* 20 (2022) 359–364; Cypess, *Women and Musical Salons*; Bunzel and Loges, *Musical Salon Culture*; Mirjam Gerber, *Zwischen Salon und musikalischer Geselligkeit: Henriette Voigt, Livia Frege und Leipzigs bürgerliches Musikleben* (Hildesheim: Olms, 2016). A valuable introduction to music in the *salons* of the 1830s and 1840s (the July Monarchy) is Constance Himmelfarb, 'Un salon de la Nouvelle-Athènes en 1839–1840: l'album inconnu de Juliette Zimmerman', *Revue de musicologie* 87 (2001) 33–65. A further introduction to music in the *salons* of the Second Empire is David Tunley, 'The Salons and Their Music', *Salons, Singers and Songs: A Background to Romantic French Song, 1830–1870* (Aldershot: Ashgate, 2002) 18–41. For a reading of a rare *opéra de salon* that textually and musically embodies the features of the *salon* itself, see Vilkner, 'Re-examining Salon Space'.

[9] Of this wide range of performance venues, only the Salle Herz has been subjected to any sustained study. See Laure Schnapper, *Henri Herz, magnat du piano: la vie musicale en France au xixe siècle (1815–1870)*, En temps et lieu 23 (Paris: Éditions de l'École des Hautes Études en Sciences Sociales, 2011) 211–222. For an overview, see Joël-Marie Fauquet and Laure Schnapper, 'Salle de concert', *Dictionnaire de la musique en France au xixe siècle*, ed. Joël-Marie Fauquet (Paris: Fayard, 2003) 1113–1114.

composer or performer; this was a more modest *lieu* where the composer or performer could bring a production of an *opéra de salon* together with an audience of influential acquaintances; the resulting *espace* was frequently an ecosystem for showcasing new works or the achievements of students. For these first three types of venues, the press was regularly invited and consistently commented on the performances in such journals as *Le ménestrel* and *La Revue et Gazette musicale de Paris*. The fourth space for *opéra de salon* was the more modest *parloir*; unmentioned by the press and consequently the hardest to document and analyse, the *parloir* was the most intimate *lieu*, which gave a home to the genre that, even when configured as a performative *espace*, might not provide diversion for any more than family members supplemented occasionally by neighbours and friends. Of the four types of venues, the first three exploited an overlapping repertory of *opéra de salon*, with the same work cropping up in an aristocratic *salon*, in the home of a sculptor, or in the Salle Herz. The repertory of the *parloir*, by contrast, was closely linked to the publication of *opéras de salon* in women's journals (*Le journal des demoiselles* and *Le magasin des demoiselles*, for the most part) and never seemed to receive performances outside of the intimate *parloir* context.

Opéra de salon was an identifiable repertorial force in Parisian culture from the early 1850s until at least 1900, but it also constitutes a significant proportion of the overall repertory of one-act *opérette* and *opéra comique* in the period from around 1850 to around 1870. Alongside approximately one thousand *opérettes*, *opéras comiques*, or related types premiered in theatres and *cafés-concerts* between 1850 and 1870, approximately 120 *opéras de salon* were composed and performed during the same period.[10] The number of performances of *opéra de salon* is incalculable. Of the approximately 120 works identified in this study, nearly two hundred performances were recorded in the press, but these were events in *salons* and studios where there was a significant audience and high levels of public interest and in such more public venues as the Salle Herz or Salle Pleyel;[11] when the less ambitious

---

[10] All figures in this chapter are derived from Everist, 'Music in the Second Empire Theatre (MitSET)'.

[11] For example, the single documented performance of Pauline Thys's *L'héritier sans le savoir* in the salon of Pierre-Michel-François Chevalier, known as Pitre-Chevalier, had already been reported as having been 'this jewel—already mounted with so much success in the *salon* of Mme d'A--- and of Mme La comtesse de C---' ('ce bijou,—déjà enchâssé avec tant de succès chez Mme d'A--- et chez Mme la comtesse de C---'; *Le ménestrel*, 11 April 1858). Neither patron can be identified, and neither is reported as having supported *opéra de salon* on other occasions; in this case, the single

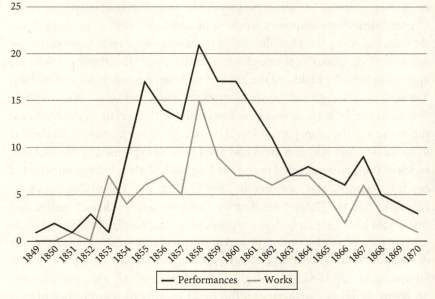

Figure 1.1. Graph of the number of works and performances of *opéra de salon*, 1849–1870.

parloir context is considered, the likely number of performances must have escalated sharply, although almost none was recorded. Distribution over time varies, with a peak in the two years before 1860, as figure 1.1 shows.

Figure 1.1 simply shows the number of new works composed and premiered in each year, and insofar as it is possible to ascertain the number of performances, this follows a similar arc. There is a discernible decline from 1858 to the end of the 1860s; this later decline may well be because the new theatres liberated by the repeal of the Napoleonic licensing laws (which had been in force since 1806/1807) in 1864 and the permission to mount stage works granted to *cafés-concerts* in 1867 squeezed *opéra de salon* out of its traditional public venues—Salle Herz, Salle Pleyel, and so on—and replaced it with one-act *opérette* in public theatres. The end of the licensing laws had its greatest effect on the development of *opérette*: either new houses opened or, more typically, theatres that had been dedicated to *vaudeville* and other forms where new composition had no place now moved to include newly

---

documentary account masks a minimum of three in total. See chapter 4 for a fuller account of *opéra de salon* in Pitre-Chevalier's home.

composed *opérettes* in their repertory. This immediately opened up a range of possibilities for composers working in *opéra de salon*, a choice that was then amplified by the 1867 decision to allow *cafés-concerts* to mount stage works with costumes, costume changes, and dance;[12] the physical spaces for *opérette* in both the regulated theatre and *café-concert* were more similar than has been assumed. *Opéra de salon*, especially when performed at such public venues as the Salle Herz, was now competing with *opérette* in the regulated theatre and in the more porous world of the *café-concert*. Some of the decline in *opéra de salon* between 1858 and 1864 may be explained by the fact that much of the change effected in the 1864 repeal had already been anticipated by, for example, the opening of the Théâtre des Folies-Concertantes/Nouvelles and the Théâtre des Bouffes-Parisiens nearly a decade earlier, and this would have encroached on the production and consumption of *opéra de salon*. There were also unsanctioned and largely unpunished performances of *opérette* at the Théâtres des Variétés, Délassements-Comiques, Folies-Dramatiques, de la Gaîté, and du Palais Royal, which also put pressure on *opéra de salon*. Furthermore, the rapid growth in the number of new *opéras de salon* in 1857 and 1858 may well have saturated the market and encouraged librettists and composers to look elsewhere.

Generic contracts between producers and consumers of *opéra de salon* and the role played by the work itself varied less in terms of venue and promoter than in the regulated theatre, where the basis of the Napoleonic

---

[12] The nature of the permission granted to *cafés-concerts* to mount *opérette* is far from clear. According to the 1864 repeal of the theatrical licensing laws, *cafés-concerts* remained within the jurisdiction of the state. Furthermore, a few months later, a police *ordonnance* made it clear not only that *cafés-concerts* were subject to their control but that 'cafés-concerts and cafés said to be "chantants"' were places 'where instrumental or vocal performances must take place in street clothes, without costume or disguise, without scenery and without mixing prose, dance or pantomime' ('les cafés-concerts et cafés dits chantants où les exécutions instrumentales ou vocales doivent avoir lieu en habit de ville, sans costume ni travestissement, sans décors et sans mélange, de prose, de danse et de pantomime'; [Symphorien-Casimir-Joseph-Edouard Boittelle], 'Police des théâtres, circulaire de M. le Préfet de Police Paris, 1er juillet 1864, art. 68', *Journal des Commissaire de Police* 10 (1864) 184. But it was clear that the legislation was never respected, perhaps because of Boittelle's elevation to the Senate in 1866. In a long and carefully argued article in the *Revue des deux mondes* a decade later, the playwright Albert Delpit explained this history and noted that by 1872, there were between 120 and 145 *cafés-concerts* in Paris; he went on to describe how artists in street clothes had begun to wear costumes, add lines of recitative to strophic songs, and adopt the conventions of *opérette*, in response to which endless complaints, even by the Société des Auteurs et Compositeurs Dramatiques, were made, all to no avail. Delpit's comments were framed in the context of a critique of the decline of serious theatre and the contribution of *cafés-concerts* to that decline (which itself could be subject to review), but his account of the legislative vacuum in which *cafés-concerts* were able to develop performances of *opérette* and related genres is incontrovertible. 'La liberté des théâtres et les cafés-concerts', *Revue des deux mondes* 25 [third series] (1878) 601–623.

legislation—in principle, at least—was to align repertory and institution.[13] Although matters of detail could vary in intriguing ways—especially between works for the *parloir* and the rest of the repertory—the conventional overarching format did not change from *parloir* to concert hall, from performer's studio to *haut-bourgeois salon*. A neighbour might attend a performance of an *opéra de salon* in an adjacent apartment in the same building and enjoy the same horizon of expectations as when they were invited to a large *salon* gathering, to a concert given by a single performer in a concert hall, or to a premiere of a new *opéra de salon* given by the family of the composer. Compared with the generic differences even between the Théâtre des Folies-Concertantes/Nouvelles and the Théâtre des Bouffes-Parisiens, especially in the 1850s, the conventions governing *opéra de salon* were consistent and comprehensible. In Hervé's and Offenbach's *opérettes* of the 1850s—newcomers to the world of the regulated theatre—experiments in generic manipulation and fragmentations of convention were the norm, against which the generic consistency of *opéra de salon* is nothing short of remarkable; only after several years of experimentation did the one-act *opérette* from the late 1850s align itself with the *opéra de salon*, which had been largely consistent since the beginning of the decade.

Opéra de salon was immune to almost all the legislative controls to which other theatrical music was subject. Neither the state nor the *préfecture* intruded into the private dwelling, although the *préfecture* had a responsibility for public safety from fire and unsanitary conditions in such venues as the Salle Herz.[14] The censors had no role whatsoever in the surveillance of *opéra de salon* in private homes, even though the numbers in the audience could match those of some public places. Libretti, however, had to be submitted to the censor for works mounted at Salle Herz, Salle Pleyel, and Salle Érard from at least 1855 to 1874.[15] The 1806–1807 legislation to manage the relationship between repertory and institution in Parisian

---

[13] For the concept of the generic contract, see Heather Dubrow, *Genre*, The Critical Idiom 42 (London: Methuen, 1982) 31–37, and Philippe Lejeune, *Le pacte autobiographique* (Paris: Seuil, 1975), assimilated into musicological study by Jeffrey Kallberg, 'The Rhetoric of Genre: Chopin's Nocturne in G Minor', *19th-Century Music* 11 (1987–1988) 243–244, 259.

[14] Schnapper, *Henri Herz*, 217–218.

[15] No account of the theatrical censorship in nineteenth-century Paris begins to approach the culture of *opéra de salon*. See the most recent general account in Karine Boulanger, 'Censure et police des théâtres', *Histoire de l'opéra français*, 3 vols., ed. Hervé Lacombe (Paris: Fayard, 2020) 2:57–64. Censors' libretti for *opéras de salon* that were performed in the more public arena of the concert hall are found in Paris, Archives Nationales, F[18] 1345–1347, 1348[B], 1349[A], 1372, 1530, and 1531. See chapter 4.

theatrical culture similarly had a marginal role to play in the culture of *opéra de salon*. Although one could envisage some interest in trying to manage the competition between events at the Salle Herz and the one-act *opéra comique* at the Théâtre-Lyrique or the Opéra-Comique, there was no energy for such scrutiny from the state, and—with both the Opéra-Comique and the Théâtre-Lyrique more interested in larger-scale works—there is no evidence of challenge from the theatres themselves, either.[16]

Opéra de salon

Opéra de salon is almost invariably in a single act with between five and eight compositions as the norm, although, as table 1.1 shows, there could be as few as two and as many as thirteen compositions in the single act; in the repertory, the most common number of compositions, and the average, is seven.

This is only a very slightly larger average than that of the more than one hundred *opérettes* composed for the two main theatres for the genre—the Théâtre des Folies-Concertantes/Nouvelles and the Théâtre des Bouffes-Parisiens, up to 1858—the year of Offenbach's *Orphée aux enfers*—where the most common number of compositions is six.[17] Dramaturgically, the number of characters and the number of scenes (since a scene change is determined by the addition or subtraction of a member of the cast) are closely related. The most frequent number of characters is either three or four, and the most frequent number of scenes is ten; the average number of characters in *opéra de salon* is 3.3, which is very close to the broader *opérette* figure of 3.3, and the average number of scenes in *opéra de salon* is 10.2 against the figure of 12.5 for the wider world of *opérette*. But *opéra de salon* is musically more consistently ambitious, with an average number of compositions for each work of 7.4 as opposed to *opérette*'s 6.3. *Opéra de salon* is largely confined to settings that are either urban or rural interiors (there are a few urban exterior settings, street scenes, and some rural exterior ones as well), all

---

[16] The inflation of *opéra comique* in the 1850s is clear from the number of three-act works that attempted to increase the number of compositions in each act, emblematized in Meyerbeer's move to *opéra comique* after his 1849 *Le prophète*: *l'étoile du Nord* (1854) and *Le pardon de Ploërmel* (1859); and in Offenbach's justification for the emergence of *opérette* itself as a counterweight to the growing dimensions of *opéra comique*. See Everist, 'L'Opéra-Comique, sous le Second Empire', *Histoire de l'opéra français*, ed. Hervé Lacombe, 3 vols. (Paris: Fayard, 2020) 2:425–434.

[17] Generalizations about the repertory of *opérette* at the regulated theatres are taken from the analysis of the structure of early *opérette* given in Everist, *Opérette: The First Twenty-Five Years*.

Table 1.1. Distribution of the number of compositions in *opéra de salon*, 1850–1870.

2 comps	4 comps	5 comps	6 comps	7 comps	8 comps	9 comps	10 comps	11 comps	12 comps	13 comps	Total
1	1	11	8	18	10	9	2	4	2	1	67
1%	1%	16%	13%	28%	16%	14%	3%	3%	3%	1%	100%

of which are so common in *opérette*.[18] But the topics in a wider range that are found in *opérette*—chivalric, military, classical antiquity, oriental, musical or literary, the hunt, and especially Offenbach's parodies—are largely absent from the repertory of *opéra de salon*. The settings for the libretti of *opéra de salon* are largely split equally between urban and rural, with a single historical setting (Jules-Laurent-Anicharsis Duprato's 1863 *Marie Stuart au château de Lochleven*)[19] and a single orientalist one (Frédéric-Étienne Barbier's *Le miroir* of 1864).[20]

Exactly what composers, librettists, and their audiences and critics called the *opéras de salon* they created is unsurprisingly difficult to grasp. The genre was described in many ways that changed over time. The theatrical *proverbe* is clearly important for the early history of the genre, but this terminology sits alongside such others as *pastorale lyrique*, *opéra comique*, *opéra comique de salon*, and *opéra de salon* itself. It is also no surprise that the use of the term *opérette* appears in the history of *opéra de salon*, after its establishment in the Théâtres des Folies-Concertantes/Nouvelles and des Bouffes-Parisiens. In 1857, Gustave Nadaud's *Porte et fenêtre* and A. Quatremère's *Les premiers*

---

[18] The data on which the comments in this paragraph are based are presented in this chapter's appendix, which includes material for every *opéra de salon* that survives with enough sources to provide the information (sixty-seven works out of a total of around 120). The appendix first gives a complete listing of all sixty-seven works, followed by lists of those pieces published (1) in *Le journal des demoiselles*, (2) in *Le magasin des demoiselles*, and (3) more conventionally through publishing houses in Paris.

[19] A published score survives which includes a complete libretto: À Mademoiselle Augusta Hoffmann./-/MARIE STUART/AU CHÂTEAU DE LOCHLEVEN, *Opérette de salon*, à un acte./ PAROLES DE M. P. BOGAERTS,/MUSIQUE DE/J. M. DUPRATO/. . ./SCHOTT FRERES/ BRUXELLES, 82 Montagne de la Cour/MAYENCE,/Les Fils de B. SCHOTT/LONDRES,/ SCHOTT ET Cº, Regent Street, 159.

[20] Barbier's *Le miroir* was originally published in *Le magasin des demoiselles* 21/1-3 (1864), both libretto and music. The score and libretto were both printed as a separate publication shortly afterwards: 21ᵉ ANNÉE. 1864-1865.—ALBUMS Nᵒˢ 1, 2, 3,/MAGASIN DES DEMOISELLES/- LE MIROIR/Opérette en un acte/PAROLES/DE M. CH. NUITTER/MUSIQUE/DE M. FRÉDÉRIC BARBIER/. . ./PARIS/ADMINISTRATIONS ET RÉDACTION DU MAGASIN DES DEMOISELLES,/51 RUE LAFFITTE, 51/-/1864-1865. The context for *opéra de salon* in such journals aimed at young unmarried women is discussed in chapter 6.

cinq francs were both advertised as *opérettes de salon*, at a time when the generic descriptor *opérette* had already gained ground—fitfully at best, however—in the regulated theatre.[21]

The anatomy of *opéra de salon* has thus far remained a closed book. An examination of two pairs of works—one from around 1855 and one from around 1870—blows a little of the dust off its pages, and the sample may serve as an introduction to establish the genre's conventional structure, against which exceptions may be judged. For each of the two pairs, one work is taken from the world of the *salon*, studio, and concert hall, while the other was published in one of the two women's journals, *Le journal des demoiselles* and *Le magasin des demoiselles* (see table 1.2).

Table 1.2 is in two parts. The upper frame gives factual and quantitative data about the four works, while the lower frame gives details of the musical compositions in each. Of the composers of the four works sampled in table 1.2, Charles-Émile Poisot was the only one who specialized in *opéras de salon*, producing six across the period from 1850 to 1870; (Dieudonné-Joseph-Guillaume-) Félix Godefroid only wrote two works for the stage, the other being *L'harpe d'or* mounted at the Théâtre-Lyrique in 1858.[22] Victor Massé, however, was the composer of some of the most revered *opéras comiques* of the mid-nineteenth century (*Galathée*, *Les noces de Jeannette*, and *La reine Topaze*, as well as five *opéras de salon*). Théophile Semet had a similar career with works at the Théâtre-Lyrique and the Opéra-Comique as well as at the Théâtre de la Gaîté after the licensing laws were repealed; *Laide*, however, was one of just two of Semet's *opéras de salon*. Three of the four librettists were well known. François-Joseph-Pierre-André Méry had been active for a quarter of a century by the time he wrote the libretto to *Le prix de famille* (his only other *opéra de salon* libretto was for Offenbach's *Le décaméron, ou La grotte d'azur*). Léocadie-Aimée de Beauvoir, known as Mme Roger de Beauvoir, was a distinguished playwright and *vaudevilliste*, although *A deux pas du bonheur* was her only libretto. While Charles Bousquet's *Rosa, la rose* was his only foray onto the lyric

---

[21] Early works mounted at the Bouffes-Parisiens to be unequivocally titled *opérette* were Offenbach's *Madame Papillon* (3 October 1855) and *Trafalgar sur un volcan* (29 December 1855), and at the Folies-Concertantes/Nouvelles Hervé's *Fifi et Nini* (15 January 1856) and Jules Bovéry's *Madame Mascarille* (1 March 1856).

[22] There is also evidence of a further untitled *opérette* by Godefroid. See chapter 4 for an account of the performance in the studio of the sculptor Henri-Joseph-Charles Cordier, 115 Boulevard Saint-Michel, on 12 January 1865. The libretto of the untitled work was by Jean-François-Eugène Tourneux, so it could not have been *A deux pas du bonheur* or *L'harpe d'or* (*La Revue et Gazette musicale de Paris*, 22 January 1865). The performance is discussed in chapter 4.

Table 1.2. Four sample *opéras de salon*: structure and contents.

Title	Composer	Author(s)	Year	Generic descriptor	Nos.	Female	Male	Scenes	Topic	Publication
A deux pas du bonheur	Godefroid	Beauvoir	1855	*proverbe lyrique*	5	1	2	5	urban domestic	*Ménestrel*/Heugel
Le prix de famille	Massé	Méry	1855	*opéra comique*	9	4	1 (travesti)	13	rural domestic	*MdD*
Rosa, la rose	Poisot	Bousquet	1868	*opérette de salon*	7	1	1	7	rural domestic	? Printed by Gheluve
Laide	Semet	Adam Boisgontier	1870	*opérette*	5	3	1	8	urban domestic	*JdD*
A deux pas du bonheur	Godefroid									Introduction [*ouverture*]; 1. *Romance* (Betty); *Chanson* (Sir Georges); 3. *Couplets* (Betty); 4. *Duo* (Betty, Sir Georges); 5. Finale: *Barcarolle* (Un Gondolier), *Romance* (Betty) *et Trio* (Betty, Sir Georges, Gondolier)
Le prix de famille	Massé									*Ouverture*; 1. *Trio* (Paul, Claire, Blanche); 2. *Couplets* (Claire); 3. *Chanson villageoise* (Claire); 4. *Romance* (Paul); 5. *Ariette* (Paul); 6. *Complainte* (Blanche, Mlle Kerbriant); 7. *Couplet rococo* (Marcelline); 8. *Air* (Marcelline); 9. Final (Marcelline, Paul, Claire, Blanche, Mlle Kerbriant)
Rosa, la rose	Poisot									Introduction [*ouverture*]; 1. *Fabliau* (Rosa); 2. *Cantabile et Valse des fleurs* (Rosa); 3. *Air* (Arnold); 4. *Duo du Latin* (Rosa, Arnold); 5. *Cantabile* (Arnold); 6. *Couplets* (Rosa); 7. *Duo finale* (Rosa, Arnold);
Laide	Semet									*Ouverture* (reuses music from the finale without the voice parts); 1. *Couplets* (Fanchette); 2. *Air* (Le Capitaine); 3. *Romance* (Elisa); 4. *Duo* (Augustine, Elisa); 5. Finale (Augustine, Elisa, Fanchette, Le Capitaine)

stage, Elisa Boisgontier, known as Mme Adam Boisgontier, was the author of no fewer than a dozen libretti for *opéra de salon*.

Le prix de famille and *Laide* were both published in two of the women's journals that included music—the first in *Le journal des demoiselles* and the second in *Le magasin des demoiselles*—fifteen years apart,[23] and *A deux pas du bonheur* was published by one of the most prestigious publishing houses of the Second Empire, Heugel.[24] But *Rosa, la rose* appears to have been published by Edmond van Gheluve, possibly before he formally took on the role of publisher and while he or his wife was still an engraver.[25] As is the case with almost all *opéras de salon* published in women's journals, there is no surviving evidence of performance for *Le prix de famille* or *Laide*, but Poisot's *Rosa, la rose* was premiered in his own studio on the rue (Catherine de) La Rochefoucauld deep in the heart of Nouvelle Athènes,[26] and Godefroid's *A deux pas du bonheur* was one of the most widely performed works of its type and was presented in all the public venues in which *opéra de salon* was found.[27]

The casts for the four works reflect broader patterns discussed in more detail later in the chapter; for the works destined for the slightly more public performance of the *salon*, studio or concert hall, roles are restricted to a single male and either a single female or a pair. In the case of the two works from women's journals, *Laide* had a single male character, while the one male character in *Le prix de famille* is a *travesti* role; female roles outnumber male

---

[23] The libretto of *Le prix de famille* was published in *Le magasin de demoiselles* 12 (1855–1856) 8–17, and the piano-vocal score was a separately paginated appendix to the first three issues of the year: MAGASIN/des Demoiselles,/*12ᵉ* - —51. Rue Lafitte 51.—*Nᵒˢ* 1.2.3/1855–1856/-/LE/PRIX/ DE FAMILLE/Opéra Comique en un acte/*Paroles*/DE/Méry/MUSIQUE/DE/VICTOR MASSÉ./ BUREAUX/51 Rue Laffitte 51/*PARIS*. The libretto of *Laide*, similarly, was published in *Le journal des demoiselles* 38 (1870) 137–141, with the piano-vocal score as a separately paginated appendix to the third issue of the year: LAIDE/OPÉRETTE EN 2 TABLEAUX/Paroles de/Mᵐᵉ ADAM BOISGONTIER/Musique de/Mʳ TH. SEMET.

[24] À DEUX PAS/DU/BONHEUR,/*Proverbe Lyrique de Salon*/en un acte,/*Paroles de*/Mᵐᵉ Roger de Beauvoir,/*Musique de*/FÉLIX/GODEFROID./. . ./*PARIS, au MÉNESTREL, Rue Vivienne, 2 bis,/ HEUGEL et Cᴵᴱ, éditeurs libraires/pour la France et l'Étranger*. The libretto is interleaved in the piano-vocal score so that the work may be read sequentially from beginning to end.

[25] ROSA, LA ROSE/Paroles de Charles Bousquet/*OPÉRETTE/de Salon*./Musique de Charles POISOT. The identification of the printer, 'Imp: Gheluve rue Montorgueil 35', is given at *ibidem*, 49, the bottom of the first page of the *duo finale*, which might imply that the number—the most complex in the work—was envisaged as a separate publication. De Gheluve only began work as a publisher in 1870 (Anik Devriès and François Lesure, *Dictionnaire des éditeurs de musique français*, 2 vols. [vol. 1 in 2 parts], Archives de l'édition musicale française 4 (Geneva: Minkoff, 1979–1988) 2:189–190), with an address at 3 rue des Martyrs and only moving (back?) to the rue Montorgueil address in 1880.

[26] Félix Clément and Pierre Larousse, *Dictionnaire des opéras (Dictionnaire lyrique)*. . . (Paris: Larousse, [1881]) 744.

[27] A full account of the performances of *A deux pas du bonheur* is given in chapter 7.

ones by three or four to one. Since the number of characters has an obvious impact on the number of scenes in the dramaturgy, this largely explains the number of thirteen for *Le prix de famille* but just five for *A deux pas du bonheur*, with the other two works in the middle range (the broader picture of the dramaturgy of *opéra de salon* is given later). The four works sampled here are good examples of the types of domestic libretti that characterize *opéra de salon*. *Le prix de famille* and *Rosa, la rose* take place in rural settings. *Laide* and *A deux pas du bonheur* are urban; unlike most libretti for *opéra de salon*, the latter specifies a location (most simply assume that urban means a Parisian apartment and rural means a provincial *chateau*), in this case, Venice, characterized musically by a *barcarolle* in the finale.

The broader scope of Méry's libretto for Massé's *Le prix de famille* is also related to the large number of compositions in the work: unlike the Godefroid and the Semet, which have five compositions in their single acts, and the seven in Poisot's *Rosa, la rose*, Massé and Méry place nine compositions in the single act of *Le prix de famille*. Where this ambition comes from is an open question. Logically, the dramatic situations for music are determined by the librettist, but Massé's one-act *opéras comiques* from the 1850s all present either seven or eight compositions, and none of them reaches nine. It seems reasonable to conclude that whichever librettist he was working with, Massé would attempt to pack a one-act work with as many compositions as possible. However, Méry's 1854 libretto for Ernest Reyer, *Maître Wolfram*, had eight numbers, and a good deal of the librettist's work for the lyric stage involved larger-scale work at the Opéra: Félicien David's 1859 *Herculanum*, the 1860 translation of Gioachino Rossini's *Semiramide*, Reyer's *Erostrate*, and ultimately Giuseppe Verdi's 1867 *Don Carlos*. Méry, then, had as much of a disposition for and the experience of writing to a much larger module than *opéra de salon*, as had Massé in packing as many compositions as he could into a single act.

Apart from the use of the duet, the types of numbers used in *opéra de salon* are the same in works for the *salon*, the studio, and the concert hall on the one hand and for the *parloir* on the other; in other words, there is very little difference in anatomy between the two types of *opéra de salon*. Each of the four works in the sample under review here includes an overture, but the scale and dramatic purpose of each is vastly different. Semet simply uses the musical material from his finale with the vocal parts removed, while Poisot presents a potpourri of musical themes from the work. Massé's overture to *Le prix de famille* begins with a 6/8 *andante mosso* which both prefigures

Marceline's *air* 'Adieu mon village' and serves as the slow introduction to a broad ternary movement with hints at a *boléro*. And while Godefroid's overture has a similar ambition in its purely musical construction, it functions in part as a large-scale *mélodrame*—of the sort that alternates spoken dialogue and composed music—and undertakes important dramatic work (example 1.1).

It breaks off on a dominant pedal while one of the characters—Sir Georges—walks onstage, sits down, and falls asleep, at which point the music of the slow introduction recurs, is developed, and moves *attacca* into the first sung number, Betty's *romance* 'Sous le ciel toute chose'; this in turn reveals the melody from the slow introduction that has been haunting Sir Georges: 'Constantly . . . this melody . . . pursues me . . ., and oppresses me. . . . Burning lie or cold truth?'.[28] Sir Georges's haunting melody serves as a running commentary throughout the work and as a key to unlocking his relationship with Betty.

There is rarely in *opéra de salon* any *introduction* on the model of the Italian *introduzione* which involves choruses, staged song (*romance, fabliau*, and so on), and other elements of *la solita forma*. Although Massé's *Le prix de famille* begins with a trio, it is for the most part a simple homophonic chorus prefaced by some melodic lines both hummed and sung. The most complex single number in *opéra de salon* is the finale; the two 'journal' operas, however, offer nothing more than a simple homophonic chorus for all their characters. *A deux pas du bonheur* gives a *barcarolle*—in 2/4 time—which is separated from a reprise of Betty's opening romance by a *tempo di mezzo* in which Sir Georges threatens to shoot the gondolier and which makes a rare use of recitative. After failing and realizing that the melody that has been haunting him had been sung by Betty all along, he also realizes that Betty loves him, at which point the dénouement concludes with a reprise of the *barcarolle*. Poisot's *Rosa, la rose* ends—ostensibly less elaborately—with a *duo finale* for the two characters, but the opening *cantabile* continues the text of the preceding spoken dialogue uninterrupted into the composed music (example 1.2).

And here also, Rosa's *fabliau*, which follows the overture, recurs, placed in Comte Arnold's mouth as he disentangles the plot by confessing to having disguised himself as a student in earlier scenes (example 1.3).

---

[28] 'Toujours . . . ce chant . . . me poursuit . . . et m'oppresse. . . . Brûlant mensonge ou froide vérité' (À DEUX PAS/DU/BONHEUR,/*Proverbe Lyrique de Salon*, 9).

Example 1.1. Félix Godefroid, *A deux pas du bonheur*, end of overture and beginning of scene 1.

Example 1.2. Charles Poisot, *Rosa, la rose*, beginning of *duo*.

Arnold.
Tout est convenu entre votre père et moi.
Rosa. *(avec douleur)*
Comment?.. vous approuvez les
projets de mon père?..
Arnold. *(avec douleur)*
Mais certainement, je les approuve et
il ne manque plus votre consentement.
Rosa. *(avec douleur)*
Mon consentement!.. c'est vous qui le
demandez, vous Monseigneur!.. (à part)
Allons tout est perdu!.. et pourtant tout à
l'heure encore, J'avais cru comprendre....

Example 1.2. Continued

The number and the opera then conclude with the waltz movement taken from the second part of the *fabliau*'s *couplets*.

Between overture and finale, the musical structure of *opéra de salon* consists of single numbers and usually no more than a single duet. Aria structures range from the simplest strophic *couplets* to more complex structures found in *opéra comique* and beyond. *Couplets* are either titled as such, or are given more elaborate generic attributions, such as the *fabliau* that opens Poisot's *Rosa, la rose*, where a pair of *couplets* are combined with the historical detail of a quasi-fairy-tale and the strummed accompaniment of the minstrel's plucked strings transferred to keyboard, or when Marceline sings her *chanson villageoise* from Massé's *Le prix de famille*.[29] Paul's *ariette*

---

[29] This number is also notable for its use of *mélodrame*, as Claire interjects spoken phrases between the ritornello and the first strophe, and Marceline does the same between the two strophes.

Example 1.3. Charles Poisot, *Rosa, la rose*, citation of *duo* in finale.

Example 1.3. Continued

'Quand on est seul' from the same work is also structured around *couplets*, as is Elisa's *romance* from *Laide* 'Allez, beau papillon', where the three stanzas are presented simultaneously in the print after an elaborate ritornello (example 1.4).

But an equally large number of arias are structured in ways that distances them from *couplets*. In general, the generic designator *air* implies a more complex structure than the strophic, as in the case of Arnold's *air* 'Ah la belle vie que celle du chasseur!' in *Rosa, la rose* and Le Capitaine's *air* 'Au bal, au bal de par ma loi!' from Semet's *Laide*, where both play off multi-section structures with and without internal reprises. The interruptions made by Sir Georges in the *romance* that begins *A deux pas du bonheur* would simply not be possible without its underlying ternary structure. Marcelline's *air* 'Adieu mon village' from Massé's *Le prix de famille* is a two-tempo aria (example 1.5 shows the transition from the end of the first section in 6/8 into the second in 2/4) familiar from nearly a century earlier, and Sir Georges's *chanson* 'Des pleurs! Des pleurs!' from *A deux pas du bonheur* is structured as an ABAB form but with none of the tonal complexities that characterize this structure in its eighteenth-century guise.

Example 1.4. Théodore Semet, *Laide*, opening of 'Allez, beau papillon'.

Example 1.4. Continued

The performance and audience of the two broad types of *opéra de salon* may well be reflected less in the structure of the arias than in the complexity of the duets. The two works published in women's journals and destined for the *parloir*—Massé's *Le prix de famille* and Semet's *Laide*—configure their duets in the simplest way possible: as strophic *couplets en duo*. The complexity of Poisot's *duo finale* in *Rosa, la rose* may be compared to the dramatized Latin lesson—the *duo du Latin*—for Rosa and Arnold that develops an ABCBDB

Example 1.5. Victor Massé, *Prix de famille*, 'Adieu mon village', transition.

Example 1.5. Continued

structure, where the B section is a repeating *vivo* passage in 3/8 that has already been heard in the overture and the C and D sections carry the grammatical weight of Rosa explaining respectively nominative and accusative and then genitive and ablative cases (example 1.6).

Godefroid's duet in *A deux pas du bonheur* again deploys a multipartite structure with a significant reprise of the first section as its penultimate portion, and it develops a range of duet discourses: spacious *cantabile* against anxious *pertichini*, simple exchanges, and intricate and interlocking *parlante*.

Passages of recitative or *mélodrame* are rare in *opéra de salon*; the *mélodrame* at the very beginning of Godefroid's *A deux pas du bonheur* is largely divorced from the main sung numbers, but it also features the single example of recitative in the sample. And here there are no examples of recitatives preceding an aria as are found in *opéra comique*; in the latter, it is quite common for the dramatic discourses to shift from dialogue, through recitative at the beginning of a number, and thence into a composed aria. The only example of recitative in this sample is found in the finale to *A deux pas du bonheur* as part of the recognition scene between Betty and Sir Georges (example 1.7).

Example 1.6. Charles Poisot, *Rosa, la rose*, extract from *duo de Latin*.

Example 1.6. Continued

46 OPÉRA DE SALON

Example 1.6. Continued

Example 1.6. Continued

The passage begins with a series of hesitant textural changes that echo Sir Georges's hesitant recognition and evolves into a formal recitative before returning to the 2/4 *allegretto* which marks the reprise of the *barcarolle* discussed earlier.

Discursive modes in *opéra de salon*, then, are largely unchanging: reflective numbers are composed and sung while kinetic action is projected in spoken dialogue. Occasional sections of *mélodrame* are also found, but recitative is confined almost exclusively to the rare instances of ensembles and to finales. However, the fact that the genre was not controlled by any form of licence—whether performed in a private home, in a public concert hall, or in a government building—meant that there was a certain amount of leeway in how discursive modes could play out. When, for example, Émile Ducellier put on a performance of his *Les deux charlatans* in 1865 and called it a *grand opéra sans choeurs mais avec balai* (*grand opéra* without chorus but with a broom; there is a play on words between *balai* and *ballet*), this meant nothing in terms of the work's discursive modes since—even given that no libretto survives—it is clear that from the vocal score that the kinetic parts of the work were in spoken dialogue.[30] This is not the case, however,

---

[30] *Dédiée aux PENSIONNATS/et/aux SOCIÉTÉS PHILHARMONIQUES./LES DEUX CHARLATANS/SAYNÈTE BOUFFE./PAROLES DE/EDOUARD DOYEN/MUSIQUE DE/ EMILE DUCELLIER/. . ./Paris, Maison L. VIEILLOT, L. LABBÉ, Succ*. Editeur, 20 rue du Croissant. The published score uses the generic descriptor *saynète bouffe*, but the programme for the *soirée* at which it was given (in the salons of Philippe-Auguste-Alfred Pittaud, known as Pittaud de Forges) called it 'Grand opéra sans choeurs, mais avec balai' (*La Revue et Gazette musicale de Paris*, 26 March 1865).

Example 1.7. Félix Godefroid, *A deux pas du bonheur*, recitative embedded in finale.

Example 1.7. Continued

50 OPÉRA DE SALON

Example 1.7. Continued

Example 1.7. Continued

Example 1.7. Continued

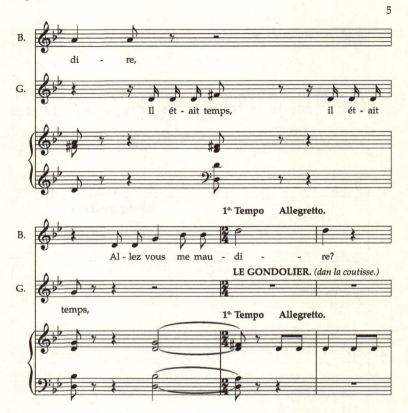

with two of the earliest *opéras de salon*: Poisot's *Le coin du feu*[31] and Duprez's *Jélyotte, ou Un passe-temps de duchesse*, the composer's first effort at the genre.[32] Despite the fact that every other *opéra de salon* mingles composed

---

[31] À Monsieur Ad. Adam/*MEMBRE DE L'INSTITUT/LE*/COIN DU FEU/Opéra de Salon/ Poëme/D'ÉTIENNE TREFEU/Musique/DE/CHARLES POISOT/. . ./*PARIS, chez Étienne CHALLIOT, Éditeur de Musique,/Rue St Honoré 354 pres la Place Vendome*. Analysis of this important early work is hampered by the fact that no libretto survives, the publication of the vocal score appears to date from 1851 (its date of accession into the Bibliothèque Nationale de France; the print has no plate number to confirm), and its first performance (identified only in the vocal score itself) was 4 February 1851 (*ibidem*, 1).

[32] Again, there is no surviving libretto, and the score survives in around two hundred manuscript pages that range from a more or less complete overture to fragments (Cambridge, MA, Harvard University, Houghton Library, MS M1500.D935 J4). Even from these partial sources, it is possible to confirm that the description in the programme for the April 1854 premiere as 'an *opérette* in one act with recitatives' ('une opérette en un acte avec récits'; *La Revue et Gazette musicale de Paris*, 9 April 1854) is correct.

Example 1.8. Charles Poisot, *Le coin du feu*, 'Il n'est pas femme à mes yeux plus charmante', accompanied recitative.

Example 1.8. Continued

Example 1.8. Continued

music and spoken dialogue, both works are through-composed with kinetic sections of the action presented in accompanied recitative. Although only extensive sketches for *Jélyotte* survive, the alternation of composed number and accompanied recitative is clear, even if the immediate continuity of the work is opaque. Poisot's *Le coin du feu*, however, was published, and here it is clear that accompanied recitative is fully assimilated into the sustained discourse of the work. Unsurprisingly, Paul's aria 'Il n'est pas femme à mes

Example 1.9. Charles Poisot, *Le coin du feu*, 'Rêve enchanteur', recitative.

Example 1.9. Continued

58 OPÉRA DE SALON

Example 1.9. Continued

Example 1.9. Continued

Example 1.9. Continued

Example 1.9. Continued

62   OPÉRA DE SALON

Example 1.9. Continued

Example 1.9. Continued

yeux plus charmante' is prefaced by an extended exchange in accompanied recitative with Cécile which plays off *tremulandi*, sustained chords, and punctuating gestures (example 1.8).[33]

Much less expected—for those familiar with either contemporary *opérette* or *opéra de salon*—is the way in which numbers are connected via accompanied recitative. Cécile's *romance* 'Rêve enchanteur d'un mois à peine' consists of two *couplets* but veers off at the end of the second into a dialogue with the character Durandin in recitative, which yields to a fragmentary reprise of the music of Cécile's *romance*, then into further accompanied recitative, now with Paul, and then moves into the duo 'Je suis coupable et m'accuse' (example 1.9).[34]

Not only does this approach to musico-poetic discourse go beyond anything found in *opérette*, but it also goes beyond anything found at the Opéra-Comique, where if this sort of writing had been presented, it would have been sorely criticized by the Opéra for overstepping its generic boundaries and trespassing on those of the Opéra itself. The fact that *opéra de salon* could develop these sorts of discourses is a direct result of its institutional positioning away from the regulated theatre, but such experiments as these would have meant that such a work as *Le coin du feu* could never have found a home in the public theatre, and this might be one explanation for why the experiment was not followed up in later decades, while a more likely reason might lie within the performative complexity of accompanied recitative that characterizes *Jélyotte* and *Le coin du feu*. Poisot immediately moved to the conventional alternation of spoken dialogue and composed number in his 1853 *Les ressources de Jacqueline* and in subsequent works. *Jélyotte* was Duprez's only attempt at *opéra de salon*, although he gave it a second performance in 1859.[35]

Patterns of Publication

Patterns of publication for *opéra de salon* differ from those for *opérette* or *opéra comique* and influence modern access to the repertory. There are three principal ones: publication where works are put on sale by commercial publishers, periodical publication in women's journals, and the issuing

---

[33] À Monsieur Ad. Adam/*MEMBRE DE L'INSTITUT*/*LE*/COIN DU FEU, 17–18.
[34] *Ibidem*, 38–42.
[35] *Le ménestrel*, 27 February 1859.

of *opéra de salon* libretti as collected works of their author. For the first and because of the nature of the venues in which *opéra de salon* was cultivated, no free-standing printed libretti were published in the same way they were put on sale in such theatres as the Opéra, Opéra-Comique, or Théâtre-Lyrique for members of the audience to follow.[36] There is some evidence of descriptive programmes being put together, but this seems to have been rare.[37] Piano-vocal scores often contained the libretto, either interleaved with the music or appended to the score; in both cases, the document could have served as a single point of access to performance of the work, and this was likely the purpose of this format. Exactly what the status of a document without any sort of publicly available libretto could have been is a question that a later discussion of *salon* and *parloir* will address. *Opéras de salon* published in this format were performed in artists' studios, concert halls, and aristocratic and *haut-bourgeois* salons; whether they were also performed in a *parloir* environment remains an open question.

A second route to publication for *opéra de salon* was in journals dedicated to the interests and activities of unmarried young women (*demoiselles*). While the publication of musical works to supplement the textual content of a journal—both specifically dedicated to music and more broadly—had been a feature on the landscape of publishing since the late eighteenth century, *Le magasin des demoiselles* and *Le journal des demoiselles* published both libretti and music of *opéras de salon* annually throughout the Second Empire and beyond. This female environment for the cultivation of *opéra de salon*—coupled with the fact that a large proportion of the repertory of *opéra de salon* was published in this format—raises broader questions about women's role in the popularity of the genre and warrants discussion beyond merely the question of publication. There is no evidence of *opéras de salon* being both published in a journal and performed in a *salon*, artist's studio, or concert hall; their publication context points unambiguously to the

---

[36] Only a tiny handful of the surviving *opéras de salon* had published libretti that resembled those prepared for performance at the regulated theatres. An example is LES RESSOURCES/ DE/JACQUELINE/COMÉDIE MÉLÉE DE CHANT/EN UN ACTE/PAROLES DE M. HENRY BOISSEAUX/MUSIQUE DE M. ANDRÉ SIMIOT/Représentée pour la première fois à Paris, le 29 mai 1854/PARIS/MICHEL LÉVY FRÈRES, LIBRAIRES-ÉDITEURS,/RUE VIVIENNE, 2 BIS./ 1854; but even here there are problems; Poisot's authorship is confused with André Simiot's, and the date of the premiere given in the printed edition is nearly a year after its premiere in the composer's own *salon* (7 June 1853; see *Le ménestrel*, 12 June 1853).

[37] This practice also seems to have been restricted to performances given by Duprez in his private theatre on the rue Turgot. For the performance of his *Samson* on 9 March 1855, a lengthy descriptive account of the work including the titles of every number was published in *Le ménestrel*, 18 March 1855. Duprez's activities are detailed in chapter 4.

parloir. Here publication, performance context, and gender are inextricably interlinked, as discussed in chapter 6.

A third and final important route for the publication of *opéra des salon* was the production of sets of libretti collected by their authors. Chief among these was *Le spectacle aux coin du feu*, published by Jean-Hyacinthe-Adonis Galoppe, known better as Cléon Galoppe d'Onquaire or just Galoppe d'Onquaire, in 1855; it included all but one of his twelve libretti that were set as *opéras de salon*.[38] Later, the composer and librettist Gustave Nadaud published the libretti of four of his five *opéras de salon*; only *La clef du secrétaire* was omitted, as it was the only one of his *opéras de salon* to set a libretto by another composer.[39] Méry, the author of the libretto to Offenbach's *Luc et Lucette* and *Le décaméron* as well as Massé's *Le prix de famille*, reworked the libretto of *Le décaméron* and *Le prix de famille* as *comédies de salon* in his *Théâtre de salon* of 1861 and *Nouveau théâtre de salon* in 1865.[40] The broader context for this type of publication—which in terms of its audience overlaps with the previous category and is discussed in chapter 6—was given by Alfred Driou's *Nouveau théâtre des jeunes demoiselles*, aimed specifically at the family and school environment.[41]

Given the engagement of the aristocracy and the *haute bourgeoisie* with *opéra de salon*, it is entirely possible, although no evidence exists, that there was a system of subventions to defray costs of publication. This might even have been the case for *opéra de salon* published in journals, although in this case, both journals published an album of music every month and the *opéra de salon* simply occupied two or three of those albums. Although when Nadaud dedicated his vocal score of *La volière* to Princesse Mathilde in 1855, it is not impossible that some sort of monetary or other exchange was envisaged or effected, but when Poisot dedicated *Les terreurs de M. Peters* to the singer Félix Marochetti or when Wilfrid d'Indy dedicated his *Deux princesses* to the predominant *artiste* of *opéra de salon*, Mme Gaveaux-Sabatier (Émilie-Perrine-Suzanne Bénazet), these gestures seem much more like acts of altruism or gratitude.

---

[38] Galoppe d'Onquaire (Jean-Hyacinthe-Adonis Galoppe), *Le spectacle au coin du feu* (Paris: Lévy, 1855).
[39] Gustave Nadaud, *Opérettes* (Paris: Plon, 1867).
[40] François-Joseph-Pierre-André Méry, *Théâtre de salon* (Paris: Michel Lévy, 1861); idem, *Nouveau théâtre de salon* (Paris: Michel Lévy, 1865).
[41] Alfred Driou, *Nouveau théâtre des jeunes demoiselles: comédies, drames, vaudevilles, opérettes et moralités bluettes propres à être jouées dans les familles et les maisons d'éducation* (Paris: Fonteney et Peltier, 1858). Driou's account of *opéra de salon* is described in chapter 6.

While both elements in the descriptor *opéra de salon*—*opéra* and *salon*—require careful handling, the generic structure of the work is clear and displays conventional characteristics that make it as recognizable as a *grande sonate*, *stretta*, or *Fantasiestück*. This is particularly remarkable since the *opéra de salon* enjoyed two types of cultivation which overlap with two types of dissemination: one discrete group was cultivated in the aristocratic and *haut-bourgeois salon*, artist's studio, and concert hall and another in the more intimate surroundings of the *parloir*; at the same time, the first group of works were printed in a conventional format by music publishers who were household names, whereas the second were circulated in periodical publications dedicated to the interests of young women between school and marriage.

While the consistency of *opéra de salon* across a range of performance environments gives focus to its generic structure and conventional forms, it also brings the genre into alignment with the emerging one-act *opérette* which appeared at precisely the same time. While *opérette* at the Théâtres des Folies-Concertantes/Nouvelles and des Bouffes-Parisiens was forged in the mid-1850s in a crucible of creative attempts to circumvent current theatrical legislation—with a wide range of experimental types as a consequence, *opéra de salon* was constrained only by the preferences of its creators and performers and by the tastes of those who populated the environments in which it was cultivated.

At the centre of this chapter has been an attempt to explain the musical and dramaturgical elements of *opéra de salon* through a sample of four representative works and to outline the background of the genre in *salon* culture of the Second Empire. But works and contexts have no meaning without their agents, and subsequent chapters will give an account of the men and women who created *opéra de salon*, who moulded *espaces* out of various forms of *lieux* for their performance, and who formed part of the human matrix that cultivated the genre. The immediate concern is with those who brought *opéra de salon* to life: the various types of vocal artist involved in its performance. It is these individuals—their training, careers, and ability to function on the improvised stages that so often characterized the shift from *lieu* to *espace*—that form the subject of this book's second chapter.

Appendix

Master List (Total: 67)

This is a list of *opéras de salon* for which there are surviving data. It includes independently published works and works appearing in *Le journal des demoiselles* and *Le magasin des demoiselles*.

Title	Composer	Author(s)	Year	Generic descriptor	Nos.	Female	Male	Chorus	Scenes	Topic	Journal	Dedication
TOTAL: 67					7,42	2,94	1,33		10,3	27 rural, 38 urban, 1 historical, 1 oriental		
Le coin du feu	Poisot	Tréfu	1852	*proverbe lyrique*	7	1	2		9	urban domestic	X	X
Les ressources de Jacqueline	Simiot	Boisseaux	1853	*pastorale lyrique*	6	1	2		8	rural domestic	X	X
Frère et soeur	Bordèse	Plouvier	1853	*opéra comique*	7	4	1	+ chorus	6	urban domestic	JdD	X
Le docteur vieuxtemps	Nadaud	Nadaud	1854	*opéra comique de salon*	8	2	3		18	urban domestic	X	X
Les échos de Rosine	Thys	Tréfu	1854	*opéra de salon*	9	1	2		11	urban domestic	X	X
A deux pas du bonheur	Godefroid	Beauvoir	1855	*proverbe lyrique*	5	1	2		5	urban domestic	X	X

Les trois clefs	Peellaert	Peellaert	1855	opéra de salon	6	3	0		9	urban domestic	JdD	X
La volière	Nadaud	Nadaud	1855	opéra comique de salon	7	1	3		15	urban domestic	X	S.A.S la Princesse Mathilde
Le coffret de Saint-Domingue	Clapisson	Deschamps	1855	opéra comique	9	4	1	+ chorus	11	urban domestic	JdD	X
Le prix de famille	Massé	Méry	1855	opéra comique	9	4	1		13	rural domestic	MdD	X
La treille du roi	Henrion	Dupeuty	1856	petit opéra comique	7	8	0	+ chorus	9	rural domestic	JdD	X
Les terreurs de M. Peters	Poisot	Stop; Muÿs	1856	opéra de salon ou de chambre	10	2	3		14	urban domestic	X	À Mr Félix Marochetti
Jaloux de soi	Marcelli	Marcelli	1856	proverbe lyrique	13	2	1		18	rural domestic	X	X
Porte et fenêtre	Nadaud	Nadaud	1857	opérette de salon	6	1	3		2	urban domestic	X	X
Le moulin des oiseaux	Bordèse	Plouvier	1857	opéra comique	8	6	1	+ chorus	10	rural domestic	MdD	X
Stella, ou Une autre Werther	O'Kelly	Montigny	1857	opéra de salon	8	1	2		8	urban domestic	X	X
Le mariage en poste	Weckerlin	Galoppe d'Onquaire	1857	opéra	9	1	2		6	rural domestic	X	X
Les revenants bretons	Weckerlin	De Guézennec de Bréhat	1857	opéra de salon	9	2	2		9	rural domestic	X	X
Les premiers cinq francs	Quatremère	Quatremère	1857	opérette de salon	12	4	4 boys		14	urban domestic	Berquin	X

Les ouvrières de qualité	Nargeot	Duflot	1858	vaudeville	5	6	1		12	urban domestic	MdD	X
La part à dieu	Laurent de Rillé	Baric	1858	opéra comique	7	6	0	+ chorus	15	urban domestic	MdD	X
La laitière de Trianon	Weckerlin	Galoppe d'Onquaire	1858	opéra de salon	8	1	1		6	rural domestic	X	X
Le médaillon d'Yvonne	Lentz	Jallais; Thiéry	1858	opérette de salon	9	2	2		9	urban domestic	JdD	X
L'amour à l'épée	Weckerlin	Galoppe d'Onquaire	1858	opéra	9	1	2		9	urban domestic	X	X
La fille du Golfe	Delibes	Nuitter	1859	opéra comique	6	5	1	+ chorus	15	rural domestic	MdD	X
Laide	Semet	Carré	1859	opérette	7	3	1		9	urban domestic	JdD	X
L'oncle Sleek			1859		7	1	2		7	urban domestic	X	X
Clara tempête	Chiaramonte	Adam-Boisgontier	1859	opérette	8	5	1		7	rural domestic	JdD	X
Les deux princesses	D'Indy	Pacini	1859	opéra comique	9	2	3		22	urban domestic	X	À Mme Gaveaux-Sabatier
Stella	O'Kelly	Montigny	1859	[opéra de salon]	10	1	2		6	urban domestic	X	X
La bohémienne	Rocheblave	Adam-Boisgontier	1860	vaudeville	5	2	2		10	rural domestic	JdD	X

L'accord parfait	Bernard	Galoppe d'Onquaire	1860	opéra comique	7	1	1		5	urban domestic	X	X
Les deux comtesses	Bordèse	Flan	1860	opéra comique	8	4	1		10	urban domestic	MdD	X
Liline et Valentin	Lecocq	De la Guette	1861	opérette de salon	5	1	1		2	urban domestic	X	X
Une reine à vingt ans	Rocheblave	Adam-Boisgontier	1861	vaudeville	5	3	2		8	urban domestic	JdD	X
Marianne	Bazin	Challamel	1861	opéra comique	7	4	0	+ chorus	16	rural domestic	MdD	X
Le proscrit	Rocheblave	Adam-Boisgontier	1862	opérette	5	3	2		9	rural domestic	JdD	X
Lanterne magique!!!	Deffès	Carré	1862	opérette	7	6	1	+ chorus	15	urban domestic	MdD	X
Un mariage par quiproquo	Sabatier-Blot	Laboureau	1862	opérette	9	2	2		13	rural domestic	X	X
Le capitaine Roch	Pfeiffer	Galoppe d'Onquaire	1862	opérette	11	2	1		11	rural domestic	X	X
La meunière de Saint-Souci	Boulanger	Carré	1863	opérette	7	5	0	+ chorus	13	urban domestic	MdD	X
Marie Stuart au château de Lochleven	Duprato	Bogaerts	1863	opérette de salon	7	4	0	+ chorus	10	historical	X	À Mademoiselle Augusta Hoffmann
Le coquelicot	Hack	Dementhe	1863	opérette	8	1	1		7	rural domestic	X	X

Deux lunatiques à Saint-Cloud	Rocheblave	Adam-Boisgontier	1863	*vaudeville*	8	3	3		11	rural domestic	*JdD*	X
Le troupier et la bonne, ou Adelaïde et Vermouth	Levassor	Levassor	1864	*saynète*	2	3	1		9	urban domestic	X	X
Favart		Dubarry	1864	*comédie-opéra*	5	1	1		3	urban domestic	X	X
Le miroir	Barbier	Nuitter	1864	*opérette*	5	3	2	+ chorus	15	urban domestic (oriental)	*MdD*	X
Grande nouvelle	Delibes	Adam-Boisgontier	1864	*opérette*	6	2	2		8	rural domestic	*JdD*	X
Le roseau chantant	Nadaud	Nadaud	1864	*opéra comique de salon*	8	1	3		15	urban domestic	X	X
L'habit ne fait pas le moine	Prévost-Rousseau	Delaunay	1864	*opérette-proverbe*	11	1	4		20	rural domestic		X
Un rendez-vous en Espagne			1864	*opéra comique*	12	2	3		11	urban domestic	X	X
Le lutin des grèves	Rocheblave	Adam-Boisgontier	1865	*opérette*	5	4	1		11	rural domestic	*JdD*	X
Jean Noël	Poise	Dubreuil	1865	*opérette*	6	3	1	+ chorus	10	rural domestic	*MdD*	X
Le compère Loriot	Perronnet	Perronnet	1865	*saynète musicale*	8	1	1		5	rural domestic	X	X

Le revenant	Hack	Sabatier	1865	opéra comique	11	2	2		13	urban domestic	X	X
La farouche ennemi	Pillevestre	Adam-Boisgontier	1866	opérette	5	3	3		12	rural domestic	JdD	X
Le marché aux servantes	Bordèse	Tréfu	1866	opérette	11	7	1	+ chorus	13	rural domestic	MdD	X
Le procès	Grisar	Adam-Boisgontier	1867	opérette	6	2	1		8	rural domestic	JdD	X
Quinolette	Legouix	Nac	1867	opérette	7	12	0	+ chorus	13	urban domestic	MdD	X
Les enfants de Perrette	Massé	Adam-Boisgontier	1868	opérette	5	5	0		11	urban domestic	JdD	X
Les valet modèles	Douay	Tourte	1868	opéra comique	6	1	1		7	urban domestic	X	X
Miss Robinson	Jonas	Carré	1868	opérette	7	6	0	+ chorus	6	urban domestic	MdD	X
Rosa, la rose	Bousquet	Poisot	1868	opérette de salon	7	1	1		7	rural domestic	X	X
Vampire et loup-garou	Reiset	Richemont	1869	opérette	4	1	2		8	urban domestic	X	X
Le feu aux poudres	Jacobi	Fournier	1869	opérette	7	5	0		10	rural domestic	X	X
Abeilles et bourdons	De Rillé	Adam-Boisgontier	1869	opérette	7	3	1	+ chorus	13	urban domestic	JdD	X
Judith et Suzon	Bordèse	Tourte	1870	opérette	7	5	0	+ chorus	10	rural domestic	MdD	X

Journal des demoiselles (Total: 18)

					6,39	3,44	1,33		9,39			
Frère et sœur	Bordèse	Plouvier	1853	opéra comique	7	4	1	+ chorus	6	urban domestic	JdD	X
Les trois clefs	Peellaert	Peellaert	1855	opéra de salon	6	3	0		9	urban domestic	JdD	X
Le coffret de Saint-Domingue	Clapisson	Deschamps	1855	opéra comique	9	4	1	+ chorus	11	urban domestic	JdD	X
La treille du roi	Henrion	Dupeuty	1856	petit opéra comique	7	8	0	+ chorus	9	rural domestic	JdD	X
Le médaillon d'Yvonne	Lentz	Jallais; Thiéry	1858	opérette de salon	9	2	2		9	urban domestic	JdD	X
Laide	Semet	Carré	1859	opérette	7	3	1	+ chorus	9	urban domestic	JdD	X
Clara tempête	Chiaramonte	Adam-Boisgontier	1859	opérette	8	5	1		7	rural domestic	JdD	X
La bohémienne	Rocheblave	Adam-Boisgontier	1860	vaudeville	5	2	2		10	rural domestic	JdD	X
Une reine à vingt ans	Rocheblave	Adam-Boisgontier	1861	vaudeville	5	3	2		8	urban domestic	JdD	X
Le proscrit	Rocheblave	Adam-Boisgontier	1862	opérette	5	3	2		9	rural domestic	JdD	X
Deux lunattiques à Saint-Cloud	Rocheblave	Adam-Boisgontier	1863	vaudeville	8	3	3		11	rural domestic	JdD	X

Grande nouvelle	Delibes	Adam-Boisgontier	1864	opérette	6	2	2		8	rural domestic	JdD	X
Le lutin des grèves	Rocheblave	Adam-Boisgontier	1865	opérette	5	4	1		11	rural domestic	JdD	X
La farouche ennemi	Pillevestre	Adam-Boisgontier	1866	opérette	5	3	3		12	rural domestic	JdD	X
Le procès	Grisar	Adam-Boisgontier	1867	opérette	6	2	1		8	rural domestic	JdD	X
Les enfants de Perrette	Massé	Adam-Boisgontier	1868	opérette	5	5	0		11	urban domestic	JdD	X
Abeilles et bourdons	De Rillé	Adam-Boisgontier	1869	opérette	7	3	1	+ chorus	13	urban domestic	JdD	X
Laide	Semet	Adam-Boisgontier	1870	opérette	5	3	1	+ chorus	8	urban domestic	JdD	X

Magasin des demoiselles (Total: 15)

					7,13	5,47	0,67		12,4			
Le prix de famille	Massé	Méry	1855	opéra comique	9	4	1		13	rural domestic	MdD	X
Le moulin des oiseaux	Bordèse	Plouvier	1857	opéra comique	8	6	1	+ chorus	10	rural domestic	MdD	X
La part à dieu	Laurent de Rillé	Baric	1858	opéra comique	7	6	0	+ chorus	15	urban domestic	MdD	X

Les ouvrières de qualité	Nargeot	Duflot	1858	vaudeville	5	6	1		12	urban domestic	MdD	X
La fille du Golfe	Delibes	Nuitter	1859	opéra comique	6	5	1	+ chorus	15	rural domestic	MdD	X
Les deux comtesses	Bordèse	Flan	1860	opéra comique	8	4	1		10	urban domestic	MdD	X
Marianne	Bazin	Challamel	1861	opéra comique	7	4	0	+ chorus	16	rural domestic	MdD	X
Lanterne magique!!!!	Deffès	Carré	1862	opérette	7	6	1	+ chorus	15	urban domestic	MdD	X
La meunière de Saint-Souci	Boulanger	Carré	1863	opérette	7	5	0	+ chorus	13	urban domestic	MdD	X
Le miroir	Barbier	Nuitter	1864	opérette	5	3	2	+ chorus	15	urban domestic (oriental)	MdD	X
Jean Noël	Poise	Dubreuil	1865	opérette	6	3	1	+ chorus	10	rural domestic	MdD	X
Le marché aux servantes	Bordèse	Tréfu	1866	opérette	11	7	1	+ chorus	13	rural domestic	MdD	X
Quinolette	Legouix	Nac	1867	opérette	7	12	0	+ chorus	13	urban domestic	MdD	X
Miss Robinson	Jonas	Carré	1868	opérette	7	6	0	+ chorus	6	urban domestic	MdD	X
Judith et Suzon	Bordèse	Tourte	1870	opérette	7	5	0	+ chorus	10	rural domestic	MdD	X

Regular (Non-Journal) Publication (Total: 34)

					7,91	1,45	1,88	9,67			
Le coin du feu	Poisot	Tréfu	1852	*proverbe lyrique*	7	1	2	9	urban domestic	X	X	
Les ressources de Jacqueline	Simiot	Boisseaux	1853	*pastorale lyrique*	6	1	2	8	rural domestic	X	X	
Les échos de Rosine	Thys	Tréfu	1854	*opéra de salon*	9	1	2	11	urban domestic	X	X	
Le docteur vieuxtemps	Nadaud	Nadaud	1854	*opéra comique de salon*	8	2	3	18	urban domestic	X	X	
A deux pas du bonheur	Godefroid	Beauvoir	1855	*proverbe lyrique*	5	1	2	5	urban domestic	X	X	
La volière	Nadaud	Nadaud	1855	*opéra comique de salon*	7	1	3	15	urban domestic	X	S.A.SlaPrincesse Mathilde
Jaloux de soi	Marcelli	Marcelli	1856	*proverbe lyrique*	13	2	1	18	rural domestic	X	X
Les terreurs de M. Peters	Poisot	Stop; Muÿs	1856	*opéra de salon ou de chambre*	10	2	3	14	urban domestic	X	À Mr Félix Marochetti
Stella, ou Une autre Werther	O'Kelly	Montigny	1857	*opéra de salon*	8	1	2	8	urban domestic	X	X

Le mariage en poste	Weckerlin	Galoppe d'Onquaire	1857	opéra	9	1	2	6	rural domestic	X	X
Porte et fenêtre	Nadaud	Nadaud	1857	opérette de salon	6	1	3	2	urban domestic	X	X
Les revenants bretons	Weckerlin	De Guézennec de Bréhat	1857	opéra de salon	9	2	2	9	rural domestic	X	X
La laitière de Trianon	Weckerlin	Galoppe d'Onquaire	1858	opéra de salon	8	1	1	6	rural domestic	X	X
L'amour à l'épée	Weckerlin	Galoppe d'Onquaire	1858	opéra	9	1	2	9	urban domestic	X	X
L'oncle Sleek			1859		7	1	2	7	urban domestic	X	X
Stella	O'Kelly	Montigny	1859	[opéra de salon]	10	1	2	6	urban domestic	X	X
Les deux princesses	D'Indy	Pacini	1859	opéra comique	9	2	3	22	urban domestic	X	À Mme Gaveaux-Sabatier
L'accord parfait	Bernard	Galoppe d'Onquaire	1860	opéra comique	7	1	1	5	urban domestic	X	X
Liline et Valentin	Lecocq	De la Guette	1861	opérette de salon	5	1	1	2	urban domestic	X	X
Le capitaine Roch	Pfeiffer	Galoppe d'Onquaire	1862	opérette	11	2	1	11	rural domestic	X	X

Un mariage par quiproquo	Sabatier-Blot	Laboureau	1862	opérette	9	2	2		13	rural domestic	X	X
Marie Stuart au château de Lochleven	Duprato	Bogaerts	1863	opérette de salon	7	4	0	+ chorus	10	historical	X	À Mademoiselle Augusta Hoffmann
Le coquelicot	Hack	Dementhe	1863	opérette	8	1	1		7	rural domestic	X	X
Favart		Dubarry	1864	comédie-opéra	5	1	1		3	urban domestic	X	X
Le roseau chantant	Nadaud	Nadaud	1864	opéra comique de salon	8	1	3		15	urban domestic	X	X
Un rendez-vous en Espagne			1864	opéra comique	12	2	3		11	urban domestic	X	X
Le troupier et la bonne, ou Adelaïde et Vermouth	Levassor	Levassor	1864	saynète	2	3	1		9	urban domestic	X	X
L'habit ne fait pas le moine	Prévost-Rousseau	Delaunay	1864	opérette-proverbe	11	1	4		20	rural domestic		X
Le compère Loriot	Perronnet	Perronnet	1865	saynète musicale	8	1	1		5	rural domestic	X	X
Le revenant	Hack	Sabatier	1865	opéra comique	11	2	2		13	urban domestic	X	X

Les valet modèles	Douay	Tourte	1868	opéra comique	6	1	1	7	urban domestic	X	X
Rosa, la rose	Poisot	Bousquet	1868	opérette de salon	7	1	1	7	rural domestic	X	X
Vampire et loup-garou	Reiset	Richemont	1869	opérette	4	1	2	8	urban domestic	X	X
Le feu aux poudres	Jacobi	Fournier	1869	opérette	7	5	0	10	rural domestic	X	X

2
Performers and the Improvised Stage

Casts, Scoring, and Instrumentation

Understanding the casts for *opéra de salon* is conditioned by the purpose of the work, its proposed venue, and its audience. *Opéras de salon* that circulated in aristocratic and *haut-* and *moyen-bourgeois salons*, in performers' studios, and in concert halls by convention had one type of cast; those destined for the *parloir* and published in women's journals had entirely different ones. In general, casts tended to be more equal in terms of male and female voices and voice types in the more public settings for *opéra de salon*, whereas in the *parloir* environment, female voices predominate. The types of *emploi* that are used to distinguish voice types in the regulated theatre—*Trial, Elleviou, Falcon*, and so on—are unknown in any of the discourses surrounding *opéra de salon*.[1]

Although there is a wide range of casting practice on display in the more public *opéra de salon*, the two most common involved (1) a single female voice accompanied by a single male or by three males and (2) a single female voice together with two males, a casting that was used in a third of all *opéras de salon* for public presentation—*salon*, studio, and concert hall.[2] In the second case, however, there was a clear distinction between the importance of the two male roles, where one was clearly subsidiary, and the dramaturgy therefore resembled that of works for a single female and a single male voice. Composers and librettists had a clear sense of the most popular performance teams in the capital and wrote works that those teams could exploit. In general, there were rarely more than two female voices involved, and when there were—in Georges Jacobi's 1869 *Le feu aux poudres*, for example—the four

---

[1] For an account of voice types in the 1830s and 1840s and a discussion of the concept of the *emploi*, see Olivier Bara, 'The Company at the Heart of the Operatic Institution: Chollet and the Changing Nature of Comic-Opera Role Types during the July Monarchy', *Music, Theater and Cultural Transfer: Paris, 1830–1914*, ed. Mark Everist and Annegret Fauser (Chicago: Chicago University Press, 2009) 11–28.

[2] These figures are taken from the data presented in the appendix of chapter 1.

Opéra de salon. Mark Everist, Oxford University Press. Oxford University Press 2025.
DOI: 10.1093/9780197695210.003.0003

female voices masked two *travesti* roles for the Colonel and Léonard;[3] and while this latter case clearly invites reflection on the type of performance envisaged (it seems to have been destined for the Salle Herz), it does not run counter to the general practice of casting for single women.

Things were very different in the *parloir*, the environment where the repertory of *opéra de salon* was published in women's journals. Here male roles are frequently entirely absent or restricted to a single minor character, and it is no stretch of the imagination to see these few roles as aimed at the paterfamilias. Female roles could range from two or three characters up to eight in Paul Henrion's 1856 *La treille du roi* or even up to twelve in Isidore Legouix's 1867 *Quinolette*.[4] The works in *Le journal des demoiselles* took a slightly more generous view of male roles, whereas they were extremely rare in *Le magasin des demoiselles*. What further marks out what might be thought of as '*opéras de parloir*' is their use of the all-female chorus, found in about half the works in *Le journal des demoiselles* but in almost all those published in *Le magasin des demoiselles*; such choruses were very likely for children and almost certainly involved unbroken male voices. But choruses were almost entirely absent from the type of *opéra de salon* mounted in *salon*, studio, and concert hall. The single example comes from a press account of a work—Jules-Edmond-Joseph, Marquis d'Aoust's *Une partie de dominos*—for which no sources survive.[5]

Unlike casting, the instrumental scoring of *opéra de salon* was largely unchanged across the entire repertory. In principle, the genre involved a piano alone with no other instruments. For the works published in *Le journal des demoiselles* and *Le magasin des demoiselles*, which were aimed at more intimate domestic performance, the piano was ideal for accompanying the two to four voices in the modest *parloirs* of the *moyenne* and *petite bourgeoisie*, but it was also used in performances across the board. There were exceptions. When Duprez established a private theatre in his own home in 1859, the accompanying ensemble—described or illustrated in a number of sources—was consistently two pianos, two harps, and an *orgue expressif*.[6] And in an 1855 performance of Charles-Casimir Manry's *Les deux espagneuls* at the

---

[3] Only the censors' libretto survives for the work: 'Pour être représenté à mon concert / du 21 mars prochain à la Salle Herz / G. Jacobi / Le feu aux poudres / - / Opérette en un Acte' (Paris, Archives Nationales F[18] 1347/9856).

[4] For the former, see *Le magasin des demoiselles* 13 (1856-1857) 4-12 (libretto) and an unpaginated appendix for the score; for the latter, *ibidem*, 24 (1867-1868) 3-11.

[5] See chapter 6 for a discussion of this performance.

[6] See the image in *Le monde illustré*, 5 February 1859, and reproduced in chapter 4, and the account of the performance of parts of *Samson*, below, where the pianists were Amédée van den Heuvel and Édouard Batiste, the organist was Léon Duprez—Duprez *fils*—with E. Gillette performing on

Établissment Hydrothérapique des Néothermes, the oboist, Louis-Stanislas-Xavier Verroust, played obligatos in the overture and in the pastoral duet for Armand and Clarisse, 'Le berger, près de sa bergère'; the fact that both the vocal score and the libretto specifically mention 'hautbois' strongly suggests that this instrumental combination was Manry's precise specification and not merely an ad hoc arrangement.[7]

Orchestras were very occasionally established to replace keyboard accompaniment, but of the nearly two hundred documented performances of *opéra de salon*, there are fewer than a dozen accounts of such a practice. For his three performances at the Salle Herz in the early 1850s (*Le trésor à Mathurin, Le décaméron, ou La grotte d'amour*, and *Luc et Lucette*), Jacques Offenbach made use of an orchestra,[8] and for a performance of Raoul de Lostanges's *Le valet poète* in 1862 in the private house of the sculptor Louis-Félix-Édouard Trinet, an orchestra of no fewer than twenty-five was assembled.[9] D'Aoust presumably used his not inconsiderable private means to form an orchestra to accompany his *opéras de salon—Une partie de dominos* and *L'amour voleur*—both at his own home in the rue de l'Université and also in the *salon*, seven houses away on the same street, of the celebrated singer Anne-Célina-Ernestine Berdalle de Lapommeraye, where he directed.[10] And unsurprisingly, there was an orchestra for the performance of Jean-Baptiste Weckerlin's *Tout est bien qui finit bien* and of Offenbach's *Les deux aveugles* in the Salle de Diane at the Tuileries in front of Napoléon III and his family in 1856.[11]

---

perhaps the single harp used in the performance (the name of no other harpist is mentioned); *Le ménestrel*, 18 March 1855.

[7] *La Revue et Gazette musicale de Paris*, 24 December 1854; *Le ménestrel*, 7 January 1855. Passages identified for oboe are *À Monsieur le D*ʳ ' Edouard Bouland./-/LES/DEUX/ÉPAGNEULS/Opéra bouffe/*en un acte et en vers*/DE Mʳ/Edouard Fournier,/Musique de CHARLES MANRY./*Représenté aux Néothermes, le 19 Décembre 1854/. . ./Etienne CHALLIOT, éditeur,/à Paris, Rue St Honoré, 354, près la Place Vendôme*, 68–75.
[8] Discussed in Everist, *Opérette: The First Twenty-Five Years*.
[9] The performance took place on 6 February 1862 and was described in *La Revue et Gazette musicale de Paris*, 9 February 1862. There is no surviving trace of either the score or the libretto of *Le valet poète*.
[10] For the performance of *Une partie de dominos*, see *Le ménestrel*, 15 March 1863; for *L'amour voleur*, see *La Revue et Gazette musicale de Paris*, 12 March 1865. The work's subsequent performance is described *ibidem*, 26 March 1865. See also 'LAPOMMERAIE [sic] (Anne Célina Ernestine BERDALLE de)', *Cantatrices de l'Opéra de Paris, L'art lyrique français* (https://www.artlyriquefr.fr/dicos/Opera%20Cantatrices.html#LABIA).
[11] *Le ménestrel*, 2 March 1856; *La Revue et Gazette musicale de Paris*, 2 March 1856.

Vocal Artists

One of the characteristics of performances of *opéra de salon* is the participation of non-professional performers, composers, and librettists, of what might today be termed 'amateurs'. Such expressions as 'amateur' or 'professional', however, require careful definition according to time and location and, in the context of *salon* cultures of the Second Empire, entail several definitions and many antinomies. In nineteenth-century France, the term 'amateur' frequently means nothing more than someone who is familiar with and appreciates a work or a performance—synonymous with the modern 'music lover', with which it is an obvious cognate. Audiences, even the best informed and most highly praised, are frequently described as consisting of 'amateurs'. So, in closing an encomium to Duprez's theatre in 1859, Hippolyte Lucas expressed the wish that the *opéras de salon* Duprez performed there should be more broadly known, since they were at that point—according to Lucas—'known up until now only by a small group of *amateurs* [emphasis added]'.[12]

Despite this ambiguity in the use of the term amateur, there was a clear opposition, in the performance of *opéra de salon*, between performers drawn from society who did not take a fee for their performance and those who were termed *artistes* or *virtuoses* and who made their living from these and other performances. The term 'professional' is never used in this culture, nor is any terminological opposition between 'amateur' and 'professional' found, and the latter concept emerges only at the end of the nineteenth century.[13] Both non-professionals and *artistes-virtuoses* nevertheless played a key part in performances of *opéra de salon* during the Second Empire, and their interaction is one of the noteworthy characteristics of its culture.[14]

Performances in more public venues were almost invariably given by *artistes* or *virtuoses*. Almost all the performances at the Salle Herz and other concert halls, for example, were given by such individuals. These artists fall into three groups: those who worked at one of the regulated theatres (mostly either the Opéra-Comique or Théâtre-Lyrique), those *artistes-virtuoses* who

---

[12] 'connues jusqu'à ce jour seulement d'un petit nombre d'amateurs' (*Le monde illustré*, 5 February 1859).

[13] The first use of the term *professionalisme* is in the domain of cycling. See *Le sport vélocipédique*, 3 February 1881.

[14] For an account of how these issues were handled at the end of the previous century, see Rebecca Dowd Geoffroy-Schwinden, *From Servant to Savant: Musical Privilege, Property, and the French Revolution* (New York: Oxford University Press, 2022) 21–50 and *passim*.

were also described in the press as *chanteurs et cantatrices de concert*, and a much smaller group of Conservatoire laureates. Members of these groups could perform independently or together, and the combination of vocal artists speaks to the types of network in which the promoter of the concert was involved.

In the early years of *opéra de salon*, Offenbach preferred artists from the regulated theatre for his performances in the Salle Herz. His *Le trésor à Mathurin* was given there by three artists from the Opéra-Comique—Marie-Charlotte-Léocadie Lemercier,[15] Marie-Stéphanie Meyer-Meillet,[16] and Sainte-Foy (the pseudonym of Charles-Louis Pubereaux)[17]—and one of Offenbach's colleagues from the Comédie-Française, Alice-Marie Théric.[18] Six years later, by which time Meyer-Meillet had moved to the Théâtre-Lyrique with her husband, Auguste-Alphonse-Edmond Meillet;[19] they joined Jules Monjauze[20]—also from the Théâtre-Lyrique—in the premiere of Pierre-Edmond Hocmelle's *La mort de Socrate*, also at the Salle Herz.[21]

But already by the time of the 1858 premiere of *La mort de Socrate*, teams of concert artists had begun to take over the roles in *opéra de salon*. Mme Gaveaux-Sabatier was not only one of the most tireless *cantatrices de concert* but also one of the first.[22] She appeared for the first time, paired with Pierre-Thomas Levassor,[23] in the performance of Dieudonné-Joseph-Guillaume-Félix Godefroid's *A deux pas du bonheur* that took place at the Palais Bourbon in the presidential *salons*, promoted by the Comte de Morny, president of the

---

[15] 'LEMERCIER Marie Charlotte Léocadie dite Léocadie', *L'art lyrique français: Opéra-Comique-Cantatrices* (https://www.artlyriquefr.fr/dicos/Opera-Comique%20Cantatrices.html#LABAT.

[16] 'Maria MEILLET-MEYER', *L'art lyrique français: Théâtre-Lyrique-Interprètes* (https://www.artlyriquefr.fr/personnages/Meillet-Meyer.html).

[17] SAINTE-FOY, *L'art lyrique français: Opéra-Comique-Chanteurs* (https://www.artlyriquefr.fr/personnages/Sainte-Foy.html).

[18] Henry Lyonnet, *Dictionnaire des comédiens français (ceux d'hier): biographie, bibliographie, iconographie*, 2 vols., Histoire du Théâtre (Geneva: Bibliothèque de la Revue Universelle Internationale Illustrée, 1902–1908; reprint Slatkine Reprints, 1969) 681.

[19] 'Auguste Alphonse Edmond MEILLET', *L'art lyrique français: Théâtre-Lyrique-Inteprètes* (https://www.artlyriquefr.fr/personnages/Meillet.html).

[20] 'Jules Sébastien MONJAUZE dit Jules MONJAUZE', *L'art lyrique français: Théâtre-Lyrique-Inteprètes* (https://www.artlyriquefr.fr/personnages/Monjauze%20Jules.html).

[21] The cast for the premiere of Hocmelle's *La mort de Socrate* is given only in the printed libretto: LA MORT DE SOCRATE/OPÉRA COMIQUE EN UN ACTE/PAR M. GALOPPE D'ONQUAIRE/MUSIQUE DE M. HOCMELLE/REPRÉSENTÉE POUR LA PREMIÈRE FOIS, A LA SALLE HERTZ, LE 7 FÉVRIER 1858/.../LAGNY. Imprimérie de A. VARIGAULT.

[22] There is a large amount of primary material gathered on Gaveaux-Sabatier in Kurt Gänzl, *Victorian Vocalists* (London: Routledge, 2018) 260–264.

[23] Levassor had a distinguished career as an actor in the regulated theatre before beginning work in *opéra de salon*, working at the Théâtre du Palais-Royal, at the Théâtre des Variétés, and then back at the Palais-Royal, where he ended his career in 1852 (Lyonnet, *Dictionnaire des comédiens français*, 361–362).

Corps Législatif.[24] She worked briefly with Louis-Joseph-Léon Fleury, who was Conservatoire-trained and had made his debut at the Opéra-Comique as long ago as 1836; but he was better known as a *sociétaire* of the Société des Concerts du Conservatoire (he had achieved that status in 1838) and made his career in the concert world.[25] It was therefore no surprise that he should drift into the culture of *opéra de salon*. Gaveaux-Sabatier then partnered with Jules-François-René Lefort for three years from 1856 to 1859, during which time the pair put on eleven documented performances (the actual number must have been much higher) of seven separate works.[26] She then worked alongside Charles-Louis Lourdel—known as Biéval—for three years (seven performances and three separate works)[27] and then apparently fell silent for most of the first half of the 1860s, to return in 1865 paired with Léon-Charles-Sigismond Hermann; Hermann, also known as Charles Hermann-Léon, was the son of Hermann-Léon (Léonard Hermann), who had been a veteran of the Opéra-Comique from his debut in 1844 to his retirement in 1856. The son, Charles Hermann-Léon, was to have a successful career as an artist specializing in images of animals, but he also had a career as a *chanteur de concert* at least during the second half of the 1860s.[28] Other key *chanteurs de concert* were Eugène-Jean-Baptiste Archainbaud, who appears in 1857 and sang regularly until at least 1870,[29] and the near-legendary brothers

---

[24] *Le ménestrel*, 18 and 25 February 1855 (she had also appeared at the semi-public rehearsal the previous week; see *ibidem*, 11 February 1855). Morny has been the subject of two modern biographies: Christopher Robert, *Le duc de Morny: "empereur" des Français sous Napoléon III* (Paris: Hachette, 1951); Agnès d'Angio-Barros, *Morny: le théâtre du pouvoir* (Paris: Belin, 2012).

[25] Constant Pierre, *Le Conservatoire National de Musique et de Déclamation: documents historiques et administratives*, 2 vols. (Paris: Imprimerie Nationale, 1900) 755.

[26] Lefort was a major figure in the *salon* culture of the Second Empire. After a false start at the Opéra in 1848, he dedicated his career to work in *salons* and to teaching. He created roles in four *opéras de salon* as well as in *L'esprit du foyer* by Charles Salvatoris (better known as Salvator) in Baden-Baden in 1858. He sang for a single season (1861–1862) at the Théâtre-Lyrique, where he took roles in just two premieres: of Théodore-Édouard Dufaure de Lajarte's *Le neveu de Gulliver* and Pauline Thys's *Le pays de Cocagne*; significantly, these were works by composers also specializing in *opéra de salon* and *opérette*, and the intimate qualities of his voice might have made him a less than suitable member of the troupe. See 'Jules François René LEFORT dit Jules LEFORT', *L'art lyrique français: le Théâtre-Lyrique, ses interprètes* (https://www.artlyriquefr.fr/personnages/Lefort%20Jules.html). There is substantial additional information in Kurt Gänzl, 'Jules Lefort: "Delight of the Parisian Salons"' (https://kurtofgerolstein.blogspot.com/2021/05/jules-lefort-delight-of-parisian-salons.html).

[27] 'Charles Louis LOURDEL dit BIÉVAL', *L'art lyrique français: Théâtre-Lyrique-Intepètes* (https://www.artlyriquefr.fr/personnages/Bieval.html).

[28] 'Herrmann-Léon', *Benezit Dictionary of Artists* (https://www.oxfordartonline.com/benezit/view/10.1093/benz/9780199773787.001.0001/acref-9780199773787-e-00086846).

[29] Multiple prize-winner at the Conservatoire, Archainbaud was a member of the Société des Concerts du Conservatoire, *maître de chapelle* at Saint Vincent-de-Paul, and professor at the Conservatoire (Pierre, *Le Conservatoire*, 2:687).

Anatole and Hippolyte Lionnet.[30] Gaveaux-Sabatier was just the best known of several *cantatrices de concert*. Although she was the female focus of *opéra de salon* throughout the Second Empire, her best-known colleagues were Fanny-Marie Cinti, known as Cinti-Damoureau—the daughter of Laure Cinti-Damoureau;[31] Mme Lefébure-Wély;[32] Marie-Joséphine-Clémence Mira (Mlle Mira); Cécile-Henriette-Eugénie d'Halbert (who used the surname Pijon until her marriage to the Opéra-Comique's Charles-Auguste-Marie Ponchard, at which point she sang in concerts and salons as Mme Ponchard.[33] After 1861, these five were joined by Blanche Peudefer.[34]

Alongside the *chanteurs* and *cantatrices de concert* and their colleagues who only very occasionally contributed from the regulated theatres were *graduands* from the Conservatoire, students who were at the end of their time at the institution and were working their way through the various levels of prizes while—or before—making their debuts at one of the regulated theatres. Thus, in the performance of Hocmelle's *En attendant de soleil* at the home of the industrialist and philanthropist Alphonse Lavallée, all three soloists were in this liminal position: at the time of the performance in February 1856, Alphonsine-Coralie-Mathilde-Françoise Dupuy had already been declared *premier accessit* for singing and *opéra comique* in 1855, would win the second prize for both disciplines in 1856, and would be engaged by the Opéra-Comique in March 1857; she would then go on to work at the Théâtre de la Monnaie in Brussels in 1859–1860, in the French provinces, in New Orleans, back at the Opéra-Comique in the late 1860s, and again in New Orleans at the end of the decade. André Pascal Dammien, known just

---

[30] Given their status in the concert life of the Second Empire, it is strange that there is relatively little trace of the Lionnet brothers in the literature. They left a set of memoirs: Anatole and Hippolyte Lionnet, *Souvenirs et anecdotes* (Paris: Ollendorff, 1888), and the little that is known is collected in Mark Everist, *Genealogies of Music and Memory: Gluck in the 19th-Century Parisian Imagination* (New York: Oxford University Press, 2021) 31–32.

[31] Cinti-Damoureau was employed for a single season at the Opéra (1862–1863) and married Weckerlin in 1856 (Pierre, *Le Conservatoire*, 2:722).

[32] There is very little evidence for Mme Lefébure-Wély's career beyond the extensive commentaries in the musical press of the Second Empire, much of which is outlined here. The only documentary account is François-Joseph Fétis, *Biographie universelle des musiciens et bibliographie générale de la musique*, 8 vols. (Brussels: Leroux, 1835–1844; 2nd ed. Paris: Firmin Didot, 1860–1865); supplement in 2 vols. by Arthur Pougin (Paris: Firmin Didot 1880–1881), Suppl. 2:92. She also put on a performance of *Le miroir du diable* in the home she shared with her husband around the same time as the Ségalas performance (*Le ménestrel*, 13 April 1856).

[33] Conservatoire-trained, Mme Ponchard had made her début at the Opéra in 1845, but her contract was terminated in 1849 (*La Revue et Gazette musicale de Paris*, 23 September 1849; Pierre, *Le Conservatoire*, 2:741).

[34] Peudefer made her debut in *opéra de salon* in Joseph O'Kelly's *Stella* in the *salon* of Antonin Prévost-Rousseau (*Le ménestrel*, 22 December 1861).

as Pascal, was *deuxième accessit* for *opéra comique* in 1856 and sang briefly at the Opéra in the mid-1860s, and Léon-Alexandre Lafont was *accessit* in *solfège* in 1846 and would win *deuxième, premier accessit*, and then first prize for *opéra comique* in successive years beginning in 1856. Appointed immediately to the Opéra-Comique, he was afflicted by illness and became one of the earliest pensioners of the Association des Artistes Musiciens.[35]

Similarly, at two performances of Jules Beer's *Les roses M. de Malesherbes*, the first at the home of the composer and the second in Rossini's salon, both in January 1861, Mira was joined by two Conservatoire *graduands*. Alexandre-Narcisse-Marie Gourdin won five prizes in 1859–1860 and made his debut at the Opéra-Comique just a few days after the performance in Rossini's salon; but after creating seven new roles in four years, he died at the age of twenty-three.[36] His exact contemporary, Joseph-Amédée-Victor Capoul, who made his Opéra-Comique debut in August 1861, stayed until 1872 and would then enjoy a stellar career that would take him to London and New York.[37]

A Conservatoire background was also important for one of the most intriguing participants in the performance of *opéra de salon*: Marie-Louise-Eugénie Dejoly (occasionally found with the orthography De Joly). On the first two occasions she sang, she was described unhelpfully as an 'amateur'—which could mean a number of things, as has been seen, but on the third, she was recognized as the winner of the 1848 *premier prix* for piano at the Conservatoire.[38] 'More than an amateur salon *prima donna*', wrote the critic Henri Blanchard as he made a bad terminological situation worse, 'she would not be out of place on any of our lyric stages, in terms of face, figure or method'. He continued that she sang the role of Clarisse in Manry's *Les deux espagneuls* at the Établissement Hydrothérapique des Néothermes in 1854 as well as she played the piano.[39] Little more is known of Dejoly, but her activity well illustrates the ambiguity that surrounds many of those described as amateurs involved in the cultivation of *opéra de salon*. Her

---

[35] Pierre, *Le Conservatoire*, 2:747, 2:824, 2:786. See *La Revue et Gazette musicale de Paris*, 24 February 1856.
[36] Pierre, *Le Conservatoire* 2:765; 'GOURDIN Alexandre Narcisse Marie', *L'art lyrique français: Opéra-Comique-Chanteurs* (https://www.artlyriquefr.fr/dicos/Opera-Comique%20Chanteurs.html#HAAS).
[37] Joël-Marie Fauquet, 'CAPOUL, Joseph-Amédée-*Victor*', *Dictionnaire de la musique en France au xixe siècle* (Paris: Fayard, 2003) 207.
[38] Pierre, *Le Conservatoire*, 2:734.
[39] 'plus qu'une *prima donna* amateur et de salon; elle ne serait déplacée sur aucune de nos scènes lyriques par la figure, la taille et la méthode' (*La Revue et Gazette musicale de Paris*, 24 December 1854).

colleagues at that performance consisted of the mysterious Belouet (perhaps Bellouet), about whom nothing is known except for his participation in three events in the mid-1850s and a single reappearance—but alongside Mme Gaveaux-Sabatier and Hermann-Léon—in 1866; his status as an artist is lamentably ambiguous. The other participants in Dejoly's Néothermes performance were Louis-Prosper Guyot and Antoine-Anatole Jal; the former had recently arrived in Paris after a ten-year career as a magistrate's clerk in Villers-Cotterêts near where he had been born, and he would make his début in Émile Jonas's *Le duel de Benjamin* in October the following year at the Théâtre des Bouffes-Parisiens, where he would take part in the premieres of eleven *opérettes* up to 1858, and then he appeared from 1862 at the Théâtre-Lyrique, where he would participate in premieres by Georges Bizet and Victorin de Joncières as well as large numbers of Italian works (Wolfgang Amadeus Mozart and Giuseppe Verdi, mostly) at the same house until 1868.[40]

These teams of *artistes* and *virtuoses* roamed across the *salons* and concert halls of Paris throughout the two decades of the Second Empire. The same group could be found with exactly the same work in concert hall or *salon*. Gaveaux-Sabatier and Lefort, together with Anna-Angelini Banderali (the daughter of the Conservatoire teacher David Banderali, she was known as Mme Barthe after her marriage to the composer Adrien Barthe in 1858), could equally easily perform d'Indy's *Les deux princesses* in early March 1859 in the Comtesse d'Indy's apartments in the rue de Bac as they could present the same work at the Salle Herz at the end of April the same year.[41] Similarly, Gaveaux-Sabatier could host the premiere of Weckerlin's *Pierrot à Paphos, ou La sérénade intérrompue* in her own studio on the rue des Petites Écuries—this time with Hermann-Léon—in February 1866, and two months later, the two could perform the same work in the rue de Taranne apartments of the civil servant and theatre manager Jean-Baptiste-Louis-Georges Benou.[42] *Artistes* and *virtuoses* appeared in a professional capacity in aristocratic, *moyen-* and *haut-bourgeois salons*, in their own studios and those of colleagues, and in concert halls. There is no evidence whatsoever that they appeared in any *parloir*, and their repertory comprehensively eschewed the works published in journals destined for the *demoiselle*.

---

[40] 'Louis Prosper GUYOT dit Prosper GUYOT', *L'art lyrique français: Théâtre-Lyrique-Inteprètes* (https://www.artlyriquefr.fr/personnages/Guyot%20Prosper.html).
[41] See *La Revue et Gazette musicale de Paris*, 27 March 1859; *ibidem*, 24 April 1859.
[42] *Le ménestrel*, 18 February 1866; *ibidem*, 29 April 1866.

Amateur singers—or *chanteurs/chanteuses du monde*, as they were called by contemporary commentators—are better defined for the Second Empire by aspiration rather than by technical ability. In other words, they are defined entirely by a lack of ambition to do anything other than the performance in which they are singing at the moment; there is no sense of developing a career as a singer and abandoning a career as a doctor, architect, or civil servant; abandoning the liberal professions for a career in music, legion as tales of this are, almost invariably took place earlier in life. The last of the performers at the production of Manry's *Les deux espagneuls* at the Néothermes, Jal, however, was a bona fide non-professional.[43] An architect, he designed hotels in Deauville and specialized in the ceramic decoration of domestic façades (still visible today at 11 Cité Malesherbes, for example), originally commissioned by the painter Pierre-Jules Jollivet;[44] Jal was perhaps best known for his work on the tomb of Alfred de Musset in the Père Lachaise Cemetery. *Les deux espagneuls* was not his only role; he had already performed in what might have been the premiere of Gustave Nadaud's *Le docteur vieuxtemps* and would also take part in a performance of the same composer's *La volière* in March 1855.[45] Jal's better-known father, Auguste, had a career as official historian of the navy and then as its *conservateur des archives* and could put in an appearance as the prompt alongside his son in a performance of Nadaud's *La volière* in 1855—a distinction that did not go unnoticed by the press.[46] This performance took place in the Louvre apartments of the minister of state Achille Fould and was one of the performances fronted by Mme Gaveaux-Sabatier as the sole *artiste-virtuose* in a cast otherwise made up of *chanteurs du monde*.

Perhaps the best known of the *chanteurs du monde* was Ernest-Louis-Victor-Jules L'Épine. He was a junior civil servant until he came to the attention of the Comte de Morny, to whom he became first secretary and then chief of staff at the Corps Législatif. He sang in the same 1855 performance as Jal in the ministerial suite at the Louvre in Nadaud's *La volière* and at its rehearsal in the *salon* of Camille Doucet, then the head of the Division of the

---

[43] Much more is known about Jal's father, for whom see 'JAL, Augustin', *Dictionnaire critique des historiens de l'art actifs en France de la Révolution à la Première Guerre mondiale* (https://www.inha.fr/dictionnaire-critique-des-historiens-de-lart-actifs-en-france-de-la-revolution-a-la-premiere-guerre-mondiale/jal-augustin-inha/).

[44] *Monumentum: Carte des monuments historiques français* (https://monumentum.fr/immeuble-pa00088963.html).

[45] *Le ménestrel*, 5 March 1854; *ibidem*, 11 and 18 February 1855.

[46] *Ibidem*, 4 March 1855.

Theatre section within the ministry of state. But L'Épine was simultaneously a committed playwright and would develop this part of his *carrière croisée* even more after Morny's death in 1865.[47] Before then, however, he had written or contributed to the libretti of two *opérettes* by Offenbach: *Monsieur Choufleuri restera chez lui le 24 janvier 1833* (1861) and *L'amour chanteur* (1864). But he had also composed the music for three *opérettes* for the Bouffes-Parisiens: *Trafalgar sur un volcan* (1855, for which Offenbach had completed the orchestration), *Forteboule*, and *Croquignole XXXVI* (both 1860).[48]

But the vogue for performances that featured *chanteurs* and *chanteuses du monde* lasted little more than the first year in which *opéra de salon* was in vogue. The first such performance was the premiere of Nadaud's *Le docteur vieuxtemps* in Pitre-Chevalier's salon (Pitre-Chevalier is discussed in chapter 4) in late February or early March 1854,[49] and the last was an outing for the same composer's *La volière* at an unspecified *salon* in the Chaussée d'Antin on 8 March the following year, a performance led by Gaveaux-Sabatier.[50] Appearances of *chanteurs* and *chanteuses du monde* after the 1854–1855 season were rare: the mysterious Belouet reappeared with Gaveaux-Sabatier in 1866,[51] and the equally mysterious Henry Le Roy—who had appeared with some regularity during the 1853–1854 season—accompanied Gaveaux-Sabatier and Hermann-Léon at Benou's *salon* in 1866 and also, with the same team, in Gaveaux-Sabatier's own *salon* a year later.[52] The move away from the use of *chanteurs* and *chanteuses du monde* was mirrored in other aspects of the professionalization of *opéra de salon*, most notably in the management of the press. The presence of journalists at many of the performances of *opéra de salon* in the Salle Herz, for example, was probably engineered by the management of the hall, but productions of

---

[47] The concept of the *carrière croisée* was adumbrated by Emmanuel Reibel as a way to trace the conflict of interests between journalists and those professionally involved in the theatre. Emmanuel Reibel, 'Carrières entre presse et opéra au xixe siècle: du mélange des genres au conflit d'intérêts', *Presse et opéra aux XVIIIe et XIXe siècles*, ed. Olivier Bara, Christophe Cave, and Marie-Ève Thérenty, *Médias* 19, 2021 (https://www.medias19.org/publications/presse-et-opera-aux-xviiie-et-xixe-siecles/carrieres-entre-presse-et-opera-au-xixe-siecle-du-melange-des-genres-au-conflit-dinterets). But the concept may be broadened in two important ways: (1) the obvious extension to other careers and combinations of careers and (2) thinking beyond the crude binary opposition that 'journalist and theatre director' implies to allow multiple careers—it is easy to think of individuals with four, if not more, *carrières croisées*, to cross in a way that begins to evoke networks of social practice.
[48] See Fétis, *Biographie universelle des musiciens*, Suppl. 2:101–102.
[49] *Le ménestrel*, 5 March 1854.
[50] *Ibidem*, 11 and 18 February 1855.
[51] *Ibidem*, 18 February 1866.
[52] *Ibidem*, 29 April 1866; 10 March 1867.

opéra de salon in private *salons* and artists' studios must have entailed some sort of liaison between the promoters of the events and the management of the journals in which the performances were reviewed.

There were as many non-professional composers and librettists as there were non-professional performers. The artist Eugène-Nicolas Trouvé was both a *salonnier* and the librettist of Louis-Gustave Canoby's *Les sabotiers* as well as a genre painter and director of a school for artists,[53] and Jules Blerzy, who wrote the libretto for *Une partie de dominos* by d'Aoust, was a retired financier.[54] Another aristocratic libretto was *Au pied du mur* by Marie-René-Napoléon Savary, 2e Duc de Rovigo (the music was by Clara Collinet). Non-professional librettists may have worked alongside non-professional composers—Blerzy and d'Aoust are an obvious pair—but the collaborations with Collinet and Canoby are difficult to analyse in that the careers—in music and outside—of both composers are unclear to the point of obscurity. Almost all the non-professional composers of *opéra de salon* had private fortunes: the titles of the Marquis d'Aoust and Comtesse Perrière-Pilté speak for themselves; Paul de Richard d'Ivry was the son of a marquis who had taught himself music in the family's fourteenth-century Chateau de Caroboeuf.[55] Mme Peigné—a shadowy figure who used the pseudonym Max Silny—was reputed to be the daughter of a famous lawyer whose identity remains obscure.[56] Manry—whose two *opéras de salon* were the sole repertory of the theatre at the Néothermes—had abandoned a career in the law when he inherited his father's fortune in 1840.[57]

One general characteristic of *opéra de salon* is the high proportion of composers who wrote their own libretti; except for the work of Hervé, writing both poetry and music was something of a rarity in *opéra comique*, in *opérette*, and—it goes without saying—in *vaudeville*.[58] Within the domain of *opéra de salon*, Nadaud, for example, wrote all four of his own libretti except for *La clef du secrétaire*, a work whose existence remains opaque,[59] and

---

[53] Trouvé's support for and creation of *opéra de salon* is discussed in chapter 4.

[54] *Le ménestrel*, 15 March 1863. He would go on to collaborate with Albéric Second on plays at the Gymnase Dramatique and the Comédie-Française. See *L'année théâtrale*, 1 (1875) 309–310. Blerzy had previously made his fortune as a stockbroker (*agent de change*).

[55] 'Paul de Richard d'Ivry (Beaune, 1829–Hyères, 1903)', *Histoire de Beaune: Ses hommes et femmes célèbres* (http://www.beaune.fr/spip.php?rubrique200#.YIKV6uvTX0r).

[56] *La Revue et Gazette musicale de Paris*, 26 May 1867.

[57] Manry's career, output, and work at the Néothermes are discussed in chapter 3.

[58] *Vaudeville* is excluded from this discussion since, as a genre, it hinges on the reuse of pre-existing *timbres* and *airs connus*.

[59] The only attribution of *La clef du secrétaire* to Nadaud is in Girod, 'L'opéra de salon'. Older sources attribute it to Poisot: Hugo Riemann, *Opern-Handbuch: Repertorium der dramatisch-musikalischen Litteratur (Opern, Operetten, Ballette, Melodramen, Pantomimen, Oratorien, dramatische Kantaten*

Thys wrote the libretti to all three of her *opéras de salon*; significantly, when she composed *La pomme de Turquie* for the Bouffes-Parisiens, she also wrote her own libretto but set Auguste Pittaud (Pittaud de Forges) for her *Le pays de Cocagne* at the more formal Théâtre-Lyrique. Eudoxe-Françoise Péan de la Roche-Jagu, whose work will be discussed in chapter 6, certainly wrote the libretto to her *Simple et coquette* and possibly others,[60] and even Weckerlin appears to have written the libretto to one of his *opéras de salon*: *Pierrot à Paphos ou La sérénade interrompue*.[61] Non-professional composers occasionally wrote their own libretti as well: Perrière-Pilté's *Jaloux de soi* and d'Ivry's *Les amants de Vérone* (the libretto of his *La maison du docteur* was by Boisseaux, however) are examples.[62] The authorship of the two works for which Auguste-Napoléon-Joseph, Marquis de Colbert-Chabanais, wrote the music for Gilbert Duprez's theatre in 1868 and 1870 is unclear. The libretto of *Les jolis racoleurs* is explicitly attributed to Édouard Duprez. The performance of *Djahn Ara* at Gilbert Duprez's theatre relies solely on a listing by Albert Soubies of libretti based on Victor Hugo's *Notre Dame de Paris* and may mask joint authorship of both music and libretto.[63]

Librettists whose *opéras de salon* were set by others also frequently worked in the regulated theatre, and names were familiar across the field. Boisseaux, for example, also wrote libretti for *opéras de salon*—Poisot's *Les ressources de Jacqueline*, Nadaud's *La clef du secrétaire*, and Lajarte's *On guérit de la peur*[64]—but he also wrote for the Opéra-Comique, Théâtre-Lyrique, Bouffes-Parisiens, and Théâtre des Fantaisies-Parisiennes. Such *opérette* librettists as Étienne Tréfeu, Armand Delbès, and several others wrote both *opéras de salon* and works for the regulated theatre and—after 1867 in the

---

u.s.w.)—ein notwediges Supplement zu jedem Musiklexikon, 2 vols. (Leipzig: Sengsbuch, 1887) 1:76; John Dennison Champlin, *Cyclopedia of Music and Musicians*, 3 vols. (New York: Scribner, 1888–1890) 3:137. Whatever the attribution, the libretto was by Caroline Berton and Henry Boisseaux.

[60] Fétis, *Bibliothèque universelle de musiciens*, Suppl. 2:578.
[61] The report in *Le ménestrel*, 10 April 1859, is explicit about Weckerlin's composition of his own libretto. Weckerlin's autograph is Paris, Bibliothèque Nationale de France MS 16905.
[62] See above for Perrière-Pilté's *Jaloux de soi*; d'Ivry's *Les amants de Vérone*—generically akin to Gilbert Duprez's own *Samson* and *Jeanne d'Arc*—is a major work in four acts, through-composed without spoken dialogue: LES AMANTS DE VÉRONE/OPÉRA en QUATRE ACTES/et/*Six Tableaux*/Imité de SHAKESPEARE/PAROLES ET MUSIQUE/DE/RICHARD YRVID/.../Paris, G. FLAXLAND Éditeur, 4, Place de la Madeleine.
[63] See *Le ménestrel*, 19 June 1870; for Soubies's list, *ibidem*, 6 June 1924.
[64] Répertoire des Théâtres, Salons & Concerts/Théâtre/ON/GUÉRIT DE LA PEUR/PAROLES DE M HENRY BOISSEAUX/MUSIQUE DE/T. DE LAJARTE/.../Paris, CHOUDENS, 371, Rue St Honoré.

case of Delbès, once *cafés-concerts* were permitted to mount *opérette*—in these regulated spaces as well.[65]

Composers' engagement with *opéra de salon* was much more varied. Nadaud, Beer, and Manry wrote for no other theatre, and Poisot and Weckerlin only wrote somewhere else on one occasion each.[66] Although these composers accounted for both most of the *opéras de salon* composed and most of the performances given, many composers contributed a small number of works to the repertory of *opéra de salon*. Offenbach, Duprato, and Laurent de Rillé wrote three *opéras de salon* each; Aristide Hignard, Charles Lecocq, Jonas, and Léo Delibes wrote two each; and a long list of composers—many of whom were more familiar from the *opéra comique* rather than the *opérette* repertory—each wrote a single *opéra de salon*.[67] However, of these, a significant number were contributors to the periodical publications that supported the genre—*Le magasin des demoiselles* and *Le journal des demoiselles*—and performances of their works seemed not to come to the attention of those who attended formal *salons*; their cultivation may well have been restricted to the *parloir*. Exceptions to this pattern were exceptions in other ways as well: Duprez's composition only extended to a single *opéra de salon*, *Jélyotte*, but he exploited the same generic culture for the promotion both of his pupils and of his larger works (*Jeanne d'Arc* and *Samson* in particular); his work for his own theatre is but a part of his output, which included works for the regulated theatre: the Théâtre-Lyrique, the Opéra-Comique, as well as the Spectacle Deburau and—much later—the Théâtre de l'Ambigu-Comique.[68] Similarly, Godefroid's *A deux pas du bonheur* with its offstage aria with harp accompaniment is paralleled by his only other stage work: his *La harpe d'or* at the Théâtre-Lyrique.[69]

---

[65] For the complete activity of these librettists within the domain of the regulated theatre, see Everist, 'Music in the Second Empire Theatre (MitSET)'.

[66] Poisot's *Le paysan*, to a libretto by Jules-Édouard Alboize de Pujol, had been premiered at the Opéra-Comique in October 1850 and did not survive its first season. Weckerlin set the same librettist's *L'organiste dans l'embarras* for the Théâtre-Lyrique in May 1853. Its fate was similar.

[67] For the wider activity of these composers within the domain of *opéra de salon* and elsewhere, see Everist, 'Music in the Second Empire Theatre (MitSET).'

[68] This varied activity is detailed in *ibidem*.

[69] LA/HARPE/D'OR/*Opéra Légende en deux actes,*/de MM/Ernest Dubreuil et Jaime fils,/ MUSIQUE/DE/FÉLIX GODEFROID/PARTITION PIANO ET CHANT/PARIS, CHOUDENS, éditeurs/rue Saint Honoré, 263, près l'Assomption. It was premiered on 9 September 1858 and ran for only nine performances.

The Improvised Stage

Vocal and instrumental artists created performances in a range of *lieux* which were transformed into performative *espaces*—in part, at least—by the creation of improvised theatres in much the same way as streets were transformed into markets, Michel de Certeau's theoretical paradigm outlined in the introduction to this book. Just as vendors set up stalls in streets and in doing so repurposed *lieux* into *espaces*, so promoters of *opéra de salon* made use of various theoretical elements to changes these *salons*, ballrooms, or studios into performative *espaces*. The growth in the use of temporary stages for *opéra de salon* involved the professionalized use of third parties for the supply of sets, costumes, lighting, and the raised stages themselves.

The higher echelons of *théâtre de société* had always brought the theatre into urban *hôtels particuliers* and rural *châteaux*, so when Comte Jules Boniface de Castellane mounted performances in his Paris home in 1837, he could bring in costumers and set designers—Pierre-Luc-Charles Ciceri, the principal designer for the Opéra, no less—to work on productions there.[70] The performances, mentioned at the beginning of this chapter, of *Tout est bien qui finit bien* and *Les deux aveugles* in front of the imperial family were fully staged with a temporary theatre, sets, and costumes, so that 'A charming theatre, raised by the Menus-Plaisirs, received at 10 o'clock the opera and the remarkable impromptu [*improvisés*] dramatic artists for which all our *salons* compete'.[71] Similarly, when Fould and his wife hosted Nadaud's *La volière* in the Louvre, the theatre was constructed at government expense.[72] Certainly, for such events as those at the Louvre, Palais Bourbon, and the Tuileries, senior imperial and government figures could call upon state resources for the performance of *opéra de salon*, as some of the most public *lieux* in the city were transformed into *espaces* for performance. This is hardly unexpected, but the more intriguing questions centre on those *salons*—such as Casimir Gide's—where the evidence is slender but allusive. Gide's elaborate performance of his own *Belphégor, ou Le grelot du diable*, which took place

---

[70] Eleanor Clare Cloutier, 'Repetitive Novelty: Italian Opera in Paris and London in the 1830s and 1840s' (PhD diss., University of California at Berkeley, 2016) 18.

[71] 'Un charmant théâtre, élevé par les Menus-Plaisirs, recevait à 10 heures l'opéra et les remarquables artistes dramatiques improvisés que tous nos salons se disputent' (*Le ménestrel*, 2 March 1855). The use of the term 'Menus-Plaisirs' is problematic, since such an office for state celebration and entertainment had not existed since the revolution of 1830; its use in 1855 is best read as a shorthand for imperial support and funding for the creation of such a theatre.

[72] *Le ménestrel*, 4 March 1855.

on the rue Bonaparte in 1858, was described as 'in his own *salons* and on a stage fashioned for him'.[73] Gide's performance must have been something of a rarity; more often, when composers put on performances of their own works, the 'theatre' consisted of the screens and trestles—the 'paravents et tréteaux' of Jacques Normand's anecdotal sketches.[74] There were probably as many solutions to producing an *opéra de salon* as there were places where it was attempted; challenges would have included spaces that were simply too small or—as in the case of the artists' workshops—required compromises with largely impossible ambitions.[75]

But it was the Salle Herz that boasted the most fully staged performances. Offenbach was not only the first to attempt some sort of improvised theatre, but he developed it with some care. The composer's first work there, *Le trésor de Mathurin*, was performed in 1853 with an orchestra at the foot of the raised stage and with the two actors in costume;[76] the following year, however, the performance of *Luc et Lucette* was furnished with a little stage set (*un petit décor de théâtre*),[77] but in 1855, one of the reviews of *Le décaméron* opened with the line: 'The curtain goes up, Mlle Poinsot sings an aria full of languor and charm', strongly suggesting that the *petit décor* of the previous year had been amplified to include a formal curtain—perhaps stage lights—as well as a stage set.[78] If Offenbach's three works were put on at the Salle Herz with progressively more elaborate staging, so, too, were Louis Clapisson's *Le coffret de Saint-Domingue* and Godefroid's *A deux pas du bonheur*.[79] The Salle Herz remained the home of fully staged performances of *opéra de salon* at least as late as 1860, and it may well be that stagings in performances after that date were simply not mentioned in the press because they were so common. No other concert hall used for the performance of *opéra de salon* apparently attempted any form of staging.

There were several examples of individuals—and not only the aristocracy and *haute bourgeoisie*—putting on performances of *opéra de salon* that had

---

[73] 'dans ses propres salons et sur un théâtre machiné à son intention' (*Le ménestrel*, 14 February 1858).

[74] Jacques-Clary-Jean Normand, *Paravents et tréteaux: fantaisies de salon et de théâtre*, 6th ed. (Paris: Calmann Lévy, 1882). The performance of *Belphégor* in Gide's apartments and the composer's attempts to restart his career are discussed in chapter 3.

[75] The smaller rooms with 'oriental'-style doorways in Cordier's studio, such as the ones depicted in chapter 4, are a case in point.

[76] *Le ménestrel*, 15 May 1853.

[77] Ibidem, 7 May 1854; *La Revue et Gazette musicale de Paris* for the same date.

[78] 'Le rideau se lève, Mlle Poinsot chante une mélodie pleine de langueur et de charme' (*La France musicale*, 6 May 1855).

[79] *La Revue et Gazette musicale de Paris*, 4 March 1855; *Le ménestrel*, 6 May 1855.

pretensions to be fully staged. Of the *salons* or cognate spaces discussed so far in this book, no fewer than half are documented as mounting productions of *opéra de salon* where serious efforts in the direction of sets and costumes were made; this proportion is probably actually higher, since reviewers frequently concentrated on the quality of the work of the singers and simply said nothing about the other aspects of the performance. Commentaries on staging were furthermore often perfunctory and oblique, even though the energy and expense expended could be significant. The prologue to Gide's 1858 *Belphégor* began self-deprecatingly:

> Gentlemen, this very small *salon*
> Devoid of luxury, with modest furniture,
> Represents, for you, a site of wilderness
> By the sea, at the bottom of an untouched valley.[80]

'Thanks to M. Séchan', the author of the prologue continued, 'our regular scene-painter / We have over there some waves'.[81] And the prologue ended explicitly:

> If our poetry and music
> Leave much to be desired,
> If our singers are ultimately subjected to criticism,
> The *mise-en-scène* at least will be entirely able to make amends.[82]

In addition to quoting the prologue that attributes the scenery to Charles Séchan—a long-standing collaborator for many Parisian theatres from the Opéra down—the review unambiguously refers to two more: Jules Diéterle and Édouard Despléchin, two of Séchan's contemporaries. It seems clear that Gide's *soirée* made use of as much formal scenic apparatus, and of as high a quality, as was physically possible.

Further evidence comes from Émile Barateau, who in an early and wide-ranging article on *opéra de salon* for *Le ménestrel* gave an enthusiastic idea of how easy it might be to set up a temporary theatre in a private residence:

---

[80] 'Messieurs, ce tout petit salon, / Exempt de luxe, au mobilier modeste, / Vous représente un site agreste / Sur le bord de la mer, au fond d'un frais vallon' (*Le ménestrel*, 14 February 1858).
[81] 'Grâce à M. Séchan, notre peintre ordinaire, / Nous avons là-bas quelques flots' (*ibidem*).
[82] 'Si nos vers et notre musique / Laissent beaucoup à désirer, / Si nos chanteurs enfin soulèvent la critique, La mise en scène au moins pourra tout réparer' (*ibidem*).

Do you need, for a single evening, a stage set? Just write a note to M. Adolphe Belloir; and, in his role as *entrepreneur général des fêtes administratives et particuliers,* he will improvise for you a forest, a cottage, an opulent *salon,* even a sumptuous palace. Do you need to add costumes? Here is M. Moreau with his universal bazaar borrowed from all over the world. Do you need an amusing and witty play whose music makes you like the libretto, and the libretto makes you like the music? Gustave Nadaud is ready.[83]

Barateau continues in a similar vein and certainly exaggerates the ease with which such an entertainment could be mounted—and he says nothing about cost—but what is interesting about this article is just how early it is. There are examples from much later in the century of companies established to take on all aspects of such a performance via the use of collapsible and portable theatres,[84] but even at the dawn of *opéra de salon,* it appears that it was already possible to commission off-the-peg temporary stages.

At his performance of Nadaud's *Le docteur vieuxtemps* in 1854, Pitre-Chevalier used a professional company, Jallot-Taboureux, which had been in business at least since 1847 and advertised itself as 'carpet-supplier, decorator' and able to undertake 'work for balls and parties';[85] the company also offered its services to the Société Centrale d'Horticulture de France in 1851.[86] Here it seems as if Pitre-Chevalier was aligning a performance of *opéra de salon* with the levels of decorative finish found in *bals et fêtes,* and the reviewer in *Le ménestrel* confirmed this when he described the cast and the sets as 'like real artists in a real theatre'.[87] And the critic for *L'artiste* went further: speaking of the curtain that rose and fell, he said, 'This red curtain was a real curtain closing off a real theatre', and at the end of the performance, 'everyone applauded, and the audience [*le public*], like a real *parterre* at a

---

[83] 'Avez-vous besoin, pour une soirée seulement, d'une décoration quelconque?—écrivez un mot à M. Adolphe Belloir; et, en sa qualité d'entrepreneur général des fêtes administratives et particulières, il vous improvisera une forêt, une chaumière, un riche salon, même un somptueux palais.—Faut-il y ajouter des costumes? voici M. Moreau avec son universel bazar emprunté à tous les pays.—Avez-vous besoin d'une pièce amusante, spirituelle, dont la musique fasse aimer le libretto et le libretto la musique? là, toujours—Nadaud est dispos' (*Le ménestrel,* 25 February 1855).

[84] Such arrangements are set out clearly, for example, in André de Lorde, *Pour jouer la comédie de salon: guide pratique du comédien mondain* (Paris: Hachette, 1908).

[85] *Annuaire général du commerce et de l'industrie, ou Almanach des 500,000 adresses* 10 (1847) 154.

[86] *Annales de la Société Centrale d'Horticulture de France* 42 (1851) 242.

[87] 'comme des vrais artiste sur un vrai théâtre' (*Le ménestrel,* 5 March 1854).

premiere, but a *parterre* without the claque [*sans romains*], shouted for the author to appear', exactly as in one of the regulated theatres.[88]

Descriptions of staging of particular performances are rare and infrequently detailed, but Gide's performance of his own *Belphégor* was perhaps no more elaborate than those given in the *salons* of Beer and Émile de Girardin,[89] and when the librettist and playwright Pittaud de Forges put on a performance of Offenbach's *Le 66!* in his own home in the rue Saint-Lazare, he also was able to profit from 'a little improvised stage, with footlights, curtain, and highly varied sets'.[90]

Very little is known of the types of improvised stages on which *artistes* and *virtuoses* performed in their own studios. What evidence survives suggests that less effort was made or indeed required given the nature of the enterprise: the promotion of works by named composers or simply the novelty of the artists in their own homes. So when Gaveaux-Sabatier put on Weckerlin's *Manche à manche* in March 1867, her studio on the rue des Petites-Écuries was lit 'with the modest glow of a row of *salon* candles'.[91] Even less is known about the staging in the *parloir* of those *opéras de salon* that were published in women's journals. But to look ahead to Honoré Daumier's engravings of *théâtre de société*, discussed in chapter 7, is to witness even in the most modest environments the use of footlights, some sort of curtain, and a sense of backstage and auditorium; without the cachet of a Weckerlin in the audience or a Gaveaux-Sabatier performing, the theatrical infrastructure must have been thrown into relief much more. But however varied the *lieux* that were repurposed through the use of the improvised theatre, the resulting *espaces*—whether in the tiny *moyen-bourgeois* apartment seating twenty or the aristocratic *salon* seating several hundred—created space for works that were largely similar in features and aesthetic ambition.

Performers who created *opéra de salon* formed an essential part of a matrix of practice that supported the genre and were as varied as the *espaces* in which they appeared. Despite a clear move away from society performers towards *artistes* and *virtuoses* in the early 1850s, *opéra de salon* brought together

---

[88] 'Ce rideau rouge était un vrai rideau fermant un vrai théâtre' ... 'tout le monde applaudit, et le public, comme un vrai parterre un soir de première représentation, mais un parterre sans romains, demande l'auteur à grands cris' (*L'artiste: journal de littérature et des beaux arts* 12 [1854] 62).

[89] There were two fully staged events in Beer's *salons*, on 18 January 1859 and 17 January 1861 (see *Le ménestral*, 23 January 1859; *La Revue et Gazette musicale de Paris*, 20 January 1861). The performance in Girardin's *salon* took place on 10 May 1857 (*ibidem*, 17 May 1857).

[90] 'une petite scène improvisée, avec rampe, rideau et décors fort bien brossés' (*La Revue et Gazette musicale de Paris*, 26 March 1865).

[91] 'aux feux modestes d'un rang de bougies de salon' (*Le ménestrel*, 10 March 1867).

those who were paid and those who paid, in performance environments that were completely different from those of the regulated theatre. Vocal artists were putting together performances of the same work in successive months in radically different surroundings: the improvised theatre in the Salle Herz, for example, but also perhaps just a curtain and some footlights in the homes of the *moyenne bourgeoisie*. The range of *lieux* repurposed as *espaces*, from the Salle de Diane in the Louvre to the most modest *parloir*, and the range of patrons, from the best-heeled aristocrat to the most aspirant member of the *moyenne bourgeoisie* and all ranks in between, were immense. The following two chapters examine different categories of patron and the varying *espaces* they could offer the culture of *opéra de salon*.

3
Performance and Places
The *Bourgeois* and the Aristocrat

Opéra de salon was marked out from the rest of the culture of Parisian music in the theatre by its mobility and the wide range of hosts who supported it. Such support was offered both in hosts' homes and in more public places. There are four categories of venue and two categories of sponsor, and the two categories overlap. Venues encompassed the *salon*, concert halls managed by piano manufacturers and other public venues, a handful of state buildings, and the *parloir*. Hosts or sponsors were either private individuals who mounted their events at their own cost or professional musicians—singers and composers—who not only put on events in their own studios, again at their own cost, but also mounted concerts including *opéra de salon* in concert halls and other public venues. While no money changed hands in the former, the commercial basis for the latter is more complex. The use of state buildings was restricted to the most powerful individuals in the land: the emperor and empress, the minister of state, and the president of the Corps Législatif. But s*alon* culture changed a great deal under the Second Empire, and domination by the largely aristocratic families of the eighteenth and the early nineteenth century was now under challenge from those who had made their own way in the world, and it was these types of *salons*, held by medical professionals, artists (beyond the field of music), literary figures, engineers, and other members of the *moyenne bourgeoisie*, as well as those from the *haute bourgeoisie*, including financiers, industrialists, and property speculators. Senior civil servants and politicians were also key to the culture of *opéra de salon*; such individuals would have probably placed themselves, had they read the recent French translation of *Le manifested du parti communiste*, somewhere between the *moyenne* and *haute bourgeoisie*. The size of the physical *lieux* and the resulting sizes of audiences not only varied from building to building but also constitute a challenge to the idea that *salons* were consistently smaller than concert halls: the former could frequently welcome the same size audience as the latter. The *salon*, concert hall, and artist's studio should be distanced from the *parloir* as the basis for an understanding of the matrix of overlapping venues and works that characterized *opéra de salon*. While the *parloir* is key to much of the intimate and the domestic discussed in chapter 6, this and the following chapters occupy themselves with those who sought to present performances in the less intimate venues of the *salon*, artist's studio, and concert hall.

Spaces and Patrons 1: The Medical Profession

In a world where medicine was already institutionalized but still a privately funded endeavour, well-known practitioners could own property of a size sufficient to host some sort of *salon*. Many doctors owned property in the Faubourg Saint-German—although at the less fashionable east end—close to the Hôpital de la Charité. Alexis-Hippolyte Bourdon was a senior figure at La Charité when he hosted a performance of Godefroid's *proverbe lyrique* titled *A deux pas du bonheur*.[1] This was in April 1855, when his home was at 32 rue de Bac, 200 metres from the front door of La Charité. Then at the height of his career, with three of his four medical treatises already published, Bourdon had already received national honours for his handling of the 1849 cholera outbreak and would become *chevalier* of the Légion d'Honneur in 1858.[2] Léon Gatayes's review of *A deux pas du bonheur* in *Le ménestrel* was as thoughtful and wide-ranging as any text on a new work at one of the regulated theatres but remarks almost not at all on the nature of the evening: 'une brillante soirée' is all he has to say beyond the work itself.[3] For Gatayes, then, Boudon's *salon* was as suitable a place for a premiere as any regulated theatre.

A very different type of event was given by an equally distinguished physician: Ulysse Trélat. This took place in the same street in the Faubourg Saint-Germain as La Charité itself, the rue des Saint-Pères. Trélat was *chirugien en chef* of all the Parisian hospitals,[4] while his wife, Anne-Marie-Renée Molinos, was a singing teacher who used her *salon* to attempt a relaunch of

---

[1] *Le ménestrel*, 6 May 1855.
[2] See Maurice Genty, ed., *Index biographique des membres, des associés et des correspondants de l'Académie de médecine: 1820–1990*, 4th ed. (Paris: Académie Nationale de Médecine, 1991) 31.
[3] *Le ménestrel*, 6 May 1855.
[4] Françoise Huguet, *Les professeurs de la faculté de médecine de Paris: dictionnaire biographique, 1794–1939* (Paris, INRP-CNRS, 1991) 478–480.

Bizet's *Les pêcheurs de perles* in 1868.[5] Although premiered in 1863 at the Théâtre-Lyrique, Bizet's work had only eighteen performances and was thought by some—including Marie Trélat—to have been judged too rapidly.[6] The performance of six extracts from *Les pêcheurs de perles* was given by the hostess, together with Marie-Félicie-Clémence de Reiset, better known as Mme de Grandval, who composed extensively under a number of pseudonyms of which Caroline de Blangy was the most common.[7] The male roles were taken by an otherwise unidentified individual, Ménars, and Charles-Philippe Robin, the eminent anatomist and biologist. These exclusively non-professional performers were directed by Delibes, and the piano accompanist was Ernest Guiraud, who is today best known for having written the recitatives to *Carmen* after Bizet's death. The event continued with Bizet himself playing four-hands Felix Mendelssohn with Louise-Aglaé Masson (Mme[e] Massart) and concluded with Camille Saint-Saëns playing an improvised transcription of the offertory from a recently premiered mass by de Grandval.[8] There is much that is atypical about this event, most obviously the fact that although the evening was set up in the same way as an *opéra de salon*, *Les pêcheurs de perles* is a very different sort of work, and it was already five years old at that point. It is also late in the history of *opéra* in the *salon* for non-professional singers to be playing such a large role, especially alongside such individuals as Delibes, Guiraud, and Bizet himself.

More conventional was the performance of Émile Durand's *Le miroir du diable* mounted at the home of Pierre-Salomon Ségalas in March 1856. Ségalas was a distinguished urologist and the inventor of the urethral

---

[5] Marie Trélat was a friend and correspondent of Bizet, who attended her *salon* frequently—*l'usine* (the factory) was how he described it. See Hervé Lacombe, *Georges Bizet: Naissance d'une identité créatrice* (Paris: Fayard, 2000), 413–416.

[6] *Ibidem*, 306.

[7] Important during the Second Empire, de Grandval became even more celebrated during the Third Republic. See Joël-Marie Fauquet, 'GRANDVAL, *Marie*-Félicie-Clémence de REISET, Mme de', *Dictionnaire de la musique en France au xixe siècle* (Paris: Fayard, 2003) 530. She wrote four works for the Second Empire stage: for the Théâtre des Bouffes-Parisiens, the Théâtre Beaumarchais, the Théâtre-Lyrique, and the Opéra-Comique.

[8] The event is described in *Le ménestrel*, 4 April 1868, as a postscript to an account of de Grandval's *Messe brève*, which had just been premiered. The six extracts from *Les pêcheurs de perles* were (1) the opening chorus 'Sur la grève en feu'; (2) the duet for Nadir and Zurga 'Au fond du temple saint'; (3) the scene for Zurga and the chorus 'Un long voile à mes yeux'; (4) Nadir's *romance* 'Je crois encore entendre'; (5) Léila's 'O Dieu Brahma'; and (6) Nadir's *chanson* 'De mon amie'. All the music was taken from act i with the exception of Nadir's act ii *chanson*. The de Grandval offertory was taken from her *Messe brève*, published the previous year (*A Madame la B*[onne] *de Caters/née Lablache/Messe Brève/Pour Soprano/Kyrie—Offertoire—O salutaris—Agnus Dei/Avec Accompagnement d'Orgue ou Harmonium/Par Madame/LA V*[tessee] *de GRANDVAL/-/Chez Madame Maeyens-Couvreur, 40 Rue du Bac/Paris*).

speculum, one of the earliest endoscopes; his scholarly contribution to medical science was immense and wide-ranging.[9] He lived in the Faubourg Saint-Honoré, a couple of minutes' walk from the home of his much younger brother, the lawyer Jean-Victor Ségalas. This matters not only because Ségalas's *salon* was geographically far removed from those other medical professionals[10] but also because Jean-Victor's wife was Anaïs Ségalas, *née* Anne-Caroline Ménard, the librettist of *Le miroir du diable*.[11] Anaïs Ségalas was the sister-in-law of a distinguished urologist, and the event was hosted at the home of a doctor, but *Le miroir du diable* was the work of a composer who had recently won the Second Grand Prix for composition at the Conservatoire, would become a teacher of both *solfège* and harmony there (Durand taught Claude Debussy), and, in addition to a large output of *romances*, would produce further *opérettes* for the Théâtre des Fantaisies-Parisiennes (*L'elixir de Cornélius*) and the Théâtre des Variétés (*L'astronome du Pont-Neuf*) later in the 1860s.[12] Furthermore, the two artists who took the principal roles in *Le miroir du diable* were two of the most celebrated on the *salon* circuit: Joséphine Court, better known as Mme Lefébure-Wély and the wife of composer Louis-James-Alfred Lefébure-Wély, and Lefort, perhaps the best-known tenor at work on the same circuit.

The importance of the Ségalas example transcends other examples here since it illustrates a phenomenon found across the culture of *opéra de salon*: a family network where one member with the physical infrastructure to support the genre offers a venue to a creative team that features another family member. Different from the practice of composers premiering or promoting their works in their own studios or in concert halls, there are four other examples of debutant composers of *opéra de salon* being supported by their parents: d'Indy's *Les deux princesses* was premiered at his mother's home on the rue du Bac,[13] while two of Thys's *opéras de salon—La perruque du bailli* and *Quand Dieu est dans le mariage, Dieu le garde*—were premiered in her parents' apartment on the rue La Bruyère.[14] Perhaps the best-known example

---

[9] Alain Ségal, 'Aperçu sur l'oeuvre de Pierre Salomon Ségalas d'Etchépare', *Histoire des sciences médicales* 42 (2008) 199–204.

[10] The Ségalas residence was at 5 Place Vendôme in the heart of the Faubourg Saint-Honoré.

[11] *Le ménestrel*, 9 March 1856.

[12] For the composer, see Joël-Marie Fauquet, 'DURAND, Émile', *Dictionnaire de la musique en France au xixe siècle*, ed. Joël-Marie Fauquet (Paris: Fayard, 2003) 413. He also put on a performance of *Le miroir du diable* on 30 March 1858 (*Le ménestrel*, 4 April 1858) with different artists.

[13] *Le ménestrel*, 27 March 1859.

[14] *Ibidem*, 1 January 1860; *ibidem*, 10 February 1861; *La Revue et Gazette musicale de Paris*, 17 February 1861.

of parental support must have been Georges Pfeiffer's *Le capitaine Roch*, two performances out of the six documented presentations of which were at the home of his parents, 18 rue Bleue.[15] Similarly, *Les matelots du Formidable*, by the Perry-Biagoli siblings Antonine and Henri, was premiered at their parents' home on the rue du Faubourg-Poissonnière.[16] With Jean-Josamed, their father a doctor—a distinguished author on issues of homeopathy for more than a quarter of a century—the Perry-Bagiolis' *Matelots du Formidable* also joins the ranks of *opéras de salon* in which members of the medical profession played a key role in their cultural network. Unlike Bourdon and Trélat, who lived in homes in the eastern Faubourg Saint-Germain, Perry and Ségalas lived in the centre of the Faubourg Saint-Honoré.

There is only evidence of single *opéra de salon* being performed in the homes of Doctors Bourdon, Trélat, Ségalas, and Perry. But the widow of another medical family, the Orfila, was an enthusiastic supporter of *opéra de salon* in the context of a wide-ranging musical *salon* that had run since the 1830s; this was Anne-Gabrielle Lesueur, who had married Mateu Josep Bonaventura Orfila i Rotger, known as Mathieu Orfila, in 1815. Orfila, like Bourdon and Trélat, lived in the Faubourg Saint-Germain, on its northeastern edge in the rue Saint-André-des-Arts; this very slight distancing, however, was regularly observed in the voluminous press coverage.[17] She seems to have picked up on the accelerating vogue for *opéra de salon* in 1858 and between then and her death in 1864 promoted at least nine performances of at least nine different works, all except one in her home in Paris (the exception was at her summer home in Passy in the summer of 1861).[18] However, Jacques-Léopold Heugel described Orfila's *salon* as 'the cradle of the genre', citing Nadaud's *La volière* (1855) and Weckerlin's *L'amour à l'épée* (1858) as early works that she supported, although there is no corroborating evidence of a performance of the latter in the Orfila *salon*.[19] The sustained

---

[15] *Ibidem*, 2 March 1862, and *Le ménestrel* for the same date; *La Revue et Gazette musicale de Paris*, 20 May 1866.

[16] *Ibidem*, 9 April 1865.

[17] Tunley, 'The Salons and Their Music', 24, is a good general introduction to the centrality of the Orfila *salon*.

[18] *Le ménestrel*, 9 June 1861.

[19] 'Mme Orfila's *salon* is the cradle of the genre; it is there that Nadaud's *La volière* made its home. Since then, a number of first performances have followed there: yesterday it was *L'amour à l'épée*, today it is *Bredouille*' ('Les salons de Mme Orfila ont été le berceau du genre: c'est là que la *Volière*, de Nadaud, a fait élection de domicile. Depuis, nombre de premières représentations s'y sont succédé: hier c'était le *Mariage à l'épée* [*L'amour à l'épée*], aujourd'hui c'est *Bredouille*'; *Le ménestrel*, 7 March 1858). Heugel's commentary is yet further proof that the surviving documented performances of *opéra de salon* in private residences is but a fraction of the total.

Table 3.1. Performances of *opéra de salon* at the home of Anne-Gabrielle Lesueur (Orfila).

Date	Title	Composer	Librettist	Performers
18 February 1855	La volière	Nadaud	Nadaud, Gustave	
March 1858	Bredouille	Bernard	Galoppe d'Onquaire	Gaveaux-Sabatier, Lefort
18 December 1858	Manche à manche	Weckerlin	Galoppe d'Onquaire	Ponchard, Romain Bussine, Prosper-Alphonse Bussine
December 1859	Loin du bruit	Bernard	Galoppe d'Onquaire	
25 November 1860	La perruque du bailli	Thys	Thys	Gaveaux-Sabatier, Biéval
June 1861 [Passy]	A la porte	Hignard	Verconsin	Gaveaux-Sabatier, Biéval
March 1862	Le capitaine Roch	Pfeiffer	Galoppe d'Onquaire	Marie-Julie-Blanche Baretti, Géraldy, Biéval
24 February 1864	A deux pas de bonheur	Godefroid	Roger de Beauvoir	Gaveaux-Sabatier, Levassor
9 May 1864	Tout est bien qui finit bien	Weckerlin	Jules Malherbe	Gaveaux-Sabatier, Lefort

commitment to *opéra de salon* is clear from the fully documented events that took place in her *salon* (table 3.1).

Commentaries on Orfila's *opéra de salon* performances stress the size, elegance, and brilliance of the audiences and of the events in general. In at least two cases—Nadaud's *La volière* (1855) and Pfeiffer's *Le capitaine Roch* (1862)—the productions at the Orfila *salon* were advertised not only as premieres but also as performances that had been preceded by formal dress rehearsals to which the press had also been invited.[20] In two cases, Paul Bernard's *Bredouille* and Pfeiffer's *Le capitaine Roch*, the composer presided at the piano.[21] The composer who concealed himself behind the name Salvator provided the accompaniment for Thys's *La perruque du*

---

[20] For *La volière*, the premiere took place in the *salon* of Doucet (see below) on 10 February 1855, with the performance at the Orfila *salon* on 18 February (*Le ménestrel*, 11, 18, and 25 February 1855); for *Le capitaine Roch*, the rehearsal took place in Pfeiffer's parents' *salon* in the rue Bleue on 23 February 1862 and the performance in the Orfila *salon* on 1 March (*La Revue et Gazette musicale de Paris*, 2 and 23 March 1862; *Le ménestrel*, 2 March 1862).

[21] See Le ménestrel for the latter; 7 March 1858 for the former.

bailli, and Adolphe Maton, about whom little is known, did the same for Godefroid's *A deux pas du bonheur*.[22] There is, furthermore, no evidence of the use of costumes or sets in the performances at the Orfila *salon*. The one exception—which may reveal that this was the rule—comes from a description of the performance of Bernard's 1859 *Loin du bruit* in December that year, at which point Orfila was co-hosting her salon with Marie-Elisabeth-Césarine Mosneron de Saint-Preux (who, the daughter of a baron, had aristocratic claims). Heugel wrote that 'the *salon* of these women represents the depths of the countryside, and we are in the presence of a Parisian from the rue des Lombards, previously a greengrocer—today dreaming of the sweetness of the *dolce far niente* in the middle of peasants, hens and cockerels from a real village, a hundred leagues from Paris'.[23] In general, performances of *opéras de salon* at the Orfila *salon* were always prefaced by a vocal recital, an instrumental recital, or a recital of both instrumental and vocal music. The performance of *Loin du bruit* just discussed, for example, was prefaced by a mixed recital; Jean-Antoine-Just Géraldy, one of his pupils, the Catalan Llorenç Pagans i Julià (Lorenzo Pagans), and Anne-Célina-Ernestine Berdalle de Lapommeraye were responsible for the vocal section of the concert, and Vincenzo Sighicelli performed a number of solos on the violin; the title of none of the works has been preserved.

So many of the descriptions of performances of *opéra de salon* are limited by the absence of any real sense of the *espaces* or *lieux* in which the performances took place. Certainly, the location in the city is significant; groupings in such key *quartiers* as the Faubourg Saint-Germain or—as will be seen—Nouvelle Athènes are important to the topography of the genre (chapter 7 is occupied in part with these questions), but once through the front door and into the main courtyard, the precise dimensions of performing spaces and auditorium frequently remain a mystery. Some sense of how this might have worked, however, comes from the two documented performances at the Établissement Hydrothérapique des Néothermes, hosted by the director Pierre Bouland in late 1854 and early 1856, just as the genre's star was in the ascendant—key moments for the history of the genre

---

[22] *Ibidem*, 2 December 1860; 15 May 1864. The biography and output of Salvator are discussed in chapter 7.

[23] 'Le salon de ces dames représente la pleine campagne, et nous sommes en présence d'un Parisien de la rue des Lombards, ci-devant épicier,—rêvant aujourd'hui les douceurs du *dolce far niente* au milieu des paysans, des poules et coqs d'un vrai village, à cent lieues de Paris' (*ibidem*, 18 December 1859). The description could be read equally plausibly as an extended metaphor for the *salon* or as a precise description of the set.

in terms of the authorship of the libretti, the composition of the music, and the balance between *artistes-virtuoses* and *chanteurs/chanteuses du monde*, as well as the obvious significance of the location.

The Néothermes was what would today be called an exclusive spa. Founded in 1831, it was sited at 56 rue de la Victoire, just north of the Boulevard, very close to the fashionable Chaussée d'Antin where Rossini would soon hold his *salon*, to the Opéra, and to the Salle Herz, which was less than a minute's walk away on the same street (to the east, no. 48). The estate was large, and in addition to Bouland's residence, the various baths, showers, treatment rooms, and consulting rooms, it included hotel rooms, a restaurant (which also provided room service), a library, a billiard room, several *parterres*, and—the space in which the two performances took place—the glazed *grande galerie* (figure 3.1).[24]

Described in the original 1832 prospectus as 30 metres long (100 *pieds*), the *galerie* seems to have been long and thin, with a slightly later (1841) image of the *galerie* that includes humans suggesting that it might have been around 8 metres wide (figure 3.2).[25]

Even so, with a footprint of around 240 square metres, this compares strikingly with the dimensions of the Salle Herz at 169 square metres and of the Salle Pleyel on the rue [Marguerite-de-] Rochechouart at 192 square metres. The latter was—like the *grande galerie des Néothermes*—long and thin: 24 metres by 8 metres. Given that the Salle Pleyel could seat 700 and the Salle Herz 660, even if not all the space in the *grande galerie* was used, that still allowed audiences to attend in their hundreds.[26]

During the quarter century before Bouland thought of using the Néothermes as a venue for *opéra de salon*, the establishment was already famous not only for its treatments and therapies but also as a place for dining, residing, and meeting. One of its most notorious residents was the author of the semi-fictionalized, not to say plagiarized, *Souvenirs de la marquise de*

---

[24] Bringol Architecte/Aug^te Fevèvre/VUE/*Intérieure des* NÉOTHERMES/Lith. de Bichebois aîné, rue de la Bibliothèque, N° 4 (Collection Centre Canadien d'Architecture/Canadian Centre for Architecture, Montréal, DR1974:0002:010:043).

There is a very full account of the facilities of the Néothermes, the treatments available, and prices in the prospectus published in 1832: *Établissment hygénique des néothermes ... prospectus* (Paris: n.p., [1832]).

[25] Arthur de Bonnard, *Description des néothermes et relation des principales guérisons obtenues par l'emploi des appareils médicaux de toute nature établis dans cette maison de bains et de santé* (Paris: Pollet, [1841]).

[26] For the dimensions of the Salle Herz, the Salle Pleyel, and others, see Fauquet and Schnapper, 'Salle de concert'.

Figure 3.1. Établissement Hydrothérapique des Néothermes, view of the *grande galerie*, 1831.

Créquy, Pierre-Marie-Jean Cousin de Courchamps. It was in the library of the Néothermes that he apparently found the inspiration for the *Souvenirs*, and he was a regular visitor—usually when escaping creditors or those wounded by his mordant wit—from at least 1841; he spent the last four years of his life living in an apartment in the building (he died in 1849).[27]

Perhaps the best-known encounter at the Néothermes took place in the billiard room. Here is Hector Berlioz writing in 1838; ill, he had been trying to get out of bed to visit Niccolò Paganini:

> In the middle of such agitations and with a heart full of so many impetuous sentiments, I shook with impatience at not being able to leave my bed. Finally, at the end of the sixth day feeling a little better, I could stand it no longer, I got dressed and ran to the Néothermes, rue de la Victoire, where Paganini was then staying. I was told that he was taking a solitary stroll in

---

[27] Alfred Marquiset, *Romieu et Courchamps* (Paris: Émile-Paul, 1913) 187 and *passim*.

Figure 3.2. Établissement Hydrothérapique des Néothermes, view of the *grande galerie*, 1841.

the billiard room. I entered; we embraced each other without being able to say a word.[28]

This was just more than a year before Paganini's death, after the loss of his lawsuit—and of his voice—and just before his escape in 1838 to relative safety in Nice, not yet part of France.

A home, then, for the dispossessed, indebted, and embattled, the Néothermes was an ideal location for those Parisians who wanted to take the

---

[28] 'Au milieu de telles agitations et le cœur gonflé de tant d'impétueux sentiments, je frémissais d'impatience de ne pouvoir quitter mon lit. Enfin au bout du sixième jour me sentant un peu mieux, je n'y pus tenir, je m'habillai et courus aux Néothermes, rue de la Victoire, où demeurait alors Paganini. On me dit qu'il se promenait seul dans la salle de billard. J'entre, nous nous embrassons sans pouvoir dire un mot.' Hector Berlioz, *Mémoires de Hector Berlioz, Membre de l'Institut de France, comprenant des voyages en Italie, en Allemagne, en Russie et en Angleterre, 1803–1865* (Paris: Lévy, 1870; reprint Farnborough: Gregg, 1969) 218. The anecdote had already been related in *Le monde illustré*, 4 June 1859.

waters but did not want to travel to Vichy, Evian, or Croisic, to say nothing of Baden.[29] On the rue de la Victoire, they could enjoy baths with water of various medicinal types including opium, steam baths of all sorts—Russian, Egyptian, mercury, or alcohol—and various sorts of showers, of which the *douche ascendante* the organization was most proud, as it soothed the urethra, rectum, and sexual organs; it was, as the 1841 description had it, 'established according to the most recent findings of medical science'.[30]

The medical networks that encompassed both the salons discussed so far and the Néothermes extended to the composer of the two *opéras de salon* that were premiered at the Néothermes: *Les deux espagneuls* and *La bourse ou la vie*.[31] Both were by Charles-Casimir Manry, the son of the pathbreaking dermatologist Jean Manry.[32] Although Charles-Casimir started training in the legal profession, when he came into his father's fortune in 1840, he was able to devote his subsequent career to composition without any concern about an income. His output consisted mainly of liturgical works (fully scored masses for St. Philippe-du-Roule and St. Roch) and instrumental compositions. He wrote a certain number of *romances*, but his theatrical output was restricted to the two works he wrote for the Néothermes. He died at the age of forty-one in 1866, but even with this short creative life turned neither to further *opéra de salon* nor to musical work in the regulated theatre.[33] Whether Manry's family background played into Bouland's choice of composer for his *opéra de salon* is an open question; it is unlikely that Bouland could have known Manry's father in any way that might have tipped his hand, although it is indisputable that Bouland and Manry—*père et fils*—were part of the same network.

Manry worked with two librettists: Édouard Fournier and Galoppe d'Onquaire; it was a novelty for both. In 1854, Fournier had as much of

---

[29] There is a further account of the Néothermes in Paul d'Artiste, *La vie et le monde du boulevard (1830–1870): (Un dandy: Nestor Roqueplan)* (Paris: Tallandier, 1930) 164–166.

[30] 'établi d'après les dernières indications de la science médicale'. Bonnard, *Description des Néotheermes*, 4.

[31] *Les deux espagneuls* was published and dedicated to Bouland: À *Monsieur le D^r/*Edouard Bouland/LES/*DEUX*/ESPAGNEULS/Opéra bouffe/*en un acte en et vers.*/*DE M^r/*Édouard Fournier,/Musique de/CHARLES MANRY./*OP. 53)/Représenté aux Néothermes, le 19 Décembre 1854/-/Partition PIANO et chant/.../Etienne CHAILLOT, éditeur,/à Paris, Rue St Honoré, 354, près la Place Vendôme.*

[32] See Jean Manry, 'Lettre de M. le professeur Hardy: Documents pour servir à l'histoire de l'hôpital St Louis au commencement de ce siècle—Alibert, Biett, Lugol, Manry, Emery', *Annales de dermatologie et de syphiligraphie*, 2nd series, 6 (1885) 629–638.

[33] See Joël-Marie Fauquet, 'MANRY, Charles', *Dictionnaire de la musique en France au xixe siècle*, ed. Joël-Marie Fauquet (Paris: Fayard, 2003) 740. More detailed are Fétis, *Biographie universelle des musiciens*, 5:431–432 and Suppl. 2:158.

a background as an antiquarian as he had as a man of the theatre: he had written an *Essai historique sur l'orthographe* in 1849 and a *Histoire des royaumes d'Argot et de Thunes* the following year, and the work for which he was perhaps best known—*Paris démoli*—appeared in 1853. Alongside this work, however, he had collaborated with Pol Mercier on *Christian and Marguerite* for the Théâtre Français in 1851 and on *Le roman du village* for the Odéon in 1853. *Les deux espagneuls* was his first essay in the lyric theatre, which he would continue with work at the Théâtre-Lyrique, the Bouffes-Parisiens and the Théâtre Déjazet in the second half of the 1850s.[34] Galoppe d'Onquaire had written a history of whist, and he had enjoyed success at the Comédie-Française and the Odéon since 1844 (*Une femme de quarante ans*); this continued until his *Les vertueux de province* appeared at the Odéon in 1860, alongside a range of such other texts as *Le diable boiteux à Paris*, with two sequels, and two philosophico-religious tracts, *Les fêtes de l'église romaine* and *Le livre des sacrements*. Although none of Galoppe d'Onquaire's libretti for *opéras de salon* was published at the time at which it was premiered, they were collected in his 1863 publication *Le spectacle au coin du feu*, and he had collaborated on two *vaudevilles* for the Variétés and the Théâtre du Vaudeville, both in 1852; this experience of aligning words and notes in such a complex environment was to make the composition of libretti for *opéra de salon* relatively straightforward.[35] In the case of both librettists, therefore, their experience at the Néothermes was the beginning of a city-wide engagement with the writing of libretti, whereas for the composer it was a sustained contribution to the forging and development of a new lyric genre.

The two performances at Bouland's Néothermes were significant in terms of performing forces. Despite the size of the venue, there was no attempt to go beyond the conventional use of a piano for accompaniment except for an unconventional obbligato oboe. More important were the ambitions of the four vocal soloists, who well illustrated a mix of *artistes-virtuoses* and *chanteurs/chanteuses du monde*. The cast for *Les deux espagneuls* was as follows:[36]

---

[34] *Grand dictionnaire universel du xixe siècle français, historique, géographique, biographique, mythologique, bibliographique, littéraire, artistique, scientifique, etc.*, 17 vols. (Paris: Grand Dictionnaire Universel, 1866) 8:682–683; Gustave Vapereau, *Dictionnaire universel des contemporains contenant toutes les personnes notables de la France et des pays étrangers*, 5th ed., 2 vols. (Paris: Hachette, 1880) 1:688.

[35] There is very little on the biography of Galoppe d'Onquaire. See *Grand dictionnaire universel du xixe siècle*, 8:971.

[36] *La Revue et Gazette musicale de Paris*, 24 December 1854; *Le ménestrel*, 7 January 1855.

Clarisse (soprano):	Marie-Louise-Eugénie Dejoly [De Joly]
Bichonnet (baryton):	Louis-Prosper Guyot
Armand (ténor):	Antoine-Anatole Jal
Fanfare (ténor):	M. Belouet
Grillemann (basse):	?

While Guyot would go on to a successful professional career and Dejoly was a Conservatoire-trained pianist, both Jal and Belouet followed careers outside of music.[37]

Manry's *La bourse ou la vie*, Bouland's offering for 1856, involved very different types of performers, two of the key figures in *opéra de salon* in the second half of the 1850s: Gaveaux-Sabatier and Lefort.[38] When they premiered Manry's second *opéra de salon*, they had only sung together in such a genre once before, at a legendary evening in the Salle de Diane, hosted by the emperor and empress in the Palais des Tuileries, where they had sung what might well have been the premiere of Weckerlin's *Tout est bien qui finit bien*.[39]

Broadening the context for the interest in *opéra de salon* on the part of medical professionals poses the question of the genre's place in the network of practices associated with experimental science and music.[40] Despite the burgeoning interest in the subject, the alignment of medicine—as opposed to experimental science—and music seems restricted to issues around mental health, vocal hygiene, and phrenology.[41] The medical concerns of those who

---

[37] See chapter 2 for the detailed accounts of the non-musical careers of *chanteurs/chanteuses du monde*, including Jal, and the ways in which they interact more broadly with the work of *artistes-virtuoses* and the generalized culture of *opéra de salon*. Belouet is completely impossible to identify. He might be the same as the poet for two of *romances* composed by Hector-Auguste Charpentier— *La colombe* and *La jeune pensionnaire*—both published in 1856, known either as T. J. Belouet or J. J. Belouet. Publication of the two *romances* by Choudens places at least some of the work in Paris, unlike the other candidate for Belouet the vocal artist: the Abbé Belouet, who seems to have come from Chaumont, as the publication of his *La pitoyade: poème héroï-comique* (Chaumont: Miot-Dadant, 1863) seems to suggest.

[38] *La Revue et Gazette musicale de Paris*, 9 March 1856.

[39] The event had taken place on 28 February 1856, hosted by the Napoléon III and the empress Eugénie. See *ibidem*, 2 March 1856 and *Le ménestrel* for the same date.

[40] A frequent *point d'appui* for such studies is John Tresch, *The Romantic Machine: Utopian Science and Technology after Napoleon* (Chicago: University of Chicago Press, 2012). For useful introductions, see Sarah Hibberd, 'Note from the Guest Editor [*Music and Science in London and Paris*]', *19th-Century Music* 39 (2015–2016) 83–86; David Trippett and Benjamin Walton, 'Introduction: The Laboratory and the Stage', *Nineteenth-Century Opera and the Scientific Imagination*, ed. David Trippett and Benjamin Walton (Cambridge: Cambridge University Press, 2019) 1–18.

[41] For mental health, see Carmel Raz, 'Operatic Fantasies in Early Nineteenth-Century Psychiatry', *Nineteenth-Century Opera and the Scientific Imagination*, ed. David Trippett and Benjamin Walton (Cambridge: Cambridge University Press, 2019) 63–83. The literature on vocal science is

cultivated *opéra de salon* were epidemiology, surgery, urology, homeopathy, hydrotherapy, anatomy, and forensic medicine; across a large range of texts published by doctors interested in *opéra de salon*, there is almost nothing about music or theatre to suggest any sort of relationship between their professional work and their artistic interests.

Spaces and Patrons 2: Entrepreneurs and the *Haute Bourgeoisie*

Although less active and much less assiduous in their cultivation of *opéra de salon*, those who made their careers in industry and banking broaden the geospatial consistency exhibited by much of the medical profession and those men of letters who also lived in the eastern reaches of the Faubourg Saint-Germain; these *haut-bourgeois* entrepreneurs built luxury dwellings in the neighbourhood at the west end of the city towards the Champs-Élysées, the Faubourg Saint-Honoré. Performances hosted by the *haut-bourgeois* also help focus questions of how *opéra de salon* could function as a locus of social power during the Second Empire for the simple reason that the attempt at the acquisition of cultural capital using financial resources to mount productions of *opéra de salon* is just so clear. Such clarity assists in judging the types of power *opéra de salon* could manipulate in other groups of patrons and hosts, as described in chapter 7.

Alphonse Lavallée, for example, made his career in shipping during the Restoration and moved to Paris in 1827, where he established the École Centrale des Arts et Manufactures in what is now the Musée Picasso in the Marais;[42] it was there that he hosted the premiere of Hocmelle's *En attendant le soleil*, the composer's first essay in the genre after nearly a decade of composing *romances*.[43] While no trace of the libretto or score of *En*

---

wide-ranging; see James Q. Davies, *Romantic Anatomies of Performance* (Berkeley: University of California Press, 2014) 13–40, 66–92, 123–151. On phrenology and music, see David Trippett, 'Exercising Musical Minds: Phrenology and Music Pedagogy in London circa 1830', *19th-Century Music* 39 (2015–2016) 99–124; Céline Frigau Manning, 'Phrenologising Opera Singers: The Scientific "Proofs of Musical Genius"', *ibidem*, 125–141.

[42] For a biography of Lavallée, see 'Alphonse Lavallée, le fondateur de l'École Centrale' (http://archive.wikiwix.com/cache/index2.php?url = http%3A%2F%2Folivier.dibos.club.fr%2FAlphLav.html).

[43] Hocmelle was a Conservatoire-trained organist who was organist at the Invalides, at the chapel of the Sénat, and then at St-Philippe-du-Roule in 1860, alongside his vocal and theatrical compositions. See Kurt Lueders, 'HOCMELLE, Pierre-Edmond', *Dictionnaire de musique en France au xixe siècle* (Paris: Fayard, 2003) 595–596.

attendant le soleil has survived, reports of the event make clear that Hocmelle himself accompanied and directed from the piano, no small achievement for an artist who had been blind since birth;[44] in addition to taking the role of prompt, he had assembled a team of very recent Conservatoire graduates on Lavallée's behalf: Dupuy, Pascal, and Lafont.[45]

The least is known about perhaps the most sumptuous private performance of an *opéra de salon*, an event that took place in the home of the brothers Isaac and Émile Pereire on the Place Vendôme, a building that now houses the Ritz hotel.[46] Entrepreneurs specializing in finance, industry, and property, the brothers offered their guests the second known performance of Beer's *En état de siège*;[47] the premiere had been at Beer's home on the rue d'Aumale a couple of months previously and had then been given by Gaveaux-Sabatier and Lefort together with Edmond-Antoine-Auguste Cabu (known as Cabel), conscripted from the Théâtre-Lyrique.[48] The telegrammatic report of the Pereire performance in *La Revue et Gazette musicale de Paris* betrays almost nothing about the lavish event of which the *opéra de salon* formed part, although it may be assumed that the same artistic team provided the performance (Lefort is the only one explicitly named in the press notice) as at the premiere.

The Pereire brothers were not only two of the most wealthy supporters of the Saint-Simonian movement, but they also supported the movement's best-known composer, David.[49] Their support might explain one of David's least understood and most fragmentary works: his incomplete and apparently unperformed *Le fermier de Franconville* to a libretto by Adolphe de Ribbing (better known by his pseudonym Adolphe de Leuven). The surviving fragments consist of an overture, three *airs*, two trios, and a duo repurposed from a rejected aria from *Le perle de Brésil*; in short, the fragments resemble around two-thirds of a typical *opéra de salon*.[50] The

---

[44] *La Revue et Gazette musicale de Paris*, 24 February 1856.
[45] See chapter 2 for a discussion of their careers and how recent Conservatoire graduates interacted with the culture of *opéra de salon* as a career move.
[46] Jean Autin, *Les frères Pereire: le bonheur d'entreprendre* (Paris: Perrin, 1984).
[47] *La Revue et Gazette musicale de Paris*, 17 April 1859.
[48] *Le ménestrel*, 18 January 1859.
[49] See Alexis Azevedo, *F. David: coup d'oeil sur sa vie et son oeuvre* (Paris: Ménestrel; Heugel, 1863) 80; Ralph P. Locke, *Music, Musicians, and the Saint-Simonians* (Chicago: University of Chicago Press, 1986) 217–218.
[50] *Le fermier de Franconville* survives in two manuscript sources: Paris, Bibliothèque Nationale de France, MS 1094^A (the first five numbers) and MS 1094^B (the overture). The trio (no. 4), based on a rejected duo from David's *La perle de Brésil*, also survives with David's autograph modifications in MS 1093. The other repertory of *opéras de salon* with surviving autographs are the works of

only point of variance between the surviving fragments of *Le fermier de Franconville* and the conventions of *opéra de salon* is that the surviving numbers are all fully scored. It is entirely possible that the Pereires were planning an *opéra de salon* to outdo other performances in the city and were contemplating a performance that went beyond the conventions of *opéra de salon* by including an orchestra. This ambitious plan might have explained the downfall of the work, with the scoring proving too much for the generic conventions of performers and audiences alike.

The industrialist Henri Binder stood at the head of a company that made carriages for both the private individual and the companies whose vehicles criss-crossed Paris daily. By the mid-1860s, his house on the rue du Colisée was of an opulence that matched that of bankers, other members of the *haute bourgeoisie*, and the aristocracy.[51] In 1864, he was able to put on the most sumptuous productions of *opéra de salon*, one of which was captured by the illustrated journal *Le monde illustré* (figure 3.3).[52]

The image is interesting for many reasons. Although we know the name of the composer and the work, no score or libretto has survived.[53] The illustration, however, is sufficiently detailed and engraved from such a wide angle that it provides useful evidence on the relationship between place and space discussed in chapter 5. And in its use of glazed walls and ceilings, it brings Binder's performance into alignment not only with other performances of *opéra de salon* in glazed spaces (conservatories) but also with Binder's own commercial interests (figure 3.4).[54]

Binder's showroom, in 1864 part of the same site on the rue du Colisée, was also constructed out of glass and may well have been contiguous with the ballroom in which *opéra de salon* took place. Whether contiguous or not,

---

Weckerlin, which are all scored for keyboard alone. See, for example 'Le mariage à l'épée/L'amour à l'épée/-/Opéra de salon' (MS 16884).

[51] See Jean-Louis Libourel, 'Binder à Paris, Henry Binder'(https://www.attelage-patrimoine.com/article-binder-a-paris-henry-binder-41052058.html).

[52] *Le monde illustré*, 9 April 1864.

[53] The composer was Charles Grisart (not Grisar, as given by some authorities), and the title of the work was *La lettre de cachet*. The name of the librettist, Adam, given as part of the legend on the engraving in *Le monde illustré*, could possibly indicate Camille Adam, the author of a single self-published *romance* also from 1864 (*Amour et respect*). Grisart was a young banker, born around 1840, and a pupil of Delibes, for whom *La lettre de cachet* was his first endeavour. He mounted other works at the Folies-Bergère (*Memnon, ou La sagesse humaine*, 1871) and the Cercle des Beaux-Arts (*Mistress Pudor*) and two *opérettes* at the Bouffes-Parisiens (*La quenouille de verre*, 1873; *Les trois Margot*, 1877). See Fétis, *Biographie universelle des musiciens*, Suppl. 2:424.

[54] Godefroy Durand, *Vue de l'établissement de HENRY BINDER, - 31, rue du Colysée* (Paris: n.p., 1863).

PERFORMANCE AND PLACES: *BOURGEOIS*, ARISTOCRAT 117

Figure 3.3. Ballroom of Henri Binder modified for performance of *opéra de salon*.

Figure 3.4. Carriage showroom of Henri Binder.

with their glazed roofs, the two *lieux* aligned themselves with other similar types of buildings where the glazed roofs—more typical of the *passages*—were associated with *espaces* and *lieux* devoted to music. Three critical ones were Princesse Mathilde's town house on the rue de Courcelles, Pauline Viardot's apartments in the rue de Douai, and the *grande galerie* of the Néothermes.[55] All used *lieux* with glazed roofs as part of the *espace* in which *salons* took place, Viardot's being the art gallery for the collection of her husband, Louis. The broader context for this *salon* activity under glass is the network of *passages* that criss-crossed Paris in the nineteenth century, made famous in different literary ways by Charles Baudelaire, Louis Aragon, and Walter Benjamin. Both the *salon* environment and the *passage* shared the same emphasis on sociability: the *passage* was a place in which not only to consume but also to conduct exchanges of all sorts; the Passage de l'Opéra, so celebrated by Aragon before its destruction in 1924, was an informal *espace* for out-of-hours stock trading, for example. Whether Binder consciously modelled his ballroom on other *salons* or this was merely a generalized interest in natural light, he cannot have been displeased with any sort of allusion to the aristocracy represented by Princess Mathilde and her glazed *salon* or to the musical significance of other glazed *lieux*.

Spaces and Patrons 3: Government and Aristocracy

Jean-Baptiste-Louis-Georges Benou was a mid-level civil servant, one of the state-appointed *commissaires-priseurs* who were responsible for overseeing auctions in the city and responsible to the local magistrate.[56] He held this position from 1829 to 1845, before moving into the management of first the Théâtre du Palais-Royal until 1858 and then the Théâtre du Vaudeville from 1860 until 1863. These were positions as *directeur-gérant* and *administrateur*, respectively, and involved purely administrative responsibilities; the creative director of the Palais-Royal at that period was Joseph Dormeuil (Joseph-Jean Contat-Desfontaines), an actor and *vaudevilliste* who had been active since the 1820s, and Bernou shared responsibility at the Vaudeville

---

[55] Princesse Mathilde's *salon* and its activities are discussed below. For the physical qualities of Viardot's *salon*, see Mark Everist, 'Enshrining Mozart: *Don Giovanni* and the Viardot Circle', *19th-Century Music* 25 (2001) 165–189; idem, *Mozart's Ghosts: Haunting the Halls of Musical Culture* (New York: Oxford University Press, 2013) 157–188.

[56] Little is known of his work as *commisseur-priseur*, except for the publication of his *Code et manuel du commissaire-priseur, ou Traité des prisées et ventes mobilières* (Paris: D'Ocagne, 1835).

with Edmond-Henri Duponchel.[57] When Benou put on a performance of Weckerlin's *L'amour à l'épée* at his home on the Boulevard Saint-Germain in 1858, he also included a play of his own—*Bureau de placement*—at which his audience, it was claimed, laughed as much as if they were at Benou's Palais-Royal.[58] In a similar way to Gide's attempt at his re-establishment as a composer after a long time away in commerce (and Gide's and Benou's performances were more or less coterminous), Benou's *soirée* seems to be an attempt at supporting his position in the world of theatrical management: *Bureau de placement* was his first—and it seems only—creative effort for the theatre, and his choice of *opéra de salon* (another libretto by Galoppe d'Onquaire) and his performing team of Mira, Biéval, and Romain Bussine demonstrate sure-footed management of theatrical resources.[59]

Camille Doucet, on the other hand, enjoyed a much higher status as a civil servant than Benou, although his origins were not dissimilar. He has already been seen in chapter 2 to have hosted a dress rehearsal in his home on the rue de Bac of Nadaud's *La volière* of 1855; this was the second of the composer-librettist's *opéras de salon*, and after the success of *Le docteur vieuxtemps* the previous year, it was no surprise that a formal—and public—dress rehearsal would be appropriate ahead of the premiere in Orfila's salon later the same month. In reviews of the performances, much was made of Doucet's position as head of division of the theatre section within the Ministry of State, and he would assume the role of *directeur général de l'administration des théâtres* in 1863, at which point he would oversee the repeal of the 1806/1807 licensing legislation in 1864 and three years later allow fully staged works a place in the rapidly emerging culture of the *café-concert*.[60] Doucet's dress rehearsal had almost the flavour of the sorts of readings before a jury that characterized practices at the Comédie-Française; his audience consisted of four named *notabilités littéraires* among a host of others who journalists considered were there to judge.[61] It is not clear if the Mélesville present at the 1855 dress rehearsal was the father or the son: Anne-Honoré-Joseph Duveyrier (Mélesville *père*) was a distinguished playwright and librettist of nearly half a century's experience by 1855, and he would continue to write

---

[57] See Wild, *Dictionnaire des théâtres parisiens*, 352, 420 (in the 2012 revision).
[58] Benou's *Bureau de placement* appears to have been unpublished.
[59] *Le ménestrel*, 14 February 1858. Gide's career and use of *opéra de salon* as an attempted point of re-entry into the creative world is discussed in chapter 4.
[60] For Doucet's biography, see Jean-Charles Roman d'Amat and Michel Prévost, eds., *Dictionnaire de biographie française*, 21 vols. (Paris: Letouzey et Ané, 1932–) 11:650–651.
[61] A detailed account is given in *Le ménestrel*, 18 February 1855.

libretti until his death in 1865; his last was set by his son, Honoré-Marie-Joseph Duveyrier, posthumously. At the time of Doucet's dress rehearsal, Mélesville *fils* was at work on an *opérette* for which he wrote both words and music, *Les deux Gilles* for Hervé's Théâtre des Folies-Nouvelles. Father, son, or both would have been worthy 'judges' for Nadaud's *La volière*.[62] He or they were accompanied by François Ponsard, the distinguished classicizing playwright; Émile Augier, the librettist for Charles Gounod's 1851 *Sapho*; and the novelist and playwright Jules Sandeau. Given that Sandeau had little or no experience of work in the lyric theatre, one wonders what his response to *La volière* might have been.[63] The performers at Doucet's rehearsal were already well known: Gaveaux-Sabatier was the single *artiste-virtuose*, accompanied by the *chanteurs du monde* Jal and Belouet, both known from the Néothermes performances. L'Épine joined the team in the role of the notary.

La volière was duly premiered in the Orfila *salon* the following week and by early March celebrated its sixth performance, described as taking place in a *salon* 'on the Chaussée d'Antin' but without further precision.[64] In the meantime, the work had also been the focus of a spectacular production in the Palais du Louvre, hosted by the wife of the minister of state Fould. Specifically, *La volière* was performed in the *salle de réception* and the *premier salon*, opened out and joined together for the event. A temporary theatre had been constructed by the imperial household, appropriate given the fact that the audience included Princesse Mathilde, Prince Napoléon (both cousins to Napoléon III), and Prince and Princesse Murat. The cast was unsurprisingly the same as it had been at the dress rehearsal in Doucet's apartments, and there was no attempt at assembling an accompaniment more elaborate than the piano; the performance of *La volière* was accompanied by a performance of Eugène Labiche's *comédie-vaudeville La fille bien gardée*. Ponsard and Augier, who had attended the dress rehearsal, joined the distinguished company in the *premier salon* alongside Auber and Halévy.[65]

---

[62] For both father and son, see Gustave Vapereau, *Dictionnaire universel des littératures* (Paris: Hachette, 1876) 687.

[63] For Ponsard, see Peter France, ed., *The New Oxford Companion to Literature in French* (Oxford: Clarendon, 1995); for Augier, see Pierre Danger, *Émile Augier ou le théâtre de l'ambiguïté: éléments pour une archéologie morale de la bourgeoisie sous le Second Empire* (Paris: Harmattan, 1998).

[64] *La Revue et Gazette musicale de Paris*, 11 March 1855.

[65] *Le ménestrel*, 4 March 1855.

Fould and his wife had no choice regarding where to hold the event. Other senior figures had more options available to them. The Comte de Morny, as president of the Corps Législatif, had the magnificent rooms in the Palais Bourbon at his disposal, as well as his private residence on the Avenue des Champs Élysées. He used both: the Salons de la Présidence for an early performance of Godefroid's *A deux pas du bonheur* in February 1855 and his own premises for a double bill consisting of Offenbach's *Ba-ta-clan* and *Pépito* a year later.[66] The second of the two performances is perhaps the more important, as it merges two very different traditions. *Pépito* had been premiered at the Variétés in 1853 and was about to be revived at the Bouffes-Parisiens with a new cast; it was this cast that performed at Morny's house on the Avenue des Champs-Élysées, and the event reads very much like the sort of dress rehearsal that Doucet had arranged for Nadaud's *La volière*.[67] On the other hand, the performance, which took place on 29 February 1856, formed part of the sequence of invitations to the international diplomatic community in Paris for the completion of the Peace of Paris that ended the Crimean War.[68] Details of Morny's event at his home on the Avenue des Champs-Élysées are sketchy at best but may be assumed to have been lavish in the extreme, especially since the imperial family had mounted a similar event just the night before—and it is difficult to ignore possible rivalry between two half-brothers—but more important, Morny was about to be sent to Saint Petersburg as the French ambassador, with the key task of renewing relations after the Crimean War. The imperial event on 28 February had clearly been extravagant: the theatre had been built in the Salle de Diane, much in the same way as Fould had arranged affairs in the Louvre the previous year, and scenery had been painted to represent the bridge over the Seine—feet from the Tuileries itself in real life—on which Offenbach's Patachon and Giraffier spent most of *Les deux aveugles*. Comte Félix Baciocchi, superintendent of court entertainments (*spectacles*), supervised the entire show, including an encore of the famous *boléro* from *Les deux aveugles*. But the evening also

---

[66] The events took place on 28 February 1855 and 29 February 1856, respectively; see *Le ménestrel*, 25 February 1855; *La Revue et Gazette musicale de Paris*, 2 March 1856.

[67] For *Pepito*, see Richard Sherr, 'Offenbach, *Pépito* and the Théâtre des Variétés: Politics and Genre in the First Year of the Second Empire', *Cambridge Opera Journal* 32 (2021) 154–186.

[68] See Jean-Claude Yon, 'En marge des négociations: mondanités et spectacles pendant le congrès de Paris', *Le congrès de Paris (1856): un événement fondateur [colloque international organisé par le Ministère des affaires étrangères et européennes, l'Université Paris IV et l'Association des amis de Napoléon III, Paris, Musée d'Orsay, 24–25 mars 2006]*, ed. Gilbert Ameil, Isabelle Nathan, and Georges-Henri Soutou (Brussels: Peter Lang, 2009) 171–184.

included the premiere of Weckerlin's *Tout est bien qui finit bien*, whose subsequent career was adorned by the publication of a piano-vocal score that formally announced that the work had been performed 'in front of their majesties in the Palais des Tuileries'.[69]

Alongside these two high-profile events, the single *opéra de salon* to have appeared at perhaps the best-known and most active imperial salon sits very easily. Mathilde-Létizia-Wilhelmine Bonaparte, cousin of Napoléon III and better known simply as Princesse Mathilde, presided over one of the most active *salons* in Paris in her *salon* in the rue de Courcelles.[70] Unsurprisingly, the performance of Nadaud's *Le docteur vieuxtemps* attracted the imperial family as well as 'all the great dignitaries of the state and members of the diplomatic corps'.[71] Again, a temporary theatre had been constructed in the middle of the main *salon* for the *opéra de salon*, which was paired with performances by Nadaud himself of *romances* and piano pieces.[72] The event was celebrated with a commemorative poem by Galoppe d'Onquaire published in *Le ménestrel* under the title 'SOIRÉE DE S[on] A[ltesse] [Impériale] Mme LA PRINCESSE MATHILDE / 100e Représentation du Docteur Vieuxtemps'.[73] It is far from clear if the reference to the hundredth performance of *Le doctor vieuxtemps* was mere hyperbole on the part of Galoppe d'Onquaire and Heugel—who published both the piano-vocal score of *Le docteur vieuxtemps* and *Le ménestrel* itself—or whether the piece could have received one hundred performances in the couple of months since it had premiered. The number one hundred could be the same sort of ironic literary hyperbole that Offenbach would use when he identified his modest apartments in the Passage Saulnier as the '32nd Lyric Theatre in Paris',[74] or it could reveal some sense of the currency of such a work as *Le docteur vieuxtemps* outside the *salons* on which the press reported, including the much more modest *parloir* with family members participating in a performance otherwise without audience.

---

[69] *Le ménestrel*, 2 March 1856, and *La Revue et Gazette musicale de Paris* for the same date.

[70] Princesse Mathilde's *salon* has been a source of fascination for more than a century. See Bled, *La société française depuis cent ans*, 1:203–237; Rièse, *Les salons littéraires parisiens*, 15–31; Nicole Vilkner, 'Sounding Streets: Music and Urban Change in Paris, 1830–1870' (PhD diss., Rutgers University, 2016) 72–77.

[71] 'tous les grands dignitaires de l'État et MM. les membres du corps diplomatique' (*Le constitutionnel*, 27 April 1854).

[72] *Le nouvelliste*, 5 May 1854.

[73] *Le ménestrel*, 30 April 1854.

[74] *Ibidem*, 2 April 1854.

This chapter has traded more in the currency of the *haute bourgeoisie* than that of the aristocracy, and a useful point of conclusion is to reflect on the nature of mid-century Parisian aristocracy. There is a continuing tension in the mid-nineteenth century generated by the revolution of 1789, which was supposed to curtail the power of the aristocracy, if not to eliminate it, but which was also complicated not only by the Bourbon restorations of 1814 and 1815 but also by the Napoleonic propensity for the creation of aristocratic titles. Those aristocrats who promoted *opéra de salon* ran the gamut of aristocratic backgrounds. Comte Jules de Castellane sprang from a family as old as the kingdom of France that weathered the decades around 1800 in ways that enabled its various branches to maintain an existence that—if not as opulent as during the *ancien régime*—was at least as wealthy as the *haute bourgeoisie*. But many of the other aristocrats held their positions largely as the result of Napoleonic favour. Princesse Mathilde was the cousin of Napoléon III and only acquired her title by marriage to Comte Anatole Demidoff, Prince of San Donato, in 1840. The Comtesse d'Indy was born Thérèse Chorier, and her husband, Théodore, was a captain in the first regiment of mounted grenadiers, whose service in the Imperial Guard gained him his title sometime before 1814. The Marquis d'Aoust was the grandson of Eustache-Jean, who had been one of the so-called *députés de la noblesse* in 1789, and his immediate noble origins remain obscure. But perhaps the most egregious aristocrat was Charles Auguste Louis Joseph Demorny, the half-brother of Napoléon III, who from the age of thirty-two styled himself 'Comte de Morny'; despite his later (1862) elevation to the status of duke, for most of his career (he died in 1865), he was effectively a member of the *haute bourgeoisie* and a hugely effective industrialist and speculator.

Opéra de salon was cultivated assiduously not only by such *moyen-bourgeois* as members of the medical profession but also by *haut-bourgeois* industrialists, bankers, property speculators, senior civil servants, and politicians, as well as by the aristocracy. Works and performers effortlessly passed from one very different environment to another—from the palatial ballroom to the surgeon's *salon*—as hosts repurposed different forms of *lieux* into performative *espaces*. Despite this artistic slippage and overlap, there must have been little ambiguity in the physical dissonance between *opéra de salon* in *haut-bourgeois* and *moyen-bourgeois* spaces, as this chapter has shown. But much *opéra de salon* was cultivated in *espaces* that were owned, or to whom access was granted, by individuals whose status is less than clear: men of letters, artists, sculptors and architects, performers, and composers as well as their audiences, who could drift between the aristocracy and the *bourgeoisie* with exactly the sort of social mobility for which the mid-nineteenth century was known. Chapter 4 examines the performative culture of *opéra de salon* in these blurred social spaces.

4
Performance and Places
Music and Letters

If the previous chapter considered the cultivation of *opéra de salon* by some clearly chiselled social groups—the *haute bourgeoisie* and the members of the *moyenne bourgeoisie* involved in medical pursuits—it concluded with an account of the much looser structures that governed those civil servants of varying levels of seniority who welcomed *opéra de salon* into their homes. The current chapter probes this ambiguity between the *haute* and *moyenne bourgeoisie* by considering further individuals with an interest in *opéra de salon* whose social position remains much less clear. Men of letters, artists, sculptors and architects, performers, composers, and librettists not only came from highly varied parts of society but moved between them with apparent ease. The first two sections of the chapter address the cultivation of *opéra de salon* in the homes of artists and of men of letters and the ways in which composers and performers used studios in their own homes to promote *opéra de salon* and their own careers. The chapter ends with an explanation of the ways in which those same musicians could exploit public places for their activities and how their work in concert halls, for example, differed from their endeavours in their own homes.

Spaces and Patrons 4: Artists and Men of Letters

Haut-bourgeois and aristocratic families possessed large homes where they could put on performances in *salons* that were effectively, or approached the size of, ballrooms or other large reception areas. Almost invariably more modest, performance *espaces* where the patron was an artist or *homme de lettres* were created out of *lieux*—*salons* or other spaces—that were complicated by the circumstances under which the artists or *hommes de lettres* themselves lived. Performances of *opéra de salon* are known to have taken place in the homes of an artist (Eugène-Nicolas Trouvé), a sculptor

(Henri-Joseph-Charles Cordier), an architect (Pierre-Marie-Félix Pigeory), and four *hommes de lettres* (Pierre-Michel-François Chevalier, known as Pitre-Chevalier; Émile de Girardin; Casimir Gide; and Philippe-Auguste-Alfred Pittaud, known as Pittaud de Forges).

Two performances of *opéra de salon* were given at the home—on the premises, perhaps—of genre painter Trouvé in Passy, where he ran a school for women artists; the two performances begin to show how complicated the relationship between *lieu, espace*, and the domestic living arrangements of those promoting the genre could be.[1] Both events took place during the winter season, which ran counter to usual practice when events in Passy would take place at the country residences of those who ran *salons* during the summer (Rossini and Mme Orfila were but two of the best-known examples).[2] So Trouvé's events were atypical in this regard, even more so since he was the librettist of both works: *Les sabotiers* and *Un tour de clef*.[3] Furthermore, the composer of *Les sabotiers* was Canoby, who was organist of the Église Notre-Dame-de-Grâce in Passy, mere metres from Trouvé's school and home. Canoby's published works consist of a small number of sacred pieces, some romances, and a few didactic works. However, he was also the composer of three *opérettes*: *Rosette*, premiered at the Théâtre des Champs-Élysées in 1864, and *La médaille* and *Un drame en l'air*, both for the Bouffes-Parisiens in 1865.[4] With *Les sabotiers* securely attributed to him, it is tempting, given the otherwise identical performance circumstances and the same librettist, to attribute *Un tour de clef* to him as well. Jules-Émile Petit, fresh from success at the Conservatoire and shortly to start a career at the Théâtre-Lyrique, took the baritone role in *Les sabotiers*,[5] and the soprano was a Mme Denizet, described as a pupil of Gabrielle-Delphine-Elisabeth Beaucé, better known as Delphine Ugalde (the former had a career in the chorus at the Théâtre-Lyrique during the 1860s).[6]

---

[1] 'Trouvé, Eugène or Nicolas Eugène', *Benezit Dictionary of Artists* (https://www.oxfordartonline.com/benezit/view/10.1093/benz/9780199773787.001.0001/acref-9780199773787-e-00185590).

[2] Trouvé's performances took place in December 1860 and October 1863; see *Le ménestrel*, 2 December 1860 and 25 October 1863.

[3] The scores of the two works have not survived.

[4] Joël-Marie Fauquet, 'CANOBY, Louis-*Gustave*', *Dictionnaire de la musique en France au xixe siècle*, ed. Joël-Marie Fauquet (Paris: Fayard, 2003) 205; for further detail, see Fétis, *Biographie universelle des musiciens*, Suppl. 2:147–148.

[5] Pierre, *Le Conservatoire*, 2:828.

[6] Thomas Joseph Walsh, *Second Empire Opera: The Théâtre Lyrique, Paris, 1851–1870*, The History of Opera (London: Calder; New York: Riverrun, 1981) 245.

But before such an event as the premiere of *Les sabotiers* is cast off as a purely provincial out-of-season event destined for the amusement of the inhabitants of Passy alone, a glance at the members of the audience and other participants suggests a greater importance. While having a pupil of Ugalde's in the cast gave some sort of weight to the occasion, nothing could match the fact that a number of distinguished professionals were present, such as sixty-nine-year-old Nicolas-Prosper Levasseur, who was the first Bertram in Meyerbeer's 1831 *Robert le diable*, and seventy-three-year-old veteran of the Opéra-Comique Louis-Antoine-Éléonore Ponchard. They were accompanied by Ponchard's son Charles, an artist who had been at the Opéra-Comique since 1848 and would continue for another decade. Charles was there with his wife, Cécile, who had enjoyed a distinguished career at the Opéra in the 1840s and still sang in concerts. Between them, these artists contributed duets from André-Ernest-Modeste Grétry's *La fausse magie*, François-Adrien Boieldieu's *Le nouveau seigneur du village* and *La dame blanche*, and Auber's *Le philtre*, not a note of which was less than thirty years old. Levasseur was Trouvé's next-door neighbour in Passy (8 and 6bis rue Vital, respectively), although the Ponchard family (who lived together) had to brave the December weather to come from their home on the Boulevard Montmartre. This musical preface to Canoby's *opéra de salon* was described deprecatingly, but anonymously, as having 'its own little merit'.[7]

While all accounts of Trouvé's performances are simply described as *chez M. Trouvé*, such accounts leave open the question of the underpinning *lieu* that was repurposed for the performances that were attended by so illustrious a company. It may be inferred that there were studio areas—*lieux*—that could have served as performative *espaces* for *opéra de salon* within the parts of Trouvé's premises dedicated to teaching. Trouvé might also have possessed a *salon* that was suitably large to have been used both for pedagogical purposes and for his own private use, which then could have been repurposed as an *espace* for performance; but this would have contradicted what is known about the studio space of the successful artist, to say nothing of an effective art teacher. Although the surviving accounts here of *opéra de salon* are insufficiently precise as to exactly how the transformation from *lieu* to *espace* was made, or indeed what the supporting *lieu* in fact was, it seems likely that Trouvé either had some sort of artistic *lieu*—unrelated to the arts of living—that would have converted to a performative *espace* with relative

---

[7] 'une préface qui avait bien son petit mérite' (*Le ménestrel*, 2 December 1860).

ease or some sort of shared private and pedagogical space, repurposed in the same way.

If the evidence for the performance of *opéra de salon* at Trouvé's school for *beaux arts* is riddled with ambiguity, one of the most intriguing performance venues for *opéra de salon* is also one of the best documented through photographic evidence. In January 1865, the galleries of sculptor Cordier were the venue for a performance of an *opéra de salon*, the title of which is unknown, performed by a Mme Michaeli; a M. Michaeli, violinist, was also on the programme performing Jean-Delphin Alard's fantasias on Auber's *La muette de Portici* and on Gaetano Donizetti's *La fille du régiment*. Mme Michaeli was described as being among Duprez's best pupils and having a mezzo-soprano voice 'as beautiful as its range is large'.[8] The fact that she was in Paris at exactly this moment must make Lovisa Charlotta Helena Michal (known as Louise Michaëli) a strong candidate,[9] although the fact that the work that was performed is not known makes the identification of the artist that much more difficult. As in the case of the Trouvé performances, the surviving information about the work is tantalizing: the *opéra de salon* performed in Cordier's studio had a libretto by Tourneux, a painter specializing in genre scenes who was also a neighbour of Cordier's in the eastern Faubourg Saint-Germain.[10] The composer was Godefroid, whose *A deux pas du bonheur* was one of the most frequently performed *opéras de salon* during the Second Empire. Apart from this, though, Godefroid's only other stage work was *La harpe d'or*, with a libretto by Adolphe Jaime and Ernest Dubreuil, premiered

---

[8] *Ibidem*, 22 January 1865.

[9] Michaëli, who was Swedish, had trained in Paris a decade earlier and had been singing professionally since the previous year; it is entirely plausible that she spent most of the documented sojourn in Paris as Duprez's pupil (the event in Cordier's galleries was the only public event of the year in which she appeared). The problem is with her description as a mezzo-soprano, since—even with the extended tessitura with which she was praised—this is hardly a suitable descriptor for an artist who would sing Mozart's Queen of the Night. Describing her as an amateur receiving her baptism as an artist might merely be ignorant, but the fact that the name 'Michaëli' was claimed to mask the name of a noble Russian family was wrong in that the family was Swedish and Lovisa was the daughter of professional singers, and the fact that it was a pseudonym (her real surname was Michal) is correct. Michaëli was, however, in Paris only a couple of years later. Dan Olsson, 'Lovisa (Louise) Charlotta Helena Michaëli', *Svenskt kvinnobiografiskt lexikon* (https://www.skbl.se/sv/artikel/LouiseMichaeli).

[10] 'Tourneux, Eugène or Jean François Eugène', *Benezit Dictionary of Artists* (https://www.oxfordartonline.com/benezit/view/10.1093/benz/9780199773787.001.0001/acref-9780199773787-e-00184531?rskey=VWynwq&result=1). Cordier's studio was at 115 Boulevard Saint-Michel, while Tourneux's was at 55 rue Cherche-Midi, on the other side of the Luxembourg Gardens. A decade earlier, Tourneux was already engaging with *opéra de salon* when he wrote a prologue to a work by Nadaud, almost certainly his *Porte et fenêtre* of 1857. See AVANT LA REPRÉSENTATION/ D'UN/OPÉRA DE G. NADAUD/PROLOGUE/PAR E. TOURNEUX/-/MARS 1857/-/PARIS/ IMPRIMERIE DE J CLAYE/DUE SAINT BENOÎT, 7.

at the Théâtre-Lyrique in September 1858; the work for the Cordier salon could therefore have been neither *A deux pas du bonheur* nor *La harpe d'or*, since neither had a libretto by Tourneux, but an apparently unknown third work. Most of Godefroid's compositions in the mid-1860s consisted of piano fantasies on operatic themes and other keyboard works, as well as works for harp, so the absence of any identification is telling in more than one respect.

There is a paradox between the anonymity of the work, performers, and composer and the fact that the Cordier event reveals so much about how the *lieu* might have been transformed into performative *espace*.[11] The audience was described as 'numerous and brilliant', and the *espace* in which the performance took place reflects precisely Cordier's legendary status as the foremost ethnographic sculptor of his generation.[12] In the wake of the re-establishment of the abolition of slavery in French colonies in 1848, Cordier began a series of busts of non-European subjects that included a series of the African Venus at the Paris Salon of 1853 and Chinese subjects at the Exposition Universelle, also in Paris, in 1855. Queen Victoria had purchased a bust entitled 'The Negro of Timbuktu' when Cordier exhibited at the Great Exhibition in London in 1851. He bought his studio at 115 Boulevard Saint-Michel in 1852 in a part of the Latin Quarter where his teacher François Rude (the sculptor of the Arc de Triomphe) and Louis Petitot (the artist responsible for part of the work on the obelisk at the Place de la Concorde) both lived and worked. Unsurprisingly, Cordier's studio and galleries were decorated in an uncompromisingly orientalist style (figures 4.1 and 4.2).[13]

The obviously itinerant Cordier abandoned his studio and many of his possessions in 1865—the same year as the *opéra de salon* performance—and a photograph survives of part of the room in which the *opéra de salon* may have been performed and where his possessions were displayed (figure 4.3).

The first of the three images (figure 4.1) that reveal the *lieu* in which Cordier worked seems to give a view through two others giving on to the

---

[11] For details of the workshop at 115 Boulevard Saint-Michel, see Anne de Buridan, 'Charles Cordier: sculpteur de l'Orient', *La revue du quartier latin* (8 July 2016) (https://archive.wikiwix. com/cache/index2.php?url=https%3A%2F%2Fwww.quartierlatin.paris%2F%3Fcharles-cordier-sculpteur-de-l-orient#federation=archive.wikiwix.com&tab=url).

[12] Pierre Dalibard, *C'était le temps où Charles Cordier unissait l'onyx et le bronze* (Buc: Tensing, 2012), is the standard biography. An important retrospective of Cordier's work was held in 2004. See Laure de Margerie et al., *Charles Cordier, 1827–1905: l'autre et l'ailleurs [exposition, Musée d'Orsay, Paris, 2 février–2 mai 2004, Musée National des Beaux-Arts, Québec, 10 juin–6 septembre 2004, Dahesh Museum of Art, New York, 12 octobre 2004–9 janvier 2005]* (Paris: La Martinière, 2004).

[13] All three images of Cordier's studio are taken from Buridan, 'Charles Cordier: sculpteur de l'Orient'.

Figure 4.1. Studio of Henri-Joseph-Charles Cordier, view through multiple arches.

Figure 4.2. Studio of Henri-Joseph-Charles Cordier, view of smaller room.

Figure 4.3. Studio of Henri-Joseph-Charles Cordier, general view of larger room.

window in the centre of the shot of the main room (figure 4.3); this would suggest a suite of rooms off to the left of that room. Figure 4.2, and this is more speculative, is either a picture of the middle room indicated in figure 4.1 or an entirely different one.

Cluttered with Cordier's objects then currently on sale, the clearly orientalist quality of the room in Cordier's studio that must have been the *espace* in which the *opéra de salon* was presented must have given a particular artistic frisson to the performance, and this is to say nothing of the orientalist door openings visible in figures 4.1 and 4.2. The décor is entirely congruent with Cordier's artistic output and professional career, but it also makes the loss of the *opéra de salon* itself that much more frustrating since it might have shared similar orientalizing traits.

Exactly how many individuals—'numerous and brilliant'—were present at Cordier's *soirée* is difficult to judge; his workshop was, however, described as 'gigantic' in a review of a display of sculpture later the same year, so it is tempting to posit the same sorts of numbers—in the hundreds—that were known at such performances given by Princesse Mathilde or the Binder family.[14] The image in figure 4.3 is clearly set up as pre-sale viewing, so it

---

[14] *Le monde illustré*, 11 March 1865.

represents neither the habitual configuration of Cordier's living space (the way in which he configured the *lieu* into an *espace* for living and sculpture) nor the way the *lieu* and *espace* might have been reconfigured for the performance of *opéra de salon*; it is equally possible that there might have been another *lieu* that was not photographed that served as a performative *espace*. However, the fact that the photograph in figure 4.3 seems to have been taken from a balcony goes some way towards explaining how such a large number of individuals could have witnessed the performance, since it seems there was a balcony on at least two of the four walls of the main *salon*.

Trouvé and Cordier appear to have restricted their activities to art and sculpture, with a sideline in pedagogy for the former. The architect Pigeory was not only responsible for *hôtels particuliers* and buildings in coastal resorts, but he also edited *La revue des beaux arts* and was a prolific author. These activities aligned him with a network of *hommes de lettres* active in both publishing and the promotion of *opéra de salon* which included the publishers Pitre-Chevalier and Émile de Girardin and the illustrator and caricaturist Charles-Albert d'Arnoux, who published under the pseudonym Berthall.

When Pigeory was able to put on an event in his home in the rue d'Amsterdam sometime in early February 1860,[15] he lived and worked not in an apartment but in an *hôtel particulier*, a free-standing building for the use of a single family and staff;[16] it therefore seems reasonable to assume that the studio and the *lieux* available for conversion to performative *espaces* were extensive. Pigeory was able to offer his guests a new work—Bernard's *L'accord parfait* to a libretto by Galoppe d'Onquaire performed by Mlle Mira,[17] who had been a younger colleague of the well-known singer of *opéra de salon* Gaveaux-Sabatier since 1857, and Gaveaux-Sabatier's frequent partner Biéval. They were joined in a performance of Bernard's *Loin du bruit* (again to a libretto by Galoppe d'Onquaire) by Sainte-Foy, then in the middle of an unbroken and distinguished career at the Opéra-Comique that had started in 1848; the last premiere in which he appeared was Delibes's *Le roi l'a dit* in May 1873.[18] The composer of both works presided at the piano.[19]

---

[15] He had designed the building himself. See 'PIGEORY, Félix', 'École des Chartes—Comité des travaux historiques et scientifiques: annuaire prosopographique' (http://cths.fr/an/savant.php?id=116005).

[16] Alexandre Gady, *Les hôtels particuliers de Paris, du moyen âge à la belle époque* (Paris: Parigramme, 2011).

[17] Pierre, *Le Conservatoire*, 2:814.

[18] 'SAINTE-FOY', *L'art lyrique français*.

[19] *Le ménestrel*, 19 February 1860.

Pitre-Chevalier was closely connected to Pigeory both by their enthusiasm for *opéra de salon* and through publishing: Pigeory was director of *La revue des beaux arts*, and Pitre-Chevalier had been editor of *Le Figaro* from 1838 and *Le musée des familles* from 1842. More important, they invested together in the spa at Villers-sur-Mer, which, by the time they were mounting productions of *opéra de salon* in their homes in Paris, amounted to more than fifty buildings and a casino.[20] The harpist and composer of *opéra de salon* Godefroid, whose contribution to *opéra de salon* has been discussed, bought property and died there.

Whether the two *opéras de salon* in Pigeory's *hôtel particulier* were staged with sets, costumes, and other attributes is something that surviving documentary accounts do not reveal, although the opulence of the surroundings and the back-to-back performances of two works suggest that some sort of temporary stage must have been present. By contrast, Pitre-Chevalier was able to mount a production in a temporary theatre in which the sets were taken from the Jallot-Taboureux company;[21] the result was that the commentator for *Le ménestrel* could describe the event as taking place at a *quatrième théâtre lyrique*. Such an accolade, once the title *troisième théâtre lyrique* had been accorded the Théâtre-Lyrique, was bestowed on the Théâtre des Bouffes-Parisiens in the 1850s and the Théâtre des Fantaisies-Parisiennes in the 1860s;[22] for this to be applied to a venue for *opéra de salon*, especially given that in 1854, Pitre-Chevalier was still in an apartment on the rue Bonaparte, was a significant achievement.[23]

Pitre-Chevalier put on what might well have been the premiere of Nadaud's *Le docteur vieuxtemps* (Nadaud wrote both the words and the music) in late February or early March 1854 in a performance with professional sets,[24] and an early performance of *L'héritier sans le savoir*, with both music and libretto by Thys, in April 1858.[25] The mostly non-professional performers (Dejoly, Jal, art dealer Le Roy, and an individual named Mounnier) of

---

[20] See Henri Hamel, *Felix Pigeory, fondateur de Villers, 1812–1873* (Trouville: Association des Amis du Musée de Trouville, 1985) for the work of the two men at Villers-sur-Mer and their connections in other artistic domains.
[21] See chapter 2.
[22] *Le ménestrel*, 5 March 1854; 6 October 1867.
[23] Pitre-Chevalier moved from the rue Bonaparte to the rue des Écuries-d'Artois in 1861, where he hosted at least one performance of *opéra de salon* in April 1863. Pierre Bonnaffé, *Pitre-Chevalier* (Paris: Leroux, 1905) 20; the performance was reviewed in *Le ménestrel*, 12 April 1863, and the performance had taken place on the fifth of the month.
[24] *Le ménestrel*, 5 March 1854.
[25] *Ibidem*, 11 April 1858.

Pitre-Chevalier's 1854 performance were replaced by *artistes-virtuoses* in 1858:[26] Mme Lefébure-Wély and Lefort were joined by Paul Malézieux. The presence of Dejoly and Jal provides a connection to events hosted by medical professionals through their participation in the performances given at the Néothermes. The 1854 performance was prefaced by a prologue read by Pitre-Chevalier himself and an otherwise unknown text by Anaïs Ségalas.[27] However elaborate the sets for *Le docteur vieuxtemps* might have been,[28] the performance was still accompanied with just a piano, executed by Charles Delioux de Savignac.[29]

His involvement in *Le musée de familles* brought Pitre-Chevalier into contact with Berthall; while the former edited the journal, the latter was one of its best-loved caricaturists. Berthall also worked extensively for the journal *Le magasin pittoresque* and illustrated dozens of books between the 1840s and 1880s; it is significant that he provided illustrations for Georges Bonnefons's *Hôtels historiques de Paris*, in which he focussed on the illustrations for the Hôtel de Bourgogne, near legendary as a home for the *théâtre de société* of which *opéra de salon* formed part. His illustration of the actor Raymond Poisson, who invented the valet roles known as 'Crispin' at the Hôtel de Bourgogne (figure 4.4) may well have been part of the same impetus that resulted in the performance of Offenbach's *Les deux aveugles* in his home on the rue Fleurus, at that unfashionable end of the Faubourg Saint-Germain now familiar as a home for *opéra de salon*.

Berthall's performance—slightly less than three years after *Les deux aveugles*'s premiere at the Théâtre des Bouffes-Parisiens—was enhanced by the presence of one of the original artists, Jean-François-Philibert Berthellier, who was paired with Sainte-Foy.[30]

Pitre-Chevalier's engagement with the journal *Le musée de familles* connected him to several other individuals variously engaging with *opéra de salon*; perhaps the most famous member of this literary network engaged with *opéra de salon* was Girardin. Girardin had founded *Le musée des*

---

[26] Dejoly's ambiguous status as *chanteuse du monde* or *artiste-virtuose* is discussed in chapter 2.

[27] Ségalas's role in the network of *opéra de salon* culture around a group of medical professionals in the eastern Faubourg Saint-Germain is discussed in chapter 3 and her role more generally as a female librettist in chapter 6.

[28] This dimension of the performance *Le docteur vieuxtemps* is discussed chapter 2.

[29] Pitre-Chevalier mounted a third performance of *opéra de salon* just nine weeks before his death, on 5 April 1863, of Barbier's *Le loup et l'agneau* (the libretto was by Étienne-Hippolyte Chol de Clercy and Hippolyte Messant) which had been premiered at the beginning of the season (30 September 1862) at the Théâtre Déjazet. See *Le ménestrel*, 12 April 1863.

[30] *La Revue et Gazette musicale de Paris*, 7 March 1858.

Figure 4.4. Raymond Poisson, engraving by Charles-Albert d'Arnoux (Berthall).

familles in 1833 shortly before the real publishing success of his career in 1836: *La presse*, with all the associations of low price and the advent of the *roman-feuilleton* that it entailed.[31] Girardin's only *soirée* to include an *opéra de salon* may well have been part of a series of events to mark his return to Parisian society after the death of his first wife, Delphine Gay, in 1855 and the introduction into his social circle of Wilhelmina Josephina Rudolphina Brunold, Comtesse de Tiefenbach, whom he had married in October 1856; the *opéra de salon* was given on 10 May 1857.[32] Girardin's opulent home on

---

[31] See Pierre Pellissier, *Émile de Girardin, prince de la presse* (Paris: Denoël, 1985); for Girardin's political career, see Guy Thullier, 'Les idées politiques d'Émile de Girardin', *Revue administrative* 68 (1959) 134–143.

[32] *La Revue et Gazette musicale de Paris*, 17 May 1857.

the corner of the Avenue des Champs Élysées and the rue Marbeuf was the venue for what was perhaps the premiere of Weckerlin's *Le mariage en poste* (libretto by Galoppe d'Onquaire).[33] It was a big event: the correspondent for *La Revue et Gazette musicale de Paris* described the premises as having being turned into a *salle de spectacle*, which might merely have meant a space with theatre-style seating, or it could just as easily have indicated a temporary theatre, as suggested by the mention of a concluding *chute du rideau*—curtain calls for the cast. Certainly, the cast for *Le mariage en poste* could hardly have been bettered: Mlle Mira was partnered with Archainbaud, for whom this was the first outing in *opéra de salon*, the beginning of a career that would last throughout the Second Empire. *Le mariage en poste* was followed by a performance of Alexandre Dumas's *L'invitation à la valse*, a preview of a work that would be formally premiered at the Gymnase Dramatique the following month. The evening ended with *Les deux font la paire*, comic scenes delivered by the Lionnet brothers.[34]

Girardin's activities lay well to the north-west of the Faubourg Saint-Germain, diametrically across from where most of the *moyenne bourgeoisie* cultivated *opéra de salon*, and closer to the homes of the *haute bourgeoisie* with similar interests in the Faubourg Saint-Honoré. He represents an intriguing case of a 'man of letters' sufficiently successful to gravitate towards the members of the *haute bourgeoisie*.

Two other men of letters, Gide and Pittaud de Forges, promoted *opéra de salon* just outside the strict geographical boundaries of the Faubourg Saint-Germain but back in the same south-east corner favoured by those medical professionals who supported the genre. Gide represents an intriguing reversal of the normal sequence where a young individual is destined for a liberal profession—the law, medicine, academia—but rejects it in favour of music. Gide had started his career as a Conservatoire-trained composer and had enjoyed success as a ballet composer at the Opéra for nearly two decades, collaborating with Halévy and Adam, among others. He inherited the family publishing business in 1847, and his compositional career stopped dead for a decade.[35] The performance put on by his spouse, Clémentine Adèle Eugénie,

---

[33] *Le mariage en poste* survives in Weckerlin's autograph (Paris, Bibliothèque Nationale de France, MS-16900).

[34] The careers of the Lionnet brothers and their engagement with *opéra de salon* are discussed in chapter 2.

[35] See, for the first part of his career, Éric Kocevar, 'GIDE, Casimir', *Dictionnaire de musique*, 514. Fétis (*Biographie universelle des musiciens*, Suppl. 1:379) notes not only *Belphégor* (wrongly as unperformed) but also a three-act *Françoise de Rimini*, also presumably composed after Gide's return to composition in 1857.

née Jacques, apparently for an all-female audience on 5 February 1858, might well represent the beginning of an attempt at musical rehabilitation, since the main attraction was her husband's *opéra de salon*, *Belphégor*. It seems no effort was spared in mounting the work; commentaries spoke of 'a charming theatre, situated in one of the most elegant *salons* on the rue Bonaparte', and of the work being mounted in front of a *parterre*.[36] *Belphégor* was prefaced by a verse prologue composed by Léon Halévy—the author of the libretto to *Belphégor*—but read by the young poet Romain Bussine.[37] In addition to the prologue, the evening include a comedy by Hilarion Ballande, *Trop tard*, and scenes from Pierre Corneille's *Le Cid*. Although the review in *La Revue et Gazette musicale de Paris* suggested that there was enthusiasm for a second performance of *Belphégor* under similar conditions, further attempts at reviving Gide's career through *opéra de salon* appear to have left no trace.

This chapter opened with an account of Trouvé's performance of an *opéra de salon* for which he himself had written the libretto. Similarly, when librettist and *vaudevilliste* Pittaud de Forges put on an evening of theatre and dance in his vast apartment in the rue Saint-Lazare in 1865,[38] the central work was Offenbach's *Le 66!* for which Pittaud de Forges had written the libretto himself a decade earlier.[39] It was accompanied by a new work—a kind of pendant to Offenbach's *Les deux aveugles*—titled *Les deux charlatans*, a 'grand opéra, without chorus, but with a broom';[40] it was composed by Ducellier, who had taken one of the roles in the evening's performance of *Le 66!*, and the libretto was by Édouard Doyen. Pittaud de Forges's contribution, however, had been not to write the libretto of *Les deux charlatans* but to provide the space for the performance. The performers were all *chanteurs* and *chanteuses du monde*: the soprano who took the role of Grettly in *Le 66!* remained anonymous as the 'daughter of a famous artistic name', and one of the performers, Filhouze, remains unknown. Ducellier—in addition to being the composer—was inspector of primary schools for the city. Pittaud

---

[36] 'Un charmant théâtre, situé dans un des plus élégants salons de la rue Bonaparte (*La Revue et Gazette musicale de Paris*, 14 February 1858).

[37] *Ibidem* and *Le ménestrel*, 14 February 1858. The brother of singer Prosper-Alphonse Bussine, Romain Bussine was a vocal teacher and poet and would cofound—with Saint-Saëns—the Société Nationale de Musique in 1871. His poetry was set by Gabriel Fauré, most notably his translation of *Après une rêve*, op. 7. See Joël-Marie Fauquet, 'BUSSINE, Prosper-Alphonse', *Dictionnaire de la musique en France au xixe siècle*, ed. Joël-Marie Fauquet (Paris: Fayard, 2003) 188.

[38] *La Revue et Gazette musicale de Paris*, 26 March 1865. The event had taken place on 21 March.

[39] Offenbach's *Le 66!* had been premiered at the Bouffes-Parisiens on 31 July 1856. Pittaud de Forges had written the libretto with Paul-Aimé Chapelle.

[40] The play on words—*balai* (a broom) and *ballet*—has been explained in chapter 1.

de Forges himself took the role of the prompt and director and, with his wife, led the dancing that closed the event. Pittaud de Forges's apartments clearly made it possible to mount an *opéra de salon* with something approaching a genuine theatrical experience, and there is no doubt that it was in the playwright's own home that the performance took place. Reports speak of each member of 'a crowd receiving the humorous and ironic "programme"' at the entrance to 'his vast apartment' before the performance.[41]

Spaces and Patrons 5: Professional Musicians

Professional musicians used their own premises to mount either their own *opéras de salon* or those of others. Teachers, performers, and composers made use of their own homes in ways that reflected their professional orientation, their location, the size of their fortunes, and—in some cases—their family origins. So when Émile Ettling and his wife gave the premiere of his *Un jour de noce* at his home at 24 rue de la Grange-Batelière on 6 March 1864, this was described as the twelfth *matinée musicale* that the couple had given, and they had been running them annually since 1852.[42] Most of Ettling's *matinées musicales* had been a mix of vocal and especially instrumental work (he himself was a violinist), but *Un jour de noce* represented his first attempt at *opéra de salon* and subsequently led to a series of *opérettes* at the *cafés-concerts* La Tertulia and Eldorado in the early 1870s.[43] Gaveaux-Sabatier was renowned for the quality of her pupils and used her home on the rue des Petites-Écuries as an environment for showing off their skill. Starting in 1866, however, she started putting on performances of *opéra de salon*, including two performances of Weckerlin's 1858 *La laitière de Trianon* in 1868, which in the press were wrongly thought to be the premiere and second performances.[44] And the same mistake had been made in the previous two

---

[41] 'De bonne heure il y avait foule dans son vaste appartement, à l'entrée duquel chaque invité recevait un programme' ('There was early on a crowd in his vast apartment at the entrance of which each guest received a programme'). Pittaud de Forges's apartments were comically renamed in the programme 'Théâtre de la Guerre' for the evening, and the artists—mimicking royal and imperial practices—were called 'Les comédiens ordinaires de la Guerre'. The performances were given on a stage with footlights, curtain, and sets (*La Revue et Gazette musicale de Paris*, 26 March 1865).

[42] *La Revue et Gazette musicale de Paris*, 13 March 1864.

[43] *Le nain* and *Le tigre* at La Tertulia in 1872 and 1873, respectively, and *L'oeil de M. L'expert* at the Eldorado in 1874. All three libretti were by the prolific Tréfeu; his career spanned a period from 1851 until the end of the century.

[44] These took place in February and March 1868. See *Le ménestrel*, 23 February 1868 and 5 April 1868.

years when Gaveaux-Sabatier's salon had been the home for performances of two other works by Weckerlin from a decade before: *Manche à manche* and *Pierrot à Paphos, ou La sérénade interrompue*.[45] What seems to have been happening in her salon in the rue des Petites-Écuries is that Gaveaux-Sabatier was reviving works that were up to a decade old in which she appeared consistently accompanied by Hermann-Léon, but because of the temporal distance between the revivals and their premieres, the press was wrongly assuming that they were new works. Given that they were all by Weckerlin, Gaveaux-Sabatier, the composer's most loyal performer, may have been attempting to canonize the composer's works.

Gaveaux-Sabatier was—as has repeatedly been shown—a central figure in the culture of *opéra de salon*; in comparison with the quantity of performances in which she was engaged in the 1850s and 1860s, the performances she gave at home were but a small part of her contribution to that culture. Gabrielle Colson, however, was a distinguished piano pedagogue who never seems to have performed outside of her own salon. From 1855 to at least 1869, she put on a concert of chamber music with piano twice a year—at the beginning (November–December) and end (April–May) of the season; she would play piano trios and quartets with some of the best-known string players in the capital, and the events would be rounded out with vocal contributions as well. On two occasions, in 1861 and 1868, she included *opéra de salon* in her programmes. On 1 April 1868, she mounted a production of Weckerlin's evergreen *Tout est bien qui finit bien* (originally from 1855), at which point the composer had probably lost count of how many performances the work had received.[46] On Christmas Day 1861, however, she had put on a performance of an *opera de salon* by Lecocq to a libretto by Jules de la Guette; this could have been one of two works: *Le baiser à la porte* or *Liline et Valentin*. Both works were subsequently mounted in the regulated theatre (at the Théâtre des Folies-Nouvelles and the Théâtre des Champs-Élysées, respectively, both in 1864), but Colson's 1861 performance might well have been the only time Lecocq had enjoyed any sort of performance between *Huis-clos* at the Folies-Nouvelles in 1859 and the performances of 1864.[47] Colson's studios were in her salon at 5 rue Saint-Benoît, on the eastern border of the Faubourg Saint-Germain, a long way from Nouvelle Athènes and the Ettling

---

[45] *Ibidem*, 10 March 1867; 18 February 1866 (the 1866 performance, although it took place in Gaveaux-Sabatier's studio, seems to have been Weckerlin's own responsibility).
[46] See *ibidem*, 12 April 1868.
[47] *Ibidem*, 5 January 1862.

and Gaveaux-Sabatier *salons*, even farther from those of Duprez, and geographically more closely aligned with the literary and medical professionals in the eastern reaches of the Faubourg Saint-Germain.

The most celebrated example of a pedagogue promoting *opéra de salon* is Duprez, who had been the best-known tenor at the Opéra from his return to Paris in 1837 to his retirement from the stage in 1850, creating roles in works from Berlioz's *Benvenuto Cellini* in 1838 to Verdi's *Jérusalem* in 1847. Legendary as being the first artist to sing the high C in Rossini's *Guillaume Tell* in chest voice, Duprez also took all the established tenor roles at the Opéra: Arnold in *Guillaume Tell*, Raoul in Meyerbeer's *Les Huguenots*, Eléazar in Halévy's *La juive*, and Masaniello in Auber's *La muette de Portici*. A pedagogue and author of vocal treatises, Duprez taught at the Conservatoire from 1842 to 1850.[48]

Duprez had the distinct advantage of not only having opened a formal singing school in 1853 but also having built a small but permanent theatre in the grounds of his house on the rue Turgot—even farther away from the rest of his professional colleagues than Gaveaux-Sabatier's salon (although only a kilometre north-west). Duprez's theatre was fully equipped with a stage and space for an orchestra, and it seated around three hundred; it even had a chandelier (figure 4.5).[49]

This engraving is an especially valuable document since it records a specific event on 30 January 1859.[50] Although the illustration did not depict an *opéra de salon*, it was a typical display of Duprez's pupils. Figure 4.5 shows one of the four female soloists, three of whom were to go on to professional careers ('Mme Raissac' was the daughter of a wealthy engineer, socialite, and amateur pupil). Caroline Monrose—who sang 'Casta diva' from Vincenzo Bellini's *Norma*—would have a career at the Opéra-Comique, as would Marie-Ernestine Marimon (an aria from Auber's *Les diamants de la couronne*). The fourth artist, Marie-Anne-Sophie Battu (half-sister of the librettist Léon Battu), would move directly to the Théâtre-Italien, thence to the Opéra from 1863 to 1865 (where she created the role of Inès in Meyerbeer's *L'africaine*), and subsequently to the Théâtre de la Monnaie in Brussels and

---

[48] The best account of Duprez's vocal career remains Fétis, *Biographie universelle des musiciens*, 3:84–85, and of his pedagogy and later career *ibidem*, Suppl. 1:292–293. See also Pierre Girod, 'Les mutations du ténor romantique' (PhD diss., Université de Rennes 2, 2015); *idem*, 'L'École Duprez (1849–1894): exercices publics et tournées dans les départements', (https://dezede.org/dossiers/id/248/).

[49] *Le monde illustré*, 5 February 1859.

[50] There is a full account of the concert in *Le ménestrel*, 6 February 1859.

Figure 4.5. Gilbert Duprez's theatre on the rue Turgot.

the Opéra-Comique. She sang an aria from Rossini's *Semiramide* at the 1859 concert, as well as a fragment of Duprez's own *opéra de salon*, his *Jélyotte*, which by then was five years old.

Real success as a composer—which for Duprez meant not just Paris but a production at the Opéra where he had enjoyed such fame as a performer—eluded him. He reconfigured the second of his two works for the Monnaie—*L'abîme de la maladetta*—as *Joanita* for the Théâtre-Lyrique in 1852, and his *La lettre au bon Dieu* appeared at the Opéra-Comique a year later. His two works that were clearly targeted at the Opéra—*Samson* and *Jeanne d'Arc*—fit in perfectly with the prevailing orthodoxy for the biblical and the historical at the Salle Le Peletier. Duprez, however, failed with both; *Jeanne d'Arc* eventually reached the stage at the short-lived Grand-Théâtre-Parisien in 1865.[51] In 1855, Duprez had mounted a summary performance of his *Samson* on

---

[51] Duprez's attempts to recruit Princesse Mathilde to the cause of a performance of *Jeanne d'Arc* at the Opéra are described in Everist, *The Empire at the Opéra*, 17–18.

the rue Turgot (but before the construction of the theatre), and a descriptive programme was published in Le ménestrel.[52] For this event, Duprez had assembled a star-studded cast: alongside the composer himself and his daughter, Caroline—who had brought her colleague, Julius Stockhausen, from the Opéra-Comique, where they both formed part of the troupe— together with Louis-Gustave-Esprit Euzet and Louis Gueymard from the Opéra. Pierre-Louis-Philippe Dietsch, head of the chorus at the Opéra (he would take over as chief music director in 1860), directed the performance. Despite the impressive cast and the successful performance, *Samson* was destined to remain silent and never escaped the confines of the rue Turgot.[53]

Trials of works destined for the regulated theatre were not the only *opéra de salon* events that Duprez hosted. He participated in the irresistible vogue for more conventional *opéra de salon* with his *Jélyotte, ou Un passe-temps de duchesse,* which he premiered in his own home in April 1854.[54] With a libretto by Duprez's brother, Édouard, *Jélyotte* was premiered by the composer assisted by Gustave-Hippolyte Roger from the Opéra, Toussaint-Eugène-Ernest Mocker from the Opéra-Comique, and two pupils, M. Rauch and Mlle Mira; the latter, as has already been seen, was to go on to a successful career as an *artiste-virtuose* in the *salon*. *Jélyotte* appeared at least twice more in Paris, always at Duprez's home and with varying casts;[55] it also played at the Grand Théâtre in Lyon as part of a double bill with Massé's *Les noces de Jeannette* in 1859.[56] As a Second Empire reinscription of the eighteenth-century *haute-contre* and composer Pierre de Jélyotte, Duprez's *opéra de salon* was pushing hard at the generic boundaries that were being set elsewhere; some of the numbers were large, multi-movement structures, and the kinetic discourse in play was not—as it was almost everywhere else in *opéra de salon*—spoken dialogue but accompanied recitative.

Apart from such teachers as Gaveaux-Sabatier or Duprez, performers almost never mounted productions in their own homes, for the obvious reason that most of them lived in much smaller apartments mostly in the Nouvelle Athènes neighbourhood and simply had insufficient room. The single example of Levassor, who put on a performance of Godefroid's *A deux*

---

[52] *Le ménestrel*, 18 March 1855. The programme gave details of the performers and the biblical sources of Dumas's libretto.
[53] Joseph d'Ortigue wrote a complimentary review in *Le journal des débats*, 19 April 1855.
[54] *La Revue et Gazette musicale de Paris*, 9 April 1854.
[55] 27 February 1859 (*Le ménestrel*); 1 February 1864 (*ibidem*, 21 February 1864). Both performances were in Duprez's own theatre.
[56] *La Revue et Gazette musicale de Paris*, 15 May 1859.

pas du bonheur in 1855, looks very much like a rehearsal for the event that Morny hosted at the Palais Bourbon a week and a half later and in which Levassor took the role of the improbable English baronet Sir Georges alongside Gaveaux-Sabatier as Betty.[57] Similarly, it is difficult to have much sense of how big Clara Pfeiffer's *salon* was on the rue Bleue, and the performance of her son Georges's *Le capitaine Roch* was also very likely a rehearsal[58] for more elaborate ones that would take place in Mme Orfila's salon and—promoted by professionals—in the Salles Érard and Pleyel.[59]

Composers, perhaps less surprisingly, were prepared to try out new works in their or others' homes. Poisot opened up his *salon* on the rue Larochefoucauld—again in Nouvelle Athènes—for the first performance of his *Les ressources de Jacqueline* in 1853[60] and his *Rosa, la rose* in 1868.[61] Pauline Thys—daughter of the composer Alphonse Thys—married Charles Sébault sometime before the end of 1859, but although she resided in Nouvelle Athènes, she enjoyed a private home (5 rue La Bruyère; it is now, since 1944, the Théâtre La Bruyère) big enough to put on performances of two of her own works: *La perruque du bailli*—which also circulated widely to the Salle Herz, the *salon* of Mme Orfila, and even a possible performance in the Hôtel de Ville of the eleventh *arrondissement*—and *Quand Dieu est dans le mariage, Dieu le garde*.[62] Indeed, the performance during the first week of February 1861 included both works as well as a number of other compositions by Thys herself. By this time, she had already had *La pomme de Turquie* performed at the Bouffes-Parisiens[63] and would look forward to *Le pays de Cocagne* appearing at the Théâtre-Lyrique in 1862.[64] Fifty metres south of the Thys-Sébault *salon* was the one hosted by Jules Beer, nephew of Meyerbeer and not only a composer of *opéra de salon*, like his neighbour, but also one who set the two-act libretto of *La fille d'Égypte* by Jules-Paul Barbier for the Théâtre-Lyrique in 1852. Beer put on performances in his *salon* in the rue d'Aumale of both his *En état de siège* and *Les roses de M. de Malesherbes*

---

[57] *Le ménestrel*, 18 and 25 February 1855.
[58] *La Revue et Gazette musicale de Paris*, 2 March 1862; *Le ménestrel* for the same date.
[59] See the account of the Orfila *salons* in chapter 3.
[60] 7 June 1853 (*Le ménestrel*, 12 June 1853).
[61] 24 February 1868. Clément and Larousse, *Dictionnaire des opéras*,744.
[62] Her premiere of *La perruque du bailli* took place in December 1859 (*Le ménestrel*, 1 January 1860) and that of *Quand Dieu est dans le mariage, Dieu le garde* in February 1861 (*ibidem*, 10 February 1861; *La Revue et Gazette musicale de Paris*, 17 February 1861).
[63] Premiered on 9 May 1857.
[64] Something of a rarity for Thys, *Le pays de Cocagne*'s libretto was by a different person, Pittaud de Forges, and was premiered on 24 May 1862.

before performances, respectively, in the *salon* of Isaac and Émile Pereire on the Place Vendôme and in Rossini's *salon* on the rue Chaussée d'Antin.[65]

Rossini's *salon*, after his return to Paris in 1855, was one of the most interesting musically in the capital and—like so many of those of his colleagues in Nouvelle Athènes—certainly played its role in the growth of *opéra de salon*. He was especially interested in the libretti by Galoppe d'Onquaire: of the four recorded instances of *opéra de salon* in Rossini's home, three are settings of works by that librettist. Weckerlin's *La laitière du Trianon* received its premiere *chez* Rossini on the rue Chaussée d'Antin in December 1858,[66] and there was production of his *Le mariage en poste* during the same season.[67] Galoppe d'Onquaire's *Loin du bruit* was set by Paul Bernard; the premiere in Rossini's *salon* was a clear benefit for the composer: 'Paul Bernard's music . . . was as usual noted for its scenic and melodic qualities, but this time it was like it received a consecration and a baptism to which the high priest of the temple, in person, had wished to associate himself in bestowing his praise and encouragement on our collaborator'.[68] Such praise could go in both directions, and at the end of the performance of *La laitière du Trianon*, when the authors were invited to acknowledge the thanks and applause, Rossini himself was the beneficiary of an *hommage* written by Galoppe d'Onquaire and set by Weckerlin.[69]

Offenbach's legendary *soirées*—first in the Passage Saulnier and then after October 1856 in the rue Laffite—occasionally overlapped with the culture of *opéra de salon* but rarely encompassed works other than those by the host. *Pépito* appeared on 28 March 1854—midway between its appearance at the Théâtre des Variétés in 1853 and its revival at the Bouffes-Parisiens in March

---

[65] For *En état de siège*, the premiere in Beer's own *salon* took place on 18 January 1859 (*Le ménestrel*, 23 January 1859), with the performance in the Orfila *salon* in April the same year (*La Revue et Gazette musicale de Paris*, 17 April 1859); it is possible that the three performers were the same (Gaveaux-Sabatier, Lefort, and Cabel), but only Lefort's name is given in the report of the Orfila performance. *Les roses de M. de Malesherbes* was given in Beer's *salon* on 17 January 1861 (*ibidem*, 20 January 1861; *La Revue et Gazette musicale de Paris* for the same date) and in Rossini's exactly a week later (*ibidem*, 27 January 1861; *Le ménestrel*, 3 February 1861). The cast was the same for both performances: Mira, Gourdin, and Capoul.

[66] *Ibidem*, 19 December 1858; *La Revue et Gazette musicale de Paris*, 26 December 1858.

[67] *Ibidem*, 6 March 1859.

[68] 'la musique de Paul Bernard . . . a été comme toujours remarquée pour ses qualités scéniques et mélodiques, mais cette fois c'était comme une consécration qu'elle venait recevoir et comme un baptême auquel le grand prêtre du temple, en personne, a bien voulu s'associer en prodiguant à notre collaborateur la louange et les encouragemens' (*Le ménestrel*, 10 June 1860).

[69] Weckerlin's *Hommage à Rossini* survives as 'Hommage à Rossini. / à propos chanté après la 1ière représentation / de la Laitière de Trianon chez Rossini / le 18 Décembre 1858 / Paroles de Galoppe d'Onquaire/Musique de J. B. Weckerlin' (Paris, Bibliothèque Nationale de France, MS-14632).

1856.[70] Three years later, now in the rue Laffite, Offenbach put on a parody of Verdi's *Le trouvère* (*Il trovatore*), which had just appeared in Emilien Pacini's French translation at the Opéra, and the *Valse des animaux—La basse cour*, which would be interpolated into Jonas's *Les petits prodiges* later in 1857.[71] There was, however, no *opéra de salon* at this performance, and in general, the performances in Offenbach's home have little in common with the broader culture of *opéra de salon*, even if—as has been seen—some of his early *opérettes* were repurposed for a *salon* context.

Spaces and Patrons 6: Public Spaces

However important were the performances of *opéra de salon* at the homes of composers and performers, they are dwarfed in number by those mounted in public spaces; no fewer than ten public buildings, mostly what would today be called concert halls, were used for the performance of *opéra de salon* before 1870. Table 4.1 gives all the surviving documented performances, together with the names of the promoters, indications of whether they were composer or performer, and the names of the works in question.[72]

---

[70] The event took place on 28 March 1854 (*Le ménestrel*, 2 April 1854).
[71] See *Le Figaro*, 29 March 1857 (the event had taken place the night before). The text from *Le Figaro* is reprinted with commentary in Jean-Claude Yon, ed., *M. Offenbach nous écrit: lettres au Figaro et autres propos* (Paris: Actes Sud and Palazetto Bru Zane, 2019) 69–76.
[72] There is an additional group of *opéras de salon* whose libretti survive in Paris, Archives Nationales, but for which there is no evidence of performance; they may well have been submitted to and approved by the censors but then abandoned. Attributions of the libretti are sometimes unclear, and composers are sometimes not mentioned. They are as follows:

Salle	Date	Composer	Librettist	Title
Herz	1857	Joseph O'Kelly	Jules Montigny	*Stella, ou Un autre Werther*
Herz	1859			*L'oncle Sleek*
Herz	1864		Armand Dubarry	*Favart*
Herz	1864			*Un rendez-vous en Espagne*
Herz	1864	Pierre-Thomas Levassor	Pierre-Thomas Levassor	*Le troupier et la bonne, ou Adelaïde et Vermouth*
Herz	1865	Alfred d'Hack	Louise Sabatier	*Le revenant*
Pleyel	1868	Georges Douay	Francis Tourte	*Les valets modèle[s]*
Herz	1873		Léonie Bonnemessier	*Le commodore*
Érard	1874			*Le chevalier de triste-figure*
Herz	1874		Amélie Perronnet	*Mousseline et Passe-Lacet*

Table 4.1. Performances of *opéra de salon* in concert halls.

Venue	Year	Promoter		Title
Sainte-Cécile	1852	Péan de la Roche-Jagu	C	*Le mariage de hasard*
Herz (T)	1853	Offenbach	C	*Le trésor à Mathurin*
Lyrique (T)	1853	Péan de la Roche-Jagu	C	*La jeunesse de Lully*
Sainte-Cécile	1853	Péan de la Roche-Jagu	C	*La jeunesse de Lully*
Herz (T)	1854	Offenbach	C	*Luc et Lucette*
Érard	1854	Guglielmi	Pvox	*Le docteur vieuxtemps*
Herz (T)	1855	Offenbach	C	*Le décaméron*
Herz	1855	Frères Lionnet	P	*Les revenants bretons*
Herz (T)	1855	Gaveaux-Sabatier	P	*A deux pas de bonheur & La volière*
Herz (T)	1855	Chaudesaigues	Pvox	*Le coffret de Saint-Domingue*
Lyrique [T]	1856	Savary	L	*Au pied du mur*
Souffleto	1856	Duclos & Briand	P	*A deux pas de bonheur*
Herz	1856	Gaveaux-Sabatier	P	*Tout est bien qui finit bien*
Herz	1857	? Mira		*Le mariage en poste*
Souffleto	1857	Péan de la Roche-Jagu	C	*Simple et coquette*
Herz	1857	Gaveaux-Sabatier	P	*Suzanne*
Herz	1857	Lefébure-Wély	P	*Les revenants bretons*
Herz	1858	Chaudesaigues (vve)	B	*Les deux aveugles*
Herz	1858	Hocmelle	C	*La mort de Socrate*
Beethoven	1858	Poisot	C	*Les deux billets*
Beethoven	1858	Ritter	C	*Le nègre de madame*
Herz	1858	Lefébure-Wély	P	*L'héritier sans le savoir*
Pleyel	1858	Huet	Ppno	*Le terreurs de M. Peters*
Sainte-Cécile	1858	Heugel	Pub	*L'amour à l'épée*
Beethoven	1859	Archainbaud	P	*Pierrot à Paphos, ou La sérénade interrompue*
Herz	1859	Banderali	P	*Les deux princesses*
Herz	1859	Gaveaux-Sabatier	P	*L'esprit du foyer*
Herz	1860	Weckerlin	C	*Jobin et Nanette*
Herz (T)	1860	Gaveaux-Sabatier	P	*La perruque du bailli*
Herz	1860	Mira	P	*Loin du bruit & Entre deux feux*

Table 4.1. Continued

Venue	Year	Promoter		Title
Herz	1861	Castel	P	Au fond du verre
Herz	1861	Mira	P	L'amour à l'épée
Herz	1862	Péan de la Roche-Jagu	C	La reine de l'onde
Herz	1862	Sabatier-Blot	C	Un mariage per quiproquo
Pleyel	1862	Pfeiffer	C	Le capitaine Roch
Pleyel	1864	Archainbaud	P	Une promenade dans un salon
Érard	1864	Ketterer	Ppno	Une promenade dans un salon
Érard	1865	Perronnet	C	Le compère Loriot
Beethoven	1865	Perry-Biagoli	C	Les matelots du Formidable
Herz	1869	Jacobi	C	Le feu aux poudres
Érard	1869	Lebouc	Pvc	Le capitaine Roch
Pleyel	1870	Pfeiffer	C	Le capitaine Roch

21 P[erformer] (piano; voice; cello); 19 C[omposer]; 1 Pub[lisher]; 1 L[ibrettist]; 1 B[enefit]
[T] = evidence of improvised theatre

Of the forty-one events listed, the majority took place in the concert halls managed by the four principal piano manufacturers: Érard, Herz, Pleyel, and Souffleto. Other venues included the Salle Beethoven, the Salle Sainte-Cécile and the Salle Lyrique. The Salle Beethoven, originally known as the Théâtre Moderne, formed part of the Passage de l'Opéra in the Galerie du Baromètre, housed a wide range of theatrical activities, and in the 1820s had given a home to the Europama, just one of the spaces for the projection of geographical images that were so much in vogue during the Restoration. From 1850 onwards, it functioned as a 250-seat concert hall that could also accommodate *opéra de salon* and, for example, Ida Bruning's visiting Deutsche Theater in 1865.[73] Very little is known about the Salle Sainte-Cécile, housed within the Casino de Paris on the rue du Chaussée d'Antin, beyond descriptions of the concerts that took place there. There was an improvised hall from as early as the late 1830s,[74] and the hall as it was known during the second half of

---

[73] Philippe Chauveau, *Les théâtres parisiens disparus (1402–1986)*, Collection 'Théâtre' (Paris: Amandier, 1999) 387–392.
[74] *Le ménestrel*, 28 January 1838.

the nineteenth century was opened in December 1848, when concerts were held before it was finally complete.[75] The Salle Lyrique, known variously as the École-Lyrique or Salle Moreau-Sainti, on the rue [Louise-Émilie] de La Tour d'Auvergne, was a fully fledged theatre where theatre pupils could practice and the audience was admitted gratis.[76] From 1859, some of its activities were dedicated to the work of the pupils in the *classe de déclamation* at the Conservatoire.

Almost all these venues were in southern Nouvelle Athènes, except for the Salle Érard on the rue du Mail north-east of the Palais-Royal and the Salle Sainte-Cécile in the south-west corner of Nouvelle Athènes; the Salle Souffleto was just south of the Boulevard on the rue Montmartre. Of these, the Salle Herz was far and away the most popular for *opéra de salon*; it was home for twenty-two productions during the period, whereas the next largest were the Salle Pleyel and Salle Érard, with only four each. The Salle Herz was also the largest and moreover the simplest shape of the four halls, which lent itself better to the temporary stages that were often installed for *opéra de salon*. It may also be that Herz offered more advantageous financial arrangements to those who wished to mount concerts, but there is no evidence to support such a claim. The Salle Pleyel relied on using adjacent rooms to accommodate larger audiences, which worked less well for dramatic performances than the single space in the Salle Herz.[77] The Salle Érard was only built in 1860 and was much smaller than the other two halls.[78] Just after a renovation in March 1858, a commentator in *La Revue et Gazette musicale de Paris* described the Salle Herz as the most elegant in the city and wrote that 'its suitable dimensions make it the choice of preference for all those artists who have enough of a reputation to hope to fill it'; he also noted that bookings for the Salle Herz filled up very quickly during the concert season.[79]

Twenty-one of the events listed in table 4.1 were mounted by performers, and this aligns clearly with the broader culture of concerts in Paris during

---

[75] *Ibidem*, 3 December 1848.
[76] Wild, *Dictionnaire des théâtres parisiens*, 124–125.
[77] Reports of these events frequently refer to the *salons* Pleyel or Pleyel-Wolff in the plural for just this reason.
[78] René Beaupain, *La maison Érard: manufacture de pianos, 1780–1859* (Paris: L'Harmattan, 2005).
[79] 'Ses dimensions convenables la font choisir de préférence par tous les artistes qui ont assez de réputation pour espérer de la remplir' (*La Revue et Gazette musicale de Paris*, 14 March 1858). The article was signed 'S. D.', an author whose name has resisted identification.

the Second Empire, where performers took the financial risk of hiring the hall, paying the fees of supporting artists, and undertaking advertising and other management. Almost all the performers took part in the *opéra de salon* that formed part of the evening (invariably the second half), but in a couple of instances, the events were mounted by singers who did not take part in the *opéra de salon* but contributed *romances* and opera arias in other parts of the event (Guglielmi and Charles-Barthélémy Chaudesaigues are two examples).[80] In a few cases, the concerts were mounted by pianists—the other biggest constituency—who performed in the concert but not in the *opéra de salon*: Marie-Honorine-Virginie Huet and Nicolas-Eugène Ketterer;[81] the cellist Charles-Joseph Lebouc also put on a concert including *opéra de salon*.[82] There are further isolated instances of one of the concerts sponsored by the journal *Le ménestrel* exploiting *opéra de salon* (Weckerlin's *L'amour à l'épée*), a benefit for the widow of Chaudesaigues (he died in 1858),[83] and an instance of a non-professional librettist (Savary) using the Salle Lyrique for his *Au pied du mur* set by Collinet, another non-professional, in May 1856.[84]

Table 4.1 also shows the wide range of public places used by composers to put on concerts that included their *opéras de salon*. The Salle Herz, unsurprisingly, was the venue of choice, with Weckerlin,[85] Jacobi,[86] Maria Sabatier-Blot,[87] and Eudoxe-Françoise Péan de la Roche-Jagu all mounting performances there. But the semi-permanent seating and stage layout in the Salle Beethoven was also attractive; Théodore Ritter's *Le nègre de madame* was performed there in 1858,[88] and Poisot mounted his *Les deux billets* there

---

[80] Guglielmi (details of his biography are unknown) put on a performance of Nadaud's *Le docteur vieuxtemps* in the Salle Érard in April 1854 (*ibidem*, 7 May 1854), and Chaudesaigues mounted the only known public performance of Clapisson's *Le coffret de Saint-Domingue* in the Salle Herz in March 1855 (*ibidem*, 4 March 1855).

[81] Huet's contribution was a performance in the Salle Pleyel of Poisot's *Les terreurs de M. Peters* in April 1858 (*ibidem*, 18 April and 2 May 1858), and Ketterer offered Alfred Mutel's *Une promenade dans un salon* in the Salle Érard in April 1864 (*ibidem*, 10 April 1864).

[82] The performance took place on 30 April 1869 and included Pfeiffer's *opéra de salon Le capitaine Roch* (*ibidem*, 25 April and 16 May 1869).

[83] *Le ménestrel*, 28 March 1858 (the event took place exactly a week before).

[84] *Ibidem*, 13 May 1856.

[85] *Jobin et Nanette* was mounted on 29 March 1860. See *La Revue et Gazette musicale de Paris*, 25 March 1860; *Le ménestrel*, 8 April 1860.

[86] Jacobi was the music director of the Bouffes-Parisiens when he premiered *Le feu aux poudres* at the Salle Herz on 21 March 1869 with a performance team brought directly from his own theatre. See *La Revue et Gazette musicale de Paris*, 4 April 1869.

[87] With a libretto by Adèle Laboureau, *Un mariage per quiproquo* was put on at the Salle Herz on 26 February 1862. See *Le ménestrel*, 2 March 1862.

[88] *La Revue et Gazette musicale de Paris* 19 July 1858 (the performance took place on 9 July).

the same year.[89] Four years later, the Perry-Bagioli brothers, Antoine and Henri, put on their *Les matelots du Formidable*.[90] Occasional performances were offered in the Salle Pleyel and the Salle Érard by Pfeiffer,[91] and Péan de la Roche-Jagu, in acts of desperation, tried out not only a performance in the Salle Souffleto but also in the Salle du Grand Orient on the rue Cadet.[92]

Opéra de salon in public spaces follows many of the patterns of the conventional concert and differs in many ways from the events held in private venues. In the concert hall and other places just mentioned, the event invariably consists of an *opéra de salon* together with either an instrumental component, a vocal element, or sometimes both. The only exceptions were Offenbach's concerts in the Salle Herz, which all involved some sort of literary endeavour, and a couple of further scattered events; for example, when Mira put on a performance of Weckerlin's *L'amour à l'épée* in 1861, also in the Salle Herz, it was prefaced by a '*proverbe*', *Le tout est de s'entendre* by Pierre-Frédéric-Eugène Verconsin,[93] and in February the following year, Péan de la Roche-Jagu's *La reine de l'onde* was paired with a reading by the author of Théodore Leclerc's *Le dernier acte de bienfaisance de M. Scribe*.[94] But for the overwhelming majority of *opéra de salon* performances in public places, the literary dimension that was so important in private performances was almost entirely absent.

Events that included *opéra de salon* could be very simple. For example, when Mme Lefébure-Wély put on a concert April 1857 with Mme Ponchard), the second half was dedicated to a performance of Weckerlin's *Les revenants bretons*, which had premiered two years earlier. The *opéra de salon* was prefaced by a single aria for each of the two artists: one from Auber's *Actéon* for Lefébure-Wély and one from Nicolas Isouard's *Cendrillon* for Ponchard. Although the Lionnet brothers took the two male roles in *Les revenants bretons*, they appear not to have participated in the first part of the

---

[89] The date is not clear, but the performance was recorded *ibidem*, 25 April 1858.
[90] 4 April 1865. See *ibidem*, 9 April 1865.
[91] Pfeiffer put on two performances of his *Le capitaine Roch* in the Salle Pleyel on 7 April 1862 (*ibidem*, 30 March and 13 April 1862) and 4 April 1870 (*ibidem*, 10 April 1870), as well as a further performance in the Salle Érard on 30 April 1869 (*ibidem*, 25 April and 16 May 1869).
[92] Both were performances of her *Simple et coquette*, in March 1857 (*ibidem*, 15 March 1857) and 28 December 1862 (*ibidem*, 11 January 1862); the latter performance may well have been fragmentary.
[93] The text seems not to have survived, although Verconsin also wrote the libretto to Hignard's *A la porte*. For the Mira performance, see *La Revue et Gazette musicale de Paris*, 27 January 1861; for the Hignard, see *Le ménestrel*, 9 June 1861.
[94] See Théodore Leclerc, *Biographie et pensées* (Paris: Richard, 1862) 20–21. *La Revue et Gazette musicale de Paris*, 9 February 1862.

performance.[95] Instrumental music could replace vocal music, as in the performance of Pfeiffer's *Le capitaine Roch* given in the Salle Pleyel in April 1862. Here the composer performed his first piano trio with the violinist Antoine Kontski and Lebouc and a couple of solo numbers, Mendelssohn's *Fantasie*, op. 28 (the *Sonate écossaise*), and the so-called *Andante Favori* attributed to Mozart but in fact by François (Franz) Bendel.[96]

Performances that mixed both instrumental and vocal solos with *opéra de salon* were rarer and usually the result of a special event. Thus, the forty-fifth concert sponsored by the journal *Le ménestrel*, given on 21 March 1858 in the Salle Sainte-Cécile, presented Weckerlin's *L'amour à l'épée* in its second half. But this was prefaced by a cornucopia of instrumental and vocal music freely intermingled. The instrumental works consisted of Camillo Sivori's apparently unpublished *Fantaisie* for violin and piano on Donizetti's *Lucia de Lammermoor*, played by the composer, and Weber's overture to *Oberon* arranged for two pianos, played by Louis Diemer and Guiraud. Marie-Caroline Miolan-Carvalho sang the variations on *Le carnaval de Venise*, and Stockhausen sang an aria from Boieldieu's *La fête du village voisin* and—standing in for the indisposed Pierre-Jules Michot—Giovanni Battista Pergolesi's *Tre giorni* and an unidentified *Lied* by Franz Schubert. Meillet sang an aria from Gounod's *Le médecin malgré lui*, and Mathilde-Jeanne Chambard (known as Mme Cambardi) sang an aria from *La traviata*. This concert was much more elaborate than most, almost certainly the result of its status as an event sponsored by *Le ménestrel*.[97]

Opéra de salon behaved very differently in the hands of men of letters and those of composers, librettists, and performers; belletrists, publishers, and authors rubbed shoulders with art historians, artists, and sculptors as the genre found a natural home in the literary, poetic, and dramatic environments that were already in place before *opéra de salon* emerged as a key part of Parisian theatrical culture. Despite a couple of exceptions—Gaveaux-Sabatier and especially Duprez—professional musicians for the most part did not enjoy the luxury of living in *lieux* that could be repurposed as *espaces* that could support performances, audiences, and the attendant

---

[95] *Ibidem*, 12 April 1857; *Le ménestrel*, 26 April 1857.
[96] *La Revue et Gazette musicale de Paris* and *Le ménestrel*, 2 March 1862.
[97] *Ibidem*, 28 March 1858.

infrastructure. Composers and performers were at the forefront of the move to exploit the concert hall and some associated performance spaces for various types of concerts, especially those that could engage with *opéra de salon*. In this regard, the relationship between regulated theatre, public performance space, and genres conceived for the private and intimate stood at its most complex.

5
Contexts and Cultivation

Contexts for Creation

Opéra de salon was not created or cultivated in a vacuum. It emerged from, and its creators, recreators, and consumers acted within, a number of related contexts. While the most obvious of these is the *salon* concert, the most important is perhaps the broader tradition of drama outside the theatre, what was known as *théâtre de société*. *Théâtre de société* encompassed a vast generic range, but two of these—the *charade* and the *proverbe*—were critical for the emergence of *opéra de salon*, and an account of this follows a discussion of the *salon* concert in this chapter.

Moving between performances in the concert hall, studio, *salon*, and *parloir*, *opéra de salon* transcended the permeable boundaries of what contemporary commentators considered the private. This permeability may be further problematized by the investigation of two linked themes that encompass the entire culture of the *opéra de salon*. First, *opéra de salon* followed a course largely parallel to that of the repertory of the regulated theatres—Opéra-Comique, Théâtre-Lyrique, and theatres for *opérette* and related genres, to say nothing of *vaudeville*. In general, there were no points at which the genre or those who supported it overlapped with the established theatres; however, there are occasional but telling examples of how *opéra de salon* and the agents involved with its creation and reception did in fact engage with these institutions that further illuminate its cultural significance. Second, in its colonization of *salon* space, *opéra de salon* was aligned with other types of activity promoted there, and as *opéra de salon* emerged in 1853, it collided with a precisely coterminous *salon* vogue for the *séance*, turning tables, and the visual, verbal, and musical involvement with the other world. Routes were established between the *séance* and *vaudeville* in the regulated theatre and then back to *opéra de salon*.

Salons—Concerts

There is an abundance of theatrical and musical contexts for the composition of *opéra de salon*. The best known within the domain of music history is the *salon* concert.[1] By the Second Empire, the format of these had become conventionalized in that they usually consisted of a *partie instrumentale* and a *partie vocale*. The singers were almost always artists from the major theatres in the capital, and instrumentalists could be either visiting soloists and local players from the Opéra orchestras or the Société des Concerts du Conservatoire (there was a large overlap between the two groups), as well as more formalized ensembles. These concerts were regularly reviewed in the music press, and such publicity added lustre to the reputation of the concert hall or *salon*, its *salonnière*, and its activities.

An example of a concert in one of the venues favoured for *opéra de salon*—the Salle Herz—was given by the Italian violinist Antonio Bazzini in May 1858.[2] Although he spent most of his early career touring, Bazzini spent the years 1852–1863 in Paris, so he was very much a local host for this concert. He was supported by three vocal artists: the soprano Anne-Euphrasie Poinsot, the tenor Italo Gardoni, and the baritone Jean Baptiste Portehaut. Poinsot was a key player at the Opéra, taking leading roles in classics: Alice in Meyerbeer's *Robert le diable*, Valentine in his *Les Huguenots*, and Berthe in his *Le prophète*.[3] Portehaut was also at the Opéra but took such minor roles as Leuthold in *Guillaume Tell*, Raimbaud in Rossini's *Le comte Ory*, Albert in Halévy's *La juive* and De Retz in *Les Huguenots*.[4] A decade before, Gardoni had been employed at both the Opéra and the Théâtre-Italien, but in the late 1850s, he was shuttling back and forth between London and Paris and is not

---

[1] The best general account of concerts in the *salon* is David Tunley, *Salons, Singers and Songs: A Background to Romantic French Song, 1830–1870* (Aldershot: Ashgate, 2002) 18–41. The Italian dimension to the *romance* in the *salon* has received a good deal of attention; see Mary Ann Smart, 'Parlor Games: Italian Music and Italian Politics in the Parisian Salon', *19th-Century Music* 34 (2010) 39–60; reprinted in shortened and slightly edited form in idem, *Waiting for Verdi: Opera and Political Opinion in Nineteenth-Century Italy, 1815–1848* (Los Angeles: University of California Press, 2018) 128–151; the revision does not, however, take account of the much wider-ranging account of Italian song in Paris in the same period in Helen Louise Macfarlane, '"*Il faut savoir l'italien pour déchiffrer une romance française*": Italian Presence in the French Romance, 1800–1850' (PhD diss., University of Southampton, 2014).

[2] Giovanni Carli Ballola and Roberta Montemorra Marvin, "Bazzini, Antonio," *Grove Music Online*, 2001 (https://www.oxfordmusiconline.com/grovemusic/view/10.1093/gmo/9781561592 630.001.0001/omo-9781561592630-e-0000002403); Karl-Josef Kutsch and Leo Riemens, *Großes Sängerlexikon*, 4 vols. (Bern: Francke, 1987–1994; 4th ed., 7 vols., Munich: Saur, 2003) 2:1266.

[3] Pierre, *Le Conservatoire*, 2:831.

[4] 'Jean-Baptiste PORTEHAUT, *L'art Lyrique français* (https://www.artlyriquefr.fr/personnages/Portehaut.html).

formally listed among the members of either house; neither was he involved in any of the performances of Verdi in the early 1850s at which the composer took such offence; he was in fact singled out as the sort of artist the composer did not want in his performances.[5]

The repertory for the concert fell exactly into the two parts just described. First was a *partie vocale* which, despite Verdi's strictures, included the following:

Giuseppe Verdi, 'Duo de *Traviata*'. ('Ah no, severo scritto mi lasciava' [act ii] or 'Parigi, o cara, noi lasceremo' [act iii]) sung by Poinsot and Gardoni.

Giuseppe Verdi, 'Air de *Trovatore*' ('Di tale amor' [act i] or 'D'amor sull' ali rosee' [act iv]), Poinsot.

Portehaut then sang an extract from:

Alfred Mutel, *Le credo des 4 saisons: chant philosophique à 4 voix*, poésie de Méry (Paris: Girod, [1864]).

The *partie instrumentale* was made up of works for violin and piano composed and performed by Bazzini himself:

Antonio Bazzini, *Fantaisie sur des motifs favoris de l'opéra 'Anna Bolena' de Donizetti, pour violon avec acompaniment de piano*, op. 24 (Paris: Richault, [1855]).

Antonio Bazzini, *L'Absence! mélodie pour violon avec accompagnement de piano*, op. 22 (Paris: Richault, [1852]).

Antonio Bazzini, *Les abeilles, 6 Morceaux caractéristiques pour le violon avec accompagnement de piano*, op. 34/2 (Paris: Richault, [1869, and therefore unpublished at the time of the concert]).

Antonio Bazzini, *La Ronde des latins . . . Scherzo fantastique pour violon avec accompt de piano*, op. 25 (Paris: Richault, [1852]).

Antonio Bazzini, Unidentifed *Serenade* for violin and piano.

Keyboard support for the whole evening was provided by Grégoire-Marc-Félix Rocheblanche, known as Véronge de la Nux. A graduate of the

---

[5] Letter from Giuseppe Verdi to Tito Ricordi, 7 November 1853, cited in Ruben Vernazza, 'Verdi e il Théâtre Italien di Parigi (1845–1856)' (PhD diss., Université de Tours and Università degli Studi de Milano, 2018) 125.

Conservatoire, he was a successful piano teacher in Paris, and his son, Paul, was a successful composer of *romances* and small piano works in the 1870s and 1880s.[6] The father was exactly the type of performer who took such a role; even when a keyboard soloist gave such a concert, the *partie vocale* would be accompanied by the sort of staff accompanist de la Nux (*père*) represented; Émile Prudent or Henri Herz did not accompany singers and only played in chamber music—usually Austro-German or Austro-German-influenced—where the piano had a soloistic role.[7]

Such concerts as Bazzini's were replicated in the *salon*. Cathinka de Dietz had been a successful touring pianist in the late 1830s and 1840s; she was Bavarian and had studied with Johann Nepomuk Hummel in Weimar and with Friedrich Kalkbrenner in Paris supported by an award from the Bavarian royal court. Throughout her career, she had cultivated courtly relationships assiduously and succeeded in being simultaneously named *Kammervirtuosin* to the queen of Bavaria and lady-in-waiting and pianist to the queen of France; she targeted her compositions with great precision, including dedications to Queen Victoria, the prince regent, and the tsarina of Russia. Clara Schumann wrote unflatteringly of her (they were almost exact contemporaries), claiming that de Dietz only played Hummel and Kalkbrenner (she regularly played Mozart, Beethoven, Schubert, and Liszt). On her marriage in 1847 to William Mackenzie Shaw, the director of the Antwerp and Rotterdam Railway, the couple established themselves in an *haut-bourgeois* villa in Saint-Germain-en-Laye; there Cathinka Mackenzie de Dietz, as she now styled herself, established a *salon*, and as *salonnière*, she sat between the *haute bourgeoisie* and those musicians who derived prestige from mounting concerts for their own benefit.[8]

De Dietz continued to perform into the 1860s, but in March 1858, she hosted a *matinée* to showcase the pianist Émilie Horst de Passardi, a pupil of Adolf Henselt in Saint Petersburg who had recently arrived in Paris. The latter played two works by Émile Albert, his *Études mélodiques*, op. 56, and his *Chanson espagnol*, op. 49, which were warmly received.[9] The *partie*

---

[6] Pierre, *Le Conservatoire*, 2:125.
[7] The event was described in *La Revue de Gazette musicale de Paris* and *Le ménestrel*, both on 9 May 1858.
[8] This paragraph is based on Heike Frey and Christiane Barlag, 'Dietz, von Dietz, de Dietz, Diez, Cathinka, Kathinka, verh. Mackenzie de Dietz', *Europäische Instrumentalistinnen des 18. und 19. Jahrhunderts*, Sophie Drinker Institut für Musikwissenschaftliche Frauen- und Geschlechterforschung (https://www.sophie-drinker-institut.de/dietz-cathinka).
[9] Émile Albert, *Études mélodiques pour piano, op. 56*, 2 vols. (Paris: Brandus et Dufour, 1858); idem, *Chanson espagnole transcrite et variée pour piano, op. 49* (Paris: Brandus, 1856). For Albert's career, see Fétis, *Biographie universelle des musiciens*, Suppl. 1:10. Horst de Passardi gave a couple

instrumentale of the concert was shared with the veteran violinist Antoine Bessems, established in Paris since 1852, who played a number of his own compositions whose titles were not recorded.[10] The *partie vocale* of the concert is more difficult to analyse: the two artists, Émile Fleury and Marie Bosc, resist identification, and the only work mentioned is an aria from Ferdinand Hérold's *Zampa*, sung by Fleury. The imprecision and incompleteness in the press are testimony to the intimacy of the event and, possibly because of the liminal status of Saint-Germain-en-Laye, to its intellectual and geographical purview, but this reveals clearly how the *salon* concert shared characteristics with those more public events in the concert hall.[11]

Théâtre de société

Equally important as part of the framework for *opéra de salon* was what was known as *théâtre de société*: the performance of plays in private spaces ranging from the most modest *parloir* to the finest *salon*.[12] Specific works were written for these types of performances, in the same way as *opéra de salon*, and collections of a single author's *théâtre de société* were published in profusion; Méry published two such collections in 1861 and 1865, for example.[13] Generic types within *théâtre de société* were as varied as in any regulated theatre, but two very popular modes were the *charade* and the *proverbe*. While the first overlapped with music to a certain degree, *proverbes* were a key link between *théâtre de société* and *opéra de salon*. Theatrical performances in non-urban *chateaux* had been known since the eighteenth century, and the nineteenth-century example of the Abbaye de Royaumont (around 50 kilometres north of Paris) was perhaps the best known, not least

---

of other concerts in Paris and settled as a teacher in the city, where she also published a handful of small-scale piano works.

[10] *Ibidem*, 1:85.
[11] The concert was reviewed in *La Revue et Gazette musicale de Paris*, 4 April 1858, and had taken place on 28 March.
[12] There is a large literature on *théâtre de société*, a term that is significantly broader in scope than *opéra de salon*; while the latter can be aligned very clearly with a well-defined repertory, *théâtre de société* is a much broader phenomenon, embracing both *charades* and *proverbes*, discussed below, and *opéra de salon* itself. See the excellent, but even now more than ten years old, collection of essays Yon and Le Gonidec, *Tréteaux et paravents*, and especially Yon's introduction, 'Le théâtre de société au xixe siècle', 13–27.
[13] Méry, *Théâtre de salon*; idem, *Nouveau théâtre de salon*. See also Stéphane Desvignes, 'Le *Théâtre de salon* de Joseph Méry, ou Les délices de l'idéal', *Tréteaux et paravents: le théâtre de société au xixe siècle*, ed. Jean-Claude Yon and Nathalie Le Gonidec (Paris: Créphis, 2012), 151–162.

because among the works performed between 1834 and 1840 was Bellini's *I Puritani* and because the composer Friedrich von Flotow had premiered some of his earliest works there: *Rob-Roy* and *Sérafine* were premiered at Royaumont in 1836, and his *Le comte de Saint-Megrin* was given there in 1838.[14] The latter work was also performed at the Parisian Théâtre de la Renaissance in 1840, which had enjoyed a precarious existence since 1838 and where Flotow had already premiered three works as he established the beginnings of a career that a decade later would result in the worldwide success of *Martha*.[15]

Flotow's *Rob-Roy* was also revived in Paris, but at the most prestigious *théâtre de société* in the private home of the Comte de Castellane.[16] This was almost exactly coterminous with the rural performances at Royaumont and apparently under the direction of Sophie Gay and the Duchesse d'Abrantès (Laure-Adelaïde-Constance Junot [née Permon] d'Abrantès), both of whom possessed literary and theatrical ambitions, if not achievements. Gay's daughter, Delphine, has already appeared in connection with the performances of *opéra de salon* in the home of her husband, Emile de Girardin. Unique at its time, the theatre that Castellane built in the garden of his home must have been the model for Duprez's theatre twenty years later, discussed in chapter 4. Flotow also wrote a work specifically for Castellane's theatre, the more ambitious two-act *Alice* in April 1837, just as he was starting to work in the regulated theatre at the Théâtre du Palais-Royal. There is no evidence of further operatic endeavour at the Théâtre Castellane, but a full account of its theatrical and musical repertory is still awaited.

The repertory of *théâtre de société* encompassed readings of plays in advance of their appearance on the regulated stage (this fundamental difference from *opéra de salon* has already been noted) but also of *vaudevilles*,

---

[14] See Yon, 'Des tréteaux dans une abbaye'. A full account of the performances at Royaumont is awaited, but Flotow's works there are listed in Peter Cohen, 'Flotow, Friedrich (Adolf Ferdinand) Freiherr von', *Grove Music Online*, 2001 (https://www.oxfordmusiconline.com/grovemusic/view/10.1093/gmo/9781561592630.001.0001/omo-9781561592630-e-0000043161). There is a little more detail on repertory in Le Gonidec, 'Le théâtre de Royaumont', *Tréteaux et paravents: le théâtre de société au xixe siècle*, ed. Jean-Claude Yon and Nathalie Le Gonidec (Paris: Créphis, 2012) 135–148.
[15] For Flotow's work at the Théâtre de la Renaissance, see Mark Everist, 'Theatres of Litigation: Stage Music at the Théâtre de la Renaissance, 1838–1840', *Cambridge Opera Journal* 16 (2004) 133–162; and idem, 'Donizetti and Wagner: *opéra de genre* at the Théâtre de la Renaissance'. *Giacomo Meyerbeer and Music Drama in 19th-Century Paris*, Variorum Collected Studies Series CS805 (Aldershot: Ashgate, 2005) 309–341.
[16] Sophie-Anne Leterrier, 'Le théâtre de Castellane: une exclusivité parisienne?', *Tréteaux et paravents: le théâtre de société au xixe siècle*, ed. Jean-Claude Yon and Nathalie Le Gonidec (Paris: Créphis, 2012) 103–116.

improvised scenes, and two specific categories: the *charade* and the *proverbe*. Each of these subgenres of *théâtre de société* had a different relationship with *opéra de salon*; some were published in similar locations—journals for young women, in particular—or shared terminological or structural similarities with *opéra de salon*.

Vaudeville is a key precursor not only to *opéra de salon* but also to the wider repertory of *opérette*. Its music, for the most part, is borrowed from pre-existing sources: other *vaudevilles*, *opéras comiques*, *romances*, the *airs* indexed in the *Clé du caveau*, instrumental works taken from the stage, and others. It was a genre exploited on several Parisian stages throughout the nineteenth century: the Théâtres de la Gaîté, des Variétés, du Palais-Royal, des Nouveautés, and so on. Like *opéra de salon*, it found its way into journals dedicated to young women, in this case, *Le journal des jeunes personnes*, which—although it was founded the same year as *Le journal des demoiselles* and published vast amounts of music—did not publish *opéras de salon*.[17] In 1843, *Le journal des jeunes personnes* published a *vaudeville* by Nicolas-Auguste Dubois titled *La réconciliation*.[18] It was carefully tailored to its environment: the cast consists of five characters—Mme de Merteuil, her two daughters, and two of their female friends from the village—and the scene is set in the garden of the de Merteuil *chateau*. The cast is clearly designed for a mother and up to four daughters, and the action takes place in ten scenes with twelve musical numbers borrowed from *romance*, *opéra*, *opéra comique*, and other *vaudeville*, some of which were indexed in the *Clé du caveau*. The origins are shown in table 5.1.

Apart from its all-female cast, *La réconciliation* behaves in much the same way as any *vaudeville* premiered in the previous half century. And while *vaudeville* continued at the regulated theatre while *opéra de salon* emerged and developed, there is very little sense of librettists and composers of *opéra de salon* taking any further interest in *vaudeville*; the only exception is the use of a terminal *vaudeville* (where the term is derived from a very different tradition from the genre of *vaudeville*) in *opéra de salon*, which triggered—especially in the works of Antoine de Rocheblave—the generic descriptor *vaudeville*, but as in the case of all *opéra de salon*, there was no question of

---

[17] See, however, the comments on the *comédie mêlée de couplets* entitled *Les suites d'une indiscrétion*, libretto by Mme Ferdinand Huard and music by Joseph-Victor-Antoine Blancou, in chapter 6.
[18] *Le journal des jeunes personnes* 13 (1843) 205–215.

Table 5.1. Sources for music in Nicolas-Auguste Dubois, *La réconciliation*.

	La réconciliation incipit	Cue	Source
1	Sans repliquer / Par un avis contraire	*Air*: Je t'aimerai (Blangini)	Henri-Jean Rigel, 'Je t'aimerai' (Blangini is a misattribution)
2	Quand je dois fuir en ce moment	*Air*: Ce que j'éprouve en vous voyant (Romagnesi)	Antoine Romagnesi, 'Ce que j'éprouve' 1819 CdC 1954
3	Pour toi, de la rose nouvelle	*Vaudeville, l'Homme vert*	Rodolphe Kreutzer, *Jadis et aujourd'hui*, opéra comique 1808
4	Aussi léger qu'un papillon	*Air: Vaudeville, Petit courrier*	Charles-François-Jean-Baptiste Moreau de Commagny and Jean-Nicolas Bouilly, *Le petit courrier, ou Comme les femmes se vengent*, comédie-vaudeville 1809
5	O douleur! O regrets	*Air: Vaudeville, Michel et Christine*	Eugène Scribe and Jean-Henri Dupin, *Michel et Christine*, comédie-vaudeville 1821
6	Il va tomber ce bosquet tutélaire	*Air: Téniers*	Joseph Pain, *Teniers*, comédie-vaudeville 1800
7	Là, chaque soir, de notre âme contente	*Air*: Te souviens-tu?	Joseph-Denis Doche, 'Te souviens-tu?' 1817
8	De la bonté parfait modèle	*Air*: De ma Céline amant modeste	CdC 1924
9	Mon premier bien est l'espoir	*Air*: Dans de caster, dame de haut lignage	?
10	Pour satisfaire un vain caprice	*Air*: Des plaisirs permis à la terre	Rodolphe Kreutzer, *Aristippe*, opéra 1808
11	Allons, plus de discorde	*Air*: Honneur à la musique	CdC 1834
12	Chacun ici-bas se tourmente	*Air: Vaudeville, Partie et revanche*	Eugène Scribe, Francis Cornu, and Nicolas Brazier, *Partie et revanche*, comédie-vaudeville 1823

borrowing pre-existing music. Rocheblave wrote five *opéras de salon* between 1860 and 1865, all to libretti by Boisgontier) and all in *Le journal des demoiselles*. Of the five, two are dubbed *vaudeville*, and both end with a *vaudeville* ensemble where each character sings a strophe, and the ensemble contributes the chorus after each.

Charade

The *charade* could take on an importance out of all proportion to its perceived content. For example, when the imperial family was at Compiègne for Christmas 1863, the playwright Ponsard was commissioned to write a *charade* for the family and entourage (around one hundred people). Ponsard had swept to prominence in 1843 with his *Lucrèce* and was a significant presence on the Parisian stage for a quarter of a century; by 1863, he was a household name and an obvious candidate for the honour of writing for the imperial family.[19] Ponsard's *charade* was titled *Harmonie* and was parsed for the purposes of the amusement as *Arme* (weapon) and *Au nid* (in the nest).[20] Each of the elements (*arme* and *au nid*) was the subject of a *tableau*: the first titled *Un chevalier arme un néophyte* and the second *L'amour au nid*, the latter divided in no fewer than five scenes. The first *tableau* had a cast of seven and the second a cast of six; all thirteen characters joined *La muse* in the third *tableau*, which depicted the entire word of the title: *Harmonie*. Music played a key role throughout and, as in *opéra de salon*, was performed at a single keyboard, by Princesse de Caraman-Chimay (Marie-Joséphine-Anatole de Montesquiou-Fézensac). Both of the first two *tableaux* opened with music, and there were musical accompaniments—marked either *guérriere*, *douce*, or *pastorale*—throughout the work, none of which appears to have survived, nor has their attribution; they function in ways analogous to *mélodrame*. The final *tableau*, dedicated to *Harmonie*, consists simply of a *choeur général*. In its use of thirteen characters, inclusion of music and stage sets (prepared by no less a figure than the renovator of Vézelay, Notre-Dame, the *collégiale* in Semu-en-Auxois, and elsewhere, Eugène-Emmanuel Viollet-le-Duc), and a structure consisting of seven scenes and three *tableaux*, *Harmonie* (*Arme–Au nid*) is as far removed from the *devinette* played in front of the fire in a *petit-bourgeois* household as possible. But its characteristics and, clearly, its performance context, align it closely with *opéra de salon*.

Even closer to the performance context of *opéra de salon* were the *charades* published in such journals as *Le musée de familles: lectures du soir*, which had been founded by Samuel-Henry Berthoud in 1833. After considerable

---

[19] Dominique Saint-Pierre, "PONSARD François", in (dir.), *Dictionnaire historique des académiciens de Lyon 1700–2016*, ed. Dominique Saint-Pierre (Lyon: Éditions de l'Académie, 2017) 1059–1060.
[20] HARMONIE/(ARME—AU NID)/CHARADE EN TROIS TABLEAUX/PAR M. PONSARD/JOUÉE AU PALAIS DE COMPIÈGNE/EN PRÉSENCE DE LEURS MAJESTÉS/LE 15 DÉCEMBRE 1863/.../PARIS/IMPRIMERIE IMPÉRIALE/-/M DCCC LXIII.

financial difficulty, *Le musée des familles* was picked up in 1849 by Pitre-Chevalier, already identified in the previous chapter as a promoter of *opéra de salon* in the 1850s and 1860s. *Le musée des familles* was aimed at families of modest means—the *petit-* and *moyen-bourgeois*—and accordingly published a wide range of articles of general interest with a strong religious bias, avoiding society news and politics but also serving as a springboard for the *feuilleton* publication of works by Honoré de Balzac, Dumas *père*, Hugo, Alphonse de Lamartine and Jules Verne.[21] It also published short plays for performances at home, and two of the most popular forms of these plays were *charades*—which, as has been seen, encoded a single word embodied in a number of ways of reading its syllables—and *proverbes*, in which the *proverbe* served as the basis for the intrigue and was usually pronounced formally as the last line of the play.

At the height of the enthusiasm for *opéra de salon* in the late 1850s, *Le musée des familles* published a *charade* in which the word *boisson* (drink) was parsed as *bois* (wood) and *son* (sound).[22] The *charade* is in three 'acts': the first an ode in verse, the second a monologue in prose, and the third a prose dialogue between the characters Simon and Mathias. There are close connections between the composition of this *charade* and contemporary *opéra de salon* demonstrating that the origins of the genre and the genre itself existed alongside each other at least until 1860. The three 'acts' of the *charade* were written by three figures well known in the cultivation of *opéra de salon*: Anaïs Ségalas, Pitre-Chevalier himself, and Verconsin. Ségalas had written the libretto to Durand's 1856 *Le miroir du diable* and must have been behind the two performances in the *salon* of her brother-in-law, the doctor Pierre-Salomon Ségalas, in 1856 and 1864 and inscribed at the centre of the discourse around *opéra de salon* and the homes of medical professionals.[23] The *Boisson charade* had closer points of contact with music as well: the first act is declaimed by La Muse, who introduces the poem and 'stands up next to the piano and recites the following ode'. More strikingly, Pitre-Chevalier's second act ends with a note: 'N.B. This second act may also be performed with song and with [instrumental] music'. Now, the nature of the musical interventions is far from clear: there is no poetry for song in the text, nor

---

[21] See Jean-Louis Mongin, *Jules Verne et le 'Musée des familles'*, Bibliothèque du Rocambole: Magasin du Club Verne 3 (Amiens: AARP–Centre Rocambole; Encrage, 2013).

[22] *Le musée des familles* 26 (1859) 259–264; the solution to the *charade* was given *ibidem*, 288.

[23] The two performances took place in early March 1856 and early April 1864; see *Le ménestrel*, 9 March 1856, and *Le monde illustré*, respectively.

Table 5.2. *Opéra de salon* based on *proverbes*.

Title	Composer	Librettist	Generic descriptor	Date
A deux pas de bonheur	Godefroid	Beauvoir	*proverbe lyrique*	1855
Jaloux de soi	Comtesse Perrière-Pilté	Comtesse Perrière-Pilté	*proverbe lyrique*	1856
Qui va à la chasse perd sa place	Bergson	Montigny	*proverbe musical*	1859
Tout chemin mène à Rome	Duc de Massa	Duc de Massa	*opéra comique*	1860
L'habit ne fait pas le moine	Prévost-Rousseau	Delaunay	*opérette-proverbe*	1864

are there any cues for music as there were, for example, in the Compiègne *Harmonie (Arme–Au nid)*, so exactly how the musical dimensions of this second act were supposed to function remains opaque.

Proverbe

Although there are no examples of *opéra de salon* based on *charades*, there are at least five based explicitly on *proverbes*: André-Philippe-Alfred Regnier, Duc de Massa's *Tout chemin mène à Rome*, Michel Bergson's *Qui va à la chasse perd sa place*, Godefroid's *A deux pas de bonheur*, the Comtesse Perrière-Pilté's *Jaloux de soi*, and Prévost-Rousseau's *L'habit ne fait pas le moine* (table 5.2).[24]

There may be others concealed under other generic descriptors whose libretti are lost and whose proverbial nature cannot therefore be established. Four of the five works in table 5.2 clearly indicate their debt to the *proverbe* tradition through their generic descriptors: *proverbe-lyrique*, *proverbe*

---

[24] For a general introduction to the *proverbe*, see Valentina Ponzetto, 'Définitions et modes d'emploi du proverbe: entre discours paratextuels et représentations métathéâtrales', *Théâtres en liberté du XVIIIe au XXe siècle: genres nouveaux, scènes marginales?*, Actes du colloque international organisé les 31 mai et 1er juin 2013 à l'Université de Genève, ed. Valentina Ponzetto and Sylvain Ledda, Publications Numériques du CÉRÉdI: Actes de colloques et journées d'étude 19 (Rouen: Centre d'Études et de Recherche Éditer/Interpréter, 2017) (http://ceredi.labos.univ-rouen.fr/public/?definitions-et-modes-d-emploi-du.html).

musical, and *opérette-proverbe*. Although Massa's *Tout chemin mène à Rome* is described as an *opéra comique*, its proverbial nature—'All roads lead to Rome'—is beyond doubt. Only a piano-vocal score survives, so it is difficult to say if the work ended with a restatement of the text or the sentiment of the *proverbe*; the final trio 'Oui j'ai donc obtenu sa promesse' makes no reference whatsoever to it, and the absence of a libretto makes tracing a citation of the *proverbe* at the end of the spoken dialogue clearly impossible.[25]

Proverbes circulated in the same way as *charades* and were found in similar types of performance contexts and publications. There were two differences, however: first, they were found more frequently in the regulated theatre in the guise of *vaudeville*; second, when *proverbes* appeared in such publications as *Le journal des demoiselles*, *Le magasin des demoiselles*, and *Le musée des familles*, they frequently made use of music. This greater concern with music clearly maps onto the interest in the *proverbe* in *opéra de salon*. Indeed, Émile Delaunay's *L'habit ne fait pas le moine* shared its *opéra de salon* subject with a *vaudeville* with the same title that had been premiered at the Théâtre du Vaudeville in 1835;[26] the latter, with a much larger cast, in three acts and with twenty-three interpolated songs, otherwise had little to do with Delaunay's *opéra de salon*, and the 1835 *vaudeville* did not even cite the *proverbe* at the end of the work. On the other hand, another *vaudeville*, *Qui mal veut, mal arrive*, by Eugène Roche and H. Chéreault, premiered at the Théâtre des Folies-Dramatiques in 1852,[27] is a conventional one-act *vaudeville*, whose musical profile is largely made up of borrowed *airs* and a very few new songs and whose action is built on the *proverbe* that gives it its title and is the final line of the work.[28]

Proverbes were a staple of such journals as *Le journal des demoiselles*, *Le magasin des demoiselles*, and *Le musée des familles*.[29] *Le musée des familles*

---

[25] TOUT CHEMIN/*MÈNE À*/ROME/Opéra Comique en Un Acte/*Paroles de M*ʳ/Le Comte de Mesgrigny/*Musique de M*ʳ/LE DUC DE MASSA/-/Paris, E. GIROD, Editeur/16, Boulevᵗ Montmartre 85–108.

[26] L'HABIT NE FAIT PAS LE MOINE,/VAUDEVILLE/EN TROIS ACTES,/De MM. Saint-Hilaire et P. Duport/MUSIQUE NOUVELLE/DE MM. Doche, Thénard et This/Représentée pour la première fois, à Paris, sur le théâtre national du Vaudeville,/le 18 août 1835./.../Impr. De J.-R. MEVREAL, passade du Caire, 54.

[27] MAGASIN THÉÂTRAL./PIÈCES NOUVELLES/JOUÉES SUR TOUS LES THÉÂTRES DE PARIS./-/*THÉÂTRE DES FOLIES—[DRAMATIQUES]*./A QUI MAL VEUT, MAL ARRIVE,/Vaudeville proverbe en un acte par MM. E. ROCHE et H. CHÉREAULT/.../PARIS./LIBRAIRIE THÉTRALE, BOULEVARD SAINT-MARTIN, 12./ANCIENNE MAISON MARCHANT./1852.

[28] The work includes twenty-one musical compositions, ranging from the most venerable *airs connus* from the *Clé du caveau* to borrowings from recent music for the stage.

[29] For theatrical *proverbes* in the *salon*, see Valentina Ponzetto, 'Le proverbe dramatique, une voie détournée pour théâtraliser l'irreprésentable?', *Les conditions du théâtre: le théâtralisable et le théâtralisé*, special issue of *Fabula-LhT* 19 (October 2017) (http://www.fabula.org/lht/19/ponze

published, in the same issue as the *Boisson charade* just discussed, a *proverbe* titled *Autant de tués que de blessés* by A. Del-Arno.[30] More ambitious than the *charade* in the same issue, *Autant de tués que de blessés* employs three characters and eleven scenes. Most important, in the stage directions at the beginning of the play are found the instructions for 'a piano, *ad libitum*',[31] and there are moments in the *comédie-proverbe*—as the work is described on its title page—when characters sing ('Il quitte sa belle, / En pensant mourir') in scene 6 and hum the same melody in scene 5.[32] It is unclear if the piano in the stage directions is supposed to accompany these musical interventions; given the musical reference elsewhere in *proverbe*, it seems likely, and the dramatic and musical effect of the scene, with the exception of the music not being specified, is indistinguishable from that of *opéra de salon*.

Other *proverbes*, also from the *Le musée des familles*, go even further in the direction of *opéra de salon* in not only indicating music to be sung in the piece but also providing the music in a supplement to the journal. Charles Wallut gave his *comédie-proverbe* the title *L'officier bleu, ou On a souvent besoin d'un plus petit que soi* when it was published in 1857.[33] In many respects, the work in one act and twelve scenes behaves straightforwardly, and the character Madeline is able to assist the brigadier Cincinnatus in matters of love to the extent that she is able to end the play with the *proverbe* declaimed verbatim.[34] But in scene 9, dedicated to just the characters Jacques and Marie, the latter sings a pair of *couplets*, whose music is attributed to Bessems and which was published in the supplement titled *Modes vraies* for April 1857;[35] here the *proverbe* is completely indistinguishable from *opéra de salon*, and Wallut would go on to write the libretto for Marcellus Müller's *Les idées de M. Pampelune* in 1874.[36]

---

tto.html); for the specifically nineteenth-century experience, see Olivier Bara, 'Des proverbes dans un fauteuil: un genre médiatique?' (unpublished typescript, 2014) (http://etudes-romantiques.ish-lyon.cnrs.fr/wa_files/Bara.pdf).

[30] 'LE SPECTACLE EN FAMILLE./AUTANT DE TUÉS QUE DE BLESSÉS .../COMÉDIE-PROVERBE EN UN ACTE', *Le musée des familles* 26 (1859) 41–48.
[31] *Ibidem*, 42.
[32] *Ibidem*, 46, 44.
[33] 'LE SPECTACLE EN FAMILLE./ - /L'OFFICIER BLEU, OU ON A SOUVENT BESOIN D'UN PLUS PETIT QUE SOI/-/COMÉDIE-PROVERBE EN UN ACTE', *Le musée des familles* 24 (1857) 17–26.
[34] *Ibidem*, 26.
[35] *Ibidem*, 24.
[36] LES IDÉES/DE/MR PAMPELUNE/Opéra-Comique/en un Acte/Paroles de Ch. WALLUT/Musique de/MARCELLUS MULLER/Paris, Maison G. FLAXLAND./DURAND, SCHOENWERK & CIE/Succeseurs/4, Place de la Madeleine, 4. The work was premiered at the short-lived Théâtre Taitbout, for which see Wild, *Dictionnaire des théâtres parisiens*, 399 (in the 2012 edition).

Opéra de salon and the Regulated Theatre

Although *opéra de salon* and the regulated theatre took parallel paths during the Second Empire, examples of where the two trajectories converge point to how the relationship functions and are well illustrated by one of the very few negative accounts of the genre, published in *La Revue et Gazette musicale de Paris* by Édouard Monnais, writing in 1861 under his *nom de plume*, Paul Smith. He asks:

> Why should one displace genres for no reason and confuse what has been carefully distinguished? *Opéra de salon* has given sufficient evidence, and one knows that there is nothing good to hope from it. Not one of these bastard works has reached the theatre and not one has opened access to its composer. Let us then leave opera in its proper place and let us only bring to the concert whatever has no need of a theatre, sets or costumes, nor of anything that demands dramatic action.[37]

Although Monnais's misunderstanding—or lack of sympathy—focusses on the idea that 'opera' belongs in the theatre and that the 'concert' should avoid the theatrical, he inadvertently dramatizes the nature of the networks in which *opéras de salon*, composers, librettists, and performers were enmeshed. These networks, which sometimes crossed over from the *salon*, studio, *parloir*, and concert hall to the theatre, were so much more complex than Monnais's tidy binary divide—however modern and therefore seductive it may be—suggests.

Different types of agents had different engagements with *opéra de salon* and the regulated theatre. Composers of *opéra de salon* interacted with broader theatrical cultures in widely differing ways. It is certainly true that no work by Nadaud or Manry, for example, reached the regulated theatre and that Poisot's and Weckerlin's only work outside of *opéra de salon* predated the genre (neither returned to the regulated theatre). Hignard, Lecocq, Jonas, and Delibes, however, each produced just a single *opéra de salon* and then moved on to work exclusively in the regulated theatre, while

---

[37] 'Pourquoi déplacer inutilement les genres et confondre ce qui doit être soigneusement distingué? L'épreuve des opéras de salon a été suffisamment faite, et l'on sait qu'il n'y a rien à en espérer de bon. Pas une de ces œuvres bâtardes n'est parvenue au théâtre et n'en a même ouvert l'accès à son auteur. Laissons donc l'opéra en son lieu propre et n'apportons au concert que ce qui n'a besoin ni de théâtre, ni de décors, ni de costumes, ni de tout ce que réclame une action dramatique' (*La Revue et Gazette musicale de Paris*, 19 May 1861).

Offenbach, Duprato and de Rillé successfully kept a foot in both camps. In general, librettists working on *opéra de salon* also worked in the regulated theatre. On the other hand, the *chanteurs* and *cantatrices de salon* had no career there; the only exceptions were very recent Conservatoire graduates or graduands whose connexion to *opéra de salon* was brief and uncommitted. Those who made their careers in *opéra de salon* neither achieved nor sought celebrity in the regulated theatre. It perhaps goes without saying, however, that the members of the same audiences who welcomed *opéra de salon* into their homes were exactly those who populated the Salle Le Peletier, the Théâtre-Italien, and the Opéra-Comique. While the dimensions (number of acts and compositions) put *opéra de salon* at a distance from the regulated theatre—there are only a few exceptions—the genre's register, with its urban or rural comedies of manners, puts it closer to that of the *vaudeville* than even to *opéra comique*, let alone contemporary *grand opéra* or imported Italian *melodramma* with Verdi at its head. And although this also aligned *opéra de salon* with the type of *opérette* that emerged in the mid-1850s, there were almost no examples of transferring works from the *salon* to the *opérette* house and vice versa.

When Pittaud de Forges put on a performance of Offenbach's ten-year-old *Le 66!* to his own libretto at his home in March 1865, he was transferring a work from the regulated theatre—in this case, the Théâtre des Bouffes-Parisiens—into the world of *opéra de salon*.[38] In 1855, Barateau expressed enthusiasm for such a transfer when he wrote that two recent one-act works for the Opéra-Comique—Albert Grisar's *Le chien du jardinier* and Massé's *Miss Fauvette*—'are, assuredly, two *opéras de salon*, easy to put on, and that will be adopted by theatres which from now on will be found in all *chateaux* and in all town houses'.[39] Despite Barateau's eagerness, there is no evidence that either work found a home in a *salon* environment. By and large, the works that were appropriated as *opéras de salon* were already quite old and were by Offenbach or Hervé, who, as theatre directors, were able to deploy their own work with greater ease than other composers and librettists. As is well known, Offenbach was also closely involved with Morny, and performances of *Ba-ta-clan* and *Pépito* were transferred from the Bouffes-Parisiens to Morny's

---

[38] Offenbach's *Le 66!* (Pittaud de Forges had written the libretto himself with Chapelle) had been premiered at the Bouffes-Parisiens on 31 July 1856.
[39] 'sont, assurément, deux opéras de salon, faciles à monter, et dont s'empareront les théâtres qui désormais, se trouveront dans tous les châteaux et dans tous les hôtels' (*Le ménestrel*, 25 February 1855).

residence on the Avenue des Champs-Élysées.[40] But Offenbach also put on shows in his own home, notably *Pépito* in March 1854 only shortly after its premiere at the Théâtre des Variétés and well before it was transferred to the Bouffes-Parisiens.[41] The motivation for the *salon* performance of *Le 66!* clearly stemmed from Pittaud de Forges himself, but Offenbach's *Les deux aveugles* was made available—quite possibly as a gesture of artistic charity—for the benefit of the widow of Chaudesaigues, Rosalie-Emilie Rodolphe,[42] and more typically featured at a *soirée* held by caricaturist and photographer Berthall;[43] these latter performances of *Les deux aveugles* featured both the original artists Berthellier and Étienne Pradeau from the first performance; Sainte-Foy replaced Pradeau at the Berthall *soirée*.

Three further works from three different decades were transferred from a regulated theatrical environment to the less regulated ecosystem of *opéra de salon*. The three were already nomads that had travelled from one regulated theatre to another, so it is hardly surprising that these ended up being employed as *opéras de salon* rather than *Le chien du jardinier* and *Miss Fauvette*, which Barateau had proposed. The three were Jean-Alexandre-Ferdinand Poise's *Bonsoir, voisin*, Pierre-Joseph-Alphonse Varney's *Le moulin joli*, and Grisar's *Les travestissements*.

Poise's *Bonsoir, voisin* had been premiered at the Théâtre-Lyrique in 1853 and had run until 1857 before finding itself the much-admired centrepiece of a *soirée* given by the distinguished urologist Ségalas in his apartments on rue Vendôme;[44] it would also get picked up by the Théâtre des Fantaisies-Parisiennes in 1866. Before its appearance at the home of an otherwise unknown M. Bélanger in 1867,[45] Varney's *Le moulin joli* had been premiered—implausibly—at the Théâtre de la Gaîté in 1849 and then—only slightly less implausibly—at the Folies-Concertantes/Nouvelles in 1859 and the Bouffes-Parisiens in 1862.[46] Even older was Grisar's *Les travestissements*, which had first appeared at the Opéra-Comique as long ago as 1839 and was

---

[40] See *La Revue et Gazette musicale de Paris*, 2 March 1856 (the performance took place on 28 February).

[41] *Pépito* was given in Offenbach's *salons* in the Passage Saulnier on 28 March 1854 (*Le ménestrel*, 2 April 1854).

[42] The performance took place in the Salle Herz in late February or early March 1855 (*La Revue et Gazette musicale de Paris*, 4 March 1855).

[43] The date is again imprecise but was late February or early March 1858 (*ibidem*, 7 March 1858).

[44] *Le monde illustré*, 6 April 1864.

[45] *La Revue et Gazette musicale de Paris*, 9 June 1867.

[46] Varney's *Le moulin joli* is the first in a series of works from the regulated theatre that shape the early history of *opérette*. See the chapter 'Theatres of Revolution' in Everist, *Opérette: The First Twenty-Five Years*.

one of the works picked up by the short-lived Opéra National in 1851. Its appearance at another physician's *soirée*, that of Bourdon, the senior figure at La Charité, in 1857 prefaced its revival at the Folies-Concertantes/Nouvelles the following year.[47]

The three works were chosen with some care. Each in one act only, the largest was Varney's *Le moulin joli*, which had four characters and nine numbers, while both Poise's *Bonsoir voisin* and Grisar's *Les travestissements* deployed only two characters each, with five numbers for the former and six for the latter. All three works, whatever their original performance venues, had atypical structures that made them ideal for appropriation to a context more fitted to *opéra de salon*.

An exception to the repurposing of venerable works from the regulated theatre as *opéras de salon* was Pitre-Chevalier's last event, just a couple of months before his death; the performance took place on 5 April 1863. He mounted Barbier's *Le loup et l'agneau*, which had been premiered with a libretto by Étienne-Hippolyte Chol de Clercy and Hippolyte Messant at the Théâtre Déjazet at the beginning of the same season, 30 September 1862.[48] This more ambitious undertaking, which went beyond Pitre-Chevalier's earlier performances in the 1850s, may have been triggered by his move from the rue Bonaparte to a more opulent apartment on the rue des Écuries-d'Artois in 1861 in the heart of the Faubourg Saint-Honoré.

In some instances, performances in a *salon* context were clearly autopsies of events that had taken place or rehearsals for shows scheduled for performance elsewhere. The attempt to rehabilitate Bizet's *Les pêcheurs de perles* in 1868 after its disappointing run of eighteen performances in 1863 brought another work from the regulated system into the domain of *opéra de salon*,[49] and when Hervé put on *Les folies dramatiques* by Dumanoir (Philippe-François Pinel) and Clairville (Louis-François Nicolaïe), a *vaudeville* with much of Hervé's own new music, on the first of the imperial dates at the Tuileries in 1853, this was the day before the work appeared at the Théâtre du Palais-Royal for the first time.[50] Neither *Les pêcheurs de perles* nor *Les folies dramatiques* was remotely similar in style or content to *opéra de salon*: the former was a much larger work, and the 1868 *salon*

---

[47] The performance in Bourdon's *salons* was given late November or early December 1857 (*Le ménestrel*, 20 December 1857).
[48] *Ibidem*, 12 April 1863.
[49] *Ibidem*, 4 April 1869.
[50] This single example shows how tenuous was Hervé's grip on *opéra de salon* (*ibidem*, 6 March 1853).

production merely offered six extracts; the latter was a *vaudeville* and consisted of five acts, each in a different genre, so Hervé's contribution was just three *airs nouveaux* to the first act, the *opéra seria* in act iii, and almost all the music for the *ballet-pantomime* in act v. Other rehearsals constituted *salon* performances, but there were preparations for events at more prestigious private venues; so when Nadaud's *La volière* was performed at Doucet's home, this was a rehearsal for performances at the home of Mme Orfila and later the Salle Herz and the Louvre.[51]

Traffic in the opposite direction—from *opéra de salon* to the regulated theatre—was even rarer. Although Offenbach reworked his 1853 *opéra de salon Le trésor à Mathurin* as *Le mariage aux lanternes* for the Bouffes-Parisiens in 1857,[52] and while *Jaloux de soi*, the *opéra de salon* for which the Comtesse Perrière-Pilté wrote the libretto and music, found its way to the Fantaisies-Parisiennes in 1873,[53] these are the only two such examples. In the same article in which he had suggested that works by Grisar and Massé could transfer from the Opéra-Comique to the world of *opéra de salon*, Barateau had pointed in the opposite direction: Godefroid's *A deux pas du bonheur*, performed (possibly its premiere) in the *salon* of one of its performers, Levassor, 'would happily augment M. Perrin's repertory' (Émile Perrin was the director of the Opéra-Comique).[54] Such transfers never took place. Given that the regulatory framework for the production of *opéra de salon* was largely non-existent, it is hardly surprising that *opéras de salon* were not transferred to the regulated theatre, since their features would have to have been reviewed to make sure that they adhered to the theatres' licence, and the libretto would have had to have been submitted to the censors (except in the case of *opéras de salon* already mounted at the Salle Herz and other concert halls). While recurring journalistic tropes emphasized the suitability of *opéra de salon* for performance at the Opéra-Comique, coupled with encouragements for its director to hire composers and librettists of *opéra de salon*, such enthusiasm failed to take account of the significant practical

---

[51] The performance took place in Doucet's home at 32 rue de Bac on 10 February 1855 (*Le ménestrel*, 11 and 18 February 1855), the Orfila performance was on 18 February 1855 in her apartments at 45 due Saint-André-des-Arts (*ibidem*, 18 and 25 February 1855), and the performance at the Salle Herz was on 25 April the same year (*ibidem*, 22 April 1855). *La volière* had by then already appeared at the Louvre on 1 March 1855 (*ibidem*, 4 March 1855).

[52] Neither of Offenbach's other two works for the Salle Herz, *Le décaméron* and *Luc et Lucette*, seems to have been repurposed at the Bouffes-Parisiens or anywhere else.

[53] *Jaloux de soi* had been premiered in the composer's own *salons* on 31 March 1856 (*Le musée des familles* 23 [1855–1856]).

[54] 'augmenterait heureusement le répertoire de M. Perrin' (*Le ménestrel*, 25 February 1855).

difficulty in making such a transition. However many examples there are of journalists identifying works from the regulated theatre as suitable for inclusion in the culture of *opéra de salon*—and there are several—there is no further trace of such a practice in the surviving documentary record.

Salon, Song, and *Séance*

Generalizing about activities in the *salon* is as dangerous as generalizing about the *salon* itself. There are, however, some widespread behaviours that help give a framework to the performance and cultivation of *opéra de salon*. Around the edges of *salon* culture are such solitary undertakings as reading, embroidery, needlepoint, the inspection of engravings and other works of art, and other diversions that largely preclude interaction with large numbers of others. It is difficult to envisage such solitary behaviours in a large *salon* of the type fostered by Princess Mathilde but much easier to imagine them in smaller *salons* where the emphasis was on family, friends, and neighbours rather than on the diversion of many highly varied guests.

Across the spectrum of *salon* activity for larger numbers of individuals, there was an array of conduct that ranges from the fully active to the completely passive. Passive activities assumed a clear difference between audience and performer and frequently involve configuring *lieux* into performative *espaces* through the use of seats in rows affording the best views to those at the front and the worst at the back. Such configurations have already been seen in almost all the engravings discussed so far in this study, and they range from such opulent surroundings as the ballroom of the Binder family to the modest surroundings of the events illustrated by Daumier. *Théâtre de société*, to which *opéra de salon* was so closely aligned, was the obvious practice that involved this configuration, but so also were recitations of poetry, dramatized *proverbes*, *tableaux vivants*, and more formalized versions of such games as *charades*. Active practices for which an audience was not an essential prerequisite—conversation, cards, dice, and *jeux de société* that might make use of cards, dice, or both—more frequently took place around a table. Conversation was not so restricted, although even without a table, the nature of the activity presupposed a certain proximity. And neither were audiences unknown: the theatrical nature of the *art de la conversation* is revealed endlessly in images of bystanders admiring the rhetorical skills of others. Communal activities in the *salon*, therefore, veered from the passive, where performer and audience are clearly separated, to the active, where most individuals present are occupied with the activity. While the most formal—and *théâtre de société* and *opéra de salon*—involved the most passive engagement (on the part of the audience), most practices sat somewhere between the two extremes, with levels of engagement in a constate state of flux and disengaged audiences moving from one activity to another but also re-engaging as the mood took them. In this distinction between active and passive zones of attention, the physical object—the table—is critical in defining behaviours and activities. It is also critical to one of the most striking *salon* activities of the early Second Empire: the *séance*.[55]

In the Paris of early 1853, just as the vogue for *opéra de salon* was developing, *séances* swamped the city's *salons* in a way the composers, librettists, and promoters of *opéra de salon* could only dream of. The fashion for various forms of table-turning—as the phenomenon was initially called—started out as the simple movement of a table under the fingers of participants, moved on to writing dictated by the spirit world, and then moved to the making of art and music similarly guided by the denizens of the beyond.[56] It emerged in parallel with *opéra de salon* and in many cases overlapped with various forms of the theatrical.

Séances well illustrate the varying zones of attention that characterize nineteenth-century salon culture. The engraving in figure 5.1 is found on the first page of the *vaudeville La table tournante* by Eugène de Mirecourt and Jules-François-Félix Fleury-Husson (better known as Champfleury), which was premiered at the Théâtre des Variétés just weeks after the vogue for the *séance* started.[57] The picture shows six participants, five around the table

---

[55] For the concept of the 'zone of attention', see James Deaville, 'The Well-Mannered Auditor: Zones of Attention and the Imposition of Silence in the Salon of the Nineteenth Century', *The Oxford Handbook of Music Listening in the 19th and 20th Centuries*, ed. Christian Thorau and Hansjakob Ziemer (New York: Oxford University Press, 2018) 55–76.

[56] The primary literature on the *séance* in the early 1850s is colossal, although its musical component has only recently been assessed; see Mark Everist, 'Resonances from beyond the Grave: Music and the Occult in Nineteenth-Century Paris', *Journal of the American Musicological Society* 78 (2025), forthcoming) to which this section of the chapter is a complement; *idem*, 'Music, Journalism and Social Justice', *Presse et musique*, special issue of *Tangence* 137 (2025),13–42. For a useful general introduction to the occult in the Second Empire and its sources, see Sophie Lachapelle, *Investigating the Supernatural: From Spiritism ad Occultism to Psychical Research and Metaphysics in France, 1853–1931* (Baltimore: Johns Hopkins University Press, 2011) 7–33, especially 'Bibliographic Essay', 179–186.

[57] MAGASIN THÉÂTRAL ILLUSTRÉ/A LA LIBRAIRIE THÉÂTRALE/BOULEVARD SAINT-MARTIN, 12/.../LA TABLE TOURNANTE/EXPÉRIENCE DE MAGNÉTISME, EN UN ACTE, MÊLÉE DE COUPLETS/PAR MM. EUGÈNE DE MIRECOURT ET CHAMPFLEURY/REPRÉSENTÉE, POUR LA PREMIÈRE FOIS, A PARIS, SUR LE THÉÂTRE DES VARIÉTÉS, LE 2 MAI 1853.

with the sixth just having stood up; the dress of the participants, the furniture, and the décor—as well as the action of the *vaudeville*—identify a *petit-bourgeois* environment for this activity and no non-participant observers. But while this might confirm the hermetic sense of the *séance* common to many accounts in popular fiction, the practice of turning or talking tables could be no less theatrical than *opéra de salon*, for example, as an exactly contemporary depiction of *séances* in a more formal *salon* clearly shows (figure 5.2).[58] Here there are no fewer than three simultaneous *séances* in progress in a *salon* significantly more elaborate than the *parloir* in figure 5.1, with large mirrors, candelabra, and opulently framed paintings on the wall, with costumes and furniture to match. The number of non-participant observers is equal to or greater than the number of those involved in the *séances* themselves; there are at least two pairs in conversation (front left and back left of the image), the second of which seems to be totally disengaged from the apparent diversions of the *séance*. Furthermore, the mechanics of the *séance*—particularly the touching of hands—seem, in the table at front right, to be as much a pretext for flirtation as for communication with the other world. The theatricality of the entire scene is confirmed by the male non-participant observers standing at the back of the scene in the same way as they formed the *loges* in the human theatre described so eloquently at the performance of *opéra de salon* in the homes of Princesse Mathilde and the Binder family.

Séances and a world dominated by mediums were saturated by references to music. Whether it was accounts of spirits filling up the spare seats at a performance of Weber's *Oberon* at the Théâtre-Lyrique in 1857–1858,[59] the drawing of Mozart's home on Jupiter by the *vaudevilliste* Victorien Sardou during a *séance*,[60] or the sustained dictation and transcription of fully notated music from the other world,[61] music featured prominently in the world of the *séance*. In the case of the formal dictation of music from beyond the grave, the *séance* in question was closely tied to philosophical principles related to the work of Charles Fourier and Henri de Saint-Simon; it was conducted by the members of the editorial board of the journal *La démocratie pacifique* which had been proscribed by Napoléon III in November 1851 but

---

[58] *L'illustration*, 14 May 1853.
[59] Allan Kardec, *Spiritisme expérimental: Le Livre des médiums, ou Guide des médiums et des évocateurs, ... pour faire suite au 'Livre des Esprits'* (Paris: Didier, Ledoyen, 1861) 205–206.
[60] Bertrand Marot, *Paris occulte: alchimistes de l'ombre, spirites inspirés, mages sulfureuses, traqueurs de fantômes et astrologues visionnaires* (Paris: Parigramme, 2018) 39.
[61] Eugène Nus, *Choses de l'autre monde* (Paris: Dentu, [1880]) 85–103.

174　OPÉRA DE SALON

Figure 5.1. A *séance* in a *parloir*, 1853.

Figure 5.2. A *séance* in the *salon*, 1853.

Table 5.3. *Vaudevilles* and *séances*.

Generic descriptor [genre]	Title	Author/composer	Theatre/venue	Date
À propos-vaudeville	*La table tournante*	Flan	Luxembourg	24 April 1853
Pochade [*vaudeville*]	*La danse des tables*	Lefebvre	Célestins, Lyon	21 May 1853
Expérience de magnétisme [*vaudeville*]	*La table tournante*	Mirecourt and Champfleury	Variétés	22 May 1853
À propos-vaudeville	*Les tables tournantes*	Seinely	Gaîté	24 May 1853
Comédie-vaudeville	*L'esprit frappeur*	Clairville and Cordier	Palais-Royal	17 December 1853
Opéra-comique [*opérette*]	*Amour et spritisme*	Robillard (libretto by Quentin and Ghédé)	Pépinière	4 November 1871
Saynette pour salon [*opéra de salon*]	*Les tables tournantes*	Marietti and Bachman (libretto by de Mongis)	Société Philotechnique	26 May 1872

continued to meet in the journal's Parisian premises on the rue de Beaune.[62] The presence of music in the rue de Beaune *séances* was the culmination of a fifteen-year history of music criticism in *La démocratie pacifique* which had brought music for the stage and in all its forms into alignment with all modes of Fouriérisme.

The theatrical nature of the *séance* made it an attractive subject for parody in the world of *vaudeville* and *opérette*. No fewer than five *vaudevilles* were mounted during 1853, and given that their titles overlap so closely, table 5.3 provides details including their frequently whimsical generic descriptors.

Attempts at conjuring the other world through the use of turning tables are used by suitors thwarted by fathers or uncles of their betrotheds to further their causes—usually by faking the outcome of the *séance*.[63] This is the basis of the intrigue in Eugène de Mirecourt and Jules-François-Félix Fleury-Husson's (pseud. Champfleury's) *La table-tournante*, which

---

[62] Everist, 'Resonances from beyond the Grave'.
[63] The only exception is Seinely's *Les tables tournantes*: Théâtre de la Gaîté/Nº 1821/20 Mai 1853/ Les tables tournantes/Apropos-Vaudeville en 1 acte (Paris, Archives Nationales, F[18] 922/1821).

the Variétés managed to assemble within barely a month of the vogue for *séances* reaching Paris in April 1853; of Hippolyte Lefebvre's *La danse des tables*, mounted at the end of the same year in Lyon;[64] and of Alexandre Flan's *La table tournante*, which managed to get onto the stage within three weeks of the phenomenon of the *séance* arriving in Paris. In Mirecourt and Champfleury's *La table-tournante*, the action is triggered by an enthusiast for Franz Mesmer's *magnétisme* reading a newspaper article about the incoming vogue for *séances* and *tables-tournantes*.[65] This depicts a very real event: a newspaper report in the *Allgemeine Zeitung* that described the arrival in Bremen of American devotees of table-turning and the background to the phenomenon.[66] This report—in the *Gazette d'Augsbourg*, as the journal was known in Paris—was published in French translation as an appendix to the *vaudeville La table-tournante* and is also referenced in *La danse des tables*[67] and in Flan's *La table tournante*.[68]

The sung numbers in *La danse des tables* almost all refer to table-turning. Anténor's *air* 'Tourne, tourne donc, c'est le refrain' from scene 7 of the work may serve as an example and includes the following: Children and adults,/ Fathers and mothers, Right up to little children,/Quite innocent,/Hold hands/And the table suddenly/Appears to get going/To this refrain:/*Tourne, tourne, donc*.[69] These sentiments are echoed throughout the work, as the subject is traded between characters whose response to the vogue for turning tables is either enthusiastic, despairing, or contemptuous. No explanation is given in the text of *La danse des tables* as to how the tables are made to dance out of the room to the accompaniment of an orchestral polka, but in the case of *La table tournante*, the turning table and also the turning hat (a key element in the drama) are explained in a note to the text which explains the

---

[64] LA/DANSE DES TABLES/POCHADE EN UN ACTE,/PAR M. H. LEFEBVRE,/ REPRÉSENTÉE POUR LA PREMIÈRE FOIS SUR LE THÉÂTRE DES CÉLESTINS/A LYON, LE 21 MAI 1853/.../LYON.—IMPRIMERIE D'AIMÉ VINGTRINIER, QUAI SAINT-ANTOINE, 36.

[65] MAGASIN THÉÂTRAL ILLUSTRÉ/A LA LIBRAIRIE THÉÂTRALE/BOULEVARD SAINT-MARTIN, 12, 1–2.

[66] *Allgemeine Zeitung*, 30 March 1853.

[67] MAGASIN THÉÂTRAL ILLUSTRÉ/A LA LIBRAIRIE THÉÂTRALE/BOULEVARD SAINT-MARTIN, 12, 7–8; LA/DANSE DES TABLES, 3–4.

[68] 'La table tournante/à propos vaudeville, en un acte/Alexandre Flan' (Paris, Archives Nationales, F^{18} 1079), [7].

[69] 'Les petits et les grands, / Les papas, les mamans, / Jusqu'aux petits enfants/Bien innocents/ Se tiennent par la main,/Et la table soudain/Semble se mettre en train/À ce refrain:/Tourne, tourne, donc' (*ibidem*, 13). The number is based on the *air connu* 'Change, change-moi, Brama', which originated in the *vaudeville* by Eugène Scribe and Mélesville *père* of 1827 titled *La chatte métamorphosée en femme*.

sleight of hand required for the stage action.⁷⁰ Such paratexts as this and the translation of the article from the *Allgemeine Zeitung*, as well as the constant reference to the current vogue for *séances*, characterize almost all of the stage works that parody them.

L'esprit frappeur, by Clairville and Jules Cordier, was produced at Paris's Théâtre du Palais-Royal just a couple of days before *La danse des tables*, and its subtitle, *Les sept merveilles du jour*, reveals the reason the protagonist Mirontaine wants to summon a spirit from the other world: in order to get a ticket to the current play at the Théâtre de la Porte Saint-Martin, *Les sept merveilles du monde*.⁷¹ Things turn out badly, as, once summoned, the *esprit frappeur* (the 'tapping spirit', and the ghost of Mirontaine's uncle) tries a *tableau vivant* of the seven wonders of the ancient world which is swiftly dismissed. Mirontaine is then taken by the *esprit frappeur* on a tour of the seven modern-day 'wonders' of the world: Paris, in other words. These include an interview with the statue of the Roman solider on the Pont d'Iéna, with Diana—not the goddess as Mirontaine hopes but Diana Bazu, a vendor of fabric on the rue du Temple, lamenting the imminent destruction of the road as part of the Hausmannien changes to the city, and a visit to the Jardin Turc, among others.

As in *La table tournante*, *L'esprit frappeur* begins with Mirontaine reading an account of turning tables in a newspaper followed by an *air* 'Ah! que de tapage à Paris!' which laments the fact that the city's *salons* are overrun with *séances*. The otherworldly action in *L'esprit frappeur* is triggered by Mirontaine's invocation of his uncle's spirit in the very first scene of the *vaudeville*, in order to assist him with obtaining a ticket to the play he is seeking; according to the conventions of the genre, the invocation is based on an *air connu* (a pre-existent melody).⁷² Mirontaine sings 'Oncle qui reposez sous une froide pierre / Reveillez-vous!' to the melody of Bertram's celebrated *évocation* from act iii of Meyerbeer's *Robert le diable* that precedes the even more celebrated ballet of the nuns (example 5.1).⁷³

---

[70] MAGASIN THÉÂTRAL ILLUSTRÉ/A LA LIBRAIRIE THÉÂTRALE/BOULEVARD SAINT-MARTIN, 12, 6.
[71] THÉÂTRE DU PALAIS-ROYAL/L'ESPRIT FRAPPEUR/OU/LES SEPT MERVEILLES DU JOUR/VAUDEVILLE EN UN ACTE,/Par MM. CLAIRVILLE et Jules CORDIER,/Représentée, pour la première fois, à Paris, sur le théâtre du PALAIS-ROYAL,/le 17 Décembre 1853./.../Paris/ BECK, LIBRAIRE, RUE DES GRANDS-AUGUSTINS, 20/-/1853.
[72] *Ibidem*, 2.
[73] Example 5.1 is constructed out of the text from THÉÂTRE DU PALAIS-ROYAL/L'ESPRIT FRAPPEUR, 2, and the music from ROBERT LE DIABLE/Opéra en 5 Actes/*Paroles de MM E. Scribe et G. Delavigne*/MUSIQUE DE/Giacomo Meyerbeer/Partition de Piano, arrangée par J. P. PIXIS/.../

Example 5.1. Clairville and Jules Cordier, *L'esprit frappeur*, reconstruction of *évocation*.

The lines sung by Mirontaine directly parody those of the opera: 'Nonnes, qui reposez sous cette froide pierre / M'entendez-vous?'. Exactly how much of the Meyerbeer scene was used in *L'esprit frappeur* is unclear, but example 5.1 gives a reconstruction of the opening of the *évocation* itself without the preceding recitative and orchestral introduction with *tremolando* strings.

Paris, chez Maurice Schlesinger, rue Richelieu N° 97/Londres, propriété de M. Monck Mason—Berlin, chez A. M. Schlesinger, 231.

Meyerbeer's opera had been a Parisian staple since its 1831 premiere; it had been given at the Académie Impériale de Musique (as the Opéra was called from 1815 to 1848) just a month earlier and would be repeated four days after the premiere of *L'esprit frappeur*.

The sources for *airs connus* in *vaudeville* evolved over the first half of the nineteenth century from a preponderance of borrowings from songs indexed in the various editions of the *Clé du caveau* to the inclusion of *romance*, instrumental works, *airs nouveaux* from other *vaudevilles*, and extracts from both *opéras comiques* and *grands opéras* from the Académie Royale de Musique. Citation of material in *vaudeville* from the Opéra-Comique and the Opéra is a much-underestimated mode of consumption for this repertory for those who could not attend performances at the two institutions, and the use here of an iconic moment from perhaps the best-known opera in Europe from the middle of the nineteenth century is entirely typical of the relationship between what might be thought high and low registral levels.

Two works from the end of the Second Empire align the culture of the *séance* with *opéra de salon* more directly. Victor Robillard's *Amour et spiritisme*, with a libretto by Léon Quentin and Cehem Ghédé, was premiered at a *café-concert*, La pépinière, in November 1871, just after the latter's opening. The protagonist in *Amour et spiritisme*, Coquillard, has arrived home full of enthusiasm for the *séance* he has just attended and, thinking he finds himself alone, begins his own:

> There!... Now I am alone, let's have some art... (rolling up his sleeves). Suppleness in the movements.... Good! Let's fascinate!... Electrify!... Magnetize! And especially let's not forget the magic words. (he makes several gestures to provoke hypnotism [*passes*]).[74]

The monologue ends, and Coquillard begins an *évocation* almost as carefully calqued on Meyerbeer's version from act iii of *Robert le diable* as the citation of the same number in *L'esprit frappeur* (example 5.2).[75]

The text of Coquillard's *évocation* mimics the prosody, rhythm, rhetoric, and some of the vocabulary of Meyerbeer's original, and the music may be

---

[74] Là! maintenant que je suis seul, opérons avec art... (Retroussant sa manche). Du moelleux dans les articulations.... Bien! fascinons!... Électrisons!... magnétisons!... et n'oublions pas surtout les mots magiques. (il fait des passes). AMOUR/ET/SPIRITISME/*Opéra-comique en un acte*/PAROLES DE/*Léon QUENTIN et GÉDHÉ*/PAROLES [sic; recte 'Musique']/DE/VICTOR ROBILLARD/.../ PARIS/Emile CHATOT éditeur/*19r. N*ᵉ *des Petits-champs, en face la Bibliothèque*, 19.

[75] *Ibidem*, 20.

Example 5.2. Victor Robillard, *Amour et spiritisme, évocation.*

compared with the version in example 5.1 (where the text is lightly modified to reflect its use in *L'esprit frappeur*. The two texts are as follows:

Meyerbeer | **Robillard**
Nonnes, qui reposez sous cette froide pierre / M'entendez-vous? | Sage, qui reposez aux pays d'outretombe / Salamalek!

Robillard's *évocation* begins with a sustained string *tremolando* in the same way as the Meyerbeer; both make use of oscillating tonic minor and leading-note diminished sevenths over a tonic pedal. Robillard's vocal line takes Meyerbeer's descending and rising minor arpeggio and simply inverts it, and both pause at the end of the first poetic line ('pierre' in Meyerbeer, 'tombe' in Robillard) before ending with an exclamation in triplet quavers ('M'entendez-vous?' in Meyerbeer, 'Salamalek' in Robillard). Robillard's use of the salutatory formula (usually with the orthography 'salamalec') invokes a generic oriental greeting known from Gérard de Nerval's *Voyages dans l'orient* of 1851, which by the early 1880s had taken on the nature of an exaggerated politeness, as seen in Joris-Karl Huysmans's early *En ménage* of 1881).[76] And Robillard's librettists ram home the similarities with *Robert le diable* at the very end of the *évocation*, when they give Coquillard a palm that he waves at the end of the number, exactly the object with which the eponymous *Robert le diable* protects himself.

From *vaudevilles* that invoke *séances* via *opérettes* that do the same, it is a small step to *opéras de salon* that return the genre back to the *salon* culture shared with the *séance*. Only the libretto survives of Jean-Antoine de Mongis's *Les tables tournantes*, premiered the year after Robillard's *Amour et spiritisme*, with music by Marietti and Bachman.[77] If the Marietti who wrote one of the numbers was the twenty-year-old Georges Marietti who had a successful career as a songwriter in the second half of the nineteenth century, then the artist who sang Adeline at the premiere—Mlle Berthe Marietti—must have been his sister; but there are problems with this identification, since Marietti is also a pseudonym for Georges-Henri-Daniel Poirotte, and

---

[76] Gérard de Nerval, *Voyage en orient*, 2 vols. (Paris: Charpentier, 1851) 2:247; Joris-Karl Huysmans, *En ménage* (Paris: Charpentier, 1880) 31.
[77] LES TABLES TOURNANTES/SAYNETTE POUR SALON/Représentée pour la première fois à la Séance publique/de la Société philotechnique, le 26 mai 1872/Par A. DE MONGIS/Extrait de l'ANNUAIRE DE LA SOCIÉTÉ PHILOTECHNIQUE—1872/-/MEULAN/IMPRIMERIE DE A. MASSON.

the composer might perfectly well be someone else. The second composer, Bachman, has likewise resisted identification. The performance context for *Les tables tournantes* fits well with other performances of *opéra de salon*. It was first given at a meeting of the Société Philotechnique in the rue de la Banque on 26 May 1872. Since at least 1832, the Société Philotechnique had held two public meetings a year, in addition to the thirty or so meetings of the members, which closed with a reading, play, concert, or—in May 1872—an *opéra de salon*.[78] The performance aligns itself with others where *opéras de salon* were used in the context of institutional celebration, such as Duprato's *La reine Mozab* at the Athénée de Paris in 1858 or at the educational institution run by Mlles Chenu and Frezzola in Versailles in 1867.[79]

The Société Philotechnique was an organization dating back to the eighteenth century that provided a point of interaction for those interested in the arts and sciences; it had sixty resident members but far many more members who corresponded from outside Paris. In addition to its almost weekly substantive meetings, it held two more ceremonial meetings each year which ended with a concert, and this is the performance context for the Marietti-Bachman *Les tables tournantes*.[80] The event was like so many other performances of *opéra de salon*, especially those outside the conventional *salon* environment, and consisted of instrumental works for *orgue expressif*, piano, and violin in various combinations and a series of opera arias and *romances* by Nicolò Isouard Étienne Méhul, Charles-Émile Poisot (the composer of other *opéras de salon*), Halévy, and Bellini.[81] *Les tables tournantes* closed the evening.[82] In terms of its structure, *Les tables tournantes* has much in common with the more modest examples of the genre. With a single act, two characters (one male, one female), and two sung numbers, it has much in common with Levassor's *Le troupier et la bonne, ou Adélaïade et Vermouth*, premiered at the Salle Herz in 1864, also titled a *saynette*. Relationships between the creative and performing teams were similarly close, with Levassor

---

[78] Comité des travaux historiques et scientifiques—Institut rattaché à l'École nationale des chartes, 'Société philotechnique—Paris' (http://cths.fr/an/societe.php?id=100746).
[79] See *La Revue et Gazette musicale de Paris*, 7 March 1858; *Le ménestrel*, 11 August 1867.
[80] Émile Loubens, 'Notice sur la Société Philotechnique', *Annuaire de la Société Philotechnique* 33 (1872) 1–4.
[81] The programme was published *ibidem*, 5–6.
[82] In addition to being published separately as LES TABLES TOURNANTES/SAYNETTE POUR SALON, the libretto of *Les tables tournantes* was printed in *Annuaire de la Société Philotechnique* 33 (1872) 72–86.

himself taking the role of Vermouth in the same way as Marietti's sister (?) had perhaps taken a role in *Les tables tournantes*.[83]

There is no evidence of *opéras de salon* being mounted in the *salon* in the rue de Beaune that had hosted the *séances* with the greatest musical significance in the early 1850s. There are, however, clear traces that link these musical *séances* and *opéra de salon*. Three individuals were invited to observe and witness the *séances* with music on the rue de Beaune:[84] Delphine Gay was an author, daughter of Sophie Gay, and wife of Girardin;[85] Émile Prudent was one of the foremost pianists of his time and a committed Saint-Simonian and Fourierist;[86] and Félicien David's Saint-Simonian credentials need little discussion.[87] Of the three, only Prudent seems to have had little contact with *opéra de salon*. The Girardins' *salon* in an opulent house on the corner of the Avenue des Champs-Élysées and the rue Marbeuf was a central meeting point for 'the elite of Parisian society',[88] and after his wife's death in 1855, Girardin mounted a performance of Weckerlin's *Le mariage en poste* at the same address at which his late wife had enthusiastically conducted *séances* just a few months earlier. By contrast, it is entirely possible that there survives an *opéra de salon* by another enthusiast for the *séance*, David. His *Le fermier de Franconville*, which might have been part of a campaign supported by the Pereire brothers for a performance in their home on the Place Vendôme, appears never to have been performed, although a good two-thirds of the work exists in draft, and its structure aligns precisely with that of *opéra de salon*.[89] Nevertheless, the links between *séance*, *opéra de salon*, and the *haute bourgeoisie* in *Le fermier de Franconville* are an allusive link between the world of the *séance* and *opéra de salon*.

[83] *La Revue et Gazette musicale de Paris*, 11 December 1864.

[84] Nus, *Choses de l'autre monde*, 90.

[85] Old accounts of the life of Delphine de Girardin—*Esprit de Mme de Girardin, avec préface par M. de Lamartine* (Paris: Hetzel, [1862]); Henri Malo, *La gloire du Vicomte de Launay: Delphine Gay de Girardin*, 6th ed. (Paris: Émile-Paul, 1925)—have been largely superseded by Melissa McCullough Wittmeier, 'Delphine Gay, Madame de Girardin, the Vicomte de Launay' (PhD diss., Stanford University, 2000).

[86] See Antoine Marmontel, *Les pianistes célèbres: silhouettes et médaillons* (Paris: Heugel, 1878), 61–69, esp. 67.

[87] Locke, *Music, Musicians, and the Saint-Simonians*.

[88] L'élite de la société parisienne' (*La Revue et Gazette musicale de Paris*, 17 May 1857, where the performance of Weckerlin's *Le mariage en poste* was described).

[89] The sources, reconstruction, and structure of *Le fermier de Franconville* are discussed in chapter 3.

The most telling relationship between *opéra de salon* and the *séances* in the rue de Beaune *salon* is the fact that Bureau, the musical stenographer for the *séance*, wrote two stage works: *Le baron de Fiferland* and *Dame Jacinthe*.[90] *Dame Jacinthe* consisted of nine numbers (*ballade, air, duo, romance, duetto, orage, prière, duo, final*), of which three were for solo voices. Although there is no surviving libretto, it is clear that there were four characters and that the kinetic action of the work proceeded in spoken dialogue. The attribution of the libretto to Michel Carré and its likely basis in a scene featuring 'Dame Jacinthe' in Dumas's 1845–1846 *Le chevalier de Maison-Rouge*,[91] however, suggest a date entirely commensurate with the period between the initiation of the rue de Beaune *séances* in early 1853 and Bureau's departure for the United States in late 1856.[92] Similarly, Bureau's *Le baron de Fifeland* consists of eight numbers (of which the sixth is missing), again with three solo numbers and four characters.[93] Both works are copied in full score as well as piano-vocal format but not published, so their status as *opéras de salon* is slightly unclear. Although all *opéras de salon* were published with piano accompaniment only, there is no clarity on what composers' autographs looked like beyond a couple of exceptions.[94] While there is no record of their performance in the regulated theatre, performance as part of the culture of *opéra de salon* could very likely be a significant part of the *opéra de salon* ecosystem that has left no trace.

The relationship between *opéra de salon* and other *salon* activities ranges from the explicit to the allusive but provides one of several contexts for the genre. There is a remarkable alignment between the chronology of *opéra de salon* and the vogue for the *séance*—table-turning and the dictation of music from the other world—that sits alongside more conventional types of *salon* activity. The relationship between the regulated theatre and *opéra de salon* is one of constant flux: although the latter was largely separate from works produced for the regulated theatre, there was a stylistic overlap between *opéra de salon* and *opérette*, with a regular view being articulated that *opéras*

---

[90] Both are described in Gabrielle Rey, *Le Fouériériste Allyre Bureau (1810–1859)*, Publications des Annales de la Faculté des Lettres Aix-en-Provence: Travaux et mémoires 21 (Aix-en-Provence: La Pensée Universitaire, 1962), 33.

[91] Alexandre Dumas, *Le chevalier de Maison-Rouge* (Paris: Chadot, 1846).

[92] *Dame Jacinthe* survives in a piano-vocal score (Pontpoint, Oise, Private Collection of Jacques Bureau, MS 3) and in full score (*ibidem*, MS 12/2).

[93] *Ibidem*, MS 12/1.

[94] Bureau's two *opéras de salon* and David's *Le fermier de Franconville* exist in autograph form with both orchestral scoring and reduction for piano; Weckerlin's corresponding works were all drafted with piano accompaniment only.

de salon were suitable for paying audiences in commercial and subsidized theatres; but the fact that these transfers almost never took place is testimony to the independence of the genre. Composers and librettists, however, moved effortlessly between the regulated theatre and *opéra de salon*, reinforcing the general sense that although *opéra de salon* and *opérette*—and related types—shared much in terms of their literary, dramatic, and musical anatomy, the performance and cultivation of the two genres remained largely discrete.

6
Performance and the *Parloir*

Women, the *Parloir*, and *Opéra de salon*

The largely domestic cultivation of **opéra de salon** depended on the role of women in its creation, recreation, and reception. This was less true when **opéra de salon** was performed in concert halls and studios rather than in **salons** or **parlors**; however, even in these more public settings, female performers and **salonnières** actively rented spaces like the Salle Herz. Performers as Mme Gaveaux-Sabatier were some of the most energetic in using studios to promote **opéra de salon**. But most of the work uniquely undertaken by women—work that was not merely shared with men—was undertaken in the formal **salon** and the less formal **parloir**. While modern access to the culture of **opéra de salon** in the **parloir** is through the publication of libretti, scores, and various forms of paratext in such women's journals as *Le magasin des demoiselles* and *Le journal des demoiselles*, the more formal **salons** were reported verbally and frequently visually in various forms of periodical publication, which resulted in an indelible and detailed record of the events. It is for precisely this sort of more formal event, therefore, that we have accounts of the performers, the members of the audience, the location, and the **salonnier/salonnière** responsible for the event. Although accounts of women's activity in these latter domains were subject to the vicissitudes and misogyny of exclusively male journalists, the record of the female librettist, composer, and—what appears as a largely female preoccupation—librettist-composer is less contentious simply by virtue of the way in which data have survived.

Publication of *opéra de salon* in *Le magasin des demoiselles* and *Le journal des demoiselles* not only stands out from other modes of dissemination that characterize *opéras de salon* discussed so far but also opens up questions of *lieu, espace,* and musico-theatrical culture that are of particular importance for women and especially the *demoiselle,* the young woman between school and marriage. Parisian journals dedicated to the specific interests of women went back deep into the *ancien régime* with *Le journal des dames* founded in 1759, and various types of journals had included music since the appearance of *Le journal de la mode et du goût* in the 1790s.[1] By the time of the Restoration and the July Monarchy, titles were established that lasted decades and were a familiar feature of the topography of the periodical press. *Le petit courrier des dames* began publication in 1822 and ran until 1864, *Le bon ton* ran from 1834 until 1884, and *Le moniteur de la mode* ran from 1843 to 1906. But these were just part of a much wider culture that encompassed dozens of journals for women, some of which lasted more than a decade, some less than a year.[2]

Le magasin des demoiselles and *Le journal des demoiselles* began publication in 1833 and 1844, respectively, but stood a little apart from the mainstream of *la presse féminine* in that they were addressed to the *demoiselle,* the young unmarried woman who needed to acquire the domestic, intellectual, and aesthetic skills to discharge future obligations as a married woman. In addition to focussing on textual modes, women's journals in general, and *Le journal des demoiselles* and *Le magasin des demoiselles* in particular, also attended to the visual and the material. The journals appeared monthly, the year starting in October for *Le magasin des demoiselles* and in January for *Le journal des demoiselles.* Texts were instructive and improving: the 1853–1854 volume of *Le magasin des demoiselles,* for example, included a biography of Friedrich Gottlieb Klopstock by Auguste-Léonce Ravergie,

---

[1] *Le journal de la mode et du goût, ou Amusemens du salon et de la toilette* was published from February 1790 to April 1793. See Rebecca Dowd Geoffroy-Schwinden, 'Fashion, Musical Taste, and the French Revolution: *Journal de la mode et du goût*', paper presented at France: Musiques, Cultures, 1789–1918 conference, Venice, July 2022.

[2] For a full listing of women's journals (*la presse féminine*) up to 1848, see Evelyne Sullerot, *Histoire de la presse féminine en France, des origines à 1848* (Paris: Armand Colin, 1966) 217–218. This should be read alongside the listing and commentary in Christine Thirion, 'La presse pour les jeunes de 1815 à 1848: essai d'analyse de contenu', *Bulletin des Bibliothèques de France* (1972/1973) 111–132 (https://bbf.enssib.fr/consulter/bbf-1972-03-0111-002).

an essay on the history of lithography by Mme Désiré Martin, a *Journal de voyage d'une jeune fille* by Louise Leneveux, and a poem by Antoine Delatour. Challenges to the intellect and the memory were frequent; for example, a question about the date and the fashion in which the royal bodyguard originated in France was posed, and each issue had a *rébus*, a graphic encoding of a proverb or similar phrase; solutions were always given in the following issue. Such relative frivolities were countered by such texts as the one headed 'MORALE' by Mme de Watteville titled 'De la prétendue indulgence du monde'.[3]

But the largest part of the journals' text involved commentaries on the visual materials they included; these consisted of watercolours and sepia tints in facsimile, steel engravings, costume engravings (the largest number of plates came under this category), and engravings of carpet, needlework, crochet, and other *petits ouvrages* involving elementary metalwork.[4] In addition, physical samples of the material were also appended to the monthly instalments of the journals as further encouragements to purchase and consume. In terms of the subjects that were promoted for education in the home, they aligned very closely with those promoted by Albertine-Adrienne Necker de Saussure's *L'éducation progressive*, which, although published between 1828 and 1832, was reprinted throughout the century, with the last edition appearing in 1887. The training programme focussed far more on education in the home, for which *Le magasin des demoiselles* and *Le journal des demoiselles* were ideally suited as resources for learning.[5]

---

[3] *Le magasin des demoiselles* 10 (1853–1854) 33–35.

[4] The wide range of non-textual material published with *Le magasin* and *Le journal des demoiselles* results in a preservation that is inconsistent at best. Even in such deposit libraries as the Bibliothèque Nationale de France, although the textual material is always preserved, engravings, dressmaking and other patterns, and especially music are frequently missing. For *Le magasin des demoiselles*, the series preserved in Paris, Bibliothèque Nationale de France, Z-4215, must be read alongside the excerpted music collection in Vm^7 8146. For *Le journal des demoiselles*, however, the chronological series is split between Paris, Bibliothèque de l'Arsenal, 8-JO-20345 for 1851–1857, and Bibliothèque Nationale de France, R-6111a.19 for 1858–1875.

[5] Albertine-Adrienne Necker de Saussure, *L'éducation progressive, ou Étude du cours de la vie*, 2 vols. (Paris: Sautelet; Paulin, 1828–1832). See the careful contextualization of the work in Rogers, *From the Salon to the Schoolroom*, 23–35 and *passim*; and an account of the author's intellectual background in Clarissa Campbell Orr, *Wollstonecraft's Daughters: Womanhood in England and France 1780–1920* (Manchester: Manchester University Press, 1996) 61–78.

Both journals began to include music in 1851. The repertory of both initially included dances for keyboard—polka, mazurka, waltz, galop, and quadrille—as well as *mélodies* and *romances*.[6] But from 1853 and 1856, respectively, *Le magasin des demoiselles* and *Le journal des demoiselles* began to include *opéra de salon*, almost invariably (table 6.1).[7]

Like the various visual contributions and the other music supplements to the journals, the vocal score of the *opéra de salon* was appended to the end of the issue in which it was found, but its libretto was integrated into the textual portion of the publication. It was also the subject of a review in the journal as part of a *revue musicale*: in the case of *Le journal des demoiselles*, Marie Lassaveur—about whom almost nothing is known—produced a sustained and well-informed series of texts that reviewed current works, explored the history of music and its technical resources, and introduced the music—and *opéra de salon*—included in the journal.

Opéras de salon in *Le magasin* and *Le journal* constitute more than a third of the total repertory; of the approximately 120 *opéras de salon* that have left some kind of trace from their origins to 1870, forty-two were published in *Le magasin des demoiselles* or *Le journal des demoiselles*. As may be seen from table 6.1, composers who were active across the Parisian lyric field—Clapisson, Grisar, Semet, Duprato, and Poise—contributed single works to one or the other of the two publications, and Massé published a single work in each. However, Bordèse wrote no fewer than

---

[6] Each month, up to four or five compositions were included, with two to three representing an average. So for June 1860, *Le magasin des demoiselles* published a single suite of *Valses allemandes* entitled *Germania* arranged by Victor Parizot, whereas for May 1854, *Le journal des demoiselles* gave its readers three keyboard dances (Paul Wagner's polka-mazurka *La rose du roi*, his waltz *Le bouquet*, and Élise Beech's polka *L'étincelle*) and two vocal works: *L'arbre de Noël, ballade* by Clapisson with words by Frédéric de Courcy; and J. Monestar's *romance L'amitié* setting a text by Émile Roustan. More typical was the pair of works offered by *Le magasin des demoiselles* in June 1865: the *duettino La cloche qui tinte* by Luigi Bordèse to words by André van Hasselt and a *Mosaïque* on themes from Mozart's *Don Giovanni* by 'Rysler', a pseudonym for the publisher Léon Grus.

[7] The inclusion of an *opéra de salon* would usually run over two or three months, so, for example, François Bazin's *Marianne* (libretto by Augustin Challamel) occupied the October and November issues of *Le magasin des demoiselles* for 1861–1862, even though all the material was published in the first of the two issues.

Table 6.1. *Opéras de salon* in *Le magasin des demoiselles*, *Le journal des demoiselles* and *Le berquin*.

LE MAGASIN DES DEMOISELLES

Volume	Year	No.	Title	Genre	Librettist and composer
10	1853–1854	1–2	Frère et soeur	opéra comique	Édouard Plouvier and Luigi Bordèse
11	1854–1855	1–5	Le coffret de Saint-Domingue	opéra comique	Émile Deschamps and Louis Clapisson
12	1855–1856	1–3	Le prix de famille	opéra comique	François-Joseph-Pierre-André Méry and Victor Massé
13	1856–1857	1–3	La treille du roi	opéra comique	Charles Depeuty and Paul Henrion
14	1857–1858	1–3	Le moulin des oiseaux	opéra comique	Édouard Plouvier and Luigi Bordèse
14	1857–1858	10	Les ouvrières de qualité	vaudeville	Joachim Duflot and Pierre-Julien Nargeot
15	1858–1859	1–3	La part à dieu	opéra comique	Jules-Jean-Antoine Baric and Laurent de Rillé
16	1859–1860	1–3	La reine Mozab	opérette	Auguste Carré and Jules-Laurent-Anicharsis Duprato
17	1860–1861	1–3	Les deux comtesses	opéra comique	Alexandre Flan and Luigi Bordèse
18	1861–1862	1–2	Marianne	opéra comique	Augustin Challamel and François Bazin
19	1862–1863	1–3	Lanterne magique!!!	opéra comique	Auguste Carré and Louis Deffès
20	1863–1864	1–3	La meunière de Sans-Souci	opérette	Auguste Carré and Ernest Boulanger
21	1864–1865	1–3	Le miroir	opérette	Charles-Louis-Étienne Truinet (Nuitter) and Frédéric-Étienne Barbier
22	1865–1866	1–3	Jean Noël	opérette	Ernest Dubreuil and Jean-Alexandre-Ferdinand Poise
23	1866–1867	1–3	Le marché aux servantes	opérette	Étienne Tréfeu and Luigi Bordèse

Table 6.1. Continued

Volume	Year	No.	Title	Genre	Librettist and composer
24	1867–1868	1–3	Quinolette	opérette	Nac and Isidore Legouix
25	1868–1869	1–3	Miss Robinson	opérette	Auguste Carré and Émile Jonas
26	1869–1870	1–3	Judith et Suzon	opérette	Francis Tourte and Luigi Bordèse
28	1872–1873	a–c	Le cigale et la fourmi	opéra comique	Alexandre Beaumont and Jean-Alexandre-Ferdinand Poise
29	1873–1874	2	Ruse contre ruse	opéra comique	Michel Carré and Joseph O'Kelly
30	1874–1875	2	La dame de compagnie	opéra comique	Alexandre Beaumont and Jean-Alexandre-Ferdinand Poise
31	1875–1876	2–3	La clef d'argent	opéra comique	Alexandre Beaumont and J. E. Legioux

LE JOURNAL DES DEMOISELLES

Volume	Year	No.	Title	Genre	Librettist and Composer
24	1856	6–8	Les trois clefs	opérette	Auguste de Pellaert
26	1858	3, 6, 7	Le medaillon d'Yvonne	opérette de salon	Amadée Jallais, Henry Thiéry, and Frédéric Lentz
27	1859	3, 5, 6	Clara tempête	opérette	Elise Boisgontier (Mme Adam Boisgontier) and Francesco Chiaromonte
28	1860	5	La bohémienne	vaudeville	Elise Boisgontier (Mme Adam Boisgontier) and Antoine Rocheblave
29	1861	5	Une reine de vingt ans	vaudeville	Elise Boisgontier (Mme Adam Boisgontier) and Antoine Rocheblave
30	1862	5	Le proscrit	opérette	Elise Boisgontier (Mme Adam Boisgontier) and Antoine Rocheblave
31	1863	5	Deux lunatiques à Saint-Cloud	vaudeville	Elise Boisgontier (Mme Adam Boisgontier) and Antoine Rocheblave

(continued)

Table 6.1. Continued

Volume	Year	No.	Title	Genre	Librettist and Composer
32	1864	5	*Grande nouvelle*	*opérette*	Elise Boisgontier (Mme Adam Boisgontier) and Léo Delibes
33	1865	5	*Le lutin des grèves*	*opérette*	Elise Boisgontier (Mme Adam Boisgontier) and Antoine Rocheglave
34	1866	5	*Le farouche ennemi*	*opérette*	Elise Boisgontier (Mme Adam Boisgontier) and Jules Pillevestre
35	1867	7	*Le procès*	*opérette*	Elise Boisgontier (Mme Adam Boisgontier) and Albert Grisar
36	1868	5	*Les enfants de Perrette*	*opérette*	Elise Boisgontier (Mme Adam Boisgontier) and Victor Massé
37	1869	5	*Abeilles et boudons*	*opérette*	Elise Boisgontier (Mme Adam Boisgontier) and Laurent de Rillé
38	1870	5	*Laide*	*opérette*	Elise Boisgontier (Mme Adam Boisgontier) and Théodore-Aimé-Émile Semet
40	1872	5	*La trouvaille*	*opérette*	Mme de Rocheblave and Victor Massé
41	1873	3	*La petite soeur d'Achille*	*opérette*	Paul Dubourg and Victor Massé
41	1873	6	*La petite soeur d'Achille*	*opérette*	Paul Dubourg and Victor Massé *suite et fin*
42	1874	7	*Une loi somptuaire*	*opérette*	Paul Dubourg and Victor Massé
43	1875	7	*Le poltron*	*opérette*	Paul Dubourg and Théodore-Aimé-Émile Semet

LE BERQUIN

1	1857–1858	2	*Les premiers cinq francs*	*opérette de salon en 2 actes*	A. Quatremère

five *opéras de salon* for *Le magasin des demoiselles*, almost his entire lyric output, and Antoine de Rocheblave similarly contributed five works to *Le journal des demoiselles*, which likewise constituted his entire theatrical oeuvre. Similarly, the libretti of these works were largely by authors whose names are familiar not only from the rest of the *opéra de salon* repertory but also from *opérette* and related genres more broadly. The shadowy Auguste Carré (he also appears to have composed) wrote five libretti for *Le magasin des demoiselles*, and although most of the librettists and all the composers of this repertory were male, the most prolific librettist was Mme Adam Boisgontier, who wrote more than a dozen libretti for *opéra de salon* in *Le journal des demoiselles*.

Unsurprisingly, generic descriptors for *opéra de salon* published in women's journals varied widely: *opéra comique, opérette, opérette de salon*, and *vaudeville* were exchanged with impunity for works with almost the same features. In some instances, the term *vaudeville* was used simply because the final number took the form of a *vaudeville*, a number where each principal sang a strophe to identical music with or without a refrain sung by the entire cast; its use had nothing to do with the structure or aesthetic of *vaudeville*, especially in its use of borrowed material.[8] *Opéras de salon* published in women's journals were almost identical in scope to their counterparts published more broadly; two-thirds of them—as well as the wider repertory—consisted of either six or seven compositions. In terms of subject matter, and like most *opéra de salon*, the focus is on the urban domestic, and the number of singing characters is also the same, mostly either three or four with occasional pieces for two or five singing characters.[9]

In chapter 5, it was seen that *Le journal des jeunes personnes* not only published instrumental music and romances but in 1843 aligned *vaudeville* with *opéra de salon*. In the same year, it published a *comédie mêlée de couplets* titled *Les suites d'une indiscrétion*, with libretto by Mme Huard and music by

---

[8] See, for example, Rocheblave's *Deux lunatiques à Saint-Cloud* to a libretto by Boisgontier. The final number is titled 'Vaudeville final'. *Le journal des demoiselles* 31 (1863) 136–137. The score is JOURNAL DES DEMOISELLES/Boulevard des Italiens, N° 1./. . ./DEUX LUNATIQUES À S^T-CLOUD/VAUDEVILLE/*Paroles* (dans le texte) de Madame/ADAM BOISGONTIER./Musique de/ A. ROCHEBLAVE/Imp. Duput Passage du Désir, 3, Paris, 14–16.

[9] These comments on the anatomy of *opéra de salon* published in *Le journal des demoiselles* and *Le magasin des demoiselles* are based on the data given in the appendix to chapter 1.

Blancou.[10] With one act in eleven scenes and a cast of four female roles and two negligible male ones, *Les suites d'une indiscrétion* deploys its eight numbers (*airs, duos,* and a *choeur général*) in the same ways as any *opéra de salon* written ten or twenty years later. The journal went to great length to explain that 'in order to give a new allure to the work, the author had interpolated *couplets, duos, choeurs,* whose music had been entrusted to a young composer full of promise, M. Blancou, first prize-winner at the Conservatoire'.[11] The attribution was a little disingenuous, since although Blancou was a prize-winner at the Conservatoire, it was for clarinet performance and not for composition. Furthermore, the work was reprinted in *Le journal des demoiselles* itself the same year. The project was not followed with any other work, probably because neither journal, although both were publishing music supplements at that point, had the ability to publish the entire score, even though *Le journal des jeunes personnes* managed to publish the *duo* for Marie and Eugène two years later in its volume for 1845.[12] Although *opéra de salon* in these types of journals had to wait a decade before it appeared again, its status as a genre deeply embedded in the lives and activities of women of all ages was already secure.

Opéras de salon published in women's journals differ from the rest of the repertory in that they almost never figure in published accounts of performances either in private homes or in concert halls; the works are therefore almost entirely absent from any form of public discourse. Of the nearly two hundred references to performances of *opéra de salon* up to 1870, only two relate to works published in women's journals. Clapisson's *Le coffret de Saint-Domingue* was mounted at a concert given in the Salle Herz by Chaudesaigues and his pianist wife in March 1855,[13] and Duprato's

---

[10] *Le journal des jeunes personnes* 11 (1843) 328–337. Mme Ferdinand Huard was presumably the wife of the poet and lyricist Ferdinand Huard, since the work is dedicated to Laure Dancla, the daughter of one of the husband's collaborators, Charles Dancla.

[11] 'Pour donner un nouvel attrait à cet ouvrage, l'auteur y a intercalé des couplets, duos, chœurs, dont la musique a été confiée à un jeune compositeur plein d'avenir, M. Blancou, premier prix du Conservatoire' (*ibidem*, 328, note 1).

[12] DUO/Extrait de la Partition des Suite[s] d'une Indiscrétion,/Comédie mêlée de Chants publiée par le Journal des Jeunes personnes/Paroles de Mme Ferdinand HUARD. Musique de M. BLANCOU, *Le journal des jeunes personnes* 13 (1845) unnumbered appendix. Strangely, the published extract bears the numbering 16–18, which has nothing to do with the organization of the journal and suggests that the score might have been published separately with no surviving trace.

[13] *La Revue et Gazette musicale de Paris*, 4 March 1855.

La reine Mozab was presented at a prize-giving ceremony at the educational institution run by Mmes Chenu and Frezzolla in Versailles in August 1867; and even these instances do not constitute performances in the most prestigious *salons*.[14] With this clear separation in mind, it is tempting to hypothesize a more intimate performance environment for *opéra de salon* published in journals for young unmarried women than that of the grander *salons*, studios, and concert halls discussed in chapters 3 and 4. Indeed, were it not for the very close alignment between the forms of the works, one might be further tempted to hypothesize a subgenre along the lines of the *opéra de parloir*, where the only audience might be the amateur domestic performing team itself, together with very close associates.

It would be wrong, despite the mutual exclusion of the repertory of *opéra de salon* published in women's journals, to insist too strongly, therefore, on a rigorous distinction between the works for the opulent and formal *salon* and those published in women's journals and the performance context one might reconstruct for each. In the introduction to his collection of plays, *vaudevilles*, and *opérettes* for young women published in 1858, Driou painted a picture of a performance of an *opéra de salon* that sat uneasily between the *parloir* as described in previous paragraphs and the fully fledged *salon*. Driou described a *soirée* given by the Vicomtesse Napoléon de Montesquiou to show off her new rooms[15] and gave an unequivocal account of a well-attended *salon* where the guests—'senators, duchesses, marquis, countesses, barons, generals, *abbés* . . . and some more vulgar names'[16]—enjoyed gambling, the wit of invited journalists and men of letters, a concert given by artists from the Conservatoire, and, towards two a.m., a dinner. The story took an unexpected turn as Driou himself went into a room where twenty young girls between the ages of eleven and fifteen were corralled while their parents enjoyed the evening. Driou's solution to a situation where the children could not agree whether to play with dolls or to play a game of

---

[14] *Le ménestrel*, 11 August 1867.

[15] Driou, *Nouveau théâtre des jeunes demoiselles*, i–viii. The Montesquiou family occupied a series of town houses on the prestigious rue de Varenne; Vicomte Napoléon and his family resided at no. 60, an eighteenth-century building attributed to the architect Dominique Pineau, together with his parents, Comte Ambroise Anatole Augustin de Montesquiou-Fézensac, formerly *aide de camp* to Louis Philippe; the Vicomte lived there until he moved into his own town house on the Boulevard La Tour-Maubourg.

[16] 'Sénateurs, duchesses, marquis, comtesses, barons, généraux, abbés, et . . . quelques noms plus vulgaires' (*ibidem*, i).

colin-maillard (blind man's buff), rejected as being too risky given the state of the furniture and decorations, was to engage the girls in 'a little comedy, a little drama in which you will yourselves play the characters, a pretty little *vaudeville* [sic] that you will play in the presence of your families and before the society that they will invite to see you and to hear you'.[17] The work in question was in fact an *opéra de salon*, *Le bonhomme Noël*, which Driou published at the end of the collection of which this account formed the prologue.[18] Girls who could sing were assigned roles, and Driou brought in musicians to play the piano, the *orgue expressif*, and the harp. The work was prepared in a week, and the performance was given in the Vicomtesse de Montesquiou's *salon* and in other locations thereafter. Driou's account intriguingly elided the engagement of the *demoiselle* associated with *opéra de salon* published in women's journals with the more opulent performance conditions from which it was usually separated.

Despite the detail given by Driou, he revealed nothing of the identity of the composer of *Le bonhomme Noël*; there is no evidence that Driou ever composed or could have prepared the music for the work himself. Given the work's evident musical ambition, this is something of a barrier to coming to terms with its significance. The single act, divided into fifteen scenes, is cast for five female characters, a single male character (the eponym, sometimes disguised as 'La mendiante'), and a female chorus. The scene is set in a girls' boarding school, the Institution Valmer. There are no fewer than twelve numbers, of which the last depends extensively but not exclusively on the first (table 6.2).

Such an ambitious structure aligns *Le bonhomme Noël* with the completely anonymous *Un rendez-vous en Espagne* that was approved by the censors for performance in the Salle Herz in April 1864 but never performed[19] and with *Les premiers cinq francs* by the mysterious Quatremère that was published in the journal *Le berquin* in 1857. Certainly—and unlike *Un rendez-vous en Espagne* and *Les premiers cinq francs*—*Le bonhomme Noël* includes no fewer than six choruses for the *demoiselles* and at least one further number that includes their participation. The first appearance of the character of Le

---

[17] 'Une petite comédie, un petit drame, dont vous serez vous-mêmes les personnages, un joli petit vaudeville que vous jouerez en présence de vos familles et devant la société qu'elle convieront à vous voir et à vous entendre' (*ibidem*, iv).

[18] *Ibidem*, 211–239.

[19] '7100/ - /18 avril 1864/Un rendez-vous/en Espagne/ - /Opéra-Comique/ - /Salle Herz' (Paris, Archives Nationales, F[18] 1346/7100).

Table 6.2. Structure of Alfred Driou, *Le bonhomme Noël*.

No.	Sc.	Character	Incipit	Notes
1	1	Choeur des élèves	'Noël! Noël! Noël!'	Accompanied by harmonium, harp, or piano
2	2	Mademoiselle de Bingrave/Choeur des élèves	'Je sors, enfants, mais restez sages'	
3	3	Marie and Jeanne	'Je ne suis point, mais point ambitieuse'	
4	3	Isabelle	'Je ne veux rien, Mesdemoiselles'	
5	3	Choeur des élèves	'Noël, Noël, toi que j'aime et vénère'	Organ prelude
6	4	Le bonhomme Noël (*mélodrame*)	'Me voilà, mes enfants; je ne fais pas attendre'	Spoken while the muted harp plays vague melodies
7	5	Choeur des élèves	'Quelle nouvelle on accourt nous apprendre!'	Accompanied by piano
8	7	La mendiante	'Aux malheureux accordez l'assistance'	Harmonium prelude
9	8	Choeur des élèves	'Beau barde, mon beau barde'	
10	12	La mendiante	'Gardez-vous de délire'	
11	13	Choeur des élèves/Sabine	'Disposons-nous, Mesdemoiselles'	
12	15	Choeur des élèves/Le bonhomme Noël	'Noël! Noël! Noël!'	Built out of Choeur des élèves (no. 1) with additional material for Le bonhomme Noël

Bonhomme Noël consists of a *mélodrame* in leisurely rolling Alexandrines over a muted harp accompaniment of 'vague melodies'.[20] Such instrumental specifications are as common in the work as they are rare in *opéra de salon* in general, and the use of preludes for both harp and *orgue expressif* (Driou prefers the term *harmonium*) betrays not only a more elaborate instrumentation than the usual keyboard but also exactly the combination of

---

[20] '[Le bonhomme Noël] parle, pendant que la harpe fait entendre en sourdine de vagues mélodies' (Driou, *Nouvel théâtre des jeunes demoiselles*, 219).

instrumental resources used by Duprez in his private theatre which was so important for *opéra de salon*.

The possibility of a generic division between different types of *opéra de salon* triggered by an exclusively female performance context prompts questions about the degree to which various forms of *opéra de salon*—bounded to varying degrees by private *lieux* and *espaces*—constitute work and recreation by and for women, both *demoiselles* and older women. Female *salonnières* had been a feature of Parisian culture since Catherine de Rambouillet and Madeleine de Scudéry established their own *salons* in the seventeenth century,[21] but at the beginning of the Second Empire, two of the most important *salonnières* had just died: Mme de Recamier in 1849 and the Comtesse de Merlin in 1852. For *opéra de salon*, this left Mme Orfila, whose salon continued until weeks before her death in 1864, and Princesse Mathilde, who would continue her *salon* activities well into the Third Republic; the women ran the two most well-established *salons* that put on *opéra de salon* during the Second Empire.[22]

Both male and female spouses were frequently identified as *salonniers/salonnières* promoting *opéra de salon*, from M. et Mme Offenbach in 1854[23] to M. et Mme Trélat in 1869.[24] There are only two examples of *opéras de salon* promoted by male *salonniers* alone. The first was Pitre-Chevalier, whose wife had died in 1859 and who may not have been able to host even as early as 1854[25] (the two other documented events at his home are in 1858 and 1863).[26] The second was Bourdon, who, although credited with hosting alone in 1855, shared the honour with his wife two years later.[27] Similar inconsistencies occur in the reports of the *soirées* given by Emile and Clara Pfeiffer for their composer son, Georges.[28]

By contrast, large numbers of single women welcomed *opéra de salon* and enthusiastic audiences into their homes; they fell into three categories: divorcées, widows, and the relatives of creative and

---

[21] The literature on seventeenth- and eighteenth-century *salons* is vast and tends to define the nature of *salon* culture—wrongly in some cases—for the nineteenth century and especially the Second Empire. See, for example, Lilti, *The World of the Salon*.

[22] There are general accounts of Orfila's salon in Bassinville, *Les salons d'autrefois*, 4:155–236. For a similarly general account of the Princesse Mathilde's *salon*, see Zucconi, 'Les salons de Mathilde et Julie Bonaparte'; Vilkner, 'Sounding Streets', 70–104.

[23] *La Revue et Gazette musicale de Paris*, 7 May 1854; *Le ménestrel*, 7 May 1854.

[24] *Ibidem*, 4 April 1869.

[25] *Ibidem*, 5 March 1854.

[26] *Ibidem*, 11 April 1858 and 12 April 1863.

[27] *Ibidem*, 25 April 1855 and 20 December 1857.

[28] The sole instance of both parents hosting an event featuring their son's work was on 23 February 1862 (see *La Revue et Gazette musicale de Paris*, 2 March 1862 and *Le ménestrel* for the same date).

performing artists. Geneviève-Lambert de Saint-Olive had married the Baron Dupuytren in 1810, and she kept her title after divorce in 1820 and alone promoted d'Indy's *Les deux princesses* in 1859 in her apartments in the Chaussée d'Antin.[29] Of more modest means but with probably more support from friends and colleagues, the newly widowed Rodolphe was the beneficiary of a concert in the Salle Herz after the death of her husband, the singer Chaudesaigues.[30] More conventional was Orfila, whose husband had died in 1853 and who frequently collaborated with Mosneron de Saint-Preux— who, as the sibling of the Baron Mosneron de Saint-Preux, may never have married—on *soirées* that included *opéra de salon*.[31]

One of the many performances of d'Indy's *Les deux princesses* was hosted by the composer's mother, the Comtesse d'Indy, in her apartments in the rue de Bac, apparently at the behest of Rossini (it is unclear why Rossini could not host in his own apartments on the Chaussée d'Antin),[32] and Pfeiffer's parents put on several performances of his *Le capitaine Roch* both in their home on the rue Bleue and also in the Salle Pleyel, just around the corner. Similarly, the wife of Prévost-Rousseau, although she did not promote her own husband's two *opérettes*, mounted a performance of O'Kelly's *Stella* in 1861.[33] And, only slightly differently, Marcelli put on a performance of *Jaloux de soi* for which she wrote both the words and the music, in her own home in 1856.[34]

Contemporary accounts of audiences for *opéra de salon* stress repeatedly the dominance of women. Some accounts make the point in neutral terms, for example, when the anonymous author of *La Revue et Gazette musicale de Paris* described the audience for *Il était une fois une roi* as 'ladies of high society more or less associated ... with members of the Cercle [de l'Union Artistique]'.[35] Aesthetic—if not discriminatory and

---

[29] *Ibidem*, 27 February 1859.

[30] *La Revue et Gazette musicale de Paris*, 7 March 1858. Offenbach's *Les deux aveugles* was performed not, as was usual, by artists who specialised in *opéra de salon*, but by performers from the Théâtre des Bouffes-Parisiens itself.

[31] See the report of the premiere of Pfeiffer's *Le capitaine Rocha* in the Orfila–Mosneron de Saint-Preux *salon* in *Le ménestrel*, 23 March 1862.

[32] *Ibidem*, 27 March 1859. Rossini had hosted *opéras de salon* in his own home on the rue de la Chaussée-d'Antin in December 1858 and February 1859 (*ibidem*, 19 December 1858; *La Revue et Gazette musicale de Paris*, 6 March 1859).

[33] *Ibidem*, 22 December 1861.

[34] *Le musée de famille*, 23 (1855–1856) 159–160 (the event took place on 31 March 1856).

[35] 'dames du grand monde plus ou moins apparentées, ... aux membres du Cercle' (*La Revue et Gazette musicale de Paris*, 14 June 1863). For what little is known of the Cercle de l'Union Artistique, see Jeffrey Cooper, *The Rise of Instrumental Music and Concert Series in Paris, 1828–1871*, Studies in Musicology 65 (Ann Arbor, MI: UMI Research Press, 1983) 225–226.

misogynistic—judgement, however, was never far behind. '*Belphégor* was given before a *parterre* made up of beautiful women'.[36] A decade later, paleness of skin would be praised: 'What a *parterre* of beautiful women and white hands to applaud!'[37] And many reports were pejorative. On three separate occasions between 1855 and 1861, the anonymous correspondent (it is not impossible that it was Heugel himself) described female members of the audiences in the same breath as diamonds and flowers: 'In the reception room, arranged as an amphitheatre, sparkled a *parterre* of women, flowers, and diamonds'; 'a genuine *parterre* of flowers, women, and diamonds'; and 'the *parterre* was dazzling with women, flowers, and diamonds'.[38] Women here are given little more of a role than mere adornments contributing to the event no more than *bijoux* or begonias.

The performing forces of *opéra de salon* were often inflected by amateur participation. In terms of soloists, men and women were equally represented. Among the men, Jal, Le Roy, Belouet, and L'Épine have already been mentioned, but they worked alongside a host of others, some of whom are known—the anatomist Robin and the composer Ducellier, for example—and others whose identification has so far resisted inquiry: Mounnier, Ménars, Filhouze, and Ferdinand Michel. These men were matched by such women as Dejoly, Bizet's friend Marie Trélat, and Mme de Grandval. The number of non-professional women soloists might be inflated by a single performance of Clapisson's *Le coffret de Saint-Domingue* where Chaudesaigues and his Conservatoire-trained wife cast the work exclusively with the relatives of well-known musicians—a fact pointed out by Blanchard.[39] The performance was given by the daughters of the composer Henrion; the Chaudesaigueses' daughter Mlle Devienne, who would have had to have been the granddaughter of the composer; Adeline Cluesmann, the daughter of the piano manufacturer; and Cécile-Antonin Biard, whose elder sister Cézarine-Anna was already well known as a performer in the city. This novelty event needs to be considered when judging the gendered focus of amateur soloists in *opéra de salon*, where the picture remains opaque.

---

[36] '*Belphégor* s'est montré devant un parterre composé de jolies femmes' (*La Revue et Gazette musicale de Paris*, 14 February 1858).

[37] 'mais quel parterre de jolies femmes et que de blanches mains pour applaudir!'(*Le ménestrel*, 10 March 1867).

[38] 'Dans la salle de réception disposée en amphithéâtre, étincelait un parterre de femmes, de fleurs et de diamants' (*Le ménestrel*, 4 March 1855); 'véritable parterre de fleurs, de femmes et de diamants' (*ibidem*, 23 January 1859); 'le parterre était éblouissant de femmes, de fleurs et de diamants' (*ibidem*, 20 January 1861).

[39] The event took place in the Salle Herz in late February or early March 1855. See Blanchard's review in *La Revue et Gazette musicale de Paris*, 4 March 1855.

Much less opaque is the appearance of society women in the chorus of *opéras de salon*. For the performance of d'Aoust's *Une partie de dominos*,[40] in a rare occurrence, the anonymous reporter listed some of the names of the society women in the chorus. In addition to the Comtesse de Molki and the Comtesse de Meffeny, who have resisted identification, the members of the chorus included Grandval, already noted as a composer of some renown; Marie-Pauline de Lanjuinais Marquise Law de Lauriston, a member of one of the country's most famous families; the Princesse de Castelcicala, who was the wife of the Neapolitan ambassador to Paris; and the Baronne de Laborde, who was to die a couple of years later at the age of twenty-three. Other members of the chorus were the Baronne de Caters (Marie Lablache, daughter of the famed Luigi Lablache) and the Marquise d'Aoust, whose talent, according to *Le ménestrel*'s author, 'was renowned on the left bank'. It is not unreasonable to suppose that works with chorus were performed with similar aristocratic forces whenever such events took place at homes of the aristocracy and the *haute bourgeoisie*.[41]

As the discussion of the casts of *opéra de salon* in chapter 2 made clear, female voices predominate in works for *salon*, studio, and concert hall and are used almost exclusively in those published in journals and destined for the *parloir*. Given the context outlined here, such conventions take on a very clear function and point to the close alignment between the largely female casts and the largely female environments for the cultivation of the genre. Driou's description above admits no male participation at all except for the title role, who spends most of the work disguised as a female beggar. The female choruses, so frequent in *opéras de salon* destined for the *parloir*, may also have employed younger sons of the family with unbroken voices.

Women Composers and Librettists

Women constituted a significant proportion of the libretti for *opéra de salon*, especially those that were published in journals aimed at the young and unmarried *demoiselles*. Several women contributed just a single libretto

---

[40] Almost nothing survives of *Une parti de dominos* except a fantasy for military band by Jules Jacob. See FANTAISIE SUR UNE PARTIE DE DOMINOS/Opéra Comique de M^r le Marquis Jules d'AOUST/L'INSTRUMENTAL/Edition GAUTROT ainé./Arr. Par. Jules JACOB./Chef de Musique du 1er Dragons/.../Paris, GAUTROT ainé, Rue Turenne, 80 et chez RICHAULT, Ed^r B^t des Italiens 4.

[41] *Le ménestrel*, 15 March 1863.

amongst a range of other literary activities. Among these were Louise Sabatier, who wrote the words to a number of *romances* by Jules Couplet and d'Hack, for whose *opéra de salon Le revenant* she supplied the libretto.[42] Jenny Sabatier (no relation since her name is a pseudonym of Jenny-Caroline Thircuir) likewise wrote the words to *romances* (two works by Amédée de Roubin) as well as the libretto to Hocmelle's *Un service d'ami*,[43] but she was much better known as a poet, and her 1863 collection, *Rêves de jeunesse*, was widely read.[44] Like Jenny Sabatier, Caroline Berton wrote words for *romances* and a libretto to an *opéra de salon*, Poisot's (perhaps Nadaud's) *La clef du secrétaire*, in collaboration with Boisseaux.[45] But Berton also wrote plays and dramatized proverbs, children's stories, and a wide range of other texts, and her continuing commitment to *opéra de salon* is witnessed by her 1893 biography of Nadaud.[46] Anaïs Ségalas, the author of collections of poetry (*Les algériennes* [1831], *Nos bons parisiens* [1865]) and works for the theatre (beginning with *La loge de l'Opéra* at the Théâtre de l'Odéon in 1847), importantly worked on two *comédies-vaudevilles* for the Théâtre de la Porte Saint-Martin and the Théâtre de la Gaîté. These served as the background to her libretto for an *opéra de salon*, *Le miroir du diable*, which was set by Durand in 1856 and premiered in her sister-in-law's *salons* on the rue Vendôme.[47]

The most remarkable woman librettist of the Second Empire must surely have been Elisabeth-Françoise Adam (1816–1876), who married the lithographer Auguste-Victor Boisgontier. The marriage apparently collapsed in the late 1830s as a result of her misconduct, but this triggered a remarkable career for Elisa Boisgontier, or Mme Adam Boisgontier, as she was subsequently known.[48] It is important to distinguish her from her almost exact

---

[42] *Le revenant* was apparently performed at the Salle Herz sometime between April and May 1865, as the censors' libretto (the only surviving trace of the work) suggests: 'Salle Herz/Lu/Oui/7557/27 avril 1865/Le Revenant/Opéra-Comique en un acte; paroles de/Mme Louise Sabatier' (Paris, Archives Nationales, F^18 1346/7557).

[43] There is no surviving evidence of a performance, but Hocmelle's score was published: À Madame de Royer/UN/SERVICE d'AMI/*Opéra Comique en un Acte*/PAROLES DE MLLE/Jenny Sabatier/Musique/DE/EDMOND HOCMELLE/*Organiste de St Philippe du Roule et de la Chapelle du Sénat/…/au MÉNESTREL, rue Vivienne, 2bis/…/chez Mr HOCMELLE, rue du Cirque, 21.*

[44] Jenny-Caroline Sabatier [Thircuir; Mme Léon Mallac], *Rêves de jeunesses … précédées de deux lettres de M. A. de Lamartine et de M. Méry* (Paris: Dentu, 1863).

[45] See chapter 2 for an account of the attribution of *La clef du secrétaire*, for which no sources survive.

[46] Caroline Berton, 'Gustave Nadaud comédien', *Nouvelle revue internationale*, 15 June 1893.

[47] The accounts in *Le ménestrel*, 9 March 1856, and in *La musée des familles* 23 (1855–1856) 192 are the only traces the work has left.

[48] Her biography is sketchy in the extreme. Élisabeth-Françoise Adam was married to the engraver Auguste-Victor Boisgontier, but the two almost immediately separated because of her alleged

contemporary, Geneviève-Elisa Boisgontier (c. 1817–1877), who had a long career as an actress in some of the same circles as Elisa from 1837 until 1872.[49] Mme Adam Boisgontier produced not only the libretti of fifteen *opéras de salon* between 1859 and 1875, all but one published in *Le journal des demoiselles* (the other was in *Le magasin des demoiselles*) but also an *opérette* titled *Qui refuse, muse* set by Hocmelle, various *comédies* and *comédies-vaudevilles* for the regulated theatre, and *charades* and *comédies* published in *Le journal des demoiselles*.[50] She also published an extended poem, *Paris nouveau*, extolling the virtues of the emerging 'new' Paris.[51] While she wrote libretti for composers who specialized in *opérette*—Jules Pillevestre, Francesco Chiaromonte, and Laurent de Rillé—Boisgontier also wrote for composers who were well known outside that world: Delibes and Grisar, for whom she wrote one libretto each; Semet, for whom she wrote two; and Massé, for whom she wrote three. The composer she worked with most was Rocheblave, whom she not only collaborated with five times but whom she also married in 1870.[52]

Although Adam Boisgontier carefully restricted her work to the composition of libretti, Anaïs Marcelli went further and wrote both libretto and score. The name concealed her identity as the Comtesse Perrière-Pilté, the widow of the industrialist Pierre Pilté, who had died in 1853.[53] By the early 1860s, she was well known for collections of poetry and the texts to a number of *romances*, by Godefroid in particular.[54] But it was her 1866 *opéra comique* *Le sorcier*, for which she wrote both words and music, that brought her out of the domain of the *salon* and into the world of the regulated theatre; the work

---

'inconduite' (Paris, Archives Nationales, F[18] 1736). Auguste-Victor left for Spain in the mid-1840s. *École Nationale des Chartes: Dictionnaire des imprimeurs-lithographes du xix siècle* (http://elec.enc.sorbonne.fr/imprimeurs/node/26739).

[49] Lyonnet, *Dictionnaire des comédiens français*, 186–187.

[50] Many of these were collected in Elisa Adam Boisgontier, *Nouveau théâtre des demoiselles* (Paris: Fonteney et Peltier, 1851) well before her engagement with *opéra de salon*.

[51] Elisa Adam Boisgontier, *Paris nouveau* (Paris: Lévy, 1857).

[52] Boisgontier's output, collaborators, and publication are all given in Everist, 'Music in the Second Empire Theatre (MitSET)'. Note that four of her libretti were written under the pseudonym 'Paul Dubourg'.

[53] Pilté had made his fortune from a monopoly of the supply of gas lamps for the streets of Paris; he also owned the building in which the Théâtre du Vaudeville was housed at the very end of the July Monarchy (Wild, *Dictionnaire des théâtres parisiens*, 419). For a comprehensive biography, see 'Pierre Pilté, industriel, directeur de théâtre, plaideur et comte posthume', *Polmorésie: histoire politique, locale, du mouvement ouvrier, de la résistance, sociale et des initiatives économiques* (http://polmoresie.over-blog.fr/2016/10/pierre-pilte-industriel-directeur-de-theatre-plaideur-et-comte-posthume.html).

[54] There is a valuable obituary of Marcelli in *Le Gaulois*, 2–3 January 1879.

was premiered at the Théâtre-Lyrique and was frequently performed during the three years following. But a decade earlier, her *Jaloux de soi*, for which she had again written both libretto and score, had been premiered in her own *salon* on the rue de Babylone in the heart of the Faubourg Saint-Germain.[55] Although it was published, *Jaloux de soi* remained in obscurity until revived by the Fantaisies-Parisiennes in 1873.[56] Marcelli never used her *salon* for the promotion of *opéras de salon* besides her own, but she was able to hire the most celebrated *opéra de salon* artists to perform it: Gaveaux-Sabatier and Lefort, accompanied by Augustine-Joséphine Zolobodjan.[57]

Eudoxe-Françoise Péan de la Roche-Jagu, like Marcelli, wrote both words and music to at least one of her eight or nine works for the stage (table 6.3).[58] It is far from clear, however, just how many of these were planned as *opéras de salon*. Péan de la Roche-Jagu is best known for her *Mémoires artistiques*, published in 1861 (she died in 1871), which cover her entire life up to the mid-1850s together with a brief conclusion for the period from 1855 to 1861.[59] The *Mémoires* are an object lesson in the difficulties of getting works onto the stage in Paris but especially the mechanics of producing *opéra de salon*, since this was the performance context for many of her works, whatever their generic origins. Three of the early works for which the composer wrote the libretto seem to have never been performed, but *Le tuteur dupé* was performed both in the family home and in the municipal theatre in Brest, the nearest large town. Despite ambitions in the direction of the regulated theatre, all the performances that Péan de la Roche-Jagu was able to mount after her arrival in Paris were at venues associated with *opéra de salon*: the Salle Sainte-Cécile, the École-Lyrique, the Salle Herz, and thanks to her family connections with Barthélémy de Las Cases, Comte de Las Cases, she was able to mount her earliest performances in Paris in the *salon* of the Hôtel de

---

[55] The event was reviewed in *Le musée des familles* 23 (1855–1856) 159–160.

[56] JALOUX DE SOI/Proverbe lyrique en un acte./Pour Chant et Piano/-/*Paroles et Musique*/de/ Mme Anaïs P. P./-/.../Lith. Ducrieux, Rue de Vaugirard, 136.

[57] Zolobodjan had won a series of Conservatoire prizes, the most recent of which was the *deuxième accessit* for voice (Pierre, *Le Conservatoire*, 2:872). She married *opéra de salon* artist Archainbaud in 1857 and on at least one occasion sang alongside her husband in a performance of *opéra de salon*: Mutel's *Promenade dans un salon* in the Salons de Pleyel-Wolff in March 1864 (see *La Revue et Gazette musicale*, 27 March 1864).

[58] The two paragraphs on Péan de la Roche-Jagu have profited from a dialogue with Richard Sherr, who is currently preparing a study of her career.

[59] Eudoxe-Françoise Péan de la Roche-Jagu, *Mémoires artistiques . . . écrits par elle-même* (Paris: Ledoyen, 1861).

Table 6.3. Eudoxe-Françoise Péan de la Roche-Jagu, lyric output.

Title	Librettist	Generic descriptor	Premiere venue	Premiere date	Subsequent performances
Le tuteur dupé	Péan de la Roche-Jagu and anonymous		Family home; Théâtre Municipale de Brest	c. 1826	
Nell, ou Le gabier d'Artimon	anonymous				
Gil Diaze	anonymous				
Le retour de Tasse	Olivier Legall	scène lyrique; grand opéra avec récitatifs	Salle Herz	13 March 1842	
La jeunesse de Lully	Galoppe d'Onquaire	opéra comique	Salle de l'Hôtel de Ville	16 March 1845	Salle de l'Hôtel de Ville, 14 March 1846; Théâtre de Montmartre, 26 December 1846; Théâtre Municipale de Brest, 14 February 1847; Salle de l'École Lyrique, 29 January 1848; Salle du Conservatoire, 12 May 1850; Salle Sainte-Cécile, 20 April 1853; Théâtre-Lyrique, 7 August 1860
Le mousquetaire	Achille and Armand d'Artois	opéra comique	Salle de l'Hôtel de Ville under the title Le jeune militaire, ou La trahison	16 December 1845	Withdrawn by librettists but offered to Georges Bousquet at the same time; premiere 1844
Paul et Julie ou la lettre supposée	Belcour	opéra comique	Salle du Casino Paganini	25 March 1851	Aborted performance because of lack of singers
Le mariage par hasard	Belcour		Salle Sainte-Cécile	30 March 1852	? Paul et Julie under a new title

Table 6.3. Continued

Title	Librettist	Generic descriptor	Premiere venue	Premiere date	Subsequent performances
Simple et coquette	Émile de Richebourg	*opéra comique*	Salle de l'École Lyrique	10 May 1856	Salons de Souffleto, 1 March 1857; Théâtre-Italien, 5 July 1859; Théâtre-Lyrique, 7 August 1860; Salle du Grand Orient, 28 December 1862
La reine de l'onde	Emile de Richebourg	*opéra comique*	Salle Herz	04 February 1862	

Ville.[60] Published reviews of these performances were as cautious as any received by composers identified by critics as noble or from society.[61]

Although Péan de la Roche-Jagu was aiming at the Opéra-Comique and—from the late 1840s onwards—the Opéra National and its successor the Théâtre-Lyrique, all her efforts were thwarted by extreme bad luck, misogynistic unfair dealing, or a lack of planning arising out of crippling debt. Negotiations with librettists and directors were frequently far advanced when directorial regimes changed, and she was forced to reopen discussions with new directors with very different priorities. This was a constant challenge to librettists and composers of both sexes. But the kinds of conspiracies that surrounded her setting of the libretto *Le mousquetaire*, by Achille and Armand d'Artois, who were trying to break into the world of *opéra comique* in 1844, feel very much like casual discrimination, using a woman composer as a pretext to develop their own careers. The d'Artois brothers used Péan de la Roche-Jagu to gain approval for their libretto at the Opéra-Comique but then—in a conspiracy with the director—judged the composer's music unplayable and passed the libretto to a recent Prix de Rome laureate, Georges Bousquet. Bousquet's *opéra comique Le mousquetaire* was premiered but

---

[60] There was a family connection with the navy, and the Comte de Las Cases had been an *aide de camp* of the navy ministers Guy-Victor Dupérré (1830-1843) and Albin Roussin (briefly replacing Dupérré in 1840). See Adolphe Robert and Gaston Cougny, *Dictionnaire des parlementaires français*, 5 vols. (Paris: Bourloton, 1889–1891) 3:612–613.

[61] The article in *La Revue et Gazette musicale de Paris*, 24 April 1853, is typical.

received only three performances. Furthermore, the d'Artois brothers tried to prevent Péan de la Roche-Jagu from performing her own music, claiming—technically correctly—that they held the rights to their libretto. When the latter tried to put on a performance of the piece, the d'Artois brothers brought an action in court, which they lost apart from agreement on new words and a new title—*Le jeune militaire, ou La trahison*—under which title the piece was performed at the Hôtel de Ville in March 1845. It is difficult to judge exactly what went on with performances that Péan de la Roche-Jagu mounted in settings more familiar from *opéra de salon*. Her accounts of not being able to assemble the funds to hire a hall or pay performing artists seem to provide evidence of optimistic, if not naive, practices that those who put on such performances successfully did not have to manage. However, the travails of Péan de la Roche-Jagu are only known because she wrote about them, whereas the endeavours of other performer- or composer-promoters who may have suffered in the same way are simply not known.[62]

Not all female composer-librettists of *opéra de salon*—and of wider-ranging genres—were as unlucky as Péan de la Roche-Jagu. Pauline Thys wrote both libretto and music for two of her three *opéras de salon* that were widely performed in the *salons* she hosted with her husband, an art dealer; they were *Le perruque du bailli* (1860), *L'héritier sans le savoir* (1858), and *Quand Dieu est dans le mariage, Dieu le garde* (1860), of which only *L'héritier sans le savoir* has left any surviving trace.[63] Thys was, however, more successful than Péan de la Roche-Jagu outside of the culture of *opéra de salon*: her first stage work, *La pomme de Turquie*, was premiered at Offenbach's Bouffes-Parisiens in 1857, and she had further success with her *Le pays de Cocagne*, to a libretto by Pittaud de Forges, at the Théâtre-Lyrique in 1862 and especially with *Le mariage de Tabarin* in 1876, given both in Paris and—as *La congiura di Chevreuse*—in Florence.[64] She was the daughter of Alphonse Thys, who had a distinguished career as a composer for the Opéra-Comique in the 1840s (his last work was *La sournoise* in 1848) but who also wrote an *opéra de salon*: *Les échos de Rosine*, which parodies Rossini's *Il barbiere di Siviglia* in at least one number.[65]

---

[62] This paragraph summarizes Péan de la Roche-Jagu, *Mémoires artistiques*, 46–59.

[63] The censors' libretto survives as 'N° 3692/8 Août 1858/L'héritier sans le savoir/Opéra Comique en un Acte./Paroles et Musique de/Mlle/Pauline Thys' (Paris, Archives Nationales, F^{18} 1531/3692).

[64] Fétis, *Biographie universelle des musiciens*, Suppl. 2:577.

[65] *Ibidem*. The work was printed, however: LES/ÉCHOS DE ROSINE/OPÉRA-COMIQUE DE SALON/REPRÉSENTÉ POUR LA PREMIÈRE FOIS A PARIS LE 13 OCTOBRE 1854/POÈME/DE/ÉTIENNE TRÉFEU/MUSIQUE/DE/A. THYS/PARIS/ETIENNE CHALLIOT, ÉDITEUR/Rue Saint-Honoré, 354, près la place Vendôme.

Performance in the *parloir* is essential to understanding *opéra de salon*. The environment in which the *opéras de salon* that were published in *Le journal des demoiselles* and *Le magasin des demoiselles* point to a cultivation by women—mothers and daughters between school and marriage—in which men played almost no role beyond the male gaze. Women and *demosielles* created performances in the *parloir* that developed the sorts of skills that would serve the latter well in life. And the *parloir* aesthetic carried over into the *salon*, as the case related by Driou exemplifies so well. Although there is a larger role for men in that at least one member of the cast in an *opéra de salon* destined for studio, concert hall, or *salon* was male, so many of the key roles in these events—most especially the audience—were taken by women that the temptation to feminize the genre of *opéra de salon*—especially the variety cultivated in the *parloir*—is almost irresistible.

The emphasis on the female cultivation of *opéra de salon* is echoed in the activity of women in the creation of the genre. In comparison with the regulated theatre, the number of women composers, librettists, and composer-librettists is very high, and in some domains—the composition of libretti for *opéra de salon* in journals—predominant. The extent to which female creative artists were able to use *opéra de salon* as a stepping stone to the regulated theatre is perhaps overestimated by mostly male critics. In many cases where women were active in the regulated theatre and in *opéra de salon*, their work in the former predated and overlapped with the latter, and their endeavours were more congruent with generalized moves towards female engagement with public life witnessed during the Second Empire and beyond.

7
Locating *Opéra de salon*

Time and Space

Opéra de salon was controlled by time and space. Time was organized by the season, space by the ways in which *lieu* could be configured and reconfigured as *espace*. Various agents interacted with these times and spaces: creative artists—librettists and composers but also set designers, costumers, and others—built or adapted, and performers of all types and ambitions formed a network with *salonniers/salonnières*, guests, and audiences, as well as with those who managed and profited from renting out concert halls. This combination of agent, time, and space created an institutional culture governed by convention that had a far-reaching effect on the structure of *opéras de salon* themselves. This chapter is devoted to an understanding of three interlocking circles of space: the precise *spatialité* in which *opéra de salon* functioned, the broader geolocative contexts of the cultivation of *opéra de salon* in the city of Paris, and the culture of *opéra de salon* beyond Paris and outside France. This understanding of space first requires a context and a grasp of how time interacts with *opéra de salon* and its cultures.

The season was critical to the functioning of the salon; it ran from December to April each year. When it began and ended was a matter for regular public comment; the first meeting of—say—Mme Orfila's salon was broadcast,[1] as was, for example, Rossini's final salon of the season.[2] Commentators would also announce the number in the series of events in a particular *salon*: when Ettling mounted the production of his *Un jour de noce* in March 1864, it was noted that this was the family's twelfth *matinée musicale* of the season.[3] The end of the season could be abrupt for some and

---

[1] '*Opéra de salon* has just made its season's entrance into the musical world . . . in the *salon* of Mmes Orfila and Mosneron de Saint-Preux' ('L'opéra de salon vient de faire son entrée de saison dans le monde musical . . . chez Mmes Orfila et Mosneron de Saint-Preux'; *Le ménestrel*, 2 December 1860). The salon of Mmes Orfila and Mosneron de Saint-Preux is discussed in chapter 3.
[2] 'The last musical event that took place in Rossini's *salon* before his departure for the country' ('La dernière réunion musicale qui a eu lieu chez Rossini avant son départ pour la campagne'; *La Revue et Gazette musicale de Paris*, 10 June 1860).
[3] *Ibidem*, 13 March 1864.

Opéra de salon. Mark Everist, Oxford University Press. Oxford University Press 2025.
DOI: 10.1093/9780197695210.003.0008

ragged for others. Weckerlin's *Tout est bien qui finit bien* was announced as the formal end of Orfila's salon as late as mid-May 1864[4] while—almost as late—when Princesse Mathilde put on Nadaud's *Le docteur vieuxtemps* in the third week of April in 1854, Horace de Viel-Castel could complain that most *salonniers/salonnières* had already closed up their city homes for the summer, but it had been raining for four days solidly, and a late *salon*—such as the one he attended—was a blessing, however late it was in the season.[5]

Rossini played fast and loose with seasonal conventions on 4 June 1860, when he put on a performance of Bernard's *Loin du bruit* in his salon in the Chaussée d'Antin. 'Last Monday', reported *Le ménestrel*, 'Maestro Rossini said farewell musically to the good city of Paris, before going to request the fresh air and the scents of the Bois de Boulogne of his new villa in Passy'.[6] It may well be that Rossini was waiting in Paris until his new villa was ready for him, but the consequences were clear: the gathering was small—'a tiny number of the chosen' (*'un petit nombre des élus'*)—and the event was chaotic. The two roles in *Loin du bruit* were to be taken by Mira and Sainte-Foy, but the latter was on duty at the Opéra-Comique, in the role of Champagne in François-Auguste Gevaert's *Le Chateau-Trompette*; to make matters worse, the Gevaert was the second work at the Opéra-Comique that evening (preceded by Paul Lagarde's *L'habit de Milord*), which meant that Sainte-Foy took his curtain calls in the Salle Favart with the cast around 11:45 p.m. and scurried across the Boulevard des Italiens to Rossini's *salon* to grab his costume for *Loin du bruit* at the stroke of midnight. In subsequent years, and with the attraction of the Villa Rossini in Passy as soon as the weather

---

[4] *Le ménestrel*, 15 May 1864.

[5] 'We leave a precocious spring to find the dark days of winter again, the cold of December or of January; the country, that calls us, has become impracticable; again we take up our padded frock coats and our woollen overcoats, to which we thought we had bidden farewell for six months; we huddle around our lighted fires; let's stay in Paris; let's resist our travelling humour. . . . The fine weather has already left us; the rain and the wind have saddened us for four days. Fatigue for parties and salons had been declared; we all aspired to rest, far from balls and concerts; the breezes of spring intoxicated us; we welcomed fields, forests, their first greenery' ('Nous sortons d'un printemps précoce pour retrouver les sombre journées de l'hiver, le froid de décembre ou de janvier; la campagne, qui nous appelait, est devenue impraticable; nous reprenons nos redingotes ouatées et nos paletots de drap, auxquels nous pensions avoir dit adieu pour six mois; nous nous pressons autour de nos foyers allumés; restons donc à Paris, refrénons notre humeur voyageuse. . . . Le beau temps nous lassait déjà; la pluie et le vent nous attristent depuis quatre jours. On se déclarait fatigué des fêtes de salons; nous aspirons tous au repos, loin des bals et des concerts; les brises du printemps nous enivrent; nous acclamions les champs, les forêts, leur première verdure'; *Le constitutionnel*, 5 May 1854). Much of Viel-Castel's review was reprinted in *Le nouvelliste*, 5 May 1854, but this passage was omitted.

[6] 'Le maestro Rossini disait musicalement adieu à la bonne ville de Paris, avant d'aller demander à sa nouvelle villa de Passy le grand air et les parfums du bois de Boulogne' (*Le ménestrel*, 10 June 1860).

improved, Rossini's *salons* were among some of the earliest to end, but then they were restarted in Passy in a different form.

Spatialité

Against this temporal backdrop, the four different locations for the cultivation of *opéra de salon*—concert halls, artists' and performers' studios, *salons*, and *parloirs*—all involve the transformation of *spatialité* in ways that have been theorized by sociologists since the end of the Second World War. What emerges from a re-reading of de Certeau's and Merleau-Ponty's theoretical engagement, discussed more fully in the introduction to this book, is the importance of contingency in the relationships between *lieu* and *espace*: theoretical models can delineate the geometrical nature of floors, walls, and ceilings and can describe cultural events that turn those *lieux* into *espaces*, but the process depends on the specific nature of the material in question. Each *lieu* transforms into *espace* in different ways, and it is these transformations that underpin the culture of *opéras de salon*.

As has been seen, concert halls were transformed into theatres throughout the Second Empire using temporary stages, footlights, sets, and costumes. Composers and performers also used their own private studios for events. Such places could range from the implausibly small to the most elaborate. Duprez's private theatre has already been seen as the most elaborate location for these types of performances, but more typical perhaps was the studio of Gaveaux-Sabatier). She has been a near-constant presence in previous chapters as one of the most celebrated performers of *opéra de salon*, and at some point around 1860, she moved into a new apartment on the rue des Petites-Écuries in the tenth *arrondissement* of Paris, which traversed the whole of the building's façade on the street side; the two rooms at the front of the building are both around 8 by 5 metres and were separated by full-width doors that could be opened to create a performance space of around 80 square metres.[7] Gaveaux-Sabatier started a sequence of performances in February 1866 with a performance of Weckerlin's *Pierrot à Paphos, ou La sérénade interrompue*; she starred with Hermann-Léon.

---

[7] I am grateful to the anonymous *concierge* of 55 rue des Petites-Écuries who granted me access to the building and enough time to make suitable estimates of the size of Gaveaux-Sabatier's apartment from both street and courtyard sides in December 2022.

Although this performance was described as Weckerlin's own enterprise 'in Mme Gaveaux-Sabatier's *salons*' rather than an undertaking by the property owner herself,[8] this was the first in a series of annual performances given on the rue des Petites-Écuries, and it was the last that Gaveaux-Sabatier undertook for someone else. She was described as the host in March 1867 when she put on Weckerlin's *Manche à manche*, again with Hermann-Léon, and in 1868 for two performances of the same composer's *La laitière de Trianon* a month apart.[9]

The types of *salon* spaces available for the performance of *opéra de salon* in private homes varied widely. They ranged from sculptors' studios in which such performances must have stretched the homeowner's resources (the studio belonging to Cordier has been discussed and illustrated in chapter 4) right up to the opulence of the *salon* of Princesse Mathilde or the ballroom of the *haut-bourgeois* Binder family. While it is difficult to generalize about the size, shape, and levels of attendance at a *salon* event, this difficulty is an important guide to the dangers in the usage of the term *salon*, so frequently pejorative but equally frequently misunderstood.

The repertory of *opéra de salon* promoted in three out of these four types of venues—concert halls, artists' and musicians' studios, and private *salons*—is shared: the same work could be heard in the Salle Herz and in the home of the Comte de Morny, at the home of a doctor in the rue de Bac, in the studio of one of the performers, or at the home of the Orfila family. A summary of the six performances of the *opéra de salon* titled *A deux pas du bonheur*, whose libretto was by Mme Roger de Beauvoir and whose score was by the celebrated harpist Godefroid, will serve as an example (table 7.1).[10]

The same work, frequently with the same performers, appears in all three categories of venue: concert hall, artist's studio, and various sorts of *salon*. The first performance was given by a performing artist in his own studio; the second, fourth, and sixth performances were mounted by *salonniers/ salonnières* in their own homes; and the third and fifth were events in

---

[8] *Le ménestrel*, 18 February 1866.
[9] *Ibidem*, 10 March 1867, 23 February 1868, 5 April 1868.
[10] *A deux pas de bonheur* was one of the four *opéras de salon* used to introduce the genre in chapter 1: À DEUX PAS/DU/BONHEUR./*Proverbe Lyrique de Salon*. The sources for table 7.1 consist of the following: *Le ménestrel*, 18 and 25 February 1855; 25 February 1855; 6 May 1855; 23 March 1856; 15 May 1864.

Table 7.1. Performances of Félix Godefroid, *A deux pas du bonheur*.

Date	Venue	Address	Salonnier/salonnière	Performers
17 February 1855	Chez Pierre-Thomas Levassor	4 Boulevard Poissonnière	Levassor	Gaveaux-Sabatier, Levassor
28 February 1855	Chez le Comte de Morny	Salon de la Présidence du Corps Législatif, Palais Bourbon, 126 rue de l'Univerisité	Comte de Morny	Gaveaux-Sabatier, Levassor
? 24 May 1855	Salle Herz	55 rue de la Victoire	Gaveaux-Sabatier	Gaveaux-Sabatier, Louis-Joseph-Léon Fleury
25 May 1855	Chez Alexis-Hippolyte Bourdon	32 rue de Bac	Bourdon	Gaveaux-Sabatier, Levassor
01 March 1856	Salons de Souffleto	171 rue Montmartre	Barbe-Éléonore Ragaine (Mme Duclos) and Paul Briand	Duclos, Briand, Fleury
09 May 1864	Chez M. et Mme Louis Orfila	? 45 rue Saint-Andree des Arts/ ? 2 rue Voltaire	M. et Mme Louis Orfila	Sainte-Foy, Talmont (Aimée-Philiberte Tillemont)

concert halls promoted by one or more performing artists. *A deux pas du bonheur* well illustrated the general principle that these *opéras de salon* effortlessly passed among the three types of performance venues and were also the same works that were distributed in conventional form by Parisian music publishers throughout the Second Empire.

The fourth type of *lieu* for *opéra de salon* was the *parloir*, and this was entirely separate from the previous three types, not only in terms of the ways in which it transformed *lieux* into *espaces* but also in the repertory, all published in *Le journal des demoiselles* and *Le magasin des demoiselles*, that was cultivated there. *Parloir* is a treacherous word that requires at least as much exegesis as the term *salon*. One nineteenth-century sense uses *parloir* as the room in which visitors were received in a convent, hospital, prison, or other type of establishment. It was, for example, the *lieu* that the teenage Hervé succeeded in turning into a performative *espace* by mounting a number of stage works at the Hospice de la Vieillesse Hommes at Bicêtre in the first half of the 1840s.[11] But *parloir* also had the same sense as the English term 'parlor', which is derived from the French but retains a much clearer distinction from *salon* than 'parlor' does from 'drawing room' in English, where '*parlour* was also widely known as the *drawing-room*', with the distinction occasionally being made on the grounds of status.[12] This is not to claim that *parloirs* were restricted to homes on the borders of the *moyenne* and *petite bourgeoisie*, since a *parloir* could be found among a suite of rooms that might be deployed—together with a *salon*, dining room, study, library, staircase, and landing—for the purposes of hosting the most prestigious *salon* event. The difference is that for the *moyenne* and *petite bourgeoisie*, the *parloir* would be the sole space available for any sort of reception or performance.[13] Balzac described a *parloir* thus: 'On the ground floor, the first room was a *parloir* lit by two windows on the courtyard side, and by two others which gave onto a garden',[14] a formulation that well describes the type of place—the *lieu*—that served as the basis for so many performances of *opéra de salon* in modest houses and apartments that were afforded access to the genre through their publication in *Le magasin des demoiselles* and *Le journal des demoiselles*. At this point in the discussion, it is worth repeating that almost none of the third of the repertory of *opéra de salon* published in journals and destined for the *parloir* (forty-odd pieces out of a total of around 120) bleeds over into the concert hall, studio, or *salon*. But the type of *opéra de salon* that was heard in the *parloir* and published in journals was largely the same as that heard in the concert hall, studio, or *salon*, and there was a certain overlap of composers and librettists between the two styles.

Identifying this more private space—the *parloir*—is something of a challenge. These places are more private and modest than those where a formal *salon* could be hosted, but sufficient expertise resided there to put on a performance of an *opéra de salon* without professional performers or any other

---

[11] Shortly before Hervé's arrival at the Bicêtre, the institution had ceased to function as a prison and was transformed into an infirmary and a hospital for the mentally ill. For a dramatic contrast in the conditions before and after this change, see the relevant entries in the 1830 and 1845 *Galignani's New Paris Guide: Containing a Detailed and Accurate Description* (Paris: Galignani, 1830) 369–374; (1845) 443–444. See Louis Schneider, *Hervé; Charles Lecocq*, Les maîtres de l'opérette française (Paris: Perrin, 1924) 7; and Everist, *Opérette: The First Twenty-Five Years*.

[12] Thad Logan, *The Victorian Parlour*, Cambridge Studies in Nineteenth-Century Literature and Culture 30 (Cambridge: Cambridge University Press, 2001; reprint 2003) 12.

[13] For the use of multiple adjacent spaces in performances in the *salon*, see Vilkner, 'Re-examining Salon Space', 226–227.

[14] 'Au rez-de-chaussée, la première pièce était un parloir éclairé par deux croisées du côté de la cour, et par deux autres qui donnaient sur un jardin'. Honoré de Balzac, *Balthazar Claës, ou la Recherche de l'absolu* (Paris: Charpentier, 1834) 121.

outside help. A starting point for understanding these spaces and practices is a series of sixteen lithographs by Daumier published in the journal *Le charivari* between April and June 1858, designed to satirize the vogue for *théâtre de société*, of which *opéra de salon* formed a part and which shared similar conditions of performance.[15] Three lithographs specifically describe *opéra de salon—opérette*, as Daumier had it; one is a caricature of a women practising her role in an *opérette* so intensely that she does not hear her child crying, so it reveals little about performance spaces. The two to be discussed here are valuable witnesses.

In the first (figure 7.1), Daumier laughs at the 'orchestra' in the household, but this is a precise illustration of the keyboard accompaniment essential to *opéra de salon* and ad hoc instrumental support that is occasionally found: the father of the household is playing the flute (Daumier's image has it backwards), and an elderly friend or relative contributes to the ensemble with the cello. The two vocal artists are both women, exactly as to be expected from the casts of *opéras de salon* published in journals. But the most interesting part of the image is the proximity of all the participants: vocal soloists on top of the cello and right next to the keyboard, with the performers barely inches from the audience. Even the family cat—in a pose conventional since at least the eighteenth century—can only find space in front of the improvised footlights, a mismatched single oil lamp and candelabra. What this image does not show, however, is the size of the audience; Daumier's second lithograph betrays much, on the other hand (figure 7.2). Behind a folding screen, a husband comforts his wife, afflicted by stage fright, while the audience waits expectantly to the right. There are four seated rows, with a couple of men standing at the back. Given that the dimensions of the room cannot allow each row to accommodate more than six or so, Daumier illustrates a gathering of no more than two dozen, an audience that might have been restricted to the residents of the apartment building in which the hosts of the *opéra de salon* lived.

The Daumier images give a clear sense of how small-scale *lieux* could be reconfigured as performative *espaces*, but they also reveal how small

---

[15] The sequence of sixteen lithographs was published in *Le charivari* between 3 April and 7 June 1858 at the height of the vogue for *opéra de salon*. See Jean-Claude Yon, 'Les comédiens de société: seize lithographies d'Honoré Daumier', *Tréteaux et paravents: le théâtre de société au xixe siècle*, ed. Jean-Claude Yon and Nathalie Le Gonidec (Paris: Créphis, 2012) 221–240, which includes reproductions of all. While all the images caricature various types of *salon* and *parlour* performance—and various levels of sophistication—the three that explicitly refer to *opéra de salon* (which Daumier calls *opérette*) are at 232, 237, and 240.

Figure 7.1. Honoré Daumier, *Les comédiens de société* i.

performing groups and audiences, as well as the physical and numerical relationship between the two groups, could be. The size of the audience was necessarily bound up with the type of *lieu* that was being used and the transformations that had been effected to create a performative *espace*. Maximum audiences at a concert hall were largely a given, but in a performer's or artist's studio or in a society *salon*, the distances between *lieux* and *espaces* could be huge, even if the size of the *lieu* in a concert hall and that in a large *salon* could be similar. For the smaller *espaces* where *opéras de salon* published in women's journals were performed in more modest *lieux*, audiences could be tiny.

In the discussion of the *opéras de salon* performed at the Néothermes, it was clear that the size of the building could allow audience numbers to rise into the hundreds and possibly reach the sizes found at the Salle Pleyel (more than six hundred) or the Salle Herz (around seven hundred). There is no doubt that the Salle Herz and similar buildings could be full for *opéra de salon*. Gaveaux-Sabatier managed to assemble an 'unprecedented number'

Figure 7.2. Honoré Daumier, *Les comédiens de société* ii.

there in April 1855,[16] although apparently nine hundred had been present for Offenbach's *Luc et Lucette* the previous year in the same hall.[17] At Morny's 1855 *soirée* in the Palais Bourbon, there had been more than five hundred, easily accommodated in the luxurious surroundings there,[18] and when Auguste Mey hired the Athénée des Arts, Sciences et Belles-Lettres on the rue de Valois for the premiere of his *Un amour de notaire* in 1858, he was chided for not having hired a larger space; the Athénée at that point was estimated by the author of the account in *La Revue et Gazette musicale de Paris* as capable of welcoming an audience of no fewer than five hundred.[19]

Private premises are harder to assess in terms of their physical dimensions and the possible sizes of audience for *opéra de salon*, but there were occasions when the author of a review formally attempted to make a judgement. Although much is known of the performances of *opéra de salon* hosted

---

[16] 'Une foule encore sans précédent' (*Le ménestral*, 6 May 1855).
[17] *Ibidem*, 7 May 1854.
[18] *Ibidem*, 25 February 1855.
[19] *La Revue et Gazette musicale de Paris*, 7 March 1858.

in Cordier's sculpture studio, the audience was merely described as 'numerous'.[20] But when the sculptor Louis-Félix-Édouard Tinant and his wife made space for the premiere of de Lostanges's *Le valet poète* in the artist's studio, the numbers attending were estimated to be between two hundred and three hundred.[21] A similar number was assessed at Beer's performances of his *En état de siège* and *Les roses de M. Malesherbes*, both given in his own home on the rue d'Aumale.[22] Although in the heart of Nouvelle Athènes, Beer's salon may have been less than typical of other musicians given his wealthy family and other connections, and the use of a sculptor's studio was obviously to permit larger audiences, so neither example might be a reliable guide to the size of most *opéra de salon* performances; however, it seems reasonable to assume that numbers up to and beyond two hundred could well have been the norm. As seen earlier in this chapter, even with the furniture that would have to have been moved around, the space in Gaveaux-Sabatier's studio left room for a performance team and from eighty to one hundred in the audience, and Duprez's private theatre seated around three hundred.

When *Le nouvelliste* sent a reporter to an early performance of Nadaud's *Le docteur vieuxtemps* in Princesse Mathilde's salon, he described the audience as follows:

> Their Majesties the Emperor and Empress arrive; they take their places in the front row. 96 women group themselves around them; these 96 women, all charmingly attired, form the *parterre*. The men, standing in the doorway and behind the women's benches, did their best to represent the [*loges d'*] *avant scène* and *loges* around the *parterre*.[23]

In other words, the men surround the women at the edge of the 'theatre' in the same way that theatre boxes surround the stalls. The description also matches nearly perfectly the engravings of both the theatre in the ballroom belonging to the Binders discussed in chapter 3[24] and the theatrical *séance*

---

[20] *Ibidem*, 22 January 1865.
[21] *Ibidem*, 9 February 1862.
[22] See chapter 4.
[23] 'Leurs Majestés l'Empereur et l'Impératrice arrivent; elles prennent place au premier rang, quatre-vingt-dix femmes se groupent autour d'elles: ces quatre-vingt-dix femmes, toutes en charmantes toilettes, forment le parterre; les hommes, debout dans les embrasures des portes et derrière les banquettes des femmes, s'efforcent de représenter les avant-scène et les loges' (*Le nouvelliste*, 5 May 1854).
[24] See chapter 3 and figure 3.3.

discussed in chapter 5.[25] While Princesse Mathilde's rooms could hold as many as two hundred without any difficulty, determining the number of members of the audience in the Binder ballroom depends on the image published in *Le monde illustré* (figure 3.3). The image gives six rows with around twenty-five in each row, yielding a total of 150 plus another dozen men standing at the side of the seating. But if the engraving depicts a view from the back of the ballroom, it would be a very strange shape indeed, and it is more likely that the viewpoint was about halfway back, with perhaps only half the audience in view; judicious calculation yields an audience of around three hundred for this performance seated, with in addition of any number of men standing at the back of the seats out of sight to the left. But whatever view is taken of the physical organization of the event or of the hierarchical division between seated women and standing men, the overwhelming majority of the audience—especially in the front four rows—is female.

Geolocation

Questions relating to *spatialité* problematize the ways in which existing places (*lieux*) are reconfigured as performative spaces (*espaces*) and are key to probing the relationships between repertories, buildings, performers, hosts, and audiences. Different social groupings employed different types of *lieux* and consequently had to reconfigure them in different ways and with different results. But these different social groupings were also conditioned by geography, with different social groupings found in different parts of the city, their boundaries clearly identified; the cultivation of *opéra de salon* therefore followed these groupings with great precision.

Establishing the geographical data for the 148 performances of *opéra de salon* between 1850 and 1870 that have been recovered plays into what has been acknowledged broadly as the 'spatial turn' in the humanities[26] but also into the more focussed question of historical mapping and its relationship

---

[25] See chapter 5 and figure 5.2.

[26] Denis Cosgrove was an early standard-bearer of the emergence of the spatial turn in the study of history; see his *Social Formation and Symbolic Landscape* (London: Croom Helm, 1984) and *Apollo's Eye: A Cartographic Genealogy of the Earth in the Western Imagination* (London: Johns Hopkins University Press, 2001). For an overview of the emergence of the concept of the spatial turn, see Angelo Torre, 'Un "tournant spatial" en histoire? Paysages, regards, ressources', *Annales: histoire, sciences sociales* 63 (2008) 1127–1144; and for a more recent analysis, Frank Zephyr, 'Spatial History as Scholarly Practice', *Between Humanities and the Digital*, ed. Patrik Svensson and David Theo Goldberg (Cambridge, MA: MIT Press, 2015) 411–428.

with digital humanities.[27] Digital mapping of music history has developed apace, with now around thirty snapshots of music history being mapped digitally for the first time,[28] and the visualization that displays Second Empire performances of *opéra de salon* adds to that number.

The administrative arrangements governing music in the nineteenth-century Parisian regulated theatre were concerned with aligning repertory with institution and with avoiding competition. The geographical organization of the theatrical world of Paris appears at first glance to mirror the legislative provisions. The principal theatres—the Comédie-Française, the Opéra, the Opéra-Comique, and the Théâtre-Italien—were all grouped in the fashionable second *arrondissement*, while the popular theatres were all huddled along the Boulevard du Temple. While this overall topography is relatively clear (figure 7.3),[29] there are some anomalies. The Théâtre-Lyrique, which in the Second Empire was the main rival to both the Opéra and the Opéra-Comique, was located at 72 Boulevard du Temple, while Offenbach's Théâtre des Bouffes-Parisiens—which has far more in common with the repertory of Hervé's Folies-Concertantes/Nouvelles, the Folies-Dramatiques, and related theatres—enjoyed the luxury of a location right next to the fashionable Théâtre-Italien and just a couple of hundred metres south of the Opéra and the Opéra-Comique.[30]

However tidy in its outlines this correlation between theatrical register and geographical situation might be, it was about to be greatly changed. Two years after the publication of the map on which figure 7.3 is based, Georges-Eugène, Baron Haussmann, launched the phase of his plan for urbanization

---

[27] For a recent study, with a focus on method, see Jen Jack Gieseking, 'Where Are We? The Method of Mapping with GIS in Digital Humanities', *American Quarterly* 70 (2018) 641–648; and for a more generally theoretical, if not critical, account of mapping in the humanities, see Mark Monmonier, *How to Lie with Maps* (Chicago: University of Chicago Press, 2018).

[28] See 'The Musical Geography Project: Mapping Place and Movement through Music History' (https://musicalgeography.org/), which is also the home of the visualization that supports the current research. See also a recent article by the director of 'The Musical Geography Project', Louis Epstein, 'The Promise and Peril of Making Digital Maps Sing', *Journal of the American Musicological Society* 77 (2024) 262–284, which carefully reviews the following digital mapping projects: Emily Thompson's 'Roaring 'Twenties' (http://nycitynoise.com/); Danielle Fosler-Lussier's companion website to her book *Music in America's Cold War Diplomacy* (https://musicdiplomacy.org/database.html); Katie Chapman's 'Troubadour Melodies Database' (https://troubadourmelodies.org/); Richard Langham Smith and Clair Rowden's 'Carmen Abroad' (https://carmenabroad.org/); Andy McGraw's 'Audible RVA' (https://audible-rva.org/); and 'The Global Jukebox' (https://theglobaljukebox.org/).

[29] The background map is Alexandre Vuillemin, *Paris nouveau, 1855* (Paris: Furne, [1855]).

[30] For a description of each of these institutions, see Nicole Wild, *Dictionnaire des théâtres parisiens*. For a map of the theatres in the second *arrondissement* c. 1830, see *ibidem*, annexe 5; for the theatres on the Boulevard du Temple in 1857, *ibidem*, annexe 6.

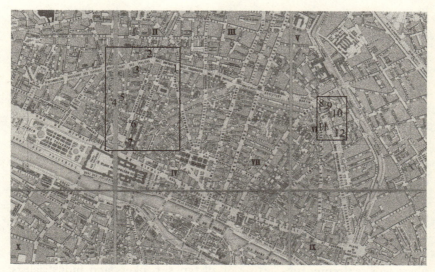

Figure 7.3. Topographical distribution of Parisian theatres, 1850s. 1: Théâtre des Variétés; 2: Opéra; 3: Opéra-Comique; 4: Théâtre Italien; 5: Théâtre des Bouffes-Parisiens; 6: Théâtre du Palais-Royal; 7: Comédie Française; 8: Théâtre Lyrique; 9: Théâtre des Folies-Dramatiques; 10: Théâtre de la Gaïté; 11: Théâtre des Delassements-Comiques; 12: Théâtre des Folies-Concertantes.

that included the demolition of the north-west corner of the Boulevard du Temple to make way for the Place de la République, and by 1862, all but one of the theatres were relocated, the Théâtre-Lyrique most notably on the Place du Châtelet. The only one to survive in place was Hervé's Folies-Concertantes, which changed its name in 1859 to the name it holds today, the Théâtre Déjazet. The resulting displacement of the theatres changed the eastern boulevards as much as the reconstruction of the Place de la République, but most of the changes kept the secondary and other minor theatres broadly speaking to the east, whereas the principal theatres in the second *arrondissement* were left untouched.[31]

The theatrical map of Paris would be further redrawn in the late 1860s, when *cafés-concerts* were allowed to mount staged productions of *opérette*, and—although several of them remained close to the eastern boulevards—some began to fill in the theatrical space between the secondary and principal

---

[31] The most striking example of relocation from the Boulevard du Temple concerned the Théâtre-Lyrique, which moved to the Place du Châtelet in 1862 (*ibidem*, 233–234).

theatres. While the Eldorado, for example, was situated on the Boulevard de Strasbourg, close to many of the secondary theatres, the Porcherons (rue Cadet), Alcazar (rue du Faubourg Poissonnière) and Folies-Bergère (rue Richer) were all established just north-west of the Opéra and the Opéra-Comique. This boundary between the ninth and tenth *arrondissements*, very close to Nouvelle Athènes, constituted a new location for music in the Parisian theatre.

But in the early Second Empire, the geography of the Parisian regulated theatre was clear, so it is even more striking that in terms of performance and urban practice, *opéra de salon* was entirely divorced from the theatrical worlds of *opéra comique*, *opérette*, *vaudeville*, and related genres—exactly those types with which the structure of *opéra de salon* had various degrees of affinity. Not only does the geolocation of *opéra de salon* not overlap with that of the main and secondary theatres, but the activities of different agents—physicians, entrepreneurs, artists of all types, bankers and industrialists, aristocrats both old and new, as outlined in chapters 3 and 4—took place in different parts of the city.[32]

The upper oval (in black) in figure 7.4 encompasses the performances mounted by composers and performers on their own premises, and the shape that broadly outlines the *quartier* of Nouvelle Athènes has been allowed to expand to include key places: Duprez's singing school with its associated theatre on the rue Turgot and Gaveaux-Sabatier's studio on the Rue des Petites-Écuries. The lower oval (in white) includes most of the activity of non-musicians at the east end of the Faubourg Saint-Germain. The white oval to the left indicates the activities of the *haute bourgeoisie* (mostly bankers and industrialists) in the Faubourg Saint-Honoré, and the black rectangle groups all the concert halls where *opéra de salon* was given during the Second Empire (with numbers of performances also given).[33]

---

[32] The culture of *opéra de salon* adumbrates the four planes of social mediation engaging with sites of performance: (1) imagined communities, (2) audiences and publics, (3) social stratifications of various types, and (4) institutional contexts. Georgina Born, 'Introduction', *Music, Sound and Space: Transformations of Public and Private Experience*, ed. Georgina Born (Cambridge: Cambridge University Press, 2013) 19–20. See the summary in George Revill, 'How Is Space Made in Sound? Spatial Mediation, Critical Phenomenology and the Political Agency of Sound', *Progress in Human Geography* 40 (2015) 245.

[33] Figure 7.4 is a screenshot from a fully interactive visualization of the topography of *opéra de salon* in Paris during the Second Empire, which allows filtering by *quartier*, date, composer, and other criteria, based on the 148 performance datasets that underpin work for this book. See '*Opéra de salon*: Paris, 1850–1870'.

LOCATING *OPÉRA DE SALON* 223

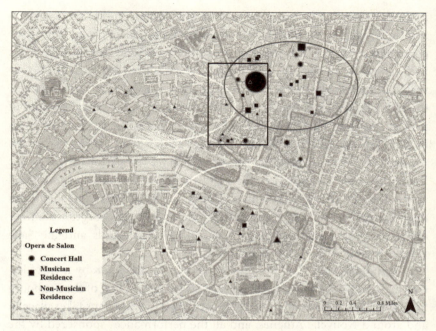

Figure 7.4. Locations of performances of *opéra de salon*.

Figure 7.4 clearly shows how the two principal zones for the cultivation of *opéra de salon*—those by musicians and by non-musicians—overlap with two of the best-identified quarters in the city: the eastern and unfashionable end of the Faubourg Saint-Germain and Nouvelle Athènes. The Faubourg Saint-Germain—*le noble faubourg*—was where all the old money was; these aristocrats at the west end of the *faubourg* did not apparently cultivate *opéra de salon* on anything like the same scale as their *moyen-bourgeois* neighbours at the eastern end, spilling over the *faubourg*'s boundaries, as figure 7.4 shows. Nouvelle Athènes—developed in the 1820s and 1830s—was, however, the crucible of French romanticism in all forms of artistic activity. It was hardly surprising that a quarter of a century later, it was where many of those who made their living from music had their homes. Furthermore, all the performances of *opéra de salon* promoted by the *haute bourgeoisie* were located in the Faubourg Saint-Honoré, a farther area distant from both Nouvelle Athènes and the eastern Faubourg Saint-Germain. Table 7.2 tabulates the data in the visualization summarized in figure 7.4 and shows the numbers of performances in each *quartier*. This shows the striking disparity, in the first instance, between the eastern and western ends of the Faubourg Saint-Germain: in the *moyen-bourgois* eastern end, there were twenty-four performances of *opéra de salon* recorded between 1850 and 1870, whereas in the western aristocratic end, there were only five. But what is also revealed is the massive preponderance of performances in Nouvelle Athènes; the sixty-six instances there constitute nearly half of the entire number of performances in the period. Table 7.2 also indicates the ten performances in the Chaussée d'Antin, although half of this total are in Rossini's *salon* at 2 rue de la Chaussée-d'Antin; the figures for Passy, a few performances on the Boulevards, and a clutch (less than 10 percent) of performances scattered across the city fall into no coherent pattern. While Passy included both *moyen-bourgeois* residents and aristocratic and *haute-bourgeois* summer exiles, the remaining groupings in table 7.2—Boulevards and the Salle Érard—remain without consequence.

In summary, almost all the promotion of *opéra de salon* by men of letters, artists, and the *moyenne bourgeoisie* is in the east end of the Faubourg Saint-Germain, almost all the activity promoted by musicians takes place in and around Nouvelle Athènes, and all the performances sponsored by the *haute bourgeoisie* are in the Faubourg Saint-Honoré. The groups of musical and non-musical promoters of *opéra de salon* are not only very clearly defined, but they are also clearly differentiated, with much unoccupied space between, and closely aligned with neighbourhoods that were already clearly self-identified. Repertory, social grouping, and geography are closely aligned.

Table 7.2. Performances of *opéra de salon*, 1850–1870, by location.

No.	Location
5	West Faubourg Saint-Germain
66	Nouvelle Athènes
14	Faubourg Saint-Honoré
24	East Faubourg Saint-Germain
10	Chaussée-d'Antin
29	Passy: 4 Boulevards: 8 Salle Érard: 3 Other: 14
148	Total

Whatever the geolocation of performance spaces for *opéra de salon*, none of these *lieux* was designed to support *opéra de salon* in the same way that a theatre was designed to provide a home for *opérette* or *comédie-vaudeville*. Conceived originally as a living area, no domestic place that was used for *opéra de salon* was designed for theatre, and the repurposing of domestic places as theatrical spaces is one of the clearest examples of de Certeau's moves from *lieu* to *espace*. This is certainly true for musicians putting on *opéra de salon* in their own homes and for men of letters and other artists undertaking similar endeavours.

Multiplicities of Power

Both composers and performers of *opéra de salon* used the genre to promote themselves, their works, and their pupils. Many of these performances were at the Salle Herz and other concert halls, but a smaller number of creative artists used their own premises. For concerts in the Salle Herz, *opéra de salon* was mounted on a financial basis: whatever artistic result was achieved, the hall was rented, artists were paid, and expenses were recouped from sales at the box office, with a maximum audience of around eight hundred. *Opéra de salon* had the ability to be deployed by creative artists in ways that went beyond hiring a space in which to sing a few arias accompanied by piano and served as a vehicle for the deployment of artistic power that was otherwise unmatched by other genres.

Many more performances of *opéra de salon* took place in the private homes of music teachers, performers, and composers, where the artistic power generated by the event was even more tightly harnessed to the works themselves. Not only were private *lieux* being transformed into more public *espaces*, but the financial basis of the cultural transactions was entirely different from that for the same artists with the same works promoted in concert halls. The use of one's own home meant that there were no hiring fees for the performing space, and given that so much of the cast consisted of the promoters themselves and their students, these costs were also negligible. Evidence is difficult to recover from the documentary record, but it seems most likely that events at the homes of such composers of *opéra de salon* as Poisot, Beer, Thys, and, of course, Offenbach treated their audiences as invited guests rather than as fee-paying customers. The same must have been the case when the composer Weckerlin had one of his many *opéras de salon* put on in the studios of Gaveaux-Sabatier. Whether the same conditions obtained in Duprez's theatre remains an open but intriguing question.

The manipulation of power, in the instances just described hinges on the ability to turn domestic *lieux* into performative *espaces*, and it is frustrating to have so little documentary record of how these transformations might have worked. The few that were documented in the nineteenth century have been discussed in previous chapters. But what cultural capital was the sculptor Cordier exploiting when he allowed his orientalist studio to serve as a performance space for the unidentified *opéra de salon* by Godefroid with a libretto by Tourneux?[34] Unlike his medical colleagues, less than a kilometre to the east, Cordier appropriates one form of cultural capital, *opéra de salon*, in support of another, the sculpture that he makes and sells to those who can afford it and who can attend his performances. He may, in his exploitation of *opéra de salon*, not be that far away from the professional interests so obvious in the performances of *opéra de salon* put on by his musical colleagues.

Performances of *opéra de salon* promoted by men of letters, medical professionals, and artists with no professional involvement in music are far more displays of cultural capital than in the case of creative and performing artists. And the financial commitment is perhaps even more obscure. So when, for example, Bourdon, the distinguished neurologist and author of *Notice sur la fièvre puerpérale*, among others, put on performances of *opéra de salon* in the mid-1850s in his apartment on the rue du Bac—the classic east end of the Faubourg Saint-Germain—he cannot have been as unconcerned about cost as some of the aristocracy or super-rich, but he nevertheless managed to hire the best artists: not just Gaveaux-Sabatier but also Levassor,[35] Biéval, and Mira.[36] Nothing in Bourdon's activity here suggests a direct benefit to his work either in private practice or at the Hôpital de la Charité, metres from his home. But the cultural capital may have had other benefits: he had reached the limits of strictly professional success by the beginning of the 1850s, but his higher recognition—as member of the Légion d'Honneur and of the Académie Nationale de Médecine—all came later in the 1850s.[37] Public recognition—so critical to the accumulation of cultural

---

[34] The performance took place in Cordier's studio at 115 Boulevard Saint-Michel on 12 January 1865 (*La Revue et Gazette musicale de Paris*, 22 January 1865).

[35] Gaveaux-Sabatier and Levassor performed Godefroid's *A deux pas du bonheur* in Bourdon's *salons* at 32 rue de Bac on 25 April 1855 (*Le ménestrel*, 6 May 1855).

[36] The two performed Grisar's by-then-venerable *Les travestissements* in early December 1857 (*ibidem*, 20 December 1857).

[37] See Genty, *Index biographique des membres*, 26.

capital—is difficult to judge. Bourdon must have been pleased that his first evening with *opéra de salon* was described at all in the music press, and even more pleased—in anticipation of further honour, perhaps—to read it described as 'a brilliant *soirée*, in the Faubourg Saint-Germain, at the home of M. le Docteur Bourdon'.[38]

It would be reasonable to assume that almost all the events in private dwellings where *opéra de salon* featured during the 1850s and 1860s treated the genre as a means of trading financial resources for cultural capital, to translate immense wealth into payment for artists, theatres, sets, costumes, refreshments, publicity, and the myriad expenses that music in the theatre demanded, in order to deploy a cultural product before those who could be impressed and influenced. Doucet's rehearsal of Nadaud's *La volière* might be thought an exception—altruistic, even—although Bouland's performances at the Néothermes may well have had a residual commercial purpose, to add a further attraction to business alongside the billiard room or library in the hope that such an act would attract further custom to his essentially commercial enterprise.

Two other instances throw into relief the critical role of the creative agent—whether composer or librettist—and the use of the ownership of a building to forward an artistic career. When Pittaud de Forges put on a production of Offenbach's *Le 66!* in his home in 1865, he was promoting a libretto of his own; it was also a work that by then was a decade old.[39] On the other hand, Marcelli never used her salon for the promotion of any *opéra de salon* except her own, but she was able to hire the most celebrated *opéra de salon* artists to perform it: Gaveaux-Sabatier and Lefort, accompanied by Zolobodjan.[40] Similarly, the d'Aoust put on performances of two of his *opéras de salon* in his own premises, again in the heart of the Faubourg Saint-Germain. His two works were to libretti by other amateurs. *Une partie de dominos* was a setting of a libretto by Blerzy, a retired financier. *L'amour voleur* was a setting of one by Pierre-Victor-Henri Berdalle de Lapommeraye, who was heavily involved in work in the Senate in the mid-1860s; the libretto was only attributed to

---

[38] 'une brillante soirée, au faubourg Saint-Germain, chez M. le docteur Bourdon' (*Le ménestrel*, 6 May 1855). The description of his home in the *faubourg*, with no further precision as to whether it was in the *moyen-bourgeois* east or the aristocratic west, can only have contributed to the cultural capital that Bourdon derived from the event and its commentary in *Le ménestrel*.

[39] *Le 66!* would be picked up, however, by the Fantaisies-Parisiennes for performance in April 1868.

[40] The performance took place on 31 March 1856 (*Le musée des familles* 23 [1855–1856] 159–160).

Henri d'Alleber, his pseudonym.[41] His sister was the distinguished singer Anne-Célina-Ernestine Berdalle de Lapommeraye. Like Marcelli, d'Aoust was also able to hire some of the best-known artists of *opéra de salon* in the capital. Although based in Nouvelle Athènes, Beer's residence on the rue d'Aumale was of a similar opulence to those of Marcelli and d'Aoust, and he was able to mount performances there of his own two *opéras de salon*— *Les roses de M. Malesherbes* and *En état de siège*—in the same way as his *haut-bourgeois* and aristocratic colleagues.[42] In all cases, non-professional composers and librettists were able to repurpose sumptuous private homes (in the rue de Babylone for Marcelli or in the rue de l'Université for d'Aoust and in a space large enough to be transformed later into a commercial theatre for Beer) as performative *espaces* in order to promote their own works.

For the *haute bourgeoisie*, the deployment of *opéra de salon* was cultural capital pure and simple. The distances between *lieu* and *espace*, furthermore, were much less marked than in the homes of the less wealthy. In the case of Binder, the survival of an illustration has made analysis of size and nature of audience possible. This room in which Grisart's *La lettre de cachet* was performed has all the qualities—size and opulence—of a ballroom. Not a domestic living area being repurposed for performance, it was already a performance *lieu*. And certainly, although the specific requirements of *opéra de salon*—the erection of a temporary stage, curtain, sets, and props—lightly repurpose the original *lieu*, the resulting *espace*, in terms of performative function, remains very close to its original use. In other words, the levels of disruption that the move from *lieu* to *espace* entailed shrank in direct proportion to the cultural capital acquired.

Such displays of cultural capital depended on distinction that went beyond the recognition of those present. The fact that an engraving appears in such a journal as *Le monde illustré* was perhaps sufficient recognition for the Binder family, but the accompanying text by no less an author than Jules Clarétie—playwright, theatre critic for *Le Figaro*, and eventually director of the Comédie-0Française—talked of 'the atmosphere of pleasure, of the visions offered by this splendid attire, these flowers, these lights, these diamonds, these smiles: all things that only the memory keeps in the

---

[41] March 1865. See *La Revue et Gazette musicale de Paris*, 26 March 1865. For Lapommeraye, see 'Lapommeraye, Pierre-Henri-Victor Berdalle de', *Revue encyclopédique* 2 (1892) 331–332.

[42] Beer's performances were on 18 January 1859 and 17 January 1861 (*Le ménestrel*, 23 January 1859; *La Revue et Gazette musicale de Paris*, 20 January 1861).

ineffaceable'.[43] Clarétie's further claim that the performers 'were all members of society but played like true actors'[44]—which would have added to the cultural power of the event had it been true—was a demonstrable falsehood, since both the professional artists, Mme Lefébure-Wély and Malézieux, were identified among the cast by other reviews of the event.[45] However overblown or inaccurate these accounts, such events were regularly described, and the attributes of distinction—taste, sensitivity, and artistic talent, among so many—were associated with the hosts and organizers of the event in question.

For such plutocrats as Binder and his entrepreneurial and financial colleagues, the quality of the review—or, rather, whether it was favourable or not—was largely irrelevant if it pointed to the chandelier and the women's diamonds. The simple publication of an account of the event was clearly enough. This may also have been the case for the members of the medical profession, artists, sculptors, and so on. But for composers and performers, simple recognition—as in the case of any review of a musical performance—was not enough on its own. And for, say, Duprez or Gaveaux-Sabatier, it was not merely oneself for whom the reviews were important but also one's pupils and junior colleagues. Recognition, in these cases and of course in the case of composers of works enjoying their premiere, was a significantly more subtle practice and one that for *opera de salon* confused the quality of musical performance or work with domestic concerns of *lieu* and *espace*.

Opéra de salon in the Provinces and Abroad

Opéra de salon occupied the city of Paris in ways that works at established theatres simply could not. A temporary stage could be erected in a ballroom, in a concert hall, or in a studio. A way of bridging the traditionally discrete domains of the concert hall and the theatre, the genre was also tied to the domestic *lieux* that divided the musicians of Nouvelle Athènes from the non-musicians of the eastern end of the Faubourg Saint-Germain. As these *lieux* were transformed into performative *espaces*, so, too, were concert halls,

---

[43] 'cette atmosphère de plaisir, du coup d'œil qu'offrent ces toilettes splendides, ces fleurs, ces lumières, ces diamants, ces sourires, toutes choses que le souvenir seul garde en traits ineffaçables' (*Le monde illustré*, 6 April 1864).
[44] 'sont tous gens du monde et jouent comme de vrais artistes' (*ibidem*).
[45] *Le petit journal*, 8 April 1864.

sculptors' studios, and even such premises as the Néothermes, discussed in chapter 3.

When Bouland took over the management of the Néothermes in the 1850s, he was already well known as the director of the baths at Enghien, 20 kilometres north-west of Paris, and he had already written a treatise on the nature and therapeutic use of the water at the spa.[46] Enghien was just one of several spa towns across France that developed as centres for taking the waters from around the 1830s.[47] Almost all of them made significant use of music for the diversion of patients, especially since most of the cures recommended staying indoors after dark, and *opéra de salon* was unsurprisingly exported to the same resorts. So when the baths at Sainte-Adresse were formally opened on 15 September 1852, there was a *matinée musicale* that featured instrumental and vocal music,[48] and in one instance, an *opéra de salon* was set in a spa town, in this case Vichy: *Tout chemin mène à Rome*, by the Duc de Massa to a libretto by Claude-François-Auguste, Marquis de Mesgrigny.[49]

Vichy was among many spa towns whose facilities encompassed music and *opéra de salon*.[50] Many were clustered on the coast of the English Channel: Dieppe, Beuzeval, Cabourg, and Sainte-Adresse, with Vichy in the centre of the country and Le Croisic on its Atlantic coast. Repertories could be elaborate and—in terms of *opéra de salon*—closely mimic the *salon* culture of Paris.[51] Le Croisic, for example, had enjoyed an *hôtel des bains* since 1847,[52] and a decade later, the proprietor, Silvain Deslandes-Orière, installed

---

[46] *La revue des beaux arts*, 15 January 1855. Pierre Bouland, *Études sur les propriétés physiques, chimiques et médicinales des eaux minérales d'Enghien* (Paris: Dentu, 1850).

[47] See Albert Lasserre, *Enghien-les-Bains: la saga des thermes et des casinos 1766–2005* (n.p.: Editions de Valhermeil, [2005]).

[48] *La Revue et Gazette musicale de Paris*, 26 September 1852.

[49] TOUT CHEMIN/MÈNE À/ROME/Opéra Comique en Un Acte. The libretto appears not to have survived.

[50] Christian Paul, *Les sociétés musicales du bassin thermal de Vichy de 1860 à 1914: contribution à l'histoire de la musique et à la connaissance du mouvement orphéonique français* (PhD diss., Université de Paris IV, 2008; Paris: Le Petit Page, 2014).

[51] There is to date no study of music in French spa towns. There is a clear overlap with music and the culture of the casino, however, for which see François Lesure, 'La villégiature lyrique ou la musique dans les casinos au xixe siècle', *D'un opéra l'autre: hommage à Jean Mongrédien*, ed. Jean Gribenski (Paris: Presses Universitaires Paris-Sorbonne, 1996) 389–398; and Etienne Jardin and Martin Guerpin, eds., *Faites vos jeux! Actes du colloque: La vie musicale dans les casinos français (XIXe–XXIe siècle), 28–29 May 2021* (Paris: Actes Sud, 2024). Although written after Lesure's article, Ian C. Bradley, *Water Music: Music Making in the Spas of Europe and North America* (Oxford: Oxford University Press, 2010), gives no space to music in French spa towns and even in the chapter on Baden treats almost exclusively composers and musicians from German-speaking states (85–112).

[52] Béatrice Verney, *Le Croisic: l'établissement de bains de mer, Silvain Deslandes de 1844 à 1893–avant–pendant–après* (Merignac: Ateliers Copy-Media, 2012).

what the anonymous correspondent for *Le ménestrel* called 'un petit théâtre ad hoc',[53] which probably resembled such temporary structures as those deployed in Parisian *salons* and concert halls.[54] Two works by Weckerlin, *Le mariage en poste* and *L'amour à l'épée*, had already been performed there by the beginning of August 1858, and two other works, Hignard's *Le joueur d'orgue* and Grisar's *Les travestissements*, were in rehearsal in the summer of 1858.[55] Although Hignard's piece is shrouded in mystery, *Les travestissements* is one of those rare cases already discussed of a work from the regulated theatre being appropriated to the culture of *opéra de salon*,[56] and the performance in Le Croisic points to boundaries between the regulated theatre and *opéra de salon* being significantly more permeable outside of Paris than in the capital itself. In support of this claim, a list of the works that Deslandes-Orière had mounted two years later at the *hôtel des bains*, given by *Le ménestrel*'s Le Croisic correspondent, makes the point very clearly. Table 7.3 puts these together with those already mentioned, with details of the works' origins.[57]

The mix is eclectic in terms of date and provenance. In addition to very recent *opéras de salon* by Weckerlin, Hignard, and Bernard, Le Croisic found space for two works from Offenbach's Théâtre des Bouffes-Parisiens (*Le 66!* and *Pépito*, although the latter had been premiered at the Théâtre des Variétés), recent successes from the Théâtre-Lyrique and Opéra-Comique (*Les noces de Jeanette*, *A Clichy*, and *Les papillottes de M. Benoist*) and also for some classics even older than *Les travestissements*: Ferdinando Paër's *Le maître de chapelle* from 1821 and, seemingly incredibly, Nicolas-Marie Dalayrac's 1799 *Adolphe et Clara*.

Repertories were brought to spa towns by the artists who had promoted them in Paris. The 1858 season in Le Croisic was dominated by a trio well known in the capital: Mira, Biéval, and Romain Bussine.[58] When they sang in Weckerlin's *L'amour à l'épée* in Le Croisic, they were replicating Parisian performances from February and March earlier the same year in the home

---

[53] *Le ménestrel*, 19 August 1860.
[54] See chapter 2.
[55] *Le ménestrel*, 1 August 1858.
[56] See chapter 4.
[57] Table 7.3 is based on material drawn from *Le ménestrel*, 1 August 1858 and 19 August 1860.
[58] *Le ménestrel*, 1 August 1858.

Table 7.3. Repertory of the *hôtel des bains*, Le Croisic, 1858–1860.

Title	Composer	Librettist	Premiere location	Premiere date
Le mariage en poste	Weckerlin	Galoppe d'Onquaire	Salle Herz [opéra de salon]	< 15 March 1857
L'amour à l'épée	Weckerlin	Galoppe d'Onquaire	Chez Benou [opéra de salon]	12 December 1858
Le joueur d'orgue	Hignard	Dubreuil		1858
Les travestissements	Grisar	Deslandes	Opéra-Comique	16 November 1839
Adolphe et Clara	Dalayrac	Benoît-Joseph Marsollier des Vivetières	Opéra-Comique	10 February 1799
A Clichy	Adam	Adolphe d'Ennery and Eugène Grangé	Théâtre-Lyrique	24 December 1854
Le 66!	Offenbach	Pittaud de Forges and Chapelle	Théâtre des Bouffes-Parisiens	31 July 1856
Les papillottes de M. Benoist	Napoléon-Henri Reber	Michel Carré and Jules-Paul Barbier	Opéra-Comique	28 December 1853
Pépito	Offenbach	Jules Moinaux and Battu	Théâtre des Variétés	28 October 1853
Le maître de chapelle	Paër	Sophie Gay	Opéra-Comique	29 March 1821
Les noces de Jeanette	Massé	Carré and Barbier	Opéra-Comique	2 February 1853
Bredouille	Bernard	Galoppe d'Onquaire	Chez Mme Orfila [opéra de salon]	< 7 March 1858

of Benou and at a concert sponsored by Heugel in the Salle Sainte-Cécile.[59] Their reception in Le Croisic could not have been bettered.

Two years later, the Archainbaud family (Eugène-Jean-Baptiste and Augustine-Joséphine *née* Zolobodjan) were was largely responsible for the cultivation of *opéra de salon* in Le Croisic, and Deslandes-Orière

---

[59] *Ibidem*, 14 February 1858; 28 March 1858. There was a later performance at the Salle Herz for Mira's benefit, but there is no record of the performers except the beneficiary (*La Revue et Gazette musicale de Paris*, 27 January 1861).

appointed the husband as director of the Le Croisic series of *opéras de salon* and concerts; the couple was accompanied by the tenor Victor-Élisabeth Verdellet and Gustave Gerpré.[60] The Archainbauds' Parisian reputation in *opéra de salon* was already well known, and Verdellet was a very recent graduate of the Conservatoire who would go on to a distinguished career in the provinces but would also later sing *opéra de salon* on at least one occasion. Gerpré was a stalwart of the Théâtre des Bouffes-Parisiens throughout its first decade and moved to the Théâtre-Lyrique in 1864; it may well be through him that the Le Croisic repertory was broadened beyond *opéra de salon* as outlined in table 7.3.

In the same vein, when Godefroid's *A deux pas du bonheur* was mounted in Vichy in 1863, it starred Amélie Faivre and an artist known only by his last name, Castel; both were well known on the Parisian *opéra de salon* circuit, although there is no evidence of either one participating in a performance of *A deux pas du bonheur* in the capital before taking it to Vichy.[61] Castel had not only participated in *opéra de salon* but had apparently performed in no fewer than forty concerts during June and July 1863 before moving to Salins (known as Salins-les-Bains after 1926) for a further series of concerts in the spa town in the Jura.[62] Godefroid established himself in Dieppe in the summer of 1861, although this was probably for harp teaching rather than the promotion of *opéra de salon*.[63] Vichy was not only a major resort, but Isaac Strauss, its music director since 1844, engaged a troupe for *vaudeville* as well as welcoming major names from the Opéra-Comique.[64]

Few of the French spa towns visited by artists specializing in *opéra de salon* could match the international social *cachet* of Baden (Baden-Baden after 1931); by the mid-nineteenth-century, the town, just over the border from France in the Grand Duchy of Baden, had become the European epicentre of summer amusements and luxury. As with Strauss in Vichy and Deslandes-Orière in Le Croisic, musical and other cultural activities were directed by a single key individual; in the case of Baden, it was Oscar-Édouard Bénazet.[65]

---

[60] *Le ménestrel*, 27 May 1860.
[61] *Ibidem*, 2 August 1863.
[62] *Ibidem*.
[63] *Ibidem*, 14 July 1861.
[64] Strauss has attracted a certain amount of attention. See Josette Rance, 'Isaac Strauss, un musicien strasbourgeois célèbre sous le Second Empire', *Recherches internationales sur la musique française* 27 (November 1988) 61–72; Laure Schnapper, *Musique et musiciens de bal: Isaac Strauss au service de Napoléon III* (Paris: Hermann, 2023) 131–174.
[65] Rolf Gustav Haebler, *Geschichte des Stadt und des Kurortes Baden-Baden*, 2 vols. (Baden-Baden: Schmidt, 1969); for Bénazet, see Dagmar Kicherer, *Kleine Geschichte der Stadt Baden-Baden* (Leinfelden-Echterdingen: Braun, 2008) 117–122.

Bénazet turned part of the *Kurhaus* into gambling rooms, gave financial support to the local newspapers, and organized such forms of external entertainment as illuminations and fireworks. The racecourse at Iffezheim, 11 kilometres from Baden, was also his creation. He established an orchestra in 1853 and a theatre in 1855, with a more elaborate building in 1862.[66]

As a result of Bénazet's endeavours, Baden was well known for the operatic premieres that took place there: Gounod's *La colombe*, Reyer's *Erostrate*, Berlioz's *Béatrice et Bénédict*, Massé's *Le cousin de Marivaux*. The *Konversationshaus* had opened in 1855 with the premiere of Clapisson's *Les amoureux de Perrette*, and his *Le sylphe* was premiered the following year.[67] Berlioz conducted the orchestra in 1853 and from 1856 to 1863, the year in which Pauline Viardot settled in the town. All of Viardot's early *opéras de salon* were composed for Baden in performances that were rarely, if ever, replicated in Paris.[68] Of the dozen or so known performances of her *Le dernier sorcier* (1869, to a libretto by Ivan Turgenev), only one—and that is doubtful—may have taken place in Viardot's Parisian home in 1889.[69] Furthermore, despite the attention the Viardot-Turgenev *salon* has received, the space in the Villa Turgenev held barely thirty individuals, and even if it is assumed that audience members could hear from other rooms and corridors, this is significantly less expansive than most performances in Paris and closer in scope to the *parloir* performers caricatured by Daumier and discussed earlier in this chapter.[70]

While there is no evidence of Viardot supporting Parisian *opéra de salon* in late-1860s Baden, it was much in evidence there during the 1850s. As in the case of French spa resorts, the repertory was triggered by visiting Parisian artists who had been singing *opéra de salon* during the winter. Baden, like everywhere else, it seemed, was dominated by the presence of Gaveaux-Sabatier, who was there—not for the first time—in 1856 with Lefort for a performance of Salvator's *Suzanne*;[71] both artists would perform the work

---

[66] Haebler, *Geschichte des Stadt*, 2:91–98.

[67] Hervé Lacombe, 'Baden-Baden vu de Paris, ou Berlioz et ses compatriotes à Bade', *Hector Berlioz: ein franzose in Deutschland*, ed. Matthias Brzoska, Hermann Hofer, and Nicole K. Strohmann (Laaber: Laaber, 2005) 184–196. For the wider repertory of stage music in Baden, see Rainer Schmusch, 'Das französische Repertoire in Baden-Baden zur Zeit von Berlioz', *ibidem*, 197–220.

[68] Viardot's activity in Baden has been endlessly discussed. See Ute Lange-Brachmann and Joachim Draheim, eds., *Pauline Viardot in Baden-Baden und Karlsruhe*, Baden-Badener Beiträge zur Musikgeschichte 4 (Baden-Baden: Nomos, 1999).

[69] Nicholas G. Zekulin, *The Story of an Operetta: 'Le dernier sorcier' by Pauline Viardot and Ivan Turgenev*, Vorträge und Abhandlungen zur Slavistik 15 (Munich: Sagner, 1989) 151.

[70] *Ibidem*, 17.

[71] *Le ménestrel*, 18 October 1856.

in the Salle Herz for Gaveaux-Sabatier's benefit the following April.[72] They returned to Baden the following year with Weckerlin's *Tout est bien qui finit bien*[73] and in 1858 premiered Salvator's *L'esprit du foyer*.[74] The latter and its composer deserve attention, as it was one of the very few *opéras de salon* composed specifically for Baden that also found its way back to Paris, since Clapisson's *Les amoureux de Perrette* and Massé's *Le cousin de Marivaux* do not seem to have returned there.

What little is known of Salvator is that he was well known in Baden, enjoying the title of *pianiste-compositeur* to its dowager grand duchess, Stéphanie de Beauharnais, who also supported the performances of at least *L'esprit du foyer* and possibly *Suzanne* as well.[75] When Beauharnais died in January 1860, this engagement with Baden ended, although Salvator had already apparently made his home in Angoulême as early as 1858, where he toured that year;[76] he was probably a member of the orchestra at the Théâtre de la Capitole in Toulouse by 1862, where he mounted a performance of an *opéra bouffe* titled *L'enlèvement d'Argentine*.[77] Both of Salvator's Baden *opéras de salon* were given in Paris: *Suzanne* in April 1857 and *L'esprit du foyer* twice, in April and May 1859.[78] All three performances were at the Salle Herz, and all three were sponsored by Gaveaux-Sabatier.

A surviving single leaf of a *romance* from *L'esprit du foyer* raises questions not only of dedication but also of the link between Salvator, Gaveaux-Sabatier, the town of Baden, and its entrepreneur Bénazet (figure 7.5).[79]

The leaf contains fragments of a *romance* 'Grand Dieu! Qu'entends-je' and a *ballade* 'Tremblez fillette', with voice, text, and figured bass. It is clearly a double album leaf dedicated to Clara Bénazet, the wife of the entrepreneur, with the *romance* copied and dedicated by the composer and the *ballade* by

---

[72] *La Revue et Gazette musicale de Paris*, 26 April 1857, and *Le ménestrel* for the same date.
[73] *La Revue et Gazette musicale de Paris*, 13 September 1857.
[74] *Ibidem*, 10 October 1858.
[75] *Le ménestrel*, 19 December 1858.
[76] *La Revue et Gazette musicale de Paris*, 14 November 1858.
[77] *La revue de l'Académie de Toulouse* 8 (1862) 181–182. Arthur Pougin mistiles the work *L'ombre d'Argentine* (the title of Alexandre Montfort's 1853 work for the Opéra-Comique) and mistakenly locates it in Toulon. Fétis, *Biographie universelle des musiciens*, Suppl. 2:479.
[78] *Le ménestrel*, 26 April 1857, and *La Revue et Gazette musicale de Paris* for the same date (*Suzanne*); *Le ménestrel*, 27 March 1859 and 10 April 1859. Salvator also accompanied Gaveaux-Sabatier and Lourdel in a performance of Thys's (she wrote both the score and the libretto) *La perruque du bailli* in the salon of Mmes Orfila and Mosneron in November 1860 (*ibidem*, 2 December 1860).
[79] The document was on sale at the Parisian Librairie Pinault in November 2022, where the dedicatee is wrongly given as Gaveaux-Sabatier herself (https://www.librairie-pinault.com/musique/1997-gaveaux-sabatier-emilie-soprano-partition-musicale-qui-lui-est-dedicacee-.html).

Figure 7.5. Autograph of Salvator, *L'esprit de foyer*.

the performer, Gaveaux-Sabatier. The Baden premiere of the work is correctly identified as 6 October (1858), and the document was prepared six days later as the inscriptions reveal.[80] The intriguing question that the document raises is the relationship between Clara and Édouard Bénazet and Gaveaux-Sabatier, whose maiden name was also Bénazet. No one called Émilie-Perrine-Suzanne exists in the Bénazet family tree, and if there had been any relationship, it would have had to have been at the level of a distant cousin. 'The true sovereign of Baden' was how *La Revue et Gazette musicale* introduced Bénazet to Parisian audiences when he spent the winter of 1860–1861 in Paris.[81] He held *soirées* at his home in the rue de la Ville-l'Evêque, and at the last of the these he put on an *opéra de salon*: *Au fond du verre* by de Rillé to a libretto by Dubreuil, preceded by a vocal and instrumental concert.[82] The work in question was cast for two male voices—given to Lefort and Castel—so it is unclear if Bénazet would have cast Gaveaux-Sabatier in

---

[80] *L'illustration de Bade*, 17 October 1858.
[81] 'le véritable souverain de Bade' (*La Revue et Gazette musicale de Paris*, 10 March 1861).
[82] *Ibidem*.

an *opéra de salon* at this home. The work was repeated the following week at the Salle Herz, hosted by Castel.[83]

Whether related to 'the true sovereign of Baden' or not, Gaveaux-Sabatier had a reputation that went well beyond the capital without straying beyond the generic boundaries of *opéra de salon*. *Opéra de salon* in the French provinces was completely dominated by Parisian performing teams, and Gaveaux-Sabatier led all of them during the last half of the 1850s; there is no evidence whatsoever of *opéra de salon* being performed by regional artists during the Second Empire. Tours by Parisian artists of *opéra de salon* tended to take place just as the Parisian season was ending in April to May or just as it was beginning in September. Gaveaux-Sabatier, together with Levassor and Louis-Joseph-Léon Fleury took Godefroid's *A deux pas du bonheur* to Orléans in April 1855,[84] seemingly the first occasion that *opéra de salon* was taken to the provinces, and together with Lefort, Gaveaux-Sabatier returned the following year with Manry's *La bourse ou la vie*.[85]

Throughout the late 1850s, Gaveaux-Sabatier and Lefort toured the provinces twice a year: Nancy, Bar-le-Duc, and Saint-Malo in 1857[86] and Angoulême, Bordeaux, and La Rochelle in 1858.[87] Their tour at the end of 1858 was accompanied by Salvator for performances of his two *opéras de salon*: *Suzanne* and *L'esprit du foyer*.[88] Similarly, in early 1860, Gaveaux-Sabatier and Lefort toured Blois, Saumur, and Tours with Hocmelle and the latter's *Un service d'ami* with a libretto by Jenny Sabatier; Hocmelle also acted as the accompanist for the performances[89] (Salvator may have done the same in 1858). When Gaveaux-Sabatier was not touring with Lefort, she travelled with other Parisian artists specializing in *opéra de salon*, with Biéval in late 1859 and with both Lefort and Castel in 1860.[90] The only challenge to Gaveaux-Sabatier's apparent supremacy came from Meyer-Meillet and her husband, Auguste-Alphonse-Edmond, who visited Rennes in 1856 with a performance of *Le secret de l'Oncle Vincent* by Lajarte and Boisseaux.[91] But the Meillets were both artists from the Théâtre-Lyrique, and *Le secret*

---

[83] *Le ménestrel*, 3 March 1861.
[84] *Ibidem*, 1 April 1856.
[85] *Ibidem*, 20 April 1856.
[86] *Ibidem*, 5 April and 6 September 1857; *La Revue et Gazette musicale de Paris*, 13 September 1857.
[87] *Ibidem*, 14 November 1858.
[88] *Le ménestrel*, 19 December 1858; *ibidem*, 2 January 1859.
[89] *Ibidem*, 15 January 1860, and *La Revue et Gazette musicale de Paris* for the same date.
[90] *Le ménestrel*, 3 September 1859; *ibidem*, 15 January 1860, and *La Revue et Gazette musicale de Paris* for the same date.
[91] *Le ménestrel*, 10 August 1856.

de l'Oncle Vincent had been premiered there a few months earlier and was still in production; furthermore, there is no evidence that *Le secret de l'Oncle Vincent* had ever been performed outside the Théâtre-Lyrique in any form of *salon* performance.

The Meillets' performance of *Le secret de l'Oncle Vincent* in Rennes, however, again points up the greater permeability between *opéra de salon* and works from the regulated theatre exhibited in the provinces. But in general, the story of *opéra de salon* there inflects the understanding of *opéra en province* in general. For example, it is striking that no *opéra de salon* toured in any of the two dozen cities that housed its own permanent *opéra* company.[92] The more pressing competition came from the small touring companies that criss-crossed the country bringing music and theatre to tiny towns; by 1855, there were forty-five companies, and by 1861, there were sixty-two, before being effectively demolished as part of the 1864 deregulation of the theatres.[93] But these touring companies could only reside in a single town or city for a week or two, so the arrival of *opéra de salon* for a single performance was unlikely to be problematic, and this also explains the interest in performances of *opéra de salon* in spa towns, since those visits were always made at the interstices of the season in April and September when peripatetic troupes were not active.[94]

What is striking in this account of *opéra de salon* in the provinces is that, unlike *vaudeville* or *opérette*, it appears to have made no impact beyond France. Leaving aside Baden, which was part of a network of spa towns, there is no evidence of *opéra de salon* in any other major European city. Its absence in Vienna and Berlin, for example, is remarkable given the rapid appearance of *opérette* in those cities, although there remains a question of Offenbach's energy in making these exports to German-speaking cities possible; the extent to which works by other composers, and from theatres other than the Théâtre des Bouffes-Parisiens, made a similar impact remains to be assessed.

---

[92] The only exception was Gaveaux-Sabatier and Lefort's tour in April 1857 (*Le ménestrel*, 5 April 1857), but its references are Delphic at best. It seems clear that Salvator's *L'enlèvement d'Argentine*, premiered in Toulouse, was not an *opéra de salon*.

[93] Katharine Ellis, *French Musical Life: Local Dynamics in the Century to World War II* (New York: Oxford University Press, 2021) 177–181. See also Sophie Horrocks, 'Performing for the Provinces: Travelling Theatre Troupes and the French Political Imaginary, 1824–1864' (PhD diss., Durham University, 2024).

[94] Peripatetic organizations—*troupes d'arrondissement* and *troupes ambulantes*—enjoyed a complex structure and an immense reach. For an early sketch of membership and activity, see *Almanach des spetacles pour 1828* (Paris: Barba, 1828) 320–350.

Opéra de salon might simply not have made its way east because it did not carry the cachet of Offenbach's authorship.

This chapter has sought to place *opéra de salon* mostly in terms of *spatialité* and geolocation but also—in its attention to the timings of the season—in temporal terms. *Opéra de salon* was developed in four types of spaces: the *salon*, the studio, the concert hall, and the *parloir*; the spaces themselves were larger than what many modern understandings of the term *salon* encompass. In all four cases, the genre existed between *lieux*, or the physical spaces of walls, floors, and ceilings, and *espaces*, or the spaces as configured in terms of usage. The various types of *opéra de salon*, especially the group of works published in women's journals, interact with these different spaces in sometimes radically different ways.

The urban location of *opéra de salon* is reflected in the cartography of the city of Paris and of the types of individual cultivating the genre; key urban spaces that emerge are the eastern end of the Faubourg Saint-Germain, especially the area around the Hôtel-Dieu (professional people with a large representation from medicine), Nouvelle Athènes (musicians and other artists), and the Faubourg Saint-Honoré (bankers and industrialists). This type of geolocation is broadened in an exploration of *opéra de salon* in the French provinces, where spa resorts were one of its most popular venues, including Baden, just over the border from the Bas-Rhin *département*. Beyond the spa, *opéra de salon* in the provinces was promoted by a small group of energetic artists, led by Gaveaux-Sabatier, who negotiated performances between established theatres and *troupes d'arrondissement*. *Opéra de salon* appears to have made no impact beyond French borders apart from Baden.

Conclusion

It might be easy to think that exposing and analysing a repertory that is completely unknown is an end in itself, and when it concerns approximately 120 unfamiliar works and the culture that supports them, such thoughts might well be justified. *Opéra de salon* takes the form—a single act, an average of seven numbers and ten scenes, with three or four characters—akin to that of *opérette* as it stabilized towards the end of the 1850s and could be considered, probably wrongly, a mere adjunct to that history. The fact that *opéra de salon* predates the emergence of *opérette* and leads the development of the genre rather than following it is striking, but this pales into insignificance alongside the broader historical arguments that explaining *opéra de salon* permit.

The study of *opéra de salon* contributes much to our broader understanding of the history of nineteenth-century music for the stage. It addresses the question of public and private at almost every turn and provides an opportunity to work with the two concepts in ways that develop their porous boundaries and subtle intersections. Such an inquiry furthermore gives a glimpse of unexceptional, quotidian musical practices that fall outside the canonic discourses associated with *grand opéra*, *opéra comique*, *melodramma*, *dramma buffo*, and other genres—even *vaudeville* and *mélodrame*—associated with the Parisian regulated theatre. *Opéra de salon* helps drives home the sense that music in the European theatre is so much broader a subject than the term 'opera' encompasses and contributes to a scholarly discourse that broadens the history of nineteenth-century music and culture.

Opéra de salon: Parisian Societies and Spaces develops work in two further domains: geolocation and *spatialité*: (1) the geolocation of performance space and the regions of the city of Paris in which *opéra de salon* was cultivated and (2) the constant interplay of *lieu* and *espace*, the largely immobile physical *lieux* that formed parts of people's homes, from the most opulent to the most modest, on the one hand, and on the other, the performative *espaces* that were temporarily created for the performance of the genre. Geolocation and *spatialité* are closely related to the status of the individuals promoting *opéra de salon*, the levels of resources they could give to its performance, and the relationship between those assets and the repertory they chose to promote.

Although little is known about the geolocation of the *parloirs* that supported *opéra de salon*, one could easily imagine them farther from the centre than even Duprez's theatre in the north-east corner of the fashionable Nouvelle Athènes or Gaveaux-Sabatier's studio in the even more fashionable tenth *arrondissement*. But the *salons* of the *moyenne bourgeoisie*, the *haute bourgeoisie*, and the aristocracy, as well as musicians' studios, displayed clear-cut spatial preferences for, respectively, the east end of the Faubourg Saint-Germain, the Faubourg Saint-Honoré, the west end of the Faubourg Saint-Germain, and Nouvelle Athènes; professional, financial, and artistic preferences were clearly echoed by location. The *espaces* that were created for the performance of *opéra de salon* differed by size and by type. Where attempts were made to create a domestic theatre, footlights, scenery, props, and costumes were frequently present, even in the most modest environment, as Daumier's engravings make clear. The supply of material for the provisional theatre was professionalized as early as the 1850s, with companies existing to put up and take down temporary stages. But the real differences lay in the underlying *lieux*, which differed enormously, from the ballroom in the opulent town house of the industrialist Binder, which could host participants in their hundreds, to the *parloir* in an apartment where participants would not exceed the low tens.

Opéra de salon was cultivated across large parts of the social spectrum. This book has given examples of performances of the same tightly focussed genre in performance venues ranging from the Louvre in front of the imperial family and an audience of hundreds to the *parloir* of the apartment of the aspirant *petit-bourgeois*. In many cases, the same has been seen to move across different performative spaces proposed by the aristocracy, as well as the *haute* and *moyenne bourgeoisie*. *Opéra de salon* entertained and enriched vastly different types of individuals across the city in ways *grand opéra* or Italian *melodramma*, on the one hand, and *comédie-vaudeville* and *mélodrame*, on the other, could only dream of. But the subtle differences are revealing, especially as the focus for a large subsection of the repertory—destined for the *parloir*—falls on the *demoiselle*, the young woman between school and marriage; here the repertory of *opéra de salon* carefully plays to the strengths of the family, with mothers and daughters much in evidence.

And as the book suggests, this *parloir* culture of *opéra de salon* was supported by a complex network of periodical publications that aligned music, its performance, and the domestic production of stage works with music to the other accomplishments that characterized the *demoiselle* at mid-century.

Opéra de salon was a largely Parisian preoccupation. Most of the regional attempts at the genre are associated with spa towns, where the clientele and audiences were largely the same as in Paris, temporarily displaced to the provinces; and even if Baden was technically outside the French empire, its culture was effectively that of Paris on summer vacation. This is not to say, however, that *opéra de salon* does not exist outside France, but it is to point up a significant lacuna in the understanding of music for the European stage. Whether, for example, the two works, both described as *opera di camera* and premiered at the Royal Gallery of Illustration in 1863 and 1869, should be assimilated into the broader European context of *opéra de salon* is a question whose answer will have to wait until the form of George Macfarren's *Jessy Lea* and Frederic Clay's *Ages Ago: A Musical Legend* and the institutional nature of the Royal Gallery of Illustration have been clarified.[1] And the broader history of such music for the private stage discussed in this book, in Italian- and German-speaking lands, to say nothing of the eastern reaches of the Austro-Hungarian empire or its Russian counterpart, remains to be written.

One of the challenges of writing about nineteenth-century music is turning proximity into distance: the immediate presence of so much nineteenth-century music at the touch of a screen in a car or on an aeroplane, is—or ought to be—a contrast to the distance at which so much nineteenth-century culture appears to sit. The introduction to *Opéra de Salon: Parisian Societies and Spaces* advanced *opéra de salon* as a genre that could bypass many of the central questions of canon that bedevil the study of nineteenth-century music, and this has been abundantly manifest throughout these pages. But a by-product of the book's evasive attitude to canon is how the focus on the differences between the nineteenth and early twenty-first centuries may so easily be preserved and enhanced. Despite the recent growth in elite 'country-house opera' in the United Kingdom, surely a product of early-twenty-first-century neoliberal restrictions on social mobility,[2] by and large people do

---

[1] For what little is known of the Royal Gallery of Illustration and its repertory, see Arthur Jacobs, 'Cradled among the Reeds: Two Victorian Operettas', *The Musical Times* 129 (1988) 234–235.

[2] There is very little critical reflection on this early-twenty-first century explosion of practices that goes back to the 1930s. For an exception, see Suzanne Aspden, 'Pastoral Retreats: Playing at Arcadia in Modern Britain', *Operatic Geographies: The Place of Opera and the Opera House*, ed. Suzanne Aspden (Chicago: University of Chicago Press, 2019) 195–212.

not mount productions of stage music in their own homes, certainly not the *moyenne bourgeoisie* and especially not those on the boundaries between the *moyenne* and the *petite bourgeoisie*. The study of *opéra de salon*—much more than, say, another analysis of *La traviata* which risks effortlessly eliding the past and present—returns us to the culture of the nineteenth century in all its vibrancy and complexity.

Bibliography

Primary Sources 1 (Manuscripts)

Cambridge, MA, Harvard University, Houghton Library, MS M1500.D935 J4: autograph of Gilbert Duprez, *Jélyotte, ou Un passe-temps de duchesse*.
Paris, Archives Nationales, F^{18} 922/1821: censors' libretto of Seinely, *Les tables tournantes*.
Paris, Archives Nationales, F^{18} 1079: censors' libretto of Alexandre Flan, *La table tournante*.
Paris, Archives Nationales, F^{18} 1345: miscellaneous censors' libretti
Paris, Archives Nationales, F^{18} 1346/7557: censors' libretto of Louis Sabatier, *Le revenant*.
Paris, Archives Nationales, F^{18} 1346/7100: censors' libretto of anonymous, *Un rendez-vous/en Espagne*.
Paris, Archives Nationales, F^{18} 1347/9856: censors' libretto of Georges Jacobi, *Le feu aux poudres*.
Paris, Archives Nationales, F^{18} 1348^B: miscellaneous censors' libretti
Paris, Archives Nationales, F^{18} 1349^A: miscellaneous censors' libretti
Paris, Archives Nationales, F^{18} 1372: miscellaneous censors' libretti
Paris, Archives Nationales, F^{18} 1531/3692: censors' libretto of Pauline Thys, *L'héritier sans le savoir*.
Paris, Archives Nationales, F^{18} 1530: miscellaneous censors' libretti
Paris, Archives Nationales, F^{18} 1531: miscellaneous censors' libretti
Paris, Bibliothèque Nationale de France, MS 1093: autograph of Félicien David, *Fermier de Franconville*.
Paris, Bibliothèque Nationale de France, MS 1094^A: autograph of Félicien David, *Fermier de Franconville*.
Paris, Bibliothèque Nationale de France, MS 1094^B: autograph of Félicien David, *Fermier de Franconville*.
Paris, Bibliothèque Nationale de France, MS 14632: autograph of Jean-Baptiste Weckerlin, *Hommage à Rossini*.
Paris, Bibliothèque Nationale de France, MS 16884: autograph of Jean-Baptiste Weckerlin, *L'amour à l'épée*.
Paris, Bibliothèque Nationale de France, MS 16900: autograph of Jean-Baptiste Weckerlin, *Le mariage en poste*.
Paris, Bibliothèque Nationale de France, MS 16905, autograph of Jean-Baptiste Weckerlin, *Pierrot à Paphos ou La sérénade interrompue*.
Pontpoint, Oise, Private Collection of Jacques Bureau, MS 3: autograph of Allyre Bureau, *Dame Jacinthe*, piano-vocal score.
Pontpoint, Oise, Private Collection of Jacques Bureau, MS 12/1: autograph of Allyre Bureau, *Le baron de Fifeland*.
Pontpoint, Oise, Private Collection of Jacques Bureau 12/2: autograph of Allyre Bureau, *Dame Jacinthe*, full score.

Primary Sources 2 (Printed Music)

21e ANNÉE. 1864–1865.—ALBUMS N°s 1, 2, 3,/MAGASIN DES DEMOISELLES/-LE MIROIR/Opérette en un acte/PAROLES/DE M. CH. NUITTER/MUSIQUE/ DE

M. FRÉDÉRIC BARBIER/. . ./PARIS/ADMINISTRATIONS ET RÉDACTION DU MAGASIN DES DEMOISELLES,/51 RUE LAFFITTE, 51/-/1864–1865.

À DEUX PAS/DU/BONHEUR,/*Proverbe Lyrique de Salon*/en un acte,/*Paroles de*/Mme Roger de Beauvoir,/*Musique de*/FÉLIX/GODEFROID./. . ./*PARIS, au MÉNESTREL, Rue Vivienne, 2 bis,/HEUGEL et CIE, éditeurs libraires/pour la France et l'Étranger.*

À Madame de Royer/UN/SERVICE D'AMI/*Opéra Comique en un Acte*/PAROLES DE MLLE/ Jenny Sabatier/*Musique*/DE/EDMOND HOCMELLE/*Organiste de St Philippe du Roule et de la Chapelle du Sénat*/. . ./*au MÉNESTREL, rue Vivienne, 2bis/. . ./chez Mr HOCMELLE, rue du Cirque, 21.*

A Madame la B^{onne} de Caters/née Lablache/Messe Brève/Pour Soprano/Kyrie—Offertoire—O salutaris—Agnus Dei/Avec Accompagnement d'Orgue ou Harmonium/Par Madame/LA V^{tessee} de GRANDVAL/-/*Chez Madame Maeyens-Couvreur, 40 Rue du Bac/Paris.*

A Mademoiselle Augusta Hoffmann./-/MARIE STUART/AU CHÂTEAU DE LOCHLEVEN, *Opérette de salon*, à un acte./PAROLES DE M. P. BOGAERTS,/MUSIQUE DE/ J. M. DUPRATO/. . ./SCHOTT FRERES/BRUXELLES, 82 Montagne de la Cour/ MAYENCE,/Les Fils de B. SCHOTT/LONDRES,/SCHOTT ET C°, Regent Street, 159.

À Monsieur Ad. Adam/*MEMBRE DE L'INSTITUT*/LE/COIN DU FEU/*Opéra de Salon*/ *Poëme*/D'ÉTIENNE TREFEU/Musique/DE/CHARLES POISOT/. . ./*PARIS, chez Étienne CHALLIOT, Éditeur de Musique,/Rue St Honoré 354 pres la Place Vendome.*

À *Monsieur le D^r ' Edouard Bouland./-/LES/DEUX/ÉPAGNEULS/Opéra bouffe/en un acte et en vers/DE M^r/Edouard Fournier,/Musique de CHARLES MANRY./Représenté aux Néothermes, le 19 Décembre 1854/. . ./Etienne CHALLIOT, éditeur,/à Paris, Rue St Honoré, 354, près la Place Vendôme.*

À *Monsieur le D^r/Edouard Bouland/LES/DEUX/ESPAGNEULS/Opéra bouffe/en un acte en vers./DE M^r/Édouard Fournier,/Musique de/CHARLES MANRY./OP. 53)/Représenté aux Néothermes, le 19 Décembre 1854/-/Partition PIANO et chant/. . ./Etienne CHAILLOT, éditeur,/à Paris, Rue St Honoré, 354, près la Place Vendôme.*

AMOUR/ET/SPIRITISME/*Opéra-comique en un acte*/PAROLES DE/*Léon QUENTIN et GÉDHÉ*/PAROLES [*sic*; recte 'Musique']/DE/VICTOR ROBILLARD/. . ./PARIS/Emile CHATOT éditeur/19r. N^e des Petits-champs, en face la Bibliothèque.

AVANT LA REPRÉSENTATION/D'UN/OPÉRA DE G. NADAUD/PROLOGUE/PAR E. TOURNEUX/-/MARS 1857/-/PARIS/IMPRIMERIE DE J CLAYE/DUE SAINT BENOÎT, 7.

Dédiée aux PENSIONNATS/et/aux SOCIÉTÉS PHILHARMONIQUES./LES DEUX CHARLATANS/*SAYNÈTE BOUFFE.*/PAROLES DE/EDOUARD DOYEN/MUSIQUE DE/EMILE DUCELLIER/. . ./Paris, Maison L. VIEILLOT, L. LABBÉ, Succ^r. Editeur, 20 rue du Croissant.

DUO/Extrait de la Partition des Suite[s] d'une Indiscrétion,/Comédie mêlée de Chants publiée par le Journal des Jeunes personnes/Paroles de Mme Ferdinand HUARD. Musique de M. BLANCOU, *Le journal des jeunes personnes* 13 (1845) unnumbered appendix.

École Nationale des Chartes: *Dictionnaire des imprimeurs-lithographes du xix siècle* (http://elec.enc.sorbonne.fr/imprimeurs/node/26739).

FANTAISIE SUR UNE PARTIE DE DOMINOS/Opéra Comique de M^r le Marquis Jules d'AOUST/L'INSTRUMENTAL/Edition GAUTROT ainé./Arr. Par. Jules JACOB./Chef de Musique du 1er Dragons/. . ./Paris, GAUTROT ainé, Rue Turenne, 80 et chez RICHAULT, Ed^r B^t des Italiens 4.

HARMONIE/(ARME—AU NID)/CHARADE EN TROIS TABLEAUX/PAR M. PONSARD/ JOUÉE AU PALAIS DE COMPIÈGNE/EN PRÉSENCE DE LEURS MAJESTÉS/LE 15 DÉCEMBRE 1863/. . ./PARIS/IMPRIMERIE IMPÉRIALE/-/M DCCC LXIII.

JALOUX DE SOI/Proverbe lyrique en un acte./Pour Chant et Piano/-/*Paroles et Musique*/de/ Mme Anaïs P. P./-/. . ./Lith. Ducrieux, Rue de Vaugirard, 136.

JOURNAL DES DEMOISELLES/Boulevard des Italiens, N° 1./. . ./DEUX LUNATIQUES À S^T-CLOUD/VAUDEVILLE/*Paroles* (dans le texte) *de Madame*/ADAM BOISGONTIER./ Musique de/A. ROCHEBLAVE/Imp. Duput Passage du Désir, 3, Paris.

LA/DANSE DES TABLES/POCHADE EN UN ACTE,/PAR M. H. LEFEBVRE,/ REPRÉSENTÉE POUR LA PREMIÈRE FOIS SUR LE THÉÂTRE DES CÉLESTINS/ A LYON, LE 21 MAI 1853/. . ./LYON.—IMPRIMERIE D'AIMÉ VINGTRINIER, QUAI SAINT-ANTOINE, 36.

LA/HARPE/D'OR/*Opéra Légende en deux actes,*/de MM/Ernest Dubreuil et Jaime fils,/ MUSIQUE/DE/FÉLIX GODEFROID/*PARTITION* PIANO *ET CHANT*/PARIS, CHOUDENS, *éditeurs/rue Saint Honoré, 263, près l'Assomption.*

LAIDE/OPÉRETTE EN 2 TABLEAUX/Paroles de/Mme ADAM BOISGONTIER/Musique de/M^r TH. SEMET.

LA MORT DE SOCRATE/OPÉRA COMIQUE EN UN ACTE/PAR M. GALOPPE D'ONQUAIRE/MUSIQUE DE M. HOCMELLE/REPRÉSENTÉE POUR LA PREMIÈRE FOIS, A LA SALLE HERTZ, LE 7 FÉVRIER 1858/. . ./LAGNY. Imprimérie de A. VARIGAULT.

LES AMANTS DE VÉRONE/OPÉRA en QUATRE ACTES/et/*Six Tableaux*/Imité de SHAKESPEARE/PAROLES ET MUSIQUE/DE/RICHARD YRVID/. . ./Paris, G. FLAXLAND Éditeur, 4, Place de la Madeleine.

LES/ÉCHOS DE ROSINE/OPÉRA-COMIQUE DE SALON/REPRÉSENTÉ POUR LA PREMIÈRE FOIS A PARIS LE 13 OCTOBRE 1854/POÈME/DE/ÉTIENNE TRÉFEU/ MUSIQUE/DE/A. THYS/PARIS/ETIENNE CHALLIOT, ÉDITEUR/Rue Saint-Honoré, 354, près la place Vendôme.

LES IDÉES/DE/MR PAMPELUNE/Opéra-Comique/en un Acte/Paroles de Ch. WALLUT/ Musique de/MARCELLUS MULLER/Paris, Miason G. FLAXLANC./DURAND, SCHOENWERK & CIE/ Succeseurs/ 4, Place de la Madeleine, 4.

'LE SPECTACLE EN FAMILLE./AUTANT DE TUÉS QUE DE BLESSÉS. . ./COMÉDIE-PROVERBE EN UN ACTE', *Le musée des familles* 26 (1859) 41–48.

'LE SPECTACLE EN FAMILLE./ - /L'OFFICIER BLEU, OU ON A SOUVENT BESOIN D'UN PLUS PETIT QUE SOI/-/COMÉDIE-PROVERBE EN UN ACTE', Le musée des familles 24 (1857) 17–26.

LES RESSOURCES/DE/JACQUELINE/COMÉDIE MÉLÉE DE CHANT/EN UN ACTE/ PAROLES DE M. HENRY BOISSEAUX/MUSIQUE DE M. ANDRÉ SIMIOT/Représentée pour la première fois à Paris, le 29 mai 1854/PARIS/MICHEL LÉVY FRÈRES, LIBRAIRES-ÉDITEURS,/RUE VIVIENNE, 2 BIS./ 1854.

LES TABLES TOURNANTES/SAYNETTE POUR SALON/Représentée pour la première fois à la Séance publique/de la Société philotechnique, le 26 mai 1872/Par A. DE MONGIS/ Extrait de l'ANNUAIRE DE LA SOCIÉTÉ PHILOTECHNIQUE—1872/ -/ MEULAN/ IMPRIMERIE DE A. MASSON.

L'HABIT NE FAIT PAS LE MOINE,/COMÉDIE-VAUDEVILLE/EN TROIS ACTES,/De MM. Saint-Hilaire et P. Duport/MUSIQUE NOUVELLE/DE MM. Doche, Thénard et This/Représentée pour la première fois, à Paris, sur le théâtre national du Vaudeville,/le 18 août 1835./. . ./Impr. De J.-R. MEVREAL, passade du Caire, 54.

MAGASIN/des Demoiselles,/12e—51. *Rue Lafitte 51.—N°s 1.2.3*/1855–1856/-/LE/PRIX/ DE FAMILLE/Opéra Comique en un acte/*Paroles*/DE/Méry/MUSIQUE/DE/VICTOR MASSÉ./BUREAUX/51 Rue Laffitte 51/*PARIS.*

MAGASIN THÉÂTRAL ILLUSTRÉ/A LA LIBRAIRIE THÉÂTRALE/BOULEVARD SAINT-MARTIN, 12/. . ./LA TABLE TOURNANTE/EXPÉRIENCE DE MAGNÉTISME, EN UN ACTE, MÉLÉE DE COUPLETS/PAR MM. EUGÈNE DE MIRECOURT ET CHAMPFLEURY/REPRÉSENTÉE, POUR LA PREMIÈRE FOIS, A PARIS, SUR LE THÉÂTRE DES VARIÉTÉS, LE 2 MAI 1853.

MAGASIN THÉÂTRAL./PIÈCES NOUVELLES/JOUÉES SUR TOUS LES THÉÂTRES DE PARIS./-/*THÉÂTRE DES FOLIES—[DRAMATIQUES]./*A QUI MAL VEUT, MAL ARRIVE./Vaudeville proverbe en un acte par MM. E. ROCHE et H. CHÉREAULT/. . ./ PARIS./LIBRAIRIE THÉTRALE, BOULEVARD SAINT-MARTIN, 12./ANCIENNE MAISON MARCHANT./1852.

Répertoire des Théâtres, Salons & Concerts/Théâtre/ON/GUÉRIT DE LA PEUR/PAROLES DE M HENRY BOISSEAUX/MUSIQUE DE/T. DE LAJARTE/. . ./Paris, CHOUDENS, 371, Rue St Honoré.
ROBERT LE DIABLE/Opéra en 5 Actes/*Paroles de MM E. Scribe et G. Delavigne*/MUSIQUE DE/Giacomo Meyerbeer/Partition de Piano, arrangée par J. P. PIXIS/. . ./*Paris, chez Maurice Schlesinger, rue Richelieu N° 97/Londres, propriété de M. Monck Mason—Berlin, chez A. M. Schlesinger.*
ROSA, LA ROSE/Paroles de Charles Bousquet/*OPÉRETTE/de Salon.*/Musique de Charles POISOT.
THÉÂTRE DU PALAIS-ROYAL/L'ESPRIT FRAPPEUR/OU/LES SEPT MERVEILLES DU JOUR/COMÉDIE-VAUDEVILLE EN UN ACTE,/Par MM. CLAIRVILLE et Jules CORDIER,/Représentée, pour la première fois, à Paris, sur le théâtre du PALAIS-ROYAL,/ le 17 Décembre 1853./ . . ./ Paris/ BECK, LIBRAIRE, RUE DES GRANDS-AUGUSTINS, 20/ -/ 1853.
TOUT CHEMIN/*MÈNE À*/ROME/Opéra Comique en Un Acte/*Paroles de M^r/Le Comte de Mesgrigny/Musique de M^r/LE DUC DE MASSA/-/Paris, E. GIROD, Editeur/ 16, Boulev^t Montmartre.*

Primary Sources 3 (Other Publications)

Albert, Émile, *Chanson espagnole transcrite et variée pour piano, op. 49* (Paris: Brandus, 1856).
Albert, Émile, *Études mélodiques pour piano, op. 56*, 2 vols. (Paris: Brandus et Dufour, 1858).
Almanach des spetacles pour 1828 (Paris: Barba, 1828).
Ancelot, Virginie, *Les salons de Paris: foyers éteints* (Paris: Tardieu, 1858).
Azevedo, Alexis, *F. David: coup d'oeil sur sa vie et son oeuvre* (Paris: Ménestrel; Heugel, 1863).
Balzac, Honoré de, *Balthazar Claës, ou la Recherche de l'absolu* (Paris: Charpentier, 1834).
Bassinville, Anaïs de, *Les salons d'autrefois: souvenirs intimes*, 4 vols. (Paris: Victorion, n.d.).
Belouet, Abbé, *La pitoyade: poème héroï-comique* (Chaumont: Miot-Dadant, 1863).
Benou, Jean-Baptiste-Louis-Georges, *Code et manuel du commissaire-priseur, ou Traité des prisées et ventes mobilières* (Paris: D'Ocagne, 1835).
Berlioz, Hector, *Mémoires de Hector Berlioz, Membre de l'Institut de France, comprenant des voyages en Italie, en Allemagne, en Russie et en Angleterre, 1803–1865* (Paris: Lévy, 1870; reprint Farnborough: Gregg, 1969).
Berton, Caroline, 'Gustave Nadaud comédien', *Nouvelle revue internationale*, 15 June 1893.
Boisgontier, Elisa Adam, *Nouveau théâtre des demoiselles* (Paris: Fonteney et Peltier, 1851).
Boisgontier, Elisa Adam, *Paris nouveau* (Paris: Lévy, 1857).
[Boittelle, Symphorien-Casimir-Joseph-Edouard], 'Police des théâtres, circulaire de M. le Préfet de Police Paris, 1er juillet 1864, art. 68', *Journal des Commissaire de Police* 10 (1864) 169–185.
Bonnard, Arthur de, *Description des néothermes et relation des principales guérisons obtenues par l'emploi des appareils médicaux de toute nature établis dans cette maison de bains et de santé* (Paris: Pollet, [1841]).
Bonninière Beaumont-Vassy, Edouard Ferdinand de la, *Les salons de Paris et la société parisienne sous Napoléon III* (Paris: Sartorius, 1868).
Bouland, Pierre, *Études sur les propriétés physiques, chimiques et médicinales des eaux minérales d'Enghien* (Paris: Dentu, 1850).
Bringol, Jean-Charles, *Intérieure des Néothermes* (Paris: Bichebois, 1853).
Champlin, John Dennison, *Cyclopedia of Music and Musicians*, 3 vols. (New York: Scribner, 1888–1890).
Clément, Félix, and Pierre Larousse, *Dictionnaire des opéras (Dictionnaire lyrique)* . . . (Paris: Larousse, [1881]).

Delpit, Albert, 'La liberté des théâtres et les cafés-concerts', *Revue des deux mondes*, 25 [third series] (1878) 601–623.
Driou, Alfred, *Nouveau théâtre des jeunes demoiselles: comédies, drames, vaudevilles, opérettes et moralités bluettes propres à être jouées dans les familles et les maisons d'éducation* (Paris: Fonteney et Peltier, 1858).
Durand, Godefroy, *Vue de l'établissement de HENRY BINDER, - 31, rue du Colysée* (Paris: n.p., 1863).
École Nationale des Chartes: Dictionnaire des imprimeurs-lithographes du xix siècle http://elec.enc.sorbonne.fr/imprimeurs/node/26739).
Établissment hygénique des néothermes...prospectus (Paris: n.p., [1832]).
Fétis, François-Joseph, *Biographie universelle des musiciens et bibliographie générale de la musique*, 8 vols. (Brussels: Leroux, 1835–1844; 2nd ed. Paris: Firmin Didot, 1860–1865); supplement in 2 vols. by Arthur Pougin (Paris: Firmin Didot, 1880–1881).
Galignani's New Paris Guide: Containing a Detailed and Accurate Description (Paris: Galiganani, 1830).
Galignani's New Paris Guide: Containing a Detailed and Accurate Description (Paris: Galiganani, 1845).
Galoppe d'Onquaire (Jean-Hyacinthe-Adonis Galoppe), *Le spectacle au coin du feu* (Paris: Lévy, 1855).
Grand dictionnaire universel du xixe siècle français, historique, géographique, biographique, mythologique, bibliographique, littéraire, artistique, scientifique, etc., 17 vols. (Paris: Grand Dictionnaire Universel, 1866).
Huysmans, Joris-Karl, *En ménage* (Paris: Charpentier, 1880).
Kardec, Allan, *Spiritisme expérimental: Le Livre des médiums, ou Guide des médiums et des évocateurs,...pour faire suite au 'Livre des Esprits'* (Paris: Didier, Ledoyen, 1861).
'Lapommeraye, Pierre-Henri-Victor Berdalle de', *Revue encyclopédique* 2 (1892) 331–332.
Leclerc, Théodore, *Biographie et pensées* (Paris: Richard, 1862).
Lionnet, Anatole and Hippolyte, *Souvenirs et anecdotes* (Paris: Ollendorff, 1888).
Lorde, André de, *Pour jouer la comédie de salon: guide pratique du comédien mondain* (Paris: Hachette, 1908).
Loubens, Émile, 'Notice sur la Société Philotechnique', *Annuaire de la Société Philotechnique* 33 (1872) 1–4.
Manry, Jean, 'Lettre de M. le professeur Hardy: Documents pour servir à l'histoire de l'hôpital St Louis au commencement de ce siècle—Alibert, Biett, Lugol, Manry, Emery', *Annales de dermatologie et de syphiligraphie*, 2nd series, 6 (1885) 629–638.
Marmontel, Antoine, *Les pianistes célèbres: silhouettes et médaillons* (Paris: Heugel, 1878).
Méry, François-Joseph-Pierre-André, *Nouveau théâtre de salon* (Paris: Michel Lévy, 1865).
Méry, François-Joseph-Pierre-André, *Théâtre de salon* (Paris: Michel Lévy, 1861).
Nadaud, Gustave, *Opérettes* (Paris: Plon, 1867).
Necker de Saussure, Albertine-Adrienne, *L'éducation progressive, ou Étude du cours de la vie*, 2 vols. (Paris: Sautelet; Paulin, 1828–1832).
Nerval, Gérard de, *Voyage en orient*, 2 vols. (Paris: Charpentier, 1851).
Normand, Jacques-Clary-Jean, *Paravents et tréteaux: fantaisies de salon et de théâtre*, 6th ed. (Paris: Calmann Lévy, 1882).
Nus, Eugène, *Choses de l'autre monde* (Paris: Dentu, [1880]).
Péan de la Roche-Jagu, Eudoxie, *Mémoires artistiques . . . écrits par elle-même* (Paris: Ledoyen, 1861).
Robert, Adolphe, and Gaston Cougny, *Dictionnaire des parlementaires français*, 5 vols. (Paris: Bourloton, 1889–1891).
Sabatier, Jenny-Caroline [Thircuir; Mme Léon Mallac], *Rêves de jeunesses...précédées de deux lettres de M. A. de Lamartine et de M. Méry* (Paris: Dentu, 1863).
Sainte-Beuve, Charles-Augustin de, *Causeries de lundi*, 15 vols. (Paris: Garnier, 1851–1862).

Vapereau, Gustave, *Dictionnaire universel des contemporains contenant toutes les personnes notables de la France et des pays étrangers*, 5th ed., 2 vols. (Paris: Hachette, 1880).
Vapereau, Gustave, *Dictionnaire universel des littératures* (Paris: Hachette; 1876).
Vuillemin, Alexandre, *Paris nouveau, 1855* (Paris: Furne, [1855]).
Yriarte, Charles, *Les cercles de Paris* (Paris: Dupray de la Mahérie, 1864).

Primary Sources 4 (Serial Publications)

Annales de la Société Centrale d'Horticulture de France.
Annuaire général du commerce et de l'industrie, ou Almanach des 500,000 adresses.
Gazette d'Augsbourg/Allgemeine Zeitung.
L'année théâtrale.
L'artiste: journal de littérature et des beaux arts.
L'illustration de Bade.
La France musicale.
La revue de l'Académie de Toulouse.
La revue des beaux arts.
La Revue et Gazette musicale de Paris.
Le berquin.
Le bon ton.
Le charivari.
Le constitutionnel.
Le Figaro.
Le Gaulois.
Le journal de la mode et du goût.
Le journal des dames.
Le journal des débats.
Le journal des demoiselles.
Le journal des jeunes personnes.
Le magasin des demoiselles.
Le magasin pittoresque.
Le ménestrel.
Le monde illustré.
Le moniteur de la mode.
Le musée des familles.
Le nouvelliste.
Le petit courrier des dames.
Le petit journal.
Le sport vélocipédique.

Secondary Sources

Agulhon, Maurice, *Le cercle dans la France bourgeoise, 1810–1848: étude d'une mutation de sociabilité*, Cahiers des annales 36 (Paris: Armand Colin, 1977).
'Alphonse Lavallée, le fondateur de l'École Centrale' (http://archive.wikiwix.com/cache/index2.php?url=http%3A%2F%2Folivier.dibos.club.fr%2FAlphLav.html).
Andrew, Edward, 'Class in Itself and Class against Capital: Karl Marx and His Classifiers', *Canadian Journal of Political Science/Revue canadienne de science politique* 16 (1983) 577–584.
Aspden, Suzanne, 'Pastoral Retreats: Playing at Arcadia in Modern Britain', *Operatic Geographies: The Place of Opera and the Opera House*, ed. Suzanne Aspden (Chicago: University of Chicago Press, 2019) 195–212.

'Auguste Alphonse Edmond MEILLET', *L'art lyrique français: Théâtre-Lyrique-Inteprètes* (https://www.artlyriquefr.fr/personnages/Meillet.html).
Autin, Jean, *Les frères Pereire: le bonheur d'entreprendre* (Paris: Perrin, 1984).
Ballola, Giovanni Carli, and Roberta Montemorra Marvin, 'Bazzini, Antonio', *Grove Music Online*, 2001 (https://www.oxfordmusiconline.com/grovemusic/view/10.1093/gmo/9781561592630.001.0001/omo-9781561592630-e-0000002403).
Bara, Olivier, 'Des proverbes dans un fauteuil: un genre médiatique?' (unpublished typescript, 2014) (http://etudes-romantiques.ish-lyon.cnrs.fr/wa_files/Bara.pdf).
Bara, Olivier, 'The Company at the Heart of the Operatic Institution: Chollet and the Changing Nature of Comic-Opera Role Types during the July Monarchy', *Music, Theater and Cultural Transfer: Paris, 1830–1914*, ed. Mark Everist and Annegret Fauser (Chicago: University of Chicago Press, 2009) 11–28.
Beaupain, René, *La maison Érard: manufacture de pianos, 1780–1859* (Paris: L'Harmattan, 2005).
Bled, Victor du, *La société française depuis cent ans: quelques salons du Second Empire*, 2 vols. (Paris: Bloud & Gay, 1923).
Bohlman, Philip V., 'On the Unremarkable in Music', *19th-Century Music* 16 (1992) 203–216.
Bonnaffé, Pierre, *Pitre-Chevalier* (Paris: Leroux, 1905).
Boon, Sonja, *The Life of Madame Necker: Sin, Redemption and the Parisian Salon* (London: Pickering and Chatto, 2011).
Born, Georgina, 'Introduction', *Music, Sound and Space: Transformations of Public and Private Experience*, ed. Georgina Born (Cambridge: Cambridge University Press, 2013) 1–69.
Boulanger, Karine, 'Censure et police des théâtres', *Histoire de l'opéra français*, 3 vols., ed. Hervé Lacombe (Paris: Fayard, 2020) 2:57–64.
Bourdieu, Pierre, 'Ökonomisches Kapital, kulturelles Kapital, soziales Kapital', *Soziale Ungleichheiten*, ed. Reinhard Kreckel, Soziale Welt: Sonderheft 2 (Göttingen: Schartz, 1983) 183–198.
Bourdieu, Pierre, and Jean-Claude Passeron, *La reproduction: éléments pour une théorie du systâeme d'enseignement*, Sens commun (Paris: Éditions de Minuit, 1970).
Bradley, Ian C., *Water Music: Music Making in the Spas of Europe and North America* (Oxford: Oxford University Press, 2010).
Bunzel, Anja, and Natasha Loges, eds., *Musical Salon Culture in the Long Nineteenth Century* (Woodbridge, UK: Boydell Press, 2019).
Bunzel, Anja, and Susan Wollenberg, 'Rethinking Salon Music: Case-Studies in Analysis', *Nineteenth-Century Music Review* 20 (2022) 359–364.
Buridan, Anne de, 'Charles Cordier: sculpteur de l'Orient', *La revue du quartier latin* (8 July 2016) (https://archive.wikiwix.com/cache/index2.php?url=https%3A%2F%2Fwww.quartierlatin.paris%2F%3Fcharles-cordier-sculpteur-de-l-orient#federation=archive.wikiwix.com&tab=url).
'Charles Louis LOURDEL dit BIÉVAL', *L'art lyrique français: Théâtre-Lyrique-Inteprètes* (https://www.artlyriquefr.fr/personnages/Bieval.html).
Chauveau, Philippe, *Les théâtres parisiens disparus (1402–1986)*, Collection 'Théâtre' (Paris: Amandier, 1999).
Chesney, Duncan McColl, 'The History of the History of the Salon', *Nineteenth-Century French Studies* 36 (2007–2008) 94–108.
Cloutier, Eleanor Clare, 'Repetitive Novelty: Italian Opera in Paris and London in the 1830s and 1840s' (PhD diss., University of California at Berkeley, 2016).
Cohen, Peter, 'Flotow, Friedrich (Adolf Ferdinand) Freiherr von', *Grove Music Online*, 2001 (https://www.oxfordmusiconline.com/grovemusic/view/10.1093/gmo/9781561592630.001.0001/omo-9781561592630-e-0000043161).
Comité des travaux historiques et scientifiques—Institut rattaché à l'École nationale des chartes, 'Société philotechnique—Paris' (http://cths.fr/an/societe.php?id=100746).

Cooper, Jeffrey, *The Rise of Instrumental Music and Concert Series in Paris, 1828–1871*, Studies in Musicology 65 (Ann Arbor, MI: UMI Research Press, 1983).

Cosgrove, Denis, *Apollo's Eye: A Cartographic Genealogy of the Earth in the Western Imagination* (London: Johns Hopkins University Press, 2001).

Cosgrove, Denis, *Social Formation and Symbolic Landscape* (London: Croom Helm, 1984).

Cypess, Rebecca, *Women and Musical Salons in the Enlightenment* (Chicago: University of Chicago Press, 2021).

Dahlhaus, Carl, *Die Musik des 19. Jahrhunderts*, Neues Handbuch der Musikwissenshaft 6 (Wiesbaden: Akademische Verlagsgesellschaft Athenaion, 1980); trans. J. Bradford Robinson as *Nineteenth-Century Music* (Berkeley: University of California Press, 1989).

Dahrendorf, Ralf, *Class and Class Conflict in Industrial Society* (Stanford, CA: Stanford University Press, 1959).

Dalibard, Pierre, *C'était le temps où Charles Cordier unissait l'onyx et le bronze* (Buc: Tensing, 2012).

D'Amat, Jean-Charles Roman, and Michel Prévost, eds, *Dictionnaire de biographie française*, 21 vols. (Paris: Letouzey et Ané, 1932–).

Danger, Pierre, *Émile Augier ou le théâtre de l'ambiguïté: éléments pour une archéologie morale de la bourgeoisie sous le Second Empire* (Paris: Harmattan, 1998),

D'Angio-Barros, Agnès, *Morny: le théâtre du pouvoir* (Paris: Belin, 2012).

D'Artiste, Paul, *La vie et le monde du boulevard (1830–1870): (Un dandy: Nestor Roqueplan)* (Paris: Tallandier, 1930).

Davies, James Q., *Romantic Anatomies of Performance* (Berkeley: University of California Press, 2014).

Deaville, James, 'The Well-Mannered Auditor: Zones of Attention and the Imposition of Silence in the Salon of the Nineteenth Century', *The Oxford Handbook of Music Listening in the 19th and 20th Centuries*, ed. Christian Thorau and Hansjakob Ziemer (New York: Oxford University Press, 2018) 55–76.

De Certeau, Michel, *L'invention du quotidien*, 2 vols. (Paris: Union Générale d'Éditions, 1980; reprint Paris: Gallimard, 1990–1994).

Desvignes, Stéphane, 'Le *Théâtre de salon* de Joseph Méry, ou Les délices de l'idéal', *Tréteaux et paravents: le théâtre de société au xixe siècle*, ed. Jean-Claude Yon and Nathalie Le Gonidec (Paris: Créphis, 2012) 151–162.

Devriès, Anik, and François Lesure, *Dictionnaire des éditeurs de musique français*, 2 vols. (vol. 1 in 2 parts), Archives de l'édition musicale française 4 (Geneva: Minkoff, 1979–1988).

Dubrow, Heather, *Genre*, The Critical Idiom 42 (London: Methuen, 1982).

Ellis, Katharine, *French Musical Life: Local Dynamics in the Century to World War II* (New York: Oxford University Press, 2021).

Epstein, Louis, 'The Promise and Peril of Making Digital Maps Sing', *Journal of the American Musicological Society* 77 (2024) 262–284.

Esprit de Mme de Girardin, avec préface par M. de Lamartine (Paris: Hetzel, [1862]).

Everist, Mark, 'Donizetti and Wagner: *opéra de genre* at the Théâtre de la Renaissance', *Giacomo Meyerbeer and Music Drama in Nineteenth-Century Paris*, Variorum Collected Studies Series CS805 (Aldershot: Ashgate, 2005) 309–341.

Everist, Mark, *The Empire at the Opéra: Theatre, Power and Music in Second Empire Paris*, Cambridge Elements of Musical Theatre (Cambridge: Cambridge University Press, 2021).

Everist, Mark, 'Enshrining Mozart: *Don Giovanni* and the Viardot Circle', *19th-Century Music* 25 (2001) 165–189.

Everist, Mark, *Genealogies of Music and Memory: Gluck in the 19th-Century Parisian Imagination* (New York: Oxford University Press, 2021).

Everist, Mark, 'Jacques Offenbach: The Music of the Past and the Image of the Present', *Music, Theater and Cultural Transfer: Paris, 1830–1914*, ed. Mark Everist and Annegret Fauser (Chicago: University of Chicago Press, 2009) 72–98.

Everist, Mark, 'L'Opéra-Comique, sous le Second Empire', *Histoire de l'opéra français*, ed. Hervé Lacombe, 3 vols. (Paris: Fayard, 2020) 2:425–434.
Everist, Mark, *Mozart's Ghosts: Haunting the Halls of Musical Culture* (New York: Oxford University Press, 2013.
Everist, Mark, 'Music in the Second Empire Theatre (MitSET)' (http://www.fmc.ac.uk/mitset/index.html?#/).
Everist, Mark, 'Music, Journalism and Social Justice', *Presse et musique*, special issue of *Tangencex* 137 (2025) 13–42.
Fauquet, Joël-Marie, 'BUSSINE, Prosper-Alphonse', *Dictionnaire de la musique en France au xixe siècle*, ed. Joël-Marie Fauquet (Paris: Fayard, 2003) 188.
Everist, Mark, 'The Music of Power: Parisian Opera and the Politics of Genre, 1806–1864', *Journal of the American Musicological Society* 67 (2014) 685–734.
Everist, Mark, 'Opéra de salon', FMC Collection 30 (http://search.fmc.ac.uk/#m-columnbrowser@||m-informationcontrol@url = html/home.php).
Everist, Mark, *Opérette: The First Twenty-Five Years* (New York: Oxford University Press, forthcoming).
Everist, Mark, 'Resonances from beyond the Grave: Music and the Occult in Nineteenth-Century Paris', *Journal of the American Musicological Society* 78 (2025) forthcoming.
Everist, Mark, 'Theatres of Litigation: Stage Music at the Théâtre de la Renaissance, 1838–1840', *Cambridge Opera Journal* 16 (2004) 133–162.
Fauquet, Joël-Marie, 'CANOBY, Louis-*Gustave*', *Dictionnaire de la musique en France au xixe siècle*, ed. Joël-Marie Fauquet (Paris: Fayard, 2003) 205.
Fauquet, Joël-Marie, 'CAPOUL, Joseph-Amédée-*Victor*', *Dictionnaire de la musique en France au xixe siècle*, ed. Joël-Marie Fauquet (Paris: Fayard, 2003) 207.
Fauquet, Joël-Marie, 'DURAND, Émile', *Dictionnaire de la musique en France au xixe siècle*, ed. Joël-Marie Fauquet (Paris: Fayard, 2003) 413.
Fauquet, Joël-Marie, 'GRANDVAL, *Marie*-Félicie-Clémence de REISET, Mme de', *Dictionnaire de la musique en France au xixe siècle*, ed. Joël-Marie Fauquet (Paris: Fayard, 2003) 530.
Fauquet, Joël-Marie, 'MANRY, Charles', *Dictionnaire de la musique en France au xixe siècle*, ed. Joël-Marie Fauquet (Paris: Fayard, 2003) 740.
Fauquet, Joël-Marie, and Laure Schnapper, 'Salle de concert', *Dictionnaire de la musique en France au xixe siècle*, ed. Joël-Marie Fauquet (Paris: Fayard, 2003) 1113–1114.
France, Peter, ed., *The New Oxford Companion to Literature in French* (Oxford: Clarendon, 1995).
Frey, Heike, and Christiane Barlag, 'Dietz, *von Dietz, de Dietz, Diez*, Cathinka, *Kathinka*, verh. Mackenzie de Dietz', *Europäische Instrumentalistinnen des 18. und 19. Jahrhunderts*, Sophie Drinker Institut für Musikwissenschaftliche Frauen- und Geschlechterforschung (https://www.sophie-drinker-institut.de/dietz-cathinka).
Gady, Alexandre, *Les hôtels particuliers de Paris, du moyen âge à la belle époque* (Paris: Parigramme, 2011).
Gänzl, Kurt, 'Jules Lefort: "Delight of the Parisian Salons"' (https://kurtofgerolstein.blogspot.com/2021/05/jules-lefort-delight-of-parisian-salons.html).
Gänzl, Kurt, *Victorian Vocalists* (London: Routledge, 2018).
Geertz, Clifford, 'Thick Description: Toward an Interpretive Theory of Culture', *The Interpretation of Cultures* (New York: Basic Books, 1973; London: Hutchinson, 1975) 3–30.
Genty, Maurice, ed., *Index biographique des membres, des associés et des correspondants de l'Académie de médecine: 1820–1990*, 4th ed. (Paris: Académie Nationale de Médecine, 1991).
Geoffroy-Schwinden, Rebecca Dowd, 'Fashion, Musical Taste, and the French Revolution: *Journal de la mode et du goût*', paper presented at France: Musiques, Cultures, 1789–1918 conference, Venice, July 2022.
Geoffroy-Schwinden, Rebecca Dowd, *From Servant to Savant: Musical Privilege, Property, and the French Revolution* (New York: Oxford University Press, 2022).

Gerber, Mirjam, *Zwischen Salon und musikalischer Geselligkeit: Henriette Voigt, Livia Frege und Leipzigs bürgerliches Musikleben* (Hildesheim: Olms, 2016).
Gieseking, Jen Jack, 'Where Are We? The Method of Mapping with GIS in Digital Humanities', *American Quarterly* 70 (2018) 641–648.
Girod, Pierre, 'L'École Duprez (1849–1894): exercices publics et tournées dans les départements' (https://dezede.org/dossiers/id/248/).
Girod, Pierre, 'Les mutations du ténor romantique' (PhD diss., Université de Rennes 2, 2015).
Girod, Pierre, 'L'opéra de salon à Paris [sic] (1851–1904)' (https://dezede.org/dossiers/opera-de-salon/).
Girod, Pierre, 'Un demi-siècle d'opéra de salon', *Histoire de l'opéra français*, 3 vols., ed. Hervé Lacombe (Paris: Fayard, 2020) 2:560–570.
'GOURDIN Alexandre Narcisse Marie', *L'art lyrique français: Opéra-Comique-Chanteurs* (https://www.artlyriquefr.fr/dicos/Opera-Comique%20Chanteurs.html#HAAS).
Haebler, Rolf Gustav, *Geschichte des Stadt und des Kurortes Baden-Baden*, 2 vols. (Baden-Baden: Schmidt, 1969).
Hamel, Henri, *Felix Pigeory, fondateur de Villers, 1812–1873* (Trouville: Association des Amis du Musée de Trouville, 1985).
'Hermann-Léon', *Benezit Dictionary of Artists* (https://www.oxfordartonline.com/benezit/view/10.1093/benz/9780199773787.001.0001/acref-9780199773787-e-00086846).
Hibberd, Sarah, 'Note from the Guest Editor [*Music and Science in London and Paris*]', *19th-Century Music* 39 (2015–2016) 83–86.
Himmelfarb, Constance, 'Un salon de la Nouvelle-Athènes en 1839–1840: l'album inconnu de Juliette Zimmerman', *Revue de musicologie* 87 (2001) 33–65.
Horrocks, Sophie, 'Performing for the Provinces: Travelling Theatre Troupes and the French Political Imaginary, 1824–1864' (PhD diss., Durham University, 2024).
Huguet, Françoise, *Les professeurs de la faculté de médecine de Paris: dictionnaire biographique, 1794–1939* (Paris, INRP-CNRS, 1991).
Jacobs, Arthur, 'Cradled among the Reeds: Two Victorian Operettas', *The Musical Times* 129 (1988) 234–235.
'JAL, Augustin', *Dictionnaire critique des historiens de l'art actifs en France de la Révolution à la Première Guerre mondiale* (https://www.inha.fr/fr/ressources/publications/publications-numeriques/dictionnaire-critique-des-historiens-de-l-art/jal-augustin.html?search-keywords=anatole+jal).
Jardin, Etienne, and Martin Guerpin, eds, *Faites vos jeux! Actes du colloque: La vie musicale dans les casinos français (XIXe–XXIe siècle), 28–29 May 2021* (Paris: Actes Sud, 2024).
'Jean-Baptiste PORTEHAUT', *L'art lyrique français* (https://www.artlyriquefr.fr/personnages/Portehaut.html).
'Jules François René LEFORT dit Jules LEFORT', *L'art lyrique français: le Théâtre-Lyrique, ses interprètes* (https://www.artlyriquefr.fr/personnages/Lefort%20Jules.html).
'Jules Sébastien MONJAUZE dit Jules MONJAUZE', *L'art lyrique français: Théâtre-Lyrique-Inteprètes* (https://www.artlyriquefr.fr/personnages/Monjauze%20Jules.html).
Kale, Steven, *French Salons: High Society and Political Sociability from the Old Regime to the Revolution of 1848* (Baltimore: Johns Hopkins University Press, 2004).
Kallberg, Jeffrey, 'The Rhetoric of Genre: Chopin's Nocturne in G Minor', *19th-Century Music* 11 (1987–1988) 238–261.
Kicherer, Dagmar, *Kleine Geschichte der Stadt Baden-Baden* (Leinfelden-Echterdingen: Braun, 2008).
Kocevar, Éric, 'GIDE, Casimir', *Dictionnaire de la musique en France au xixe siècle*, ed. Joël-Marie Fauquet (Paris: Fayard, 2003) 514.
Kutsch, Karl-Josef, and Leo Riemens, *Großes Sängerlexikon*, 4 vols. (Bern: Francke, 1987–1994; 4th ed., 7 vols., Munich: Saur, 2003).

Lachapelle, Sophie, *Investigating the Supernatural: From Spiritism ad Occultism to Psychical Research and Metaphysics in France, 1853–1931* (Baltimore: Johns Hopkins University Press, 2011).
Lacombe, Hervé, 'Baden-Baden vu de Paris, ou Berlioz et ses compatriotes à Bade', *Hector Berlioz: ein franzose in Deutschland*, ed. Matthias Brzoska, Hermann Hofer, and Nicole K. Strohmann (Laaber: Laaber, 2005) 184–196.
Lacombe, Hervé, *Georges Bizet: Naissance d'une identité créatrice* (Paris: Fayard, 2000).
Lange-Brachmann, Ute, and Joachim Draheim, eds., *Pauline Viardot in Baden-Baden und Karlsruhe*, Baden-Badener Beiträge zur Musikgeschichte 4 (Baden-Baden: Nomos, 1999).
'LAPOMMERAIE [sic] (Anne Célina Ernestine BERDALLE de)', *Cantatrices de l'Opéra de Paris*, *L'art lyrique français* (https://www.artlyriquefr.fr/dicos/Opera%20Cantatrices.html#LABIA).
Lardic, Sabine Teulon, 'L'opéra de salon ou un salon à l'opéra: les contributions de Ferdinand Poise au *Magasin des demoiselles* (1865–1880)', *Presse et opéra aux XVIIIe et XIXe siècles*, ed. Olivier Bara, Christophe Cave, and Marie-Ève Thérenty, 2018 (http://www.medias19.org/index.php?id=24101).
Lasserre, Albert, *Enghien-les-Bains: la saga des thermes et des casinos 1766–2005* (n.p.: Editions de Valhermeil, [2005]).
Latour, Bruno, *Reassembling the Social: An Introduction to Actor-Network Theory*, Clarendon Lectures in Management Studies (Oxford: Oxford University Press, 2005).
Lefebvre, Henri, *La production de l'espace*, Société et urbanisme (Paris: Anthropos, 1976).
Le Gonidec, Nathalie, 'Le théâtre de Royaumont', *Tréteaux et paravents: le théâtre de société au xixe siècle*, ed. Jean-Claude Yon and Nathalie Le Gonidec (Paris: Créphis, 2012) 135–148.
Lejeune, Philippe, *Le pacte autobiographique* (Paris: Seuil, 1975).
'LEMERCIER Marie Charlotte Léocadie dite Léocadie', *L'art lyrique français: Opéra-Comique-Cantatrices* (https://www.artlyriquefr.fr/dicos/Opera-Comique%20Cantatrices.html#LABAT).
Lesure, François, 'La villégiature lyrique ou la musique dans les casinos au xixe siècle', *D'un opéra l'autre: hommage à Jean Mongrédien*, ed. Jean Gribenski (Paris: Presses Universitaires Paris-Sorbonne, 1996) 389–398.
Leterrier, Sophie-Anne, 'Le théâtre de Castellane: une exclusivité parisienne?', *Tréteaux et paravents: le théâtre de société au xixe siècle*, ed. Jean-Claude Yon and Nathalie Le Gonidec (Paris: Créphis, 2012) 103–116.
Libourel, Jean-Louis, 'Binder à Paris: Henry Binder' (https://www.attelage-patrimoine.com/article-binder-a-paris-henry-binder-41052058.html).
Lilti, Antoine, *Le monde des salons: sociabilité et mondanité à Paris au XVIIIe siècle* (Paris: Fayard, 2005), trans. as *The World of the Salon: Sociability and Worldliness in Eighteenth-Century Paris* (New York: Oxford University Press, 2015).
Locke, Ralph P., *Music, Musicians, and the Saint-Simonians* (Chicago: University of Chicago Press, 1986).
Logan, Thad, *The Victorian Parlour*, Cambridge Studies in Nineteenth-Century Literature and Culture 30 (Cambridge: Cambridge University Press, 2001; reprint 2003).
'Louis Prosper GUYOT dit Prosper GUYOT', *L'art lyrique français: Théâtre-Lyrique-Inteprètes* (https://www.artlyriquefr.fr/personnages/Guyot%20Prosper.html).
Lueders, Kurt, 'HOCMELLE, Pierre-Edmond', *Dictionnaire de la musique en France au xixe siècle* (Paris: Fayard, 2003) 595–596.
Lyonnet, Henry, *Dictionnaire des comédiens français (ceux d'hier): biographie, bibliographie, iconographie*, 2 vols., Histoire du Théâtre (Geneva: Bibliothèque de la Revue Universelle Internationale Illustrée, 1902–1908; reprint Slatkine Reprints, 1969).
Macfarlane, Helen Louise, '"*Il faut savoir l'italien pour déchiffrer une romance française*": Italian Presence in the French Romance, 1800–1850' (PhD diss., University of Southampton, 2014).
Malo, Henri, *La gloire du Vicomte de Launay: Delphine Gay de Girardin*, 6th ed. (Paris: Émile-Paul, 1925).

Manning, Céline Frigau, 'Phrenologising Opera Singers: The Scientific "Proofs of Musical Genius"', *19th-Century Music* 39 (2015–2016) 125–141.
'Maria MEILLET-MEYER', *L'art lyrique français: Théâtre-Lyrique-Interprètes* (https://www.artlyriquefr.fr/personnages/Meillet-Meyer.html).
Margerie, Laure de, et al., *Charles Cordier, 1827–1905: l'autre et l'ailleurs [exposition, Musée d'Orsay, Paris, 2 février–2 mai 2004, Musée National des Beaux-Arts, Québec, 10 juin–6 septembre 2004, Dahesh Museum of Art, New York, 12 octobre 2004–9 janvier 2005]* (Paris: La Martinière, 2004).
Marot, Bertrand, *Paris occulte: alchimistes de l'ombre, sprirites inspirés, mages sulfureuses, traqueurs de fantômes et astrologues visionnaires* (Paris: Parigramme, 2018).
Marquiset, Alfred, *Romieu et Courchamps* (Paris: Émile-Paul, 1913).
Martin-Fugier, Anne, 'La cour et la ville sous la Monarchie de Juillet d'après les feuilletons mondains', *Revue historique* 278 (1987) 121.
Martin-Fugier, Anne, *La vie élégante ou La formation de tout-Paris* (Paris: Fayard, 1993).
Maton, Karl, 'Habitus', *Pierre Bourdieu: Key Concepts*, 2nd ed., ed. Michael Grenfell (Abingdon: Routledge, 2014) 48–64.
Merleau-Ponty, Maurice, *Phénoménologie de la perception*, Bibliothèque des idées (Paris: Gallimard, 1945; reprint 1992).
Mongin, Jean-Louis, *Jules Verne et le 'Musée des familles'*, Bibliothèque du Rocambole: Magasin du Club Verne 3 (Amiens: AARP–Centre Rocambole; Encrage, 2013).
Monmonier, Mark, *How to Lie with Maps* (Chicago: University of Chicago Press, 2018).
Monumentum: Carte des monuments historiques français (https://monumentum.fr/immeuble-pa00088963.html).
'The Musical Geography Project: Mapping Place and Movement through Music History' (https://musicalgeography.org/).
Olsson, Dan, 'Lovisa (Louise) Charlotta Helena Michaëli', *Svenskt kvinnobiografiskt lexikon* (https://www.skbl.se/sv/artikel/LouiseMichaeli).
'*Opéra de salon*: Paris, 1850–1870' (https://musicalgeography.org/opera-de-salon/).
Orr, Clarissa Campbell, *Wollstonecraft's Daughters: Womanhood in England and France 1780–1920* (Manchester: Manchester University Press, 1996).
Paul, Christian, *Les sociétés musicales du bassin thermal de Vichy de 1860 à 1914: contribution à l'histoire de la musique et à la connaissance du mouvement orphéonique français* (PhD diss., Université de Paris IV, 2008; Paris: Le Petit Page, 2014).
'Paul de Richard d'Ivry (Beaune, 1829 – Hyères, 1903)', *Histoire de Beaune: Ses hommes et femmes célèbres* (http://www.beaune.fr/spip.php?rubrique200#.YIKV6uvTX0r).
Pellissier, Pierre, *Émile de Girardin, prince de la presse* (Paris: Denoël, 1985).
Petersen, Richard A., and Albert Simkus, 'How Musical Tastes Mark Occupational Status Groups', *Cultivating Difference: Symbolic Boundaries and the Making of Inequality*, ed. Michèle Lamont and Marcel Fournier (Chicago: University of Chicago Press, 1992) 152–186.
Pierre, Constant, *Le Conservatoire National de Musique et de Déclamation: documents historiques et administratives*, 2 vols. (Paris: Imprimerie Nationale, 1900).
'Pierre Pilté, industriel, directeur de théâtre, plaideur et comte posthume', *Polmorésie: histoire politique, locale, du mouvement ouvrier, de la résistance, sociale et des initiatives économiques* (http://polmoresie.over-blog.fr/2016/10/pierre-pilte-industriel-directeur-de-theatre-plaideur-et-comte-posthume.html).
'PIGEORY, Félix', 'École des Chartes—Comité des travaux historiques et scientifiques: annuaire prosopographique' (http://cths.fr/an/savant.php?id=116005).
Ponzetto, Valentina, 'Définitions et modes d'emploi du proverbe: entre discours paratextuels et représentations métathéâtrales', *Théâtres en liberté du XVIIIe au XXe siècle: genres nouveaux, scènes marginales?, Actes du colloque international organisé les 31 mai et 1er juin 2013 à l'Université de Genève*, ed. Valentina Ponzetto and Sylvain Ledda, Publications Numériques du CÉREdI: Actes de colloques et journées d'étude 19 (Rouen: Centre d'Études et de

Recherche Éditer/Interpréter, 2017) (http://ceredi.labos.univ-rouen.fr/public/?definitions-et-modes-d-emploi-du.html).

Ponzetto, Valentina, 'Le proverbe dramatique, une voie détournée pour théâtraliser l'irreprésentable?', *Les conditions du théâtre: le théâtralisable et le théâtralisé*, special issue of *Fabula-LhT* 19 (October 2017) (http://www.fabula.org/lht/19/ponzetto.html).

Rance, Josette, 'Isaac Strauss, un musicien strasbourgeois célèbre sous le Second Empire', *Recherches internationales sur la musique française* 27 (November 1988) 61–72.

Raz, Carmel, 'Operatic Fantasies in Early Nineteenth-Century Psychiatry', *Nineteenth-Century Opera and the Scientific Imagination*, ed. David Trippett and Benjamin Walton (Cambridge: Cambridge University Press, 2019) 63–83.

Reibel, Emmanuel, 'Carrières entre presse et opéra au xixe siècle: du mélange des genres au conflit d'intérêts', *Presse et opéra aux XVIIIe et XIXe siècles*, ed. Olivier Bara, Christophe Cave, and Marie-Ève Thérenty, *Médias* 19, 2021 (https://www.medias19.org/publications/presse-et-opera-aux-xviiie-et-xixe-siecles/carrieres-entre-presse-et-opera-au-xixe-siecle-du-melange-des-genres-au-conflit-dinterets).

Revill, George, 'How Is Space Made in Sound? Spatial Mediation, Critical Phenomenology and the Political Agency of Sound', *Progress in Human Geography* 40 (2015) 240–256.

Rey, Gabrielle, *Le Fouériériste Allyre Bureau (1810–1859)*, Publications des Annales de la Faculté des Lettres Aix-en-Provence: Travaux et mémoires 21 (Aix-en-Provence: La Pensée Universitaire, 1962).

Riemann, Hugo, *Opern-Handbuch: Repertorium der dramatisch-musikalischen Litteratur (Opern, Operetten, Ballette, Melodramen, Pantomimen, Oratorien, dramatische Kantaten u.s.w.)—ein notwediges Supplement zu jedem Musiklexikon*, 2 vols. (Leipzig: Sengsbuch, 1887).

Rièse, Laure, *Les salons littéraires parisiens du Second Empire à nos jours* (Paris: Privat, 1962).

Robert, Christopher, *Le duc de Morny: "empereur" des Français sous Napoléon III* (Paris: Hachette, 1951).

Rogers, Rebecca, *From the Salon to the Schoolroom: Educating Bourgeois Girls in Nineteenth-Century France* (University Park: Pennsylvania State University Press, 2005).

'SAINTE-FOY', *L'art lyrique français: Opéra-Comique-Chanteurs* (https://www.artlyriquefr.fr/personnages/Sainte-Foy.html).

Saint-Pierre, Dominique, 'PONSARD François', *Dictionnaire historique des académiciens de Lyon 1700–2016*, ed. Dominique Saint-Pierre (Lyon: Éditions de l'Académie, 2017) 1059–1060.

Schmusch, Rainer, 'Das französische Repertoire in Baden-Baden zur Zeit von Berlioz', *Hector Berlioz: ein franzose in Deutschland*, ed. Matthias Brzoska, Hermann Hofer, and Nicole K. Strohmann (Laaber: Laaber, 2005) 197–220.

Schnapper, Laure, *Henri Herz, magnat du piano: la vie musicale en France au xixe siècle (1815–1870)*, En temps et lieu 23 (Paris: Éditions de l'École des Hautes Études en Sciences Sociales, 2011).

Schnapper, Laure, *Musique et musiciens de bal: Isaac Strauss au service de Napoléon III* (Paris: Hermann, 2023).

Schneider, Louis, *Hervé; Charles Lecocq*, Les maîtres de l'opérette française (Paris: Perrin, 1924).

Ségal, Alain, 'Aperçu sur l'oeuvre de Pierre Salomon Ségalas d'Etchépare', *Histoire des sciences médicales* 42 (2008) 199–204.

Sherr, Richard, 'Offenbach, *Pépito* and the Théâtre des Variétés: Politics and Genre in the First Year of the Second Empire', *Cambridge Opera Journal* 32 (2021) 154–186.

Smart, Mary Ann, 'Parlor Games: Italian Music and Italian Politics in the Parisian Salon', *19th-Century Music* 34 (2010) 39–60; reprinted in shortened and slightly edited form in *idem*, *Waiting for Verdi: Opera and Political Opinion in Nineteenth-Century Italy, 1815–1848* (Los Angeles: University of California Press, 2018) 128–151.

Sullerot, Evelyne, *Histoire de la presse féminine en France, des origines à 1848* (Paris: Armand Colin, 1966).

Thirion, Christine, 'La presse pour les jeunes de 1815 à 1848: essai d'analyse de contenu', *Bulletin des Bibliothèques de France* (1972/1973) 111–132 (https://bbf.enssib.fr/consulter/bbf-1972-03-0111-002).
Thullier, Guy, 'Les idées politiques d'Émile de Girardin', *Revue administrative* 68 (1959) 134–143.
Tomlinson, Gary, 'The Web of Culture: A Context for Musicology', *19th-Century Music* 7 (1984) 350–362.
Torre, Angelo, 'Un "tournant spatial" en histoire? Paysages, regards, ressources', *Annales: histoire, sciences sociales* 63 (2008) 1127–1144.
'Tourneux, Eugène or Jean François Eugène', *Benezit Dictionary of Artists*. (https://www.oxfordartonline.com/benezit/view/10.1093/benz/9780199773787.001.0001/acref-9780199773787-e-00184531?rskey=VWynwq&result=1.
Tresch, John, *The Romantic Machine: Utopian Science and Technology after Napoleon* (Chicago: University of Chicago Press, 2012).
Trippett, David, 'Exercising Musical Minds: Phrenology and Music Pedagogy in London circa 1830', *19th-Century Music* 39 (2015–2016) 99–124.
Trippett, David, and Benjamin Walton, 'Introduction: The Laboratory and the Stage', *Nineteenth-Century Opera and the Scientific Imagination*, ed. David Trippett and Benjamin Walton (Cambridge: Cambridge University Press, 2019) 1–18.
'Trouvé, Eugène or Nicolas Eugène', *Benezit Dictionary of Artists* (https://www.oxfordartonline.com/benezit/view/10.1093/benz/9780199773787.001.0001/acref-9780199773787-e-00185590).
Tunley, David, *Salons, Singers and Songs: A Background to Romantic French Song, 1830–1870* (Aldershot: Ashgate, 2002).
Tunley, David, 'The Salons and Their Music', *Salons, Singers and Songs: A Background to Romantic French Song, 1830–1870)* (Aldershot: Ashgate, 2002) 18–41.
Vernazza, Ruben, 'Verdi e il Théâtre Italien di Parigi (1845–1856)' (PhD diss., Université de Tours and Università degli studi di Milano, 2018).
Verney, Béatrice, *Le Croisic: l'établissement de bains de mer, Silvain Deslandes de 1844 à 1893– avant–pendant–après* (Merignac: Ateliers Copy-Media, 2012).
Vilkner, Nicole, 'Re-examining Salon Space: Structuring Audiences and Music at Parisian Receptions', *Journal of the Royal Musical Association* 147 (2022) 221–248.
Vilkner, Nicole, 'Sounding Streets: Music and Urban Change in Paris, 1830–1870' (PhD diss., Rutgers University, 2016).
Walsh, Thomas Joseph, *Second Empire Opera: The Théâtre Lyrique, Paris, 1851–1870*, The History of Opera (London: Calder; New York: Riverrun, 1981).
Weber, William. 'The Muddle of the Middle Classes', *19th-Century Music* 3 (1979) 175–185.
Weliver, Phyllis, *Mary Gladstone and the Victorian Salon: Music, Literature, Liberalism* (Cambridge: Cambridge University Press, 2017).
Wild, Nicole, *Dictionnaire des théâtres parisiens au xixe siècle: les théâtres et la musique* (Paris: Amateurs des Livres, 1989), revised and enlarged as *Dictionnaire des théâtres parisiens (1807–1914)*, collection Perpetuum mobile (Lyon: Symétrie, 2012).
Wittmeier, Melissa McCullough, 'Delphine Gay, Madame de Girardin, the Vicomte de Launay' (PhD diss., Stanford University, 2000).
Yon, Jean-Claude, 'Des tréteaux dans une abbaye: la comédie de société à Royaumont sous la monarchie de Juillet', *Royaumont au xixe siècle: les métamorphoses d'une abbaye*, ed. Jean-François Belhoste and Nathalie Le Gonidec (Paris: Créaphis, 2008) 137–147.
Yon, Jean-Claude, 'En marge des négociations: mondanités et spectacles pendant le congrès de Paris', *Le congrès de Paris (1856): un événement fondateur [colloque international organisé par le Ministère des affaires étrangères et européennes, l'Université Paris IV et l'Association des amis de Napoléon III, Paris, Musée d'Orsay, 24–25 mars 2006]*, ed. Gilbert Ameil, Isabelle Nathan, and Georges-Henri Soutou (Brussels: Peter Lang, 2009) 171–184.

Yon, Jean-Claude, 'Les comédiens de société: seize lithographies d'Honoré Daumier', *Tréteaux et paravents: le théâtre de socméiété au xixe siècle*, ed. Jean-Claude Yon and Nathalie Le Gonidec (Paris: Créphis, 2012) 221–240.

Yon, Jean-Claude, 'Le théâtre de société au xixe siècle: une pratique à redécouvrir', *Tréteaux et paravents: le théâtre de société au xixe siècle*, ed. Jean-Claude Yon and Nathalie Le Gonidec (Paris: Créphis, 2012) 13–27.

Yon, Jean-Claude, ed., *M. Offenbach nous écrit: lettres au Figaro et autres propos* (Paris: Actes Sud and Palazetto Bru Zane, 2019).

Yon, Jan-Claude, and Nathalie Le Gonidec, eds., *Tréteaux et paravents: le théâtre de société au xixe siècle* (Paris: Créphis, 2012).

Zbigniew, A. Jordan, ed., *Karl Marx: Economy, Class and Social Revolution* (London: Thomas Nelson and Sons, 1972).

Zekulin, Nicholas G., *The Story of an Operetta: 'Le dernier sorcier' by Pauline Viardot and Ivan Turgenev*, Vorträge und Abhandlungen zur Slavistik 15 (Munich: Sagner, 1989).

Zephyr, Frank, 'Spatial History as Scholarly Practice', *Between Humanities and the Digital*, ed. Patrik Svensson and David Theo Goldberg (Cambridge, MA: MIT Press, 2015) 411–428.

Zucconi, Antonietta Angelica, 'Les salons de Mathilde et Julie Bonaparte sous le Second Empire', *Napoleonica: la revue* 11 (2011–2012) 151–183.

Index

For the benefit of digital users, indexed terms that span two pages (e.g., 52–53) may, on occasion, appear on only one of those pages.

General note: Press sources appear frequently throughout this work. To avoid an overly dense index, they are included only when a journal is discussed in its own right, particularly its editorship, readership, or influence. This approach ensures the index remains a useful guide to substantive discussions rather than a comprehensive list of references.

1806/1807 legislation. *See* regulation

Abbaye de Royaumont, 8–9, 157–58
Académie Impérial de Musique, 5–6, 178–79
Adam, Adolphe, 18, 136–37, 231, 232*t*
Adam, Elisabeth-Françoise. *See* Boisgontier, Elise
Alard, Jean-Delphin, 128–29
Albert, Émile, 156–57
Alcazar, 221–22
amateur, as a term, 84, 88–89.
    See also *chanteur/chanteuse du monde*
ancien régime, 123, 186–87
Angoulême, 235, 237–38
Aragon, Louis, 116–18
Archainbaud, Eugène-Jean-Baptiste, 85–87, 134–36, 146*t*, 204n.57, 232–33
artiste-virtuose, defined, 14–15, 84–87, 89, 99
Association des Artistes Musiciens, 87–88
Athénée des Arts, Sciences et Belles-Lettres, 181–82, 216–17
attention, 2–3, 7, 8, 171–73
Auber, Daniel, 18, 120, 127–29, 140–41, 150–51
audience
    composition, 15–16, 19–20, 23–24, 106–7, 118–25, 127, 137–38, 167–68, 184–85, 186–201, 208, 228, 242
    entry, 6–7, 225–26
    placement, 8, 134–36, 148–50, 171–72, 199–200, 215–16, 218–19
    size, 1–2, 6–7, 19–20, 27–28, 101–2, 108, 118–19, 131–32, 215–19, 225, 228, 234, 241–42
Augier, Émile, 120

Bachman (*Les tables tournantes*), 175*t*, 181–83
Baden, 13n.19, 86n.26, 110–11, 230n.51, 233–37, 238–39, 242
Ballande, Hilarion, 136–37
ballet-pantomime, 17, 169–70
Balzac, Honoré de, 161–62, 213–14
Banderali, Anna-Angelini (Mme Barthe), 89, 146*t*
Banderali, David, 89
Barateau, Émile, 97–98, 167–68, 170–71
Barbier, Frédéric-Étienne
    Le loup et l'agneau, 134n.29, 169
    Le miroir, 28–29, 190*t*
Barbier, Jules-Paul, 143–44, 232*t*
Baretti, Marie-Julie-Blanche, 106*t*
Baric, Jules-Jean-Antoine, 190*t*
Bar-le-Duc, 237–38
Barthe, Adrien, 89
Barthe, Mme. *See* Banderali, Anna-Angelini
Batiste, Édouard, 82–83n.6
Battu, Léon, 140–41, 232*t*
Battu, Marie-Anne-Sophie, 140–41
Baudelaire, Charles, 116–18
Bavaria, 156
Bazin, François (*Marianne*), 189n.7, 190*t*
Bazzini, Antonio, 154–56
Beauharnais, Stéphanie de, 235
Beaumont, Alexandre, 190*t*
Beauvoir, Mme Roger de (Léocadie-Aimée de Beauvoir), 30–32, 31*t*, 106*t*, 163*t*, 212
Beer, Jules
    En état de siège, 115, 143–44, 217–18, 227–28
    host, 88, 99, 115, 143–44, 217–18, 225–26, 227–28
    Les roses M. de Malesherbes, 88, 143–44, 217–18, 227–28
    output, 94
Beethoven, Ludwig van, 156

Bélanger, M, 168–69
Belcour, 205*t*
Bellini, Vincenzo, 140–41, 157–58, 182–83
Belouet (or Bellouet), 88–89, 91–92, 113, 119–20, 200
Bénazet, Émilie-Perrine-Suzanne. *See* Gaveaux-Sabatier, Mme
Bénazet, Oscar-Édouard, 233–37
Bendel, François (Franz), 150–51
Benjamin, Walter, 116–18
Benou, Jean-Baptiste-Louis-Georges, 89, 91–92, 118–20, 231–32, 232*t*
Berdalle de Lapommeraye, Anne-Célina-Ernestine, 83, 106–7, 227–28
Berdalle de Lapommeraye, Pierre-Victor-Henri (Henri d'Alleber, n.d.p.), 227–28
Bergson, Michel (*Qui va à la chasse perd sa place*), 163*t*, 163
Berlin, 17, 238–39
Berlioz, Hector, 109–10, 140, 234
Bernard, Paul
  Bredouille, 106*t*, 106–7, 232*t*
  L'accord parfait, 132
  Le Croisic, 231
  Loin du bruit, 106*t*, 106–7, 132, 144, 146*t*, 210–11
Berthall (Charles-Albert d'Arnoux), 132, 134, 167–68
Berthellier, Jean-François-Philibert, 134, 167–68
Berton, Caroline, 201–2
Bessems, Antonin, 156–57, 165
Beuzeval, 230–31
Biard, Cécile-Antonin, 200
Biéval (Charles-Louis Lourdel), 85–87, 106*t*, 118–19, 132, 226–27, 231–32, 235n.78, 237–38
Binder, Henri
  audience composition, 131–32, 172–73, 218–19, 241
  profession and residence, 116–18, 171–72, 212, 228–29
Bizet, Georges, 88–89, 102–3, 169–70, 200
Blanchard, Henri, 88–89, 200
Blancou, Joseph-Victor-Antoine (*Les suites d'une indiscrétion*), 159n.17, 193–94
Blangini, 160*t*
Blangy, Caroline de. *See* Grandval, Mme de
Blerzy, Jules, 92, 227–28
Blois, 237–38
Boieldieu, François-Adrien, 127, 151
Boisgontier, Elise (Mme Adam Boisgontier; Elisabeth-Françoise Adam), 30–32,
159–60, 189–93, 202–4.
  See also Dubourg, Paul
Boisseaux, 92–94, 201–2, 237–38
Bonnefons, Georges, 134
Bonnemessier, Léonie, 145n.72
Bordeaux, 237–38
Bordèse, Luigi
  Frère et soeur, 190*t*
  Judith et Suzon, 190*t*
  Le marché aux servantes, 190*t*
  Le moulin des oiseaux, 190*t*
  Les deux comtesses, 190*t*
  publication, 189n.6, 189–93
Bosc, Marie, 156–57
Bouilly, Jean-Nicolas, 160*t*
Bouland, Pierre, 107–9, 111–13, 227, 230
Boulanger, Ernest (*La meunière de Sans-Souci*), 190*t*
Bourbon restorations, 21–22, 123, 186–87
Bourdieu, Pierre, 11n.15, 13–14
Bourdon, Alexis-Hippolyte, 102, 104–6, 168–69, 198, 213*t*, 226–27
Bousquet, Charles, 30–32, 31*t*
Bousquet, Georges, 205*t*, 206–7
Brazier, Nicolas, 160*t*
Briand, Paul, 146*t*, 213*t*
Bureau, Allyre, 184
Bussine, Prosper-Alphonse, 106*t*, 137n.37
Bussine, Romain, 106*t*, 118–19, 136–37, 231–32

Cabel (Edmond-Antoine-Auguste Cabu), 115, 144n.65
Cabourg, 230–31
cafés-concerts
  regulation, 5–6, 25–26, 93–94, 119–22
  venue for music, 24–26, 138–39, 179
Cambardi, Mme (Mathilde-Jeanne Chambard), 151
Canoby, Louis-Gustave
  career and works, 92, 126
  Les sabotiers, 92, 126–27
  Un tour de clef, 126
canon, 2–3, 4, 18, 138–39, 242–43
Capoul, Joseph-Amédée-Victor, 88, 144n.65
Caraman-Chimay, Princesse de (Marie-Joséphine-Anatole de Montesquiou-Fézensac), 161
Carré, Auguste, 189–93, 190*t*
Carré, Michel, 184, 190*t*, 232*t*
Castel, 146*t*, 233, 235–38
Castellane, Comte Jules Boniface de, 95–96, 123, 158

casts. *See* scoring
cello, 146*t*, 215
censors. *See* regulation
cercle, 7–8, 22
Certeau, Michel de, 16–17, 95, 211, 225
Challamel, Augustin, 189n.7, 190*t*
Champfleury (Jules-François-Félix Fleury-Husson), 172–73, 175*t*, 175–76
chanteur/cantatrice de concert, defined, 84–88
chanteur/chanteuse du monde, defined, 90–92
Chapelle, Paul-Aimé, 137n.39, 167n.38, 232*t*
charade
   Boisson, 162–65
   Harmonie, 161–63
   publication, 161–62, 164, 202–3
   relationship with *opéra de salon*, 8–9, 153, 157–59, 161–63
   salon activity, 171–72
Chaudesaigues, Charles-Barthélémy, 146*t*, 148–49, 194–95, 198–200
Chaudesaigues, Rosalie-Emilie Rodolphe, 146*t*, 148–49, 167–68, 194–95, 198–200
Chaussée d'Antin, 223–24, 224*t*
Chiaromonte, Francesco, 202–3
   Clara tempête, 191*t*
Chol de Clercy, Étienne-Hippolyte, 134n.29, 169
chorus/*choeur général*, 34, 47–64, 82, 103n.8, 126, 137–38, 141–42, 159–61, 193–94, 196–98, 201
Ciceri, Pierre-Luc-Charles, 95–96
Cinti, Fanny-Marie (Cinti-Damoureau), 85–87
Clairville (Louis-François Nicolaïe), 169–70
   L'esprit frappeur, 175*t*, 177–81, 178*f*
Clapisson, Louis
   Le coffret de Saint-Domingue, 96, 146*t*, 149n.80, 190*t*, 194–95, 200
   Les amoureux de Perrette, 234–35
   output, 189n.6, 189–93, 234
claque, 98–99
Clarétie, Jules, 228–29
Clay, Frederic, 242
Clé du caveau, 159, 164n.28, 179
Cluesmann, Adeline, 200
Colbert-Chabanais, Auguste-Napoléon-Joseph, Marquis de, 92–93
Collinet, Clara (*Au pied du mur*), 92, 146*t*, 148–49
Colson, Gabrielle, 139–40
Comédie-Française, 4–5, 85, 92n.54, 111–12, 119–20, 220, 221*f*, 228–29
comédie-vaudeville, 120, 160*t*, 175*t*, 201–3, 225, 241–42

Commagny, Charles-François-Jean-Baptiste Moreau de, 160*t*
Conservatoire de Paris
   affiliation with the Salle Lyrique, 147–48
   artists, 195–96
   composers, 103–4, 136–37, 193–94
   organist, 114n.43
   pianists, 88–89, 113, 155–56, 200
   professors, 89, 140
   singers, 84–89, 115, 126, 166–67, 204n.57, 232–33
Cordier, Henri-Joseph-Charles, 30n.22, 96n.75, 125–26, 128–32, 212, 217–18, 226
Cordier, Jules, 175*t*, 177–79
Corneille, Pierre, 136–37
Cornu, Francis, 160*t*
Couplet, Jules, 201–2
Court, Joséphine. *See* Lefébure-Wély, Mme
Cousin de Courchamps, Pierre-Marie-Jean, 108–9
cultural capital, 10–11, 13–14, 114, 225–29

d'Abrantès, Duchesse (Laure-Adelaïde-Constance Junot [*née* Permon] d'Abrantès), 158
d'Aoust, Marquis, Julie-Edmond-Joseph
   host, 227–28
   L'amour voleur, 83, 227–28
   non-professional singers, 201
   title, 123
   Une partie de dominos, 82–83, 92, 201, 227–28
d'Artois, Achille and Armand, 205*t*, 206–7
d'Ennery, Adolphe, 232*t*
d'Hack, Alfred (*Le revenant*), 145n.72, 201–2
d'Halbert, Cécile-Henriette-Eugénie. *See* Ponchard, Mme
d'Indy, Comtesse (Thérèse Chorier), 89, 123, 199
d'Indy, Wilfrid
   Les deux princesses, 66, 89, 104–5, 146*t*, 198–99
d'Ivry, Paul de Richard, 92
   La Maison du docteur, 92–93
   Les amants de Vérone, 92–93
Dahlhaus, Carl, 3–4
Dalayrac, Nicolas-Marie (*Adolphe et Clara*), 231, 232*t*
Dammien, André Pascal. *See* Pascal
Dancla, Charles, 194n.10
Daumier, Honoré, 99, 171–72, 214–16, 217*f*, 234, 241

David, Félicien
  Le fermier de Franconville, 115–16, 183
  Le perle de Brésil, 115–16
de Dietz, Cathinka Mackenzie, 156–57
de la Guette, Jules, 139–40
de Las Cases, Barthélémy, Comte de Las Cases, 204–6
de Lostanges, Raoul (*Le valet poète*), 83, 217–18
de Passardi, Émilie Horst, 156–57
de Savignac, Charles Delioux, 133–34
Debussy, Claude, 103–4
Deffès, Louis (*Lanterne magique!!!!*), 190*t*
Dejoly, Marie-Louise-Eugénie, 88–89, 113, 133–34, 200
Délassements-Comiques, 25–26, 221*f*
Delatour, Antoine, 187–88
Delaunay, Émile (*L'habit de fait pas le moine*), 163*t*, 163, 164
Delbès, Armand, 93–94
Delibes, Léo, 94, 102–3, 116n.53, 132, 166–67, 202–3
  Grande nouvelle, 191*t*
Delpit, Albert, 26n.12
Demorny, Charles Auguste Louis Joseph. See Morny, Compte de
Denizet, Mme, 126
Depeuty, Charles, 190*t*
Deschamps, Émile, 190*t*
description, theory of, 11–13
Deslandes-Orière, Silvain, 230–31, 232*t*, 232–34
Diemer, Louis, 151
Dieppe, 230–31, 233
Dietsch, Pierre-Louis-Philippe, 141–42
Djahn Ara, 92–93
Doche, Jospeph-Denis, 160*t*
Donizetti, Gaetano, 128–29, 151, 155
Dormeuil, Joseph (Joseph-Jean Contat-Desfontaines), 118–19
Douay, Georges (*Les valets modèle[s]*), 145n.72
Doucet, Camille, 90–91, 106n.20, 119–22, 169–70, 227
Doyen, Édouard, 137–38
dramma buffo, 240
Driou, Alfred, 66, 201, 208
  Le bonhomme Noël, 195–98, 197*t*
Dubarry, Armand, 145n.72
Dubois, Nicolas-Auguste, 159–60, 160*t*
Dubourg, Paul, 191*t*. See also Boisgontier, Elisa
Dubreuil, Ernest, 128–29, 190*t*, 232*t*, 235–37
Ducellier, Émile
  Les deux charlatans, 47–64, 137–38
  performer, 200

Duclos, Mme (Barbe-Éléonore Ragaine), 146*t*, 213*t*
Duflot, Joachim, 190*t*
Dumanoir (Philippe-François Pinel), 169–70
Dumas, Alexandre, *père*, 134–36, 161–62, 184
Dupin, Jean-Henri, 160*t*
Duponchel, Edmond-Henry, 118–19
Duprato, Jules-Laurent-Anicharsis
  La reine Mozab, 181–82, 190*t*, 194–95
  Marie Stuart au château de Lochleven, 28–29
  output, 94, 166–67, 189–93
Duprez, Caroline, 141–42
Duprez, Édouard, 92–93, 142
Duprez, Gilbert
  composer for regulated theatre, 141–42
  host, 140–43, 151–52
  Jélyotte, ou Un passe-temps de duchesse, 47–64, 94, 140–42
  pedagogue, 94, 128–29, 140–43, 222, 229
  private theatre (*see* Duprez, private theatre)
  Samson, 65n.37, 82n.6, 93n.62, 94, 141–42
Duprez, Léon, 82n.6
Duprez, private theatre
  description of, 140, 211–12, 217–18, 225–26
  descriptive programme, 65n.37
  ensemble, 82–83, 196–98
  illustration of, 141*f*
  immunity from regulation, 6–7
  inspiration, 158
  lieu, 17
  location, 139–40, 222, 241
  works for, 84, 92–93
Dupuy, Alphonsine-Coralie-Mathilde-Françoise, 87–88, 114–15
Dupuytren, Baron, 198–99
Durand, Émile (*Le miroir du diable*), 103–4, 162–63, 201–2

École-Lyrique *or* Salle de L'École Lyrique. See Salle Lyrique
Eldorado, 138–39, 221–22
emergence and decline of *opéra de salon*, 6, 12–13, 24–26, 240
Enghien, 230
Entre deux feux, 146*t*
espaces
  Cordier, 129–32
  defined, 16–17, 95–96, 211, 225, 240–41
  display of power, 225–28
  geographical boundaries, 219, 229–30
  petite bourgeoisie, 19–20

INDEX 265

seating, 171–72
types, 23–24, 99–100, 107–8, 116–18, 123–28, 151–52, 212–16, 239, 241
women, in relation to, 186–87, 198
See also stages, temporary
Établissment Hydrothérapique des Néothermes
   description, 108–11, 116–18, 216–17, 229–30
   performances, 82–83, 88–90, 92, 107–8, 111–13, 119–20, 133–34, 227
Ettling, Émile
   salon, 139–40
   Un jour de noce, 138–39, 209–10
Euzet, Louis-Gustave-Esprit, 141–42

Faivre, Amélie, 233
Faubourg Saint-Germain, 15, 104–6, 107–8, 134, 139–40, 203–4, 222–24, 224*t*, 226–30, 239, 241
Faubourg Saint-Honoré, 15, 103–5, 114, 136, 169, 222–24, 224*t*, 239, 241
female singing roles. *See* scoring
Filhouze, 137–38, 200
Flan, Alexandre, 190*t*
   La table tournante, 175*t*, 175–76
Fleury, Émile, 156–57
Fleury, Louis-Joseph-Léon, 85–87, 213*t*, 237
Fleury-Husson, Jules-François-Félix. *See* Champfleury
flute, 215
Folies-Bergère, 116n.53, 221–22
Folies-Concertantes. *See* Théâtre des Folies-Concertantes
form, 1–2, 6, 9–11, 13–14, 28–64, 67, 115–16, 142, 161, 169, 182–83, 193, 196, 197*t*, 240
Fould, Achille, 90, 95–96, 120–22
Fourier, Charles, 173–75, 183
Fournier, Édouard, 111–12

Galoppe d'Onquaire, Jean-Hycinthe-Adonis (Cléon), 66, 106*t*, 111–12, 118–19, 122, 132, 134–36, 144, 205*t*, 232*t*
Gardoni, Italo, 154–55
Gaveaux-Sabatier, Émilie-Perrine-Suzanne Bénazet
   audience size, 216–18
   Baden, 234–37
   benefit, 234–35
   host, 89, 91–92, 99, 138–40, 142–43, 151–52, 211–12, 213*t*
   promoter at the Herz, 146*t*, 235

provinces, 234–35, 237–38, 238n.92, 239
pupils, 138–39, 142–43, 229
singer, 66, 85–92, 99, 106*t*, 113, 115, 119–20, 132, 138–40, 142–43, 144n.65, 203–4, 213*t*, 226–28, 235
studio, 139–40, 186–201, 211–12, 217–18, 222, 225–26, 241
Gay, Delphine, 134–36, 158, 183
Gay, Sophie, 158, 183, 232*t*
Geertz, Clifford, *The Interpretation of Cultures*, 12
geolocation, 2–3, 11–12, 13n.21, 15–16, 209, 219–25, 238–39, 240–41
Géraldy, Jean-Antoine-Just, 106*t*, 106–7
Gerpré, Gustave, 232–33
Gevaert, François-Auguste, 210–11
Ghédé, Cehem, 175*t*, 179
Gheluve, Edmond van, 31*t*, 32
Gide, Casimir
   Belphégor, ou Le grelot du diable, 95–97, 99, 136–37, 199–200
   career, 118–19, 136–37
   hosting, 95–96, 125–26, 136–37
Gide (*née* Jacques), Clémentine Adèle Eugénie, 136–37
Girardin, Émile de, 99, 125–26, 132, 134–36, 158, 183
Gladstone, Mary, 2–3
glazed spaces, 108, 116–18
Godefroid, Félix
   A deux pas du bonheur, 31*t*, 32–34, 35*f*, 43, 48*f*, 68, 85–87, 94, 96, 102, 106*t*, 106–7, 121–22, 128–29, 142–43, 146*t*, 163*t*, 163, 170–71, 212–13, 213*t*, 226n.35, 233, 237
   death, 133
   Dieppe, 233
   harp, 133, 212, 233
   Orléans, 237
   output, 30–32, 94, 128–29, 203–4, 226
   Villers-sur-Mer, 133
Gounod, Charles, 120, 151, 234
Gourdin, Alexandre-Narcisse-Marie, 88, 144n.65
grand opéra, 4–6, 17, 47–64, 137–38, 166–67, 179, 205*t*, 240–42
Grand Théâtre in Lyon, 142
Grand-Théâtre-Parisien, 141
Grandval, Mme de (Marie-Félicie-Clémence de Reiset; Caroline de Blangy), 103, 199–200
Grangé, Eugène, 232*t*
Grétry, André-Ernest-Modeste, 127

Grisar, Albert
   Le procès, 189–93, 191*t*, 202–3
   Les travestissements, 168–69, 226n.36, 230–31, 232*t*
   works that could transfer to the *salon*, 167–68, 170–71
Grisart, Charles (*La lettre de cachet*), 116n.53, 228
Gueymard, Louis, 141–42, 146*t*
Guglielmi, 146*t*, 148–49
Guiraud, Ernest, 102–3, 151
Guyot, Louis-Prosper, 88–89, 113
Gymnase Dramatique, 5–6, 92n.54, 134–36

Halévy, Fromental, 18, 120, 136–37, 140, 154–55, 182–83
Halévy, Léon, 136–37
harmonium. See *orgue expressif*
harp accompaniment, 82–83, 94, 195–98, 197*t*
Haussmann, Baron Georges-Eugène, 220–21
Henrion, Paul
  daughters, 200
  La treille du roi, 82, 190*t*
Henselt, Adolf, 156–57
Hermann-Léon, Charles (Léon-Charles-Sigismond Hermann), 85–87, 88–89, 91–92, 138–39, 211–12
Hérold, Ferdinand, 156–57
Hervé (Louis-Auguste-Florimond Ronger), 6, 26–27, 92–93, 119–20, 167–68, 169–70, 213–14
Herz, Henri, 155–56
Heugel, Jacques-Léopold, 31*t*, 32, 105–7, 122, 146*t*, 199–200, 231–32
Heuvel, Amédée van den, 82–83n.6
Hignard, Aristide
  A la porte, 106*t*, 150n.93
  Le joueur d'orgue, 230–31, 232*t*
  output, 94, 166–67, 231
Hocmelle, Pierre-Edmond
  accompanist, 114–15, 237–38
  En attendant de soleil, 87–88, 114–15
  La mort de Socrate, 85–87, 146*t*
  other works, 114–15, 202–3
  Un service d'ami, 201–2, 237–38
Hospice de la Vieillesse Hommes, 213–14
Hôtel de Ville, eleventh *arrondissement*, 143–44
Hôtel de Ville, Salle de, 204–7, 205*t*
Huet, Marie-Honorine-Virginie, 146*t*, 148–49
Hugo, Victor, 92–93, 161–62
Hummel, Johann Nepomuk, 156
Huysmans, Joris-Karl, 181

Il était une fois une roi, 199–200
imperial family, 18–19, 83, 95–96, 113, 120–22, 161, 218
instrumentation. See scoring
Isouard, Nicolas, 150–51

Jacobi, Georges
  Le feu aux poudres, 81–82, 146*t*
  organizer at the Salle Herz, 149–50
Jaime, Adolphe, 128–29
Jal, Antoine-Anatole, 88–89, 90, 112–13, 119–20, 133–34, 200
Jallais, Amadée, 191*t*
Jallot-Taboureux, 98–99, 133
Jélyotte, Pierre de, 142
Jonas, Émile
  Miss Robinson, 190*t*
  output, 88–89, 94, 144–45, 166–67
Joncières, Victorin de, 88–89
July Monarchy, 7n.12, 7–8, 22–23, 23n.8, 186–87, 203n.53
July Revolution, 7–8, 21–22

Kalkbrenner, Friedrich, 156
Ketterer, Nicolas-Eugène, 146*t*, 148–49
Klopstock, Friedrich Gottlieb, 187–88
Kreutzer, Rodolphe, 160*t*

L'Épine, Ernest-Louis-Victor-Jules, 90–91, 119–20, 200
La démocratie pacifique. See rue de Beaune *séances*
La Revue et Gazette musicale de Paris, 12–13, 18–19, 23–24
La Rochelle, 237–38
La Tertulia, 138–39
Lafont, Léon-Alexandre, 87–88, 114–15
Lagarde, Paul, 210–11
Lajarte, Théodore-Édouard Dufaure de
  Le secret de l'Oncle Vincent, 237–38
  On guérit de la peur, 93–94
Lamartine, Alphonse de, 161–62
Lassaveur, Marie, 189
Latour, Bruno, 12–13
Lavallée, Alphonse, 87–88, 114–15
Le berquin, 192*t*, 196–98
Le bon ton, 186–87
Le charivari, 214–15
Le Croisic, 110–11, 230–34, 232*t*
Le journal de la mode et du goût, 186–87
Le journal des dames, 186–87
Le journal des débats, 12–13

Le journal des demoiselles, 23–24, 30, 32, 65–66, 82–83, 94, 164–65, 186–94, 191*t*, 193n.9, 202–3, 208, 213–14
Le journal des jeunes personnes, 159, 193–94
Le magasin des demoiselles, 23–24, 30, 32, 65–66, 82–83, 94, 164–65, 186–93, 190*t*, 193n.9, 202–3, 208, 213–14
Le ménestrel, 12–19, 23–24, 97–98
Le moniteur de la mode, 186–87
Le musée des familles: lectures du soir, 12–13, 133, 134–36, 161–65
Le petit courrier des dames, 186–87
Le Roy, Henry, 91–92, 133–34, 200
Lebouc, 146*t*, 148–51
Lecocq, Charles
　La baiser à la porte, 139–40
　Liline et Valentin, 139–40
　output, 94, 166–67
Lefébure-Wély, Louis-James-Alfred, 103–4
Lefébure-Wély, Mme, 85–87, 103–4, 133–34, 146*t*, 150–51, 228–29
Lefebvre, Henri, 16–17
Lefebvre, Hippolyte, 175*t*, 175–77
Lefort, Jules-François-René, 85–87, 89, 103–4, 106*t*, 113, 115, 133–34, 144n.65, 203–4, 227–28, 234–38, 238n.92
Legall, Oliver, 205*t*
Legioux, J. E. (*La clef d'argent*), 190*t*
legislation. *See* regulation
Legouix, Nac and Isidore (*Quinolette*), 82, 190*t*
Lemercier, Marie-Charlotte-Léocadie, 85
Leneveux, Louise, 187–88
Lentz, Frédéric (*Le medaillon d'Yvonne*), 191*t*
Lesueur, Anne-Gabrielle. *See* Orfila, Anne-Gabrielle
Leuven, Adolphe de (Adolphe de Ribbing), 115–16
Levasseur, Nicolas-Prosper, 127
Levassor, Pierre-Thomas
　host, 142–43, 170–71, 213*t*
　Le troupier et la bonne, ou Adélaïade et Vermouth, 145n.72, 182–83
　performer, 85–87, 106*t*, 142–43, 170–71, 182–83, 213*t*, 226–27, 237
lieux. *See espaces*
Lionnet, Anatole and Hippolyte, 85–87, 134–36, 146*t*, 150–51
listening. *See* attention
Liszt, Franz, 156
London, 2–3, 17, 88, 129, 154–55
Lourdel, Charles-Louis. *See* Biéval
Louvre. *See* Palais du Louvre
Lucas, Hippolyte, 84

Macfarren, George, 242
male singing roles. *See* scoring
Malézieux, Paul, 133–34, 228–29
Malherbe, Jules, 106*t*
Manry, Charles-Casimir
　La bourse ou la vie, 111, 113, 237
　Les deux espagneuls, 82–83, 88–89, 90, 111–13
　librettists, 111–12
　life and works, 92, 94, 111, 166–67
Marcelli, Anaïs (Comtesse Perrière-Pilté)
　biography, 92, 203–6
　hosting, 203–4, 227–28
　Jaloux de soi, 92–93, 163*t*, 163, 170–71, 199, 203–4
Marietti (*Les tables tournantes*), 175*t*, 181–83
Marochetti, Félix, 66
Marsollier des Vivetières, Benoît-Joseph, 232*t*
Martin, Mme Désiré, 187–88
Marx, Karl, 13–14
Massa, André-Philippe-Alfred Regnier, Duc de (*Tout chemin mène à Rome*), 163*t*, 163–64, 230
Massé, Victor
　La petite soeur d'Achille, 191*t*
　La trouvaille, 191*t*
　Le cousin de Marivaux, 234–35
　Le prix de famille, 30–34, 31*t*, 37–39, 41–43*f*
　Les enfants de Perrette, 191*t*
　Les noces de Jeanette, 231, 232*t*
　66, 190*t*
　libretti, 202–3
　Miss Fauvette, 167–68
　opéras comiques, 30–32, 170–71
　publication, 189–93, 191*t*
　Une loi somptuaire, 191*t*
Masson, Louise-Aglaé (Mme^e Massart), 102–3
Mathilde, Princesse (Mathilde-Létizia-Wilhelmine Bonaparte), 66, 116–18, 120, 122, 123, 131–32, 141n.51, 171, 172–73, 198, 209–10, 212, 218–19
matinée musicale, 138–39, 156–57, 209–10, 230
Maton, Adolphe, 106–7
Méhul, Étienne, 182–83
Meillet, Auguste-Alphonse-Edmond, 85, 151, 237–38
Mélesville (either Anne-Honoré-Joseph Duveyrier or Honoré-Marie-Joseph Duveyrier), 119–20, 176n.69
mélodrame, 4–6, 4–5n.9, 17, 18, 34, 37n.29, 43–64, 161, 196–98, 197*t*, 240–42
melodramma, 21, 166–67, 240–42

Ménars, 102–3, 200
Mendelssohn, Felix, 102–3, 150–51
Mercier, Pol, 111–12
Merleau-Ponty, Maurice, 13–14, 16–17, 211
Merlin, Comtesse de, 198
Méry, François-Joseph-Pierre-André, 30–32, 31t, 33, 66, 155, 157–58, 190t
Mesgrigny, Claude-François-Auguste, Marquis de, 230
Messant, Hippolyte, 169
Mey, Auguste (*Un amour de notaire*), 216–17
Meyer-Meillet, Marie-Stéphanie, 85, 237–38
Meyerbeer, 18, 28n.16, 127, 140–41, 143–44, 154–55, 177–81
Michaëli, Louise (Lovisa Charlotta Helena Michal), 128–29
Michaeli, Mme and M, 128–29
Michel, Ferdinand, 200
Michot, Pierre-Jules, 151
Miolan-Carvalho, Caroline, 151
Mira, Marie-Joséphine-Clémence
  benefit, 232n.59
  Le Croisic, 231–32
  promoter, 146t, 150
  singer, 85–88, 118–19, 132, 134–36, 142, 144n.65, 210–11, 226–27
Mirecourt, Eugène de (*La table tournante*), 172–73, 175t, 175–76
Mocker, Toussaint-Eugène-Ernest, 142
Moinaux, Jules, 232t
Molinos, Anne-Marie-Renée, 102–3
Mongis, Jean-Antoine de, 175t, 181–82
Monjauze, Jules, 85
Monnais, Édouard (Paul Smith), 166
Montesquiou, Vicomtesse Napoléon de, 195–96
Montigny, Jules, 145n.72, 163t
Morny, Comte de (Charles Auguste Louis Joseph Demorny)
  audience size, 216–17
  career, 123
  L'Épine, 90–91
  Offenbach, 167–68
  promoter, 85–87, 121–22, 142–43, 212, 213t
Mosneron de Saint-Preux, Marie-Elisabeth-Césarine, 106–7, 198–99, 209n.1, 235n.78
Mounnier, 133–34, 200
Mozart, Wolfgang Amadeus, 18, 88–89, 128n.9, 150–51, 156, 173–75, 189n.6
Müller, Marcellus, 165
Murat, Prince and Princess, 120
musique de scène, 17, 18
Mutel, Alfred (*Une promenade dans un salon*), 146t, 149n.81

Nadaud, Gustave
  author of his own libretti, 92–93
  biography by Caroline Berton, 201–2
  imperial family, 122
  La clef du secrétaire, 66, 92–94, 201–2
  La volière, 68, 77, 90–92, 95–96, 105–7, 106t, 119–22, 146t, 169–70, 227
  Le docteur vieuxtemps, 68, 77, 90–92, 98–99, 119–20, 122, 133–34, 146t, 149n.80, 209–10, 217–19
  Le roseau chantant, 68, 77
  Louvre, 95–96
  output, 94, 166–67
  Porte et fenêtre, 29–30, 68, 77, 128n.10
  promotion in *Le Ministrel*, 98
  publication, 66
Nancy, 237–38
Napoléon III, 1n.1, 21, 83, 113, 120, 122–23, 173–75, 218
Napoléon, 5–6, 25–27
Napoléon, Prince, 120
Nargeot, Pierre-Julien (*Les ouvrières de qualité*), 190t
Néothermes. *See* Établissment Hydrothérapique des Néothermes
Nerval, Gérard de, 181
New Orleans, 87–88
New York, 88
Nicolo, 182–83
Nouvelle Athènes, 15, 32, 107–8, 139–40, 142–44, 148, 217–18, 221–24, 224t, 227–30, 239, 241
Nuitter. *See* Truinet

O'Kelly, Joseph
  Ruse contre ruse, 190t
  Stella, ou Une autre Werther, 87n.34, 145n.72, 199
oboe, 82–83, 112
Offenbach, Jacques. *See also* Théâtre des Bouffes-Parisiens
  Ba-ta-clan, 121–22, 167–68
  canon, 18
  composer of three *opéras de salon*, 94
  exchange between regulated theatre and *opéra de salon*, 166–68, 170–71
  host, 122, 144–45, 167–68, 225–26
  Le 66!, 99, 137–38, 167–68, 227–28, 231, 232t
  Le décaméron, ou La grotte d'amour, 30–32, 66, 83, 96, 146t, 170n.52
  Le trésor à Mathurin, 83, 85, 96, 146t, 170–71
  Les deux aveugles, 83, 95–96, 121–22, 134, 137–38, 146t, 167–68, 199n.30

Luc et Lucette, 66, 83, 96, 146*t*, 170n.52, 216–17
   opérette, 9–11, 17, 18, 26–27, 28n.16, 28–29, 30n.21, 90–91, 238–39
   orchestra, 83
   Orphée aux enfers, 10–11, 28–29
   Pépito, 121–22, 144–45, 167–68, 231, 232*t*
   promoter, 146*t*, 150, 167–68, 198, 238–39
   singers, professional, 85
   staging, 96, 99
Opéra, the
   attention, 8
   audience, 166–67
   citation in *vaudeville*, 179
   comparison with *opéra de salon*, 18–19
   composers, 18, 136–37
   designs and scenery, 95–97
   instrumentalists from, 154
   libbrettist, 33
   libretti, printed, 64–65
   location, 108, 220–22
   non-overlap with the Opéra-Comique, 64
   performances, 144–45, 178–79
   politics, 10–11
   schedule, 18
   singers, 84–85, 86n.26, 87n.31, 87n.33, 87–88, 127, 140–42, 154–55
Opéra-Comique
   audience, 166–67
   citation in *vaudeville*, 179
   comparison with *opéra de salon*, 18–19, 153
   composers, 18, 30–32, 93–94, 103n.7, 141–42, 167–68, 206–8
   controls (legislative), 27–28, 64
   libretti, printed, 64–65
   location, 220–22
   performances, 94n.66, 168–69, 231, 232*t*, 235n.77
   schedule, 18
   singers, 84–88, 127, 132, 140–42, 210–11, 233
   théâtre de société, 8–9
   transfer with *opéra de salon*, 168–71
opéra comique de salon, 21, 29–30
opéra comique, 1, 4–6, 21, 24–25, 27–30, 31*t*, 37–39, 43, 64–65, 87–88, 92–94, 159, 160*t*, 163*t*, 166–67, 190*t*, 193, 203–4, 205*t*, 206–7, 222, 240
opéra de parloir, 9, 82, 194–95
Opéra National, 5–6, 206–7, 220–21. *See also* Théâtre-Lyrique
opérette
   composers, 86n.26, 90–93, 103–4, 116n.53, 119–20, 126, 138–39
   described, 28–30, 64, 214–16

   emergence, 5–6, 168n.46, 240
   librettists, 92–94, 119–20, 189–93, 202–3
   opérette-proverbe, 163*t*, 163–64
   outside France, 238–39
   overlap with *opéra de salon*, 1, 3–4, 9–11, 18, 21, 24–25, 26–27, 67, 166–67, 184–85, 193, 240
   overtaking *opéra de salon*, 25–26
   publication, 64–65
   séance, 175*t*, 175, 181–82
   singers, 88–89
   theatre, in the, 5–6, 15–16, 153, 221–22, 225
   works, 30n.22, 31*t*, 52n.32, 94, 190*t*, 191*t*, 192*t*
   See also Offenbach, Jacques
orchestral accompaniment, 83, 96, 115–16, 215
Orfila, Anne-Gabrielle Lesueur, 105–7, 106*t*, 119–20, 126, 142–44, 169–70, 198–99, 209–10, 212, 232*t*, 235n.78
Orfila, M. and Mme Louis, 213*t*
Orfila, Mathieu (Mateu Josep Bonaventura Orfila i Rotger), 105–6
orgue expressif (harmonium), 82–83, 103n.8, 182–83, 195–98, 197*t*
Orléans, 237

Paër, Ferdinando, 231, 232*t*
Paganini, Niccolò, 109–10
Pagans, Lorenzo (Llorenç Pagans i Julià), 106–7
Palais Bourbon, 85–87, 95–96, 121–22, 142–43, 213*t*, 216–17
Palais des Tuileries, 83, 95–96, 113, 121–22, 169–70
Palais du Louvre, 18–19, 90–91, 95–96, 99–100, 120–22, 169–70, 241–42
Pascal (Dammien, André Pascal), 87–88, 114–15
Passage de l'Opéra, 116–18
Passy, 105–6, 106*t*, 126–27, 210–11, 223–24, 224*t*
Péan de la Roche-Jagu, Eudoxe-Françoise
   career, 204–7
   Gil Diaze, 205*t*
   hall rental, 149–50
   La jeunesse de Lully, 146*t*, 205*t*
   La reine de l'onde, 146*t*, 150, 205*t*
   Le mariage de hasard, 146*t*, 205*t*
   Le mousquetaire (*Le jeune militaire, ou La trahison*), 205*t*, 206–7
   Le retour de Tasse, 205*t*
   Le tuteur dupé, 204–6, 205*t*
   literary pairing, 205*t*
   Nell, ou Le Gabier d'Artimon, 205*t*
   Paul et Julie ou la lettre supposée, 205*t*
   Simple et coquette, 92–93, 146*t*, 150n.92, 205*t*

Peigné, Mme (Max Silny), 92
Pellaert, Auguste de, 191*t*
Pereire, Isaac and Émile, 115–16, 143–44, 183
Pergolesi, Giovanni Battista, 151
Perrière-Pilté, Comtesse. *See* Marcelli, Anaïs
Perrin, Émile, 170–71
Perronnet, Amélie, 145n.72
Perronnet (*Le compère Loriot*), 146*t*
Perry-Biagoli, Antonine and Henri (*Les matelots du Formidable*), 104–6, 146*t*, 149–50
Petit, Jules-Émile, 126
Peudefer, Blanche, 85–87
Pfeiffer, Clara, 104–5, 142–43, 198, 199
Pfeiffer, Emile, 104–5, 198, 199
Pfeiffer, Georges (*Le capitaine Roch*), 104–5, 106*t*, 106–7, 142–43, 146*t*, 149n.82, 150n.91, 150–51, 198, 199n.31, 199
piano
    accompaniment for *opéra de salon*, 1–2, 32nn.23–24, 37–39, 82–83, 102–3, 112, 115–16n.50, 120, 121–22, 133–34, 146*t*, 155–56, 184, 194–98, 197*t*, 215, 225
    accompaniment for *proverbes*, 163–65
    accompaniment in *charades*, 161–63
    composer as accompanist, 106–7, 114–15, 132
piano manufacturers. *See* Salle Érard; Salle Herz; Salle Pleyel; Salle Souffleto
Pigeory, Pierre-Marie-Félix, 125–26, 132–33
Pijon, Mme. *See* Ponchard, Mme
Pillevestre, Jules (*Le farouche ennemi*), 191*t*, 202–3
Pitre-Chevalier (Pierre-Michel-François Chevalier)
    author of part of a *charade*, 162–63
    host, 24–25n.11, 91–92, 98–99, 125–26, 133–36, 169, 198
    publisher, 132, 133–36, 161–62
Pittaud de Forges (Philippe-Auguste-Alfred Pittaud), 47n.30, 92–93, 99, 125–26, 136–38, 143n.64, 167–68, 207, 227–28, 232*t*
Plouvier, Édouard, 190*t*
Poinsot, Anne-Euphrasie, 96, 154–55
Poise, Jean-Alexandre-Ferdinand
    Bonsoir, voisin, 168–69
    Jean Noël, 190*t*
    La dame de compagnie, 190*t*
    Le cigale et la fourmi, 190*t*
    output, 4n.6, 189–93
Poisot, Charles
    host, 32, 143–44, 225–26
    La clef du secrétaire, 66, 92–94, 201–2
    Le coin du feu, 47–64, 53*f*, 56*f*
    Les deux billets, 146*t*, 149–50

Les ressources de Jacqueline, 64, 65n.36, 93–94, 143–44
Les terreurs de M. Peters, 66, 146*t*, 149n.81
output, 30–32, 65n.36, 94, 166–67, 182–83
Rosa, la rose, 30–43, 31*t*, 36*f*, 38*f*, 44*f*, 142–44
Poisson, Raymond, 134, 135*f*
Ponchard, Charles and Cécile, 103–4
Ponchard, Charles-Auguste-Marie, 85–87
Ponchard, Luis-Antoine-Éléonore, 103–4
Ponchard, Mme (Cécile-Henriette-Eugénie d'Halbert; Pijon), 85–87, 106*t*, 150–51
Ponsard, François, 119–20, 161
Porcherons, 221–22
Portehaut, Jean Baptiste, 154–55
Pradeau, Étienne, 167–68
press coverage, 1–2, 6–7, 10–13, 18–19, 23–25, 82, 91–92, 96–99, 102, 105–7, 115, 119–20, 122, 138–39, 154, 156–57, 166, 170–71, 186–201, 204–6, 217–18, 226–29
Prévost-Rousseau, Antonin
    L'habit ne fait pas le moine, 163*t*, 163
    salon, 87n.34
    wife, 199
professional, as a term, 14–15, 84
proverb, 150, 187–88
proverbe
    A deux pas du bonheur (*see* Godefroid, Felix)
    description, 161–65
    relationship with *opéra de salon*, 8–9, 29–30, 153, 157–59, 163*t*, 164–65
    salon activity, 171–72
Prudent, Émile, 155–56, 183
Pubereaux, Charles-Louis. *See* Sainte-Foy

Quatremère, A. (*Les premiers cinq francs*), 29–30, 192*t*, 196–98
Queen Victoria, 156
Quentin, Léon, 175*t*, 179

Rambouillet, Catherine de, 198
Rauch, M., 142
Ravergie, Auguste-Léonce, 187–88
Reber, Napoléon-Henri (*Les papillottes de M. Benoisti*), 231, 232*t*
Recamier, Mme de, 198
recital, vocal, as a preface for an *opéra de salon*, 106–7
recitative, 26n.12, 34, 42*f*, 43–64, 44*f*, 48*f*, 53*f*, 142, 178–79. *See also mélodrame*
regulated theatre
    composers, 94, 202–4
    geography, 220–22
    librettists, 93–94

opéra de salon in the regulated theatre, 139–40, 166–67, 170–71, 184–85
regulated theatre in the salon, 141–42, 167–70, 237–38
relation to *opéra de salon*, 2–11, 19–20, 25–28, 28n.17, 29–30, 64, 65n.36, 98–100, 102, 151–53, 158–60, 166–71, 184–85, 208, 240
relation to *théâtre de société*, 157–60, 164
singers, 14–15, 81, 84–85, 87–88
See also regulation
regulation
censors, 6–7, 10–11, 27–28, 82n.3, 145n.72, 170–71, 196–98, 202n.42, 207n.63
legislative controls, 2–3, 5–6, 25–26, 26n.12, 27–28, 47–64, 119–20, 220, 238
traffic control, 6–7
See also regulated theatre
Reiset, Marie-Félicie-Clémence de. *See* Grandval, Mme de
Rennes, 237–38
reviews. *See* press coverage
revolution of 1789, 5–8, 21–22, 123
Reyer, Ernest, 33, 234
Ribbing, Adolphe de. *See* Leuven, Adolphe de
Richebourg, Émile de, 205*t*
Rigel, Henri-Jean, 160*t*
Rillé, Laurent de
  Abeilles et boudons, 191*t*
  Au fond du verre, 146*t*, 235–37
  La part à dieu, 190*t*
  output, 94, 166–67, 202–3
Ritter, Théodore (*Le nègre de madame*), 146*t*, 149–50
Robillard, Victor, 175*t*, 179–82
Robin, Charles-Philippe, 102–3, 200
Rocheblave, Antoine de
  Deux lunatiques à Saint-Cloud, 191*t*
  La bohémienne, 191*t*
  Le lutin des grèves, 191*t*
  Le proscrit, 191*t*
  librettist, 202–3
  output, 159–60, 189–93, 193n.8
  Une reine de vingt ans, 191*t*
Rocheblave, Mme de, 191*t*
Roger, Gustave-Hippolyte, 142
roles, vocal. *See* scoring
Romagnesi, Antoine, 160*t*
Rossini, Gioacchino
  librettists, 33
  operas, 154–55, 207
  salon, 88, 108, 126, 143–44, 199, 223–24
  season, 209–11
  singers, 140–41

Roubin, Amédée de, 201–2
Royal Gallery of Illustration, 242
rue de Beaune *séances*, 173–75, 183–84

Sabatier-Blot, Maria, 149–50
Sabatier, Jenny (Jenny-Caroline Thircuir), 201–2, 237–38
Sabatier, Louise, 145n.72, 201–2
Saint-Beuve, Charles-Augustin de, 22–23
Saint-Germain-en-Laye, 156–57
Saint-Malo, 237–38
Saint-Olive, Geneviève-Lambert de, 198–99
Saint-Preux, Marie-Elisabeth-Césarine Mosneron de, 106–7, 198–99, 209n.1
Saint-Saëns, Camille, 102–3, 137n.37
Saint-Simon, Henri de, 173–75
Saint-Simonianism, 115–16, 183
Sainte-Adresse, 230–31
Sainte-Foy (Charles-Louis Pubereaux), 85, 132, 134, 167–68, 210–11, 213*t*
Salle Beethoven (originally Théâtre Moderne), 146*t*, 147–50
Salle de Diane, 18–19, 83, 99–100, 113, 121–22
Salle du Grand Orient, 149–50, 205*t*
Salle Érard
  controls, 6–7, 27–28, 145n.72
  description, 148
  parties vocales/instrumentales, 8–9, 23–24
  performances of *opéra de salon*, 142–43, 146*t*, 147–48, 149nn.80–81, 149–50, 223–24, 224*t*
Salle Favart, 210–11
Salle Herz
  benefit, 198–99, 232n.59, 234–35
  boundaries between public and private, 19–20
  censorship, 6–7, 27–28, 170–71, 196–98
  location, 108
  orchestra, 83
  performances of *opéra de salon*, 81–82, 82n.3, 143–44, 145n.72, 146*t*, 149n.80, 149–50, 154–55, 168n.42, 169–70, 170n.52, 182–83, 194–95, 196–98, 200n.39, 202n.42, 213*t*, 232*t*, 232n.59, 235–37
  programming, 150, 154–55, 204–6, 205*t*
  rental, 186–201, 225
  reviews, 18–19, 24–25, 91–92
  singers, 85, 89
  size, 19–20, 24–25, 108, 148, 216–17, 225
  staging, 96, 99–100
  type of *opéra de salon*, 23–24, 212
  venue for *opéra de salon*, 8–9, 23–26, 84–85, 147–50
Salle Le Peletier, 141–42, 166–67

Salle Lyrique (École-Lyrique, Salle Moreau-Sainti), 146*t*, 147–49, 204–6, 205*t*
Salle Pleyel
  attentiveness, 7
  censorship, 6–7, 27–28
  performances of *opéra de salon*, 142–43, 145n.72, 146*t*, 148, 149n.81, 149–51, 199
  size, 108, 148, 216–17
  venue for *opéra de salon*, 8–9, 23–26, 147–48
Salle Sainte-Cécile, 146*t*, 147–48, 151, 204–6, 205*t*, 231–32
Salle Souffleto, 8–9, 23–24, 146*t*, 147–50, 205*t*, 213*t*
salon, Second Empire, 7–8, 21–28, 67, 198
Salons de la Présidence, 121–22
Salons de Pleyel-Wolff, 148n.77, 204n.57
Salvator (Charles Salvatoris)
  career, 86n.26, 106–7, 235, 238n.92
  L'esprit du foyer, 146*t*, 234–38, 236*f*
  Suzanne, 146*t*, 234–35, 237–38
Saumur, 237–38
Savary, Marie-René-Napoléon, 2e Duc de Rovigo, 92, 146*t*, 148–49
saynette, 175*t*, 182–83
scenery. *See* set design
Schubert, Franz, 151, 156
Schumann, Clara, 156
scoring of *opéra de salon*
  instrumentation, 82–83, 112, 196–98, 215, 216*f*
  voice types, 1–2, 31*t*, 32–33, 81–82, 102–3, 150–51, 159–60, 182–83, 193–94, 196, 200–1, 235–37
  See also orchestral accompaniment; piano
Scribe, Eugène, 150, 160*t*, 176n.69
Scudéry, Madeleine de, 198
séances, 21, 153, 171–85, 218–19
Séchan, Charles, 97
Ségalas, Anaïs (Anne Caroline Ménard), 87n.32, 103–5, 133–34, 162–63, 201–2
Ségalas, Jean-Victor, 103–5
Ségalas, Pierre-Salomon, 103–6, 162–63, 168–69
Seinely, 175*t*
Semet, Théophile-Aimé-Émile
  career, 30–32, 189–93, 202–3
  Laide, 31*t*, 33–34, 39–43, 40*f*, 191*t*
  Le poltron, 191*t*
set design, 10–11, 95–99, 106–7, 121–22, 133–34, 138n.41, 161, 166, 209, 211–12, 227, 228, 241. *See also* stages, temporary
showrooms of piano manufacturers. *See* Salle Érard; Salle Herz; Salle Pleyel; Salle Souffleto

Sighicelli, Vincenzo, 106–7
Silny, Max. *See* Peigné, Mme
Sivori, Camillo, 151
Société des Concerts du Conservatoire, 85–87, 86n.29, 154
Société Philotechnique, 175*t*, 181–83
Soubies, Albert, 92–93
spa towns, 22, 133, 229–39, 242
spatialité, 2–3, 11–12, 16–17, 209, 211–19, 239–41
stages, temporary, 15–16, 17, 95–100, 133–36, 138n.41, 211–12, 215, 228–30, 241.
  See also *espaces*; set design
state intervention. *See* regulation
Stockhausen, 141–42, 151
Strauss, Isaac, 233–34
structure, musical. *See* form

Talmont (Aimée-Philiberte Tillemont), 213*t*
terms and labels for *opéra de salon*, 9, 29–30, 163*t*, 193
Théâtre Castellane. *See* Castellane, Comte de
Théâtre de la Gaîté, 25–26, 30–32, 159, 168–69, 175*t*, 175n.63, 201–2, 221*f*
Théâtre de la Monnaie, 87–88, 140–42
Théâtre de la Renaissance, 5–6, 157–58
théâtre de société
  audience engagement, 171–72
  description, 8–9, 95–96, 153, 157–60
  engravings and illustrations, 99, 134, 214–15
Théâtre Déjazet, 111–12, 134n.29, 169, 220–21
Théâtre des Bouffes-Parisiens
  comparison with *opéra de salon*, 6, 9–10, 28–30, 67
  competitor with opéra de *salon*, 25–26
  composers, 90–91, 103–4, 116n.53, 126, 143–44, 207, 238–39
  description, 25–26, 133
  director, 149n.86
  genre, 26–27, 30n.21
  librettists, 92–94, 111–12
  location, 220, 221*f*
  movement of works between the theatre and salon, 167–71, 231, 232*t*
  overlap with *opéra de salon*, 9–10
  performances, 121–22, 134, 137n.39, 144–45
  regulation, 5–6
  singers, 88–89, 199n.30, 232–33
Théâtre des Célestins, Lyon, 175*t*
Théâtre des Fantaisies-Parisiennes, 93–94, 103–4, 133, 168–71, 203–4, 227n.39
Théâtre des Folies-Concertantes/Nouvelles

comparison with *opéra de salon*, 6, 9–10, 25–30, 67
competitor with *opéra de salon*, 25–26
composers, 119–20, 139–40
genre, 26–27
location, 220–21, 221f
movement of works between the theatre and salon, 168–69
overlap with *opéra de salon*, 9–10
regulation, 5–6
Théâtre des Folies-Dramatiques, 25–26, 164, 220, 221f
Théâtre des Variétés
  La table tournante, 172–73, 175t, 175–76
  location, 221f
  opérettes, 25–26, 103–4
  Pépito, 121–22, 144–45, 167–68, 231, 232t
  performances, unsanctioned, 25–26
  singers, 85n.23
  vaudevilles, 111–12, 159
Théâtre du Luxembourg, 175t
Théâtre du Palais-Royal, 85n.23, 118–19, 148, 158, 159, 169–70, 175t, 177, 221f
Théâtre du Vaudeville, 111–12, 118–19, 164
Théâtre Moderne. *See* Salle Beethoven
Théâtre-Italien, 5–6, 166–67
  audience, 166–67
  comparison with *opéra de salon*, 17
  legislation, 5–6
  location, 220, 221f
  performances, 205t
  schedule, 18
  singers, 15, 140–41, 154–55
  théâtre de société, 8–9
Théâtre-Lyrique, 231
  comparison with *opéra de salon*, 27–28, 133, 153
  composers, 18, 30–32, 94, 103n.7, 203–4
  gatekeeping, gendered, 206–7
  libretti, printed, 64–65
  librettists, 92–94, 111–12, 203–4
  location, 220–21, 221f
  Opéra National, 5–6
  performances, 30–32, 102–3, 128–29, 141–44, 168–69, 173–75, 203–4, 205t, 207, 231, 232t, 237–38
  singers, 84–85, 86n.26, 88–89, 115, 126, 232–33, 237–38
Théric, Alice-Marie, 85
Thiéry, Henry, 191t
Third Republic, 1n.1, 103n.7, 198

Thys, Alphonse
  daughter Pauline, 143–44, 207
  Les échos de Rosine, 207
Thys, Pauline, 92–93, 207
  host, 143–44, 207, 225–26
  La perruque du bailli, 104–5, 106t, 106–7, 143–44, 146t, 207, 235n.78
  La pomme de Turquie, 92–93, 143–44, 207
  Le mariage de Tabarin, 207
  Le pays de Cocagne, 86n.26, 92–93, 143–44, 207
  L'héritier sans le savoir, 24–25n.11, 133–34, 146t, 207
  librettist, 92–93, 133–34
  Quand Dieu est dans le mariage, Dieu le garde, 104–5, 143–44, 207
Tiefenbach, Wilhelmina Josephina Rudolphina Brunold Comtesse de, 134–36
Tinant, Louis-Félix-Édouard, 217–18
Tourneux, Jean-François-Eugène, 30n.22, 128–29, 226
Tours, 237–38
Tourte, Francis, 145n.72, 190t
travesti role, 32–33, 81–82
Tréfeu, Étienne, 93–94, 138n.43, 190t
Trélat, Marie, 102–3, 198, 200
Trélat, Ulysse, 102–3, 104–6, 198
troupes ambulantes, 238n.94
troupes d'arrondissement, 238n.94, 239
Trouvé, Eugène-Nicolas, 92, 125–29, 132, 137–38
Truinet (Nuitter), Charles-Louis-Étienne, 190t
Turgenev, Ivan, 234

Ugalde, Delphine (Gabrielle-Delphine-Elisabeth Beaucé), 126–27
Un rendez-vous en Espagne, 145n.72, 196–98

Varney, Pierre-Joseph-Alphonse (*Le moulin joli*), 168–69
vaudeville, 4–6, 4–5n.9, 8–9, 15–18, 25–26, 92–93, 111–12, 153, 158–60, 164, 166–67, 169–70, 172–82, 190t, 191t, 193–96, 222, 233, 238–240. *See also* Mirecourt, Eugène de, *La table tournante*
Verconsin, Pierre-Frédéric-Eugène, 106t, 150, 162–63
Verdellet, Victor-Élisabeth, 232–33
Verdi, Giuseppe, 33, 88–89, 144–45, 151, 154–55, 161–62, 166–67, 242–43
Verne, Jules, 161–62
Véronge de La Nux, Paul, 155–56

Véronge de la Nux (Rocheblanche, Grégoire-Marc-Félix), 155–56
Verroust, Louis-Stanislas-Xavier, 82–83
Viardot, Louis, 116–18
Viardot, Pauline, 13n.19, 116–18, 234–35
   Le dernier sorcier, 234
Vichy, 110–11, 230–31, 233–34
Viel-Castel, Horace de, 209–10
Vienna, 17, 238–39
Villa Rossini, 210–11
Villers-sur-Mer, 133
Viollet-le-Duc, Eugène-Emmanuel, 161
virtuose. See *artiste-virtuose*
voice types. *See* scoring
von Flotow, Friedrich, 157–58

Watteville, Mme de, 187–88
Weber, Carl Maria von, 18, 151, 173–75
Weber, William, 13–14
Weckerlin, Jean-Baptiste
   Gaveaux-Sabatier, 89, 99, 138–40, 211–12, 225–26
   homage to Rossini, 144

Jobin et Nanette, 146t, 149n.85
L'amour à l'épée, 105–6, 105n.19, 115–16n.50, 118–19, 146t, 148–151, 230–32, 232t
La laitière de Trianon, 138–39, 144, 211–12
Le mariage en poste, 134–36, 144, 146t, 183, 230–31, 232t
Les revenants bretons, 146t, 150–51
libretti, 92–93
Manche à manche, 99, 106t, 138–39, 211–12
marriage, 87n.31
outside Paris, 231–32, 232t, 234–35
piano accompaniment, 184n.94
Pierrot à Paphos, ou La sérénade intérrompue, 89, 92–93, 138–39, 146t, 211–12
promoter at the Herz, 146t, 149–50
regulated theatre, 94, 166–67
Tout est bien qui finit bien, 83, 95–96, 106t, 113, 121–22, 139–40, 146t, 209–10, 234–35

Zolobodjan, Augustine-Joséphine, 203–4, 227–28, 232–33